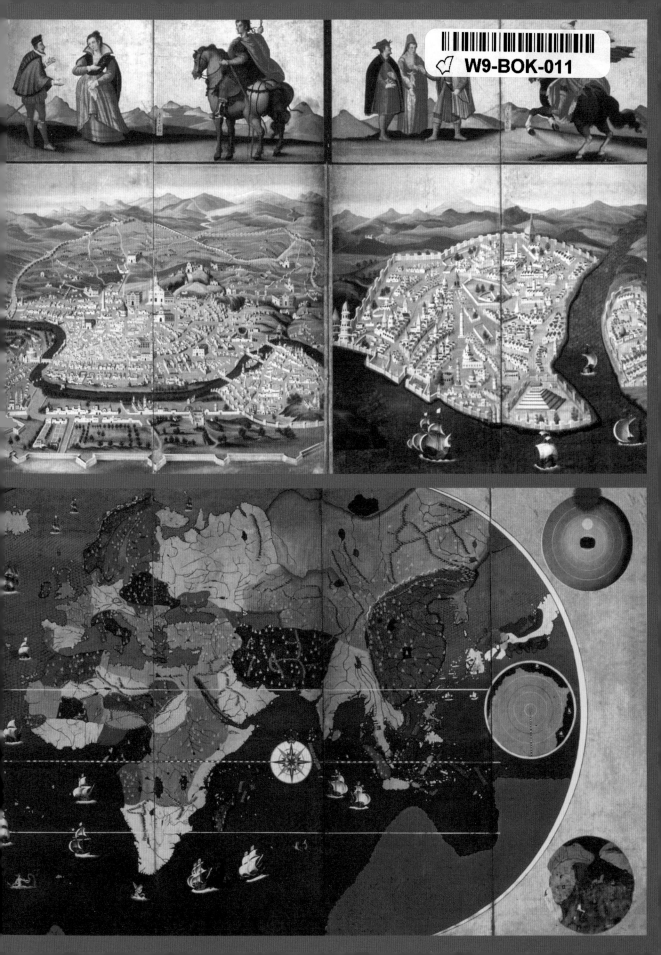

1616

The World in Motion

1616

The World in Motion

Thomas Christensen

COUNTERPOINT

BERKELEY

Title page frontispiece (pp. 2–3): Arrival of a Portuguese Ship, early seventeenth century (detail). Japan. Folding screen, one of a pair; ink, colors, and gold on paper, 333 x 173 cm (overall). Asian Art Museum, The Avery Brundage Collection, B60D77+.

See p. 68 for more of the screen.

Hardcover edition endsheets: Four Large Cities of the World (top) and Map of the World (bottom), 1610–1620. Japan. Pair of eight-panel screens; ink color, and gold on paper, each 478 x 159 cm. Kobe City Museum.

These two large screens, conceived as a set, incorporate new geographical information brought to Japan by Portuguese and Dutch visitors; at the same time they reveal a greater knowledge of Japan (shown at an exaggerated size) and East Asia than was available to Europeans. As a result they represent some of the most sophisticated geographical knowledge of the early seventeenth century.

Two of the six circular insets show a solar and a lunar eclipse, reflecting the importance of astronomical observation during the period (see "Witch Hunters and Truth Seekers," p. 187). The other insets show the arctic and antarctic poles, and globes centered on Japan and Brazil, which were considered antipodes. Four major cities of the Mediterranean region are depicted: Lisbon, home to the Portuguese sailors who traveled east to Asia around the Cape of Good Hope; Seville, home to the Spanish who traveled west to America and on from there to Asia; Rome, center of the Catholic religion; and Istanbul, representing the realm of Islam.

In captions dimensions are rounded to the nearest centimeter. Width is given before height.

Archaic spelling is sometimes retained in period quotations to give the flavor of the time.

Library of Congress Cataloging-in-Publication data is available

Printed in China

ISBN: 978-1-58243-774-3

COUNTERPOINT
1919 Fifth Street
Berkeley, CA 94710
www.counterpointpress.com

Book design by the author
www.rightreading.com

Permission credits appear on p. 379, which constitutes a continuation of this copyright page.

Distributed by Publishers Group West

10 9 8 7 6 5 4 3 2 1

Motion and transformation take place in both quality and quantity —
in the very substance of things.
  — Mulla Sadra (ca. 1571–1641), Persian philosopher

I will direct my mind to the human breast, and to the heart itself, and see
how it is driven by perpetual motion for as long as life remains; for life ends
when the motion is taken away, damaged, or hindered. It is natural there-
fore for man to move from place to place, from region to region, until he can
see into himself, above himself, and around himself.
  — Michael Maier (1569–1622), German physician, alchemist, author

◑

This book is for Carol, Claire, Ellen, Verle, and Anne

Contents

Opposite: Karna, one of the Kauravas, Slays the Pandavas' Nephew Ghatotkacha with a Weapon Given to Him by Indra, the King of the Gods, from a Manuscript of the *Razmnama* (detail), 1616–1617. India, perhaps Burhanpur, Madhya Pradesh state. Ink, opaque watercolors and gold on paper, 23 x 33 cm. Asian Art Museum, Gift of the Connoisseurs' Council with additional funding from Fred M. and Nancy Livingston Levin, the Shenson Foundation, in memory of A. Jess Shenson, 2003.6.

The *Razmnama* is a Persian translation of the Mahabharata, one of the great Hindu epics.

Preface

One morning in September 2009 I woke up in my bedroom in the San Francisco Bay Area with the date 1616 in my head and the resolution to research and write about that year already formed. It was a strange resolve in many ways, not just because it seemed to come from nowhere. My academic training had been in literary modernism and postmodernism, and my professional work had centered around trade book publishing, literary translation, and the design and production of museum art catalogues. Nevertheless, from that day on I researched that year with a single-mindedness that bordered on obsession.

Some years — 1066, 1492, 1776, 1945 — are so associated with momentous events that they are emblazoned in everyone's consciousness. The year 1616, despite such notable developments as those this book chronicles, is, for the most part, not one of these. This seems to me a good thing. Cathartic events can so dominate an era that they make it difficult to see the deeper forces that drive long-term change. In 1616, on the other hand, it is possible to make out intimations of modernity in developing globalism, militarism, imperialism, diasporism, colonialism, capitalism, rationalism, bureaucratization, urbanization, individualism, and so on.

I was vague on historical developments during this period in many parts of the world, but I knew one thing about the year from the outset. On April 23, 1616, two literary giants, William Shakespeare and Miguel de Cervantes, accomplished the feat of dying on the same date but different days. Mainly for the reason of their shared date of death, the United Nations named April 23 the international Day of the Book.

Shakespeare, seven years the younger, went first, on Tuesday. Miguel de Cervantes, despite a life of hardship, held on another week and a half, until Saturday. This was possible because Spain had adopted the Gregorian calendar proposed in 1582 by Pope Gregory XIII. Britain, however, recoiling at any whiff of papism, did not adopt the new calendar until 1752, and it lagged, in 1616, ten days behind. Although Shakespeare's death date is traditionally given as April 23, according to the new calendar he would have died on May 3.

At that time there was as little agreement about when the year began as about what day it was. In many parts of Europe it had been traditional to consider a date such as Annunciation Day — the day nine months before Christmas when it was revealed to Mary that she would bear a child — as

Opposite: Don Quixote Driven Mad by Reading, by Gustave Doré. Illustration for *Don Quixote* by Miguel de Cervantes, 1863. Hachette and Co., Paris. Engraving.

the beginning of the year; standardizing on January 1 was a newfangled notion based on an ancient tradition, the Roman consular year. The European states adopted the new date for the new year each in its time: Venice in 1522, Spain in 1556, France in 1564, Scotland in 1600, Russia in 1700, and so on. The January 1, 1616, masque that is the focus of the following section of this book would have been thought of by Londoners of its time as falling in the eleventh month of 1615.

Matters become even more confounding when considering non-Western cultures. Some, like the Persians, who thought of the period we call 1616 as made up of parts of the years 994 and 995, celebrated the new year around the spring equinox. Others related the new year not just to the solar cycle but also to the phases of the moon: lunar new years were celebrated in East Asia, the Himalayas, and many parts of Southeast Asia. Some calendars reflected ancient histories: in China the year was 4252–4253; in the Maya long count it was probably 4730; in the Hebrew reckoning — in which the new year began in the fall — it was 5376–5377.

All of which makes the study of a single calendar year an arbitrary and confused construct. It is not always certain which system a recorded date belongs to — historical documents give the impression that William III of England set sail from the Netherlands on November 11 and arrived in England on November 5. In some cases, more than one system was used at any given time: for many years both "old style" (*stilo vetere*) and "new style" (*stilo novo*) dates were in use in England. In East Asia, a year might be designated by a reign date or identified only by its associated zodiac animal, so that a reference to an event in the year of the dragon might point to 1616, or 1628, or some other year.

The reader will see that I move forward and backward from 1616 freely in telling my story, which is ultimately that of the interconnectivity of the early modern world rather than a single year's events. But the year 1616 serves as a base that helps to keep those travels grounded.

Even a single year provides much more material than can be managed in a book of this size, and so I have had to be selective: instead of surveying all of the visual arts I have mostly concentrated on painting, instead of considering all of the sciences I have mostly focused on astronomy, and so on. Even within those limits I could only provide a variety of angles from which to view some aspects of the early seventeenth century: following the overview of the prologue, the first essay deals mainly with the new maritime globalism, especially the pan-Pacific trade in silver and silk; the second discusses emerging roles for women; the third considers some developments in visual arts, in particular the counterbalance between

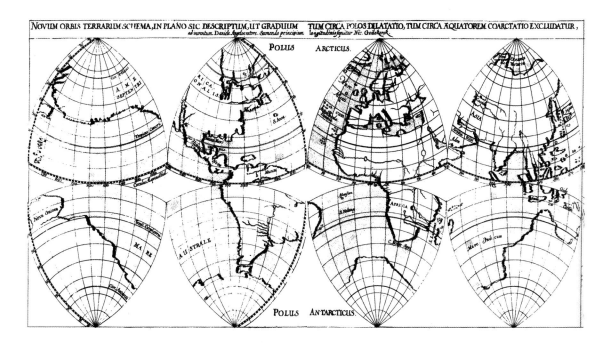

NOVUM ORBIS TERRARUM SCHEMA, IN PLANO SIC DESCRIPTUM, UT GRADUUM   TUM CIRCA POLOS DILATATIO, TUM CIRCA ÆQUATOREM COARCTATIO EXCLUDATUR,
ad inventum Daniele Angelocratore. Sumendo principium   longitudinis sequitur Nic: Geilkerken

ancient models and new directions; the fourth explores the tension between developing scientific attitudes and magical beliefs; and the fifth offers an overview of the movement of peoples — the world in motion.

Beginning in the late nineteenth century, some historians started to think of themselves as social scientists. Over the course of the twentieth century this meant that many historians concentrated on accumulating and analyzing data and constructing detailed and reasoned arguments based on the results. Certainly there is a need for such work, and it is welcome. But the origins of history lie in storytelling, and historians should not be afraid to make use of the arsenal of narrative effects available to literary writers, such as plot, story, character, metaphor and rhetoric, humor, and poetry. In the broadest sense, all history writing is narrative: it should not be thought of as the objective revelation of absolute truths. Historians, in effect, are always inventing the past, which changes as each generation views it in a new way, by reference to a new present.

Through it all "my" year spoke to me pretty clearly. Not for an instant did I lose interest as I retraced its 365-day cycle of day and night, yin and yang, clarity and obscurity. I hope that in the book that follows the reader will find some fraction of the enthusiasm that I felt in reliving the year 1616.

World Map, probably 1616, by Nicolaas Geelkercken, reproduced by Daniel Angelocrator.

Nicolaas Geelkercken was a draftsman, engraver, publisher, and surveyor who was working in Amsterdam in 1616 when he probably made the original of this map of the world as it was then known. The newly independent Dutch Republic was intensely interested in overseas trade. Geelkerken's original map has been lost, and this version was produced by Daniel Angelocrator, a Calvinist minister of Germany, who may have contributed the unusual projection by which each hemisphere is separated into four rounded equilateral triangular quadrants, each with a point at the pole and two on the equator.

As seen at upper left, Geelkerken had the impression that North America extended nearly to Japan. In fact the Pacific crossing was the longest and most difficult journey in the history of sailing. Yet the survival of the Spanish colony in Manila depended upon it, and massive amounts of American silver and Chinese silks were transported between Manila and Acapulco. This exchange was a major component of the global economy in 1616.

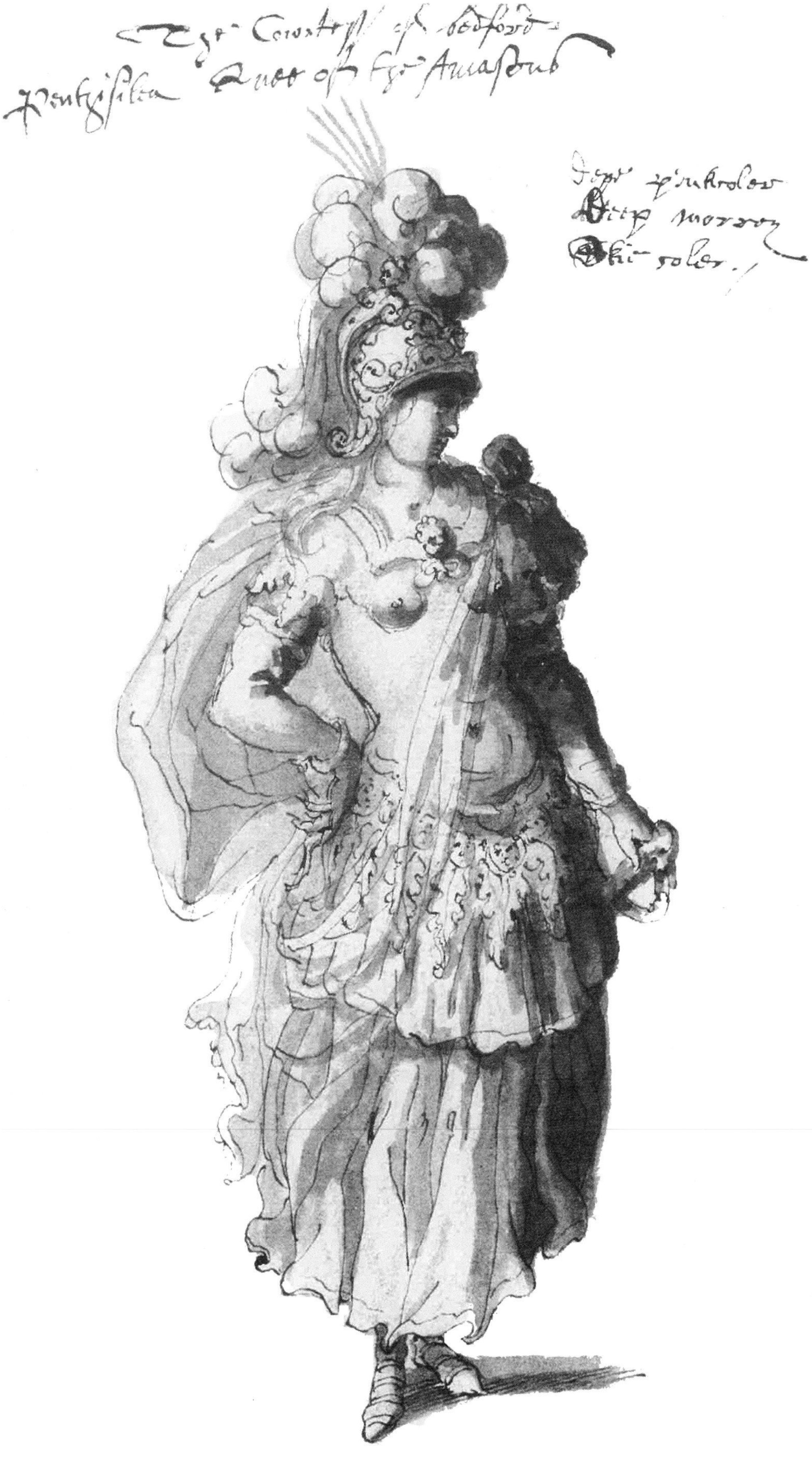
The Countesse of Bedford
Penthisilea Queen of the Amasons

Prologue: The Golden Age Restored

On the first day of January in 1616, King James I of England and his wife of twenty-seven years, Anne of Denmark, gathered with their court in their London palace of Whitehall for a performance of a masque entitled *The Golden Age Restored.* The masque — a sort of combination pageant, drama, ballet, and ballroom dance — had been written by Ben Jonson, the top playwright of the day now that Will Shakespeare, who was in failing health, was losing touch. The veteran actor had not appeared on stage since 1603, when he had performed in one of Jonson's plays. Recently his *Measure for Measure* and *Macbeth* both had to be sent to a young script doctor named Thomas Middleton to be punched up for modern audiences.

These days audiences wanted a spectacle, not, as Jonson said, actors waving rusty swords across a bare stage. The elaborate stage machinery, sets, and costumery for the masque had been devised by Inigo Jones, who had also designed the expansive Queen's House at Greenwich, which would begin construction this same year. Some said that Jones's stagecraft was more important to the success of the masques than were Jonson's words. To Jonson's annoyance, Jones was one of those who said so. While Jonson insisted that the masques were "the mirrors of man's life," Jones said they were "nothing else but pictures with Light and Motion."

Jones's architectural projects interested the king, who had long thought London in need of an upgrade; his cousin Elizabeth, her mind on other matters, had neglected this aspect of her rule, just as (to his good fortune) she had failed to provide an heir. But the theater was not the king's main love, and he had several times been observed napping during performances. Anne, on the other hand, loved all kinds of dance and display. It was she who was the great patron of the arts. Jones had begun his career in her employ on the recommendation of her brother, King Christian IV of Denmark; Jonson's first important patron was the first lady of her entourage; and the queen was responsible for advancing the careers of many other writers, artists, and performers.

James preferred arguing fine points of governance and religion with the learned elite, and he was fond of sharing his wisdom with his subjects, sometimes through speeches and other times in writing. His most popular publication was entitled *Daemonologie,* which delved eruditely into such matters as spirits and ghosts, as well as magic, sorcery, and witchcraft.

Opposite: Penthesilea, 1609, by Inigo Jones. Design for a masque.

The Masque of Queens, commissioned by Queen Anne, was the first Jonsonian masque to integrate all the elements that would make up a classical court masque. It contains the first fully developed antimasque, in which a coterie of witches is presented as foils to the queens.

For the part of Penthesilea, Queen of the Amazons, played by Lucy Harington Russell, Countess of Bedford, Inigo Jones designed a plumed helmet, sword, nearly transparent corselet, and deep pink skirts. Lady Bedford was the second most influential patroness of the arts in Jacobean England after Queen Anne herself. Her power and that of other women at the court was the target of a sarcastic verse by her cousin Sir John Harington:

These entertayne great princes; these
    have lerned
The tongues, toyes, tricks of Room, of
    Spain, of Fraunce
    These can Currentos and Lavoltas
    dance,
And though they foot yt false tis nere
    discerned,
The vertues of these dames are so
    transcendent,
    Themselves ar learnd, and their
    Heroyk sperit
    Can make disgrace an honor, sinn
    a merit.
All penns, all praysers ar on them
    dependent.

The Duke of Buckingham, the favorite of King James I of England,
was famous for his shapely legs,
which he displayed on the dance
floor in court masques and other
festivities.

By 1616 painters had largely
abandoned the martial poses and
military regalia in which courtiers
had traditionally been portrayed.
In the new world order of the early
seventeenth century nobility was
adorned instead with the trappings of culture.

It is hard to imagine anyone going to battle in the shoes Buckingham is wearing in this portrait.

Witches and ghosts were causing serious trouble not just in Britain but throughout the world in the early seventeenth century. In the hamlet of Spa in the Netherlands more than a dozen witches were being investigated at this very moment, while in Leonberg, in the triply misnamed Holy Roman Empire, action was being initiated against another suspected witch, Katharina Kepler, mother of the astronomer Johannes Kepler. Garroting and burning were common punishments for witchcraft. Aware of the king's interest in this subject, the script doctor Middleton had expanded a mention of witches in the play that, in order to flatter the Scottish king, Shakespeare had set in Scotland.

Kepler, Galileo, and others sought to replace magical thinking with empirical observation and rational argumentation. But Galileo argued the point a little too strenuously, and in 1616 he would be taken to task by Pope Paul V for overstepping his bounds.

Differences of taste were not the only strain between the monarchs. Their relations had never been easy. James had described marriage as "the greatest earthly felicitie or miserie, that can come to a man." The king and queen led separate lives. Anne had never fully forgiven him for taking their son Henry from her when he was a young child and forbidding her to see him for fear that she would infect him with her Catholic tendencies — issues of religion were inflaming passions around the world, and the seventeenth century has been called "the age of religious wars." Anne had fought hard to regain custody of her son, but James had formally commanded the boy's wards not to release him to anyone, not even to his mother, without permission from the king's own mouth.

Moreover, despite rumors of affairs with ladies of the court, James was known to have "inward" tendencies — to be more fond of his male companions than of the company of women. On public occasions he sometimes amused himself by grabbing his courtiers' codpieces. His "favorite," or chief advisor, for the past decade had been Robert Carr, the Earl of Somerset, a young man who quickly rose to fame and fortune, only to fall equally precipitously. Somerset had been best known for his good looks and his access to the king until the previous October, when during trials of members of his circle the accusation came out that he had been involved in the poisoning of one of his intimates. This had resulted in the most serious scandal of James's reign.

Now, even as the murmuring audience in Whitehall was called to attention by the "lowd musick" that announced the beginning of the masque and watched the goddess Pallas Athena (a role once played by the queen herself) descend from the heavens on her chariot, Somerset languished in prison awaiting his trial. Meanwhile, the king had found a new favorite in George Villiers, the Duke of Buckingham, who was famous for his shapely legs.

The theme of the masque, the reform of a corrupt court, was well chosen by Jonson to play against the Somerset scandal, which was still on everyone's tongue. The masque presented James, by analogy to the supreme Roman deity Jove, as a reforming king who was clearing his court of evil influences. This conceit so pleased James that he would call for a second performance five days later and present Jonson with an annual pension of a thousand marks. This would largely free the forty-three-year-old author from the need to earn his living, and though he would continue writing masques, he would not pen another play for a decade.

In his marital relations, James did not benefit from the example of his parents. As a young widow his mother, Mary Queen of Scots, had chosen for her second husband her cousin Henry Stuart. After an initial moment of ardor, the two royals discovered that they detested each other. Henry became suspicious of Mary's Italian secretary (who was rumored, almost certainly falsely, to be James's real father), and he fell in with a group of plotters who were embroiled in palace intrigues,

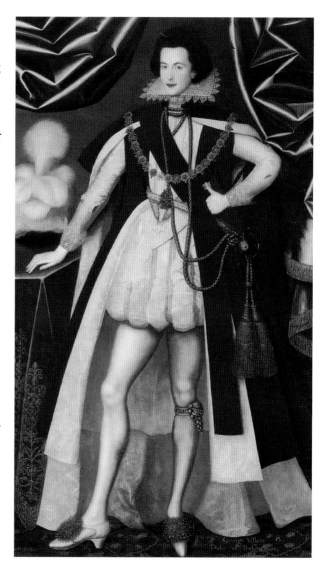

goaded on by anti-papist hysteria. The schemers contrived to murder the secretary, with Mary forced to witness the brutality. Pregnant with James at the time, Mary felt, not unreasonably, that she and her unborn son would be the next targets, as that would clear the way for Henry to rule. But she wisely disguised her fury, and not long afterward Henry was found inside a building that had exploded around him (the same thing nearly happened to James in the Guy Fawkes Gunpowder Plot of 1605).

Then it was discovered that it was not the explosion that killed Henry — he had been strangled prior to the blast. Mary, who had imprudently married Henry's chief enemy, was imprisoned and forced to abdicate. She escaped and fled Scotland for London, never to see her son again. In London she remained under the watchful custody of Elizabeth for nearly twenty years, until she became implicated in far-fetched plots against her cousin's throne. When Elizabeth ordered her execution, James, now king of Scotland, turned a cold face, seemingly little moved by his mother's plight.

It was a dangerous time to have close blood ties to a reigning monarch. Although many royals eased into lives of privilege, palace intrigues could often turn injurious or deadly, as had been the case with several of the world's current rulers. Louis XIII of France (who was branded by his prime minister, Richelieu, as "Louis the Just" to avoid his being known as "Louis the Stammerer"), having assassinated his mother's favorite, the regent, then led an army against her. Shah Abbas, who made Safavid Persia a player on the international stage, had his first son murdered, and his second and third sons blinded. In India the Mughal emperor Jahangir, a great patron of the arts, likewise had a son blinded to prevent him from challenging the throne. The stepmother and half brother of the Japanese shogun Tokugawa Hidetada were both killed by his father, Ieyasu, the first shogun of the long Tokugawa (Edo) era, on suspicion of plotting against him. Mehmed III, sultan of the Ottoman empire from 1595 to 1603, had all nineteen of his brothers killed.

In *The Golden Age Restored*, Jove, the king of heaven, oversees the action, just as James, the king of England, was overseeing the masque. Now Pallas Athena, having alighted, announces that Golden Age and Astraea, goddess of justice, are to be restored to earth. But this plan is temporarily thwarted by Iron Age and his twelve attendant evils — Avarice, Fraud, Slander, Corruption, Ambition, Pride, Scorn, Force, Rapine, Treachery, Folly, and Ignorance — who threaten to disrupt the order of Jove's dominions "and teach them all our Pyrrhick dance." Finally Pallas puts them to flight and Golden Age and Astraea descend in the company of four English poets laureate. They introduce the masquers, who dance about the hall to the delight of all.

A desire to replace the fragmentation of the medieval world with something resembling the far-reaching cultural and political cohesion of ancient Rome was an impetus for the European Renaissance, as first voiced by writers such as Petrarch in the fourteenth century; the Golden Age of the masque is a lingering expression of that ideal. Fueled by the ancients' example of greatness (and by the movable metal type printing press, an East Asian invention reverse engineered in Germany), Europeans reconfigured their society in a remarkably short time. During the age of Shakespeare it had seemed that anything was possible, and that the whole chain of being could be encompassed within a single vision. But now cracks were appearing in the old unities. Some Europeans were questioning the applicability of the ancient models — "'Tis all in pieces," John Donne had written five years earlier, "all coherence gone" — and the European world was teetering on a pivot that could propel it in different directions.

Throughout the nineteenth and much of the twentieth century, Western scholars, mindful of European success in colonizing other areas, viewed Europe as historically exceptional, developing in radically different ways from other regions. The West was seen as more dynamic, rational, and democratic than any part of Asia, which was portrayed as monolithic and static, unchanging across centuries. But in fact the early seventeenth century was a time of enormous change in most regions of the world, change largely driven by a new maritime globalism that accelerated trade and exchange of goods and ideas. In the face of such unsettling changes, many cultures looked back nostalgically to earlier times as "golden ages," and these eras served also as models legitimizing emerging states that were consolidating regions once made up of numerous small, independent principalities. In Europe five or six hundred political units would eventually merge into just a couple of dozen; in mainland Southeast Asia a couple of dozen states would resolve into just a handful; and so on. Contributing to this consolidation was the new availability of firearms and cannonry, which compounded the political advantages of centers of wealth. While Renaissance Europe looked back to ancient Rome, Ming China looked back to the pre-Mongol Song dynasty as a golden age, Tokugawa Japan to the pre–civil war Kawakura and Muromachi periods, Romanov Muscovy to early Orthodox Christian Kiev Rus, Burma to Pagan, Siam to Angkor, and the Vietnamese states to Confucian Dai Viet. The three Muslim empires, the Anatolia-based Ottomans, the Persia-based Safavids, and the South Asia–based Mughals, though each possessing Turkic lineage, all respected Persian culture and looked to the Perso-Islamic reign of the fifteenth-century Timurid ruler Sultan Husain Baiqara of Herat as a golden age of art and literature. Throughout the world, artists, writers, and political leaders were now struggling between evolving new forms and respecting the models of the glorious past.

Though it was an age of colorful figures and flamboyant gestures, with the growth of the modern state also came the beginnings of the state as a faceless bureaucracy. Shah Abbas of Persia, one of the age's most extravagant rulers, remarked that "the king of Spain and other Christians do not get any pleasure out of ruling." While the image of Abbas as a capricious despot making life-and-death decisions on a whim owes much to the Western orientalizing impulse, there is substance to his criticism. A member of the court of the Spanish king, Philip III, commented that "no secretary in the world uses more paper than His Majesty." Philip passed his days reviewing document after document — he once signed four hundred documents in a single day; by contrast, his grandfather, Charles V, had once called for a pen and found that there was not a single one to be located in the entire palace. But it was not just in Europe that some courts had become stultifying bureaucracies. The same charge could be leveled at the Ottoman court under Abbas's colorless counterpart Ahmed I, while in China the Wanli emperor spent his days engaged in mechanical rituals and endless paperwork.

Inigo Jones's designs for *The Golden Age Restored* have not survived, and we don't know exactly how the masque was produced. In general, masques were elaborate and expensive affairs. For 1608's *The Masque of Beauty,* another Jonson and Jones collaboration, we know that the ladies were opulently adorned with pearls and jewels, and an Italian observer claimed a single outfit could cost better than 100,000 pounds. Records of the king's keeper of accounts detail payments of nearly 6,000 pounds on such items as gold and silver lace, gold chains, silks, linens, and other luxury items. Although it is hard to establish equivalents, in modern currency this might approach half a million dollars for the evening's entertainment.

Courtiers too were expected to live large and spend lavishly. Lord Hay, a gentleman of the king's bedchamber, commissioned a masque entitled *Lovers Made Men* for a private reception in honor of an ambassador from France. For the occasion he spent more than 2,200 pounds on the dinner alone, employing thirty chefs over the course of twelve days. Finally, on the occasion of the feast, a splendid meal was placed on the table and uncovered … and cleared away before a bite was taken. This gesture was intended only to stimulate the guests' appetites, and a second, even more magnificent meal was then set before them.

A reception in 1606 for the queen's brother, Christian IV of Denmark, was said by an observer to have devolved into a sloppy, drunken spectacle:

> In good sooth the parliament did kindly to provide his Majestie so seasonably with money, for there hath been no lack of good living; shews, sights, and banquetings, from morn to eve…. One day, a great feast was held, and, after dinner, the representation of Solomon his Temple and the coming of the Queen of Sheba was made, or (as I may better say) was meant to have been made, before their Majesties, by device of the Earl of Salisbury and others….The Lady who did play the Queen's part, did carry most precious gifts to both their Majesties; but, forgetting the steppes arising to the canopy, overset her caskets into his

Danish Majesties lap, and fell at his feet, tho I rather think it was in his face.... Now did enter, in rich dress, Hope, Faith, and Charity: Hope did assay to speak, but wine rendered her endeavours so feeble that she withdrew, and hoped the King would excuse her brevity: Faith was then all alone, for I am certain she was not joyned with good works, and left the court in a staggering condition.... Hope and Faith ... were both sick and spewing in the lower hall. Next came Victory, in bright armour, and presented a rich sword to the King ... after much lamentable utterance, she was led away like a silly captive, and laid to sleep in the outer steps of the ante-chamber.

The result of all this was that by 1616 the English monarchy was in dire financial straits, and *The Golden Age* was probably scaled back from the earlier level of excess. Records related to the masque of 1612 show an outlay of only 280 pounds, although by 1617 the price had again risen to 2,000 pounds. Having squeezed about as much in "loans" from his subjects as he could manage, James would now turn in desperation to the aging adventurer Sir Walter Raleigh, whom he had kept locked inside the Tower of London for the past thirteen years on suspicion of treason. Raleigh would be released at last to search for the gold mines of El Dorado, which he claimed to have discovered in Venezuela during his 1594 voyage to America. But the new expedition would be likely to bring him into conflict with the Spanish, a prospect that made the English king extremely nervous.

For the previous hundred years Spain had been the preeminent Western power. Its might would soon be exposed as something of an illusion, since it rested on the foundation of an unsound and antiquated economy at home. But it was kept churning through vast amounts of gold and silver from Mexico and above all by silver from the rich mines of Potosí in present-day Bolivia. Mexico and South America at this time produced 80 percent of the world's silver and 70 percent of its gold. In Spanish there is an expression that is still used today: *Vale un Potosí*. It's worth a Potosí. It's worth a fortune. To extract the silver from the mines the Spanish used first native labor and then slaves imported from Africa.

Slavery was common in many parts of the world. Miguel de Cervantes, author of the *Quixote* — like Shakespeare, now in the final months of his life — had once been captured by North African corsairs (state-sponsored pirates) and forced to labor as a slave for five years. Corsairs in the service of the Ottomans were the most feared power in the Mediterranean. The most prominent of these was Yusuf Reis — or Jack Ward, as the onetime common sailor from Kent had been known before he converted to Islam. Now he had grown wealthy and lived lavishly, attended by Christian slaves captured in the waters of the Mediterranean by his swift raiding ships, in a majestic palace in Tangiers. A popular ballad portrayed him taunting King James:

> Go tell the King of England, go tell him this from me,
> If he reign king of all the land, I will reign king at sea.

Slaves were often treated cruelly, but traditionally they had been regarded as people rather than subhuman commodities. Some slaves rose to positions of power. Malik Ambar, an Ethiopian slave who was traded several times, ended up in India, where he became prime minister of a sultanate in the Deccan region. There, as a pioneer of guerilla warfare, he was currently a thorn in the side of the mighty Mughal ruler Jahangir. But the American slave trade that was now being developed by Portugal — the first African slave would be brought to the Bahamas this year — was different in nature. These slavers subjected their captives to horrific and degrading conditions that surpassed anything previously seen.

In the Potosí silver mines of the Bolivian Andes conditions were harsh, and the life-expectancy of the miners was no more than a handful of years. Many died of poisoning from the mercury that was used to separate the silver. In the early months of 1616 a native of the Andes named Guaman Poma — his name means Falcon Puma in the Quechua language, and he claimed to be descended from Inca royalty — completed his monumental *The First New Chronicle and Good Government*, which detailed the abuses of the Spaniards. He had worked obsessively on the book for years and now was anxious to send it to Philip III of Spain in order to instigate reforms. But there is no evidence that the Spanish king ever saw the book, and it ended up in a royal library in Denmark, where it was not rediscovered until a German researcher happened upon it in the twentieth century.

Much of the Potosí silver was sent to Mexico, where it was made into Spanish dollars. The dollars were worth eight times another unit of Spanish currency, the *real* (a Spanish word meaning "royal"). Because of this, the Spanish dollars were known to English speakers as "pieces of eight," and they were the basic unit of the seventeenth-century global economy. Nearly two hundred years later, when the United States would come into existence, it would match its dollar to this one. Until the summer of 1997, equities on the U.S. stock exchange were priced in ⅛-dollar increments as a legacy of the pieces of eight.

Apart from precious metals, the most coveted commodity on the international market in 1616 was silk, either raw or in the form of sumptuous

The former African slave Malik Ambar rose to the position of prime minister of a state in the central Indian plateau, where he led resistance against Mughal expansion. The Mughal emperor Jahangir never managed to kill Malik Ambar, but this dreamlike painting expresses his wish to do so.

In the painting Jahangir, whose name means "seizer of the world," stands on a globe, which shows India at the center. On the stand at right are emblems of Mughal ancestors going back to Tamerlane. The fish and ox at the bottom of the painting convey that Jahangir's dominion extends over land and sea. Though the Mughal court was Muslim, the fish is a symbol drawn from a Hindu creation myth, while the angels at top are of Christian origin and reflect the presence of Portuguese, centered nearby in Goa on the Indian Ocean coast.

Punishments of Miners, by Guaman Poma, drawing 325 from *El Primer Nueva Coronica y Buen Gobierno* ("The First New Chronicle and Good Government"), 1615–1616, by Guaman Poma. Bound book; ink and colors on paper, 119 x 205 cm. Det Kongelige Bibliotek, Copenhagen, Denmark.

The native Andean writer Guaman Poma completed his massive *The First New Chronicle and Good Government* in 1616 with the goal of persuading King Philip III of Spain to institute reforms to curtail abuses of native people in Peru (which at the time included modern Bolivia, where the silver mines of Potosí were located).

textiles, and the most important producer of these was China. In *The Golden Age Restored* the goddess Pallas Athena sings the praises of the new golden age:

> Then earth unplough'd shall yield her crop,
> Pure honey from the oak shall drop,
> The fountain shall run milk:
> The thistle shall the lilly bear,
> And every bramble roses wear,
> And every worm make silk.

Chinese silks, along with other goods, were brought to Manila in the Philippines on large sea-going junks that carried 200–400 men each. There the silks would be traded for the silver of the Americas, now in the form of Spanish dollars. Those dollars served as the basic currency of China.

At one time China had experimented with paper currency, but that system had been abandoned centuries before. Now, in the declining years of the Ming, China's last native dynasty, the Wanli emperor, supported by twenty thousand eunuchs and ten thousand serving women in his massive palace complex known as the Forbidden City — the largest in the world — luxuriated in the vast wealth the American silver represented. To him the king of Spain, Philip III, was known as "the King of Silver." To maximize the value of the silk trade he had required every major farmer to devote a portion of his land to the mulberry trees that the silkworms favored. As a result, a single year's silk trade could be worth two or three million dollars. In a good year the value of the silver that crossed the Pacific in the Manila galleons was greater than that of the entire trans-Atlantic trade.

In most years between twenty and sixty Chinese junks made the trip to Manila, but in 1616 only seven junks arrived. From Manila one to four galleons would make the hellish eastward passage to Acapulco each year. The massive ships would set sail around midsummer and usually arrive in Acapulco in January or February. An Italian traveler who made the trip later in the century reported that "the Voyage from the Philippine Islands to America, may be call'd the longest and most dreadful of any in the World." But both of the galleons departing from Manila in 1616 would be forced to return to port.

For more than half a century Spain had dominated much of the Pacific, which had come to be known as "the Spanish Lake." What was the cause of the failure of the Pacific trade in 1616? It may have been attributable in part to a new presence in the Pacific, one that threatened the very existence of the Spanish colony in the Philippines and the foundations of the Spanish empire.

Even as James and his court watched and participated in their extravagant masque, a ship under the Dutch captain Willem Schouten was approaching the southern tip of South America. There Schouten would discover a new passage to the Pacific through chilly waters overlooked by a promontory he would name Kaap Hoorn, after his birthplace in the Netherlands; the English, betrayed by the false cognate *Hoorn,* would call this Cape Horn. It was not an easy passage: a tradition would develop that any sailor who had made it across earned special privileges, such as the right to wear a gold loop earring and to dine with one foot on the table. Meanwhile, other Dutch vessels under Joris van Spilbergen, having navigated the narrow Straits of Magellan, had already made their way up the Pacific coast of the Americas, plundering and terrorizing the Spanish along the way.

Suddenly the Pacific was a stage of battle between the Chinese, Japanese, Spanish, Portuguese, Dutch, and English, along with various local kingdoms. The conflicts spilled over into South and West Asia, where the Turks, Persians, and Mughal Indians vied for supremacy. With the rounding of Cape Horn and the new global economy based on American silver, globalism had become a reality.

Van Spilbergen was in the service of a powerful entity that was challenging the preeminence of Spain. This was a new kind of power that would soon make the Habsburg empire of loosely confederated monarchies seem positively quaint. Van Spilbergen had been charged with sailing across the Pacific to Java, an important source of spices (nutmeg was more valuable than gold at this time), by the Dutch East India Company — the Vereenigde Oost-Indische Compagnie, or VOC. The States-General of the Netherlands had granted the VOC a monopoly on trade in Asia. Even though Spain and the Netherlands had made uneasy peace in 1603, the VOC retained for itself the right to wage war if it saw the need to do

Portrait of a Civil Official, early seventeenth century. China. Ink and colors on silk, 89 x 157 cm (image). Asian Art Museum, 2007.25.

Over the long span of the Ming dynasty (1368–1644), China's meritocracy, built on command of the Confucian classics as demonstrated in examinations, produced a large bureaucracy in which civil officials were often at odds with the emperor and the eunuchs of the Forbidden City. Resulting governmental inefficiencies contributed to the weakening of the state, which in 1644 would give way to the Manchurians of the Qing dynasty.

so — in distant locations agreements made back home were not always observed. It could also coin its own money, establish colonies, and make treaties with other powers. The company had issued stock to international investors to whom it would pay dividends. Rather than finance expeditions on a one-off basis as had been the mode until now, the VOC was looking for long-range profit from a coordinated series of ventures. The English East India Company was formed around the same time along similar lines. These new powers were, in short, the world's first megacorporations.

Warfare was pervasive. In the Americas, constant warfare together with epidemic diseases had over the past century reduced the native population to less than 10 percent of pre-contact numbers. Europe was on the brink of the prolonged and devastating conflagration known at the Thirty Years War. It would be the most traumatic European war prior to World War I. Japan, on the other hand, exhausted from its own internal battles, was entering a new era of uneasy peace. Korea, scarred and recoiling from two brutal invasions by the Japanese, was also retreating into isolationism.

The third East Asian power, China, which had sent large numbers of troops to defend Korea, was also tired. The Wanli emperor had reached an impasse with the civil bureaucrats of his regime, who objected to his personal excesses. In effect, both sides had a sort of veto power over much of the workings of the government, with no mechanism for resolving disagreements. As a result the corpulent emperor had withdrawn inside his inner palace, and the government was effectively paralyzed. China was widely seen as rich but weak, and Mongols, Japanese, and Spaniards were among those watching for an opportunity to go in for the kill. Even the Manchu vassals to China's northeast mocked its claim to be the center of the world to which all other states must pay tribute. In 1616 a Manchu leader named Nurhaci — who had observed that Chinese generals sent to check him usually just made a few meaningless maneuvers and then falsified their reports — would have the audacity to proclaim himself the head of a new dynasty.

In Southeast Asia all the world's major powers were engaged in a messy fight for supremacy in trade profiteering. Portugal, once the principal European power in the region, was struggling to maintain its bases in Goa and Melaka. Spain knew that it had to confront the Dutch and English, but the defeat of its armada in the English Channel in 1588 and subsequent military setbacks in the Netherlands, on its border with France, and in its own principality of Naples had undone the optimism of the allied European defeat of the Ottomans at Lepanto and the surprising successes of Spain's outmanned conquistadors in the Americas. Now, in Manila, it was assembling a new armada that would be by far the greatest naval force ever seen in those waters, and it hoped this time to have greater success.

Around the Indian Ocean the Portuguese had been a commanding presence throughout the sixteenth century, but now their dominance was declining. Even at its height it was never as great as Western historians used to suggest — power shifts in the region had been as much the result of the rise of the three great Islamic empires, the Ottomans of Turkey, the Safavids of Persia, and the Mughals of India, as they had been of the entry of the Portuguese into the region. Having rounded Africa, the Portuguese had fastened onto existing networks of trade and exchange. They had mostly been content to establish a chain of fortified coastal cities to support their maritime activities. But now the Dutch and the English had begun penetrating into the interior of many parts of Asia.

The Dutch and English competed in Asia not just with preestablished powers but also with each other. In 1616 they did battle over the tiny island of Run in the Moluccas archipelago, which was rich in nutmeg, a single sack of which could set a man up for life. The Dutch were led by the ruthless Jan Pieterszoon Coen, whose motto was "Spare your enemies not, for God is with us." True to his word, he would later massacre virtually the entire population of the Banda Islands, in one of history's most notorious incidents of genicide. Ultimately the English lost the Spice Islands of Southeast Asia to the Dutch, and they were forced to concentrate their activites farther north. (The two powers later signed a treaty by which England conceded its claim to the Spice Islands, receiving. Manhattan in exchange. It seemed to the Dutch a good deal at the time.) In 1616 England sent its first official ambassador to the Mughal court of Jahangir.

The three Islamic powers derived the authority and legitimacy for their regimes in different ways. The Ottomans, who had little genuine claim to dynastic rule, derived their prestige from military might; they asserted no religious authority except through their role as warriors for Islam. The Mughals carried the prestige of an illustrious dynastic pedigree. Religious figures had influence but little aspiration to political power in Mughal India (where the majority subject population was Hindu), but in Safavid Persia, where authority depended on religious righteousness, they went so far as to claim that even political power should reside in the religious leadership — an aspiration finally realized centuries later, in 1979. All three powers were engaged in territorial battles. Mughal leaders sought to consolidate and expand their territories south through India while holding ground against Safavid Persia in current Pakistan

and Afghanistan. The success of Shah Abbas in overcoming Persian factionalism allowed him to check the expansionist ambitions of the Ottomans, who were unable to fully pursue their long-standing battle with Christian Europe because of the Persian threat from the east and the encroachments of cossacks from the Russian steppes to the north. Pressured on all fronts, and damaged economically by the influx of American silver into Europe, the Ottomans would eventually be forced to abandon their goal of expanding farther into Europe.

Suffering through what is known as its Time of Troubles, Russia seemed hopelessly ensnared in conflict. After the deaths of Ivan the Terrible and his successor Boris Gudonov, the country was desperately searching for a new leader. But only impostors appeared to claim the throne, and legitimate heirs ran away when they heard the call to assume the role of tsar. Finally, kicking and screaming, a young man named Mikhail I Fyodorovich Romanov had been hauled to the throne, and the long rule of the Romanovs had tottered off on its iffy beginnings, as the nearly leaderless country was locked in seemingly hopeless battle against the formidable powers of Sweden and Poland.

Even the Jesuits had turned militaristic. In South America they had formed what they called "reductions." These were utopian societies of native peoples whom the priests armed and trained as military forces to repel *bandeirantes* — slavers and fortune-hunters — from Brazil. In 1616 nearly three hundred Belgian Jesuits would travel to the Rio Plate to join the heavily armed, cultlike, millenarian communities.

But attitudes toward warfare were slowly changing. In the West, members of the aristocracy had traditionally been defined by their prowess as warriors, and in paintings they had nearly always been depicted in martial poses. Now a courtier like Buckingham could advance through prowess not on the battlefield but on the dance floor, and the elite were as likely to be painted as scholars surrounded by books as they were to be depicted as military leaders. In Japan military prowess was giving way to ritual symbolism, and samurai armor, designed for ceremonies, would eventually become so stylized as to be impractical for battle. In 1616 the Dutch painter Rubens was still doing martial studies of young men in armor, but within a few years he would turn from celebrating warfare to depicting its atrocities and devastations; a similar change would occur later in the century in the paintings of Spanish artists such as Diego Velázquez.

In China some of the educated elite, disgusted with the excesses and corruption of the imperial court, withdrew from it entirely. They retreated to country cottages to write poems or paint landscapes. One

Opposite: Shah Abbas I and a Pageboy, 1627, by Muhammad Qasim. Isfahan, Iran. Ink, opaque watercolor, gold, and silver on paper. *Louvre, Paris.*

Shah Abbas I "The Great" made Safavid Persia an important player on the world stage. Under his rule Persia became a significant check on the power of the Ottoman empire. Abbas also established diplomatic relations with European powers, and several European travelers visited him at his court in Isfahan, which he made his capital in 1598.

It has been suggested that this scene depicts a New Year's feast. In Persia the new year began on March 21. The inscription reads "May life bring you all you desire of three lips: the lip of your lover, the lip of the stream, and the lip of the cup."

This is one of the last portraits of Abbas, who is recognizable by his distinctive drooping moustache. The artist, Muhammad Qasim, shows an awareness of both European and Chinese painting styles, reflecting both Persia's strategic geographic position and the effects of nascent globalization in the early seventeenth century.

Susanna and the Elders is the first dated and signed work by Artemisia Gentileschi; it was painted when she was seventeen years old, prior to the rape and notorious trial that resulted in her moving to Florence, where she became a member of the academy of painters in 1616.

In the biblical story, Susanna is a virtuous women who was sexually harassed by the elders of her community. Male artists of the Italian Renaissance had typically depicted Susanna as flirtatious, but Gentileschi depicts her recoiling from the menacing elders' attentions.

Gentileschi was raped by a painter named Agostino Tassi, a colleague of her father. In 1616 Tassi was painting frescos in the Quirinale Palace in Rome that depicted ambassadors to the Vatican from Persia, Japan, and elsewhere (pp. 252, 335). It is possible that unwelcome male attentions contributed to Gentileschi's unusual interpretation of the traditional scene.

writer, calling himself "the Scoffing Scholar of Lanling," devoted years to constructing an elaborate erotic novel that reached a length of 2,923 woodblock-printed pages.

Significant changes were being seen in social roles. While witchcraft, formerly gender-neutral, had increasingly come to be associated with women, in other areas women were beginning to break into once exclusively male domains. In Florence the artist Artemisia Gentileschi would be accepted this year into the academy of painters, the first woman so honored. This was a remarkable triumph, as only a few years before she had fled to Florence from Rome, where she had been the focus of a scandalous and humiliating trial. She had been raped by an associate of her father. To test her truthfulness the authorities had invasively examined and cruelly tortured her.

This was also the year the Powhatan maiden Matoaka — also known as Rebecca Rolfe but best known as Pocahontas — would travel to England, where she would witness a court masque entitled *The Vision of Delight,* featuring Buckingham, the king's new favorite. Although most of the world's population spent their lives within about twenty miles of their homes, there were many remarkable travelers like Matoaka, several of whom have left accounts of foreign wonders. In addition to adventurers and fortune-seekers, especially from England, Spain, Portugal, Italy, the Netherlands, China, and Japan, there were traveling peddlers and merchants — Malay merchants were helping to spread Islam throughout Southeast Asia — and there were also traveling diplomats, refugees, slaves, explorers, pilgrims, artesans, missionaries, and even a few tourists, traveling not in any of those capacities but for personal gratification. A wandering Scot named William Lithgow traversed Europe and crossed North Africa, dining along the way with the corsair Yusuf Reis in his palace in Tangiers. Lithgow's countryman the scholar and linguist George Strahan traveled to Isfahan in Persia and conversed with Shah Abbas. Another European traveler in West Asia was an Italian named Pietro Della Valle, who carved his name on a pyramid in Egypt and got a souvenir tattoo on a visit to the holy land. In 1616 della Valle joined a caravan to Baghdad, where he married a woman who had grown up there, in the heart of the Ottoman empire; together they would continue on to Isfahan, the new capital recently constructed by the Persian shah, and from there head on to India.

One of the most curious travelers was an ambitious author on the fringes of Ben Jonson's circle named Thomas Coryate. He had made a literary splash with an account of his travels through Europe — almost all on foot, in a single pair of shoes (which he subsequently displayed in his hometown church, where they continued to hang until the nineteenth century). The book was

Thomas Coryate,

TRAVAILER
For the English wits, and the good of this Kingdom:

To all his inferiour Countreymen, Greeting: Espe-
*cially to the Sirenicall Gentlemen, that meet the first Friday of euerie
Moneth,* at the Mermaide in Breadstreet. From the Court of
the great *Mogul, resident at the Towne of* Asmere, *in the Easterne*
India.

Printed by W. Iaggard, and Henry Fetherston.
1616.

*Greeting from the Court of the
Great Mogul,* 1616. Cover of
a book by Thomas Coryate.
London.

Thomas Coryate described his European travels in 1611 in a hefty but
entertaining travelogue entitled
Coryat's Crudities, which became a
best-seller.

Five years later, determined to
outdo that success, he set out on new
travels through the eastern Mediterranean and West Asia, ending up in
1616 in India, where he addressed
the Mughal emperor Jahangir. A
collection of his letters from India
was collected in this small book
published in London in 1616.

entitled *Coryat's Crudities: Hastily Gobbled up
in Five Months Travels in France, Italy, Rhetia
Commonly called the Grisons Country, Helvetia
Alias Switzerland, Some Parts of High Germany
and the Netherlands; Newly Digested in the
Hungry Aire of Odcombe in the County of Somerset, and Now Dispersed to the Nourishment of
the Travelling Members of this Kingdome;* it had
become a literary sensation. Eager to outdo that
best-seller, Coryate decided to extend his range,
and from Turkey he hiked to India, where he
addressed Jahangir; 1616 found him in India,
concerned that he had bitten off more than he
could chew and despairing of ever returning to
publish his new volume.

Another notable traveler was a samurai
named Yamada Nagamasa. Japan was one of
the most active powers in East and Southeast
Asia in the early years of the seventeenth century. Some of the vessels that departed almost
every day from its harbors were known as "red
seal ships." These were combination merchant
ships and warships — in this respect rather like
those of the Dutch VOC — and they traded
actively in the Philippines, Vietnam, Thailand, and elsewhere. Traveling
on these ships, some Japanese founded colonies in such far-away places
as Vietnam and Thailand. Yamada Nagamasa, a Zen practitioner who became a samurai warrior and was said to have proved his mettle by quelling
ghosts and witches in his native Japan, journeyed in one of the red seal
ships to Thailand. There, thanks to his skill as a warrior and the superiority
of Japanese swords, which were the finest in the world, he played a role in
installing a new king on the throne of Ayutthaya, as the kingdom of Thailand was then known. For years he ruled as the governor of a province in
southern Thailand.

He was not the only samurai to travel great distances. In November
1616 Pope Paul V welcomed a samurai named Hasekura Tsunenaga to
St. Paul's in the Vatican. Hasekura's embassy was unprecedented. He had
crossed the Pacific to Acapulco and traveled by donkey across New Spain
to Veracruz on the Caribbean coast. From there he had sailed to Seville in
Spain on his way to Rome; on the return he would pass by way of Manila.

His arduous journey was intended to secure trade agreements between Japan and the European powers.

But over the years Hasekura had been away Shogun Hidetada had grown alarmed by inroads made into Japan by evangelical Europeans, and he had decided to outlaw Christianity and slam the door on all outsiders. Once the missionaries gain a foothold, can the soldiers be far behind? Over the course of the current year he would increasingly impose restrictions and penalties on foreign contact, finally almost entirely closing Japan off to the outside world, a closure that the country would sustain for two and a half centuries — Japan's next embassy to Europe would not occur until 1862.

Japan had largely withdrawn, but there were still plenty of masquers on the international stage to take part in 1616's "pyrrhic dance." In London's Whitehall, Astraea, the goddess of justice, appeared to have the final word. As the masque drew to a close, she predicted the advent of a new world order:

Harlequin, early seventeenth century. Murano (Veneto), Italy. Glassware. *Castel Vecchio Museum, Trent, Italy.*

Murano glass workers were among the best in the world. Their expertise contributed to the refinement of the telescope by Galileo.

Harlequin began as an acrobatic comic servant in the Commedia dell'Arte. His original patchwork costume was already starting to assume its later more regular diamond pattern in this piece of glassware.

> It is become a heaven on earth,
> And Jove is present here,
> I feel the God-head: nor will doubt
> But he can fill the place throughout,
> Whose power is every where.
>
> This, this, and only such as this,
> The bright Astræa's region is,
> Where she would pray to live,
> And in the midst of so much gold,
> Unbought with grace or fear unsold,
> The law to mortals give.

Forging a heaven on earth is a tall order. Would Astraea really have the final word? How would the masque's aristocratic fantasia compare to the reality of the year 1616? Would the golden age be restored? Were the revelers the vanguard of a new world order? Or were they just lost in a masquerade?

1　Silk and Silver

The China Road was not much of a road. Little more than a furrow spattered with mule droppings, it wound for more than two hundred miles from the capital on its high plateau through rugged mountains, dense Brazilwood forests, and desolate plains before giving itself up onto the broad, deep bay. The trip usually took about a week to ten days and required several river crossings. Constructed by native laborers and first opened to pack animal travel in 1573, the road was not made passable for wheeled vehicles until 1927. Around the bay spread a village of barely a thousand souls — Filipinos, Malays, Chinese, mestizos, runaway slaves — who lived out a hand-to-mouth existence in rude shacks. Mixed in with the dwellings was a handful of public buildings: a church, a convent, a hospital, a treasury office. With its punishing heat, pestilent marshes, venomous snakes, relentless insects, and scarcity of fresh water, the town was unfondly known as "the door to hell."

High granite walls encircled the arc of the bay, plunging down to the sea, except for the thin strip on which the town rested. They reflected and amplified the tropical light, flooding it onto the town. The mountain walls extinguished any hope of cooling sea breezes (in the eighteenth century an opening was cut through them to bring some relief), but the sheer slopes also made the bay extraordinarily deep, right up to the shelf of the sunbaked shore. As a result, large ocean-going vessels could come so close that the seamen would sometimes just tie up to a tree rather than anchor farther out in the bay. The bay's semicircular shape, together with an island that divided it into two parts, created an inner harbor that sheltered ships from sea winds. One world traveler who passed through in the 1600s rated it "the best and safest harbor in the world."

It had a reputation as an unhealthful place, a reputation that didn't improve over time. In the sixteenth century Spanish bureaucrats stationed there called it "a hot and sickly land" and begged to be "freed from the captivity" of their posts. In the seventeenth century an Italian traveler dismissed it as "mean and wretched," littered with houses "made of nothing but wood, mud, and straw." In the eighteenth century a governor of the Philippines described it as "an abbreviated inferno" full of "venomous serpents," while a French navy captain called it "a miserable little place, though dignified with the name of a city; and being surrounded with volcanic mountains its atmosphere is constantly thick and unwholesome." In

Opposite: Acapulco Bay (detail), color lithograph from a 1628 watercolor probably by Johannes Vingboons based on a drawing by Adrian Boot. Benson Latin American Collection, University of Texas at Austin.

Adrian Boot designed and oversaw the construction of the Castilo San Diego in 1616 to protect the only authorized American port for the lucrative Asian galleon trade. In this lithograph based on a drawing by Boot himself and bearing his signature, the five-sided fort can be seen on its promontory overlooking the bay, below and to the right of the figure arriving on horseback by way of the China Road from Mexico City. Below the fort lies the sparse settlement of the town itself, and the drawing shows the advantageous situation of the bay as a harbor for vessels.

For the complicated provenance of this image and those of Mexico City and Veracruz on pages 39 and 81, see the Source Notes section, p. 362.

COME WITH **ELVIS** TO FABULOUS ACAPULCO!

Promotional poster for the film
Fun in Acapulco, 1963.

The 1963 movie starring Elvis Pres-
ley and Ursula Andress promoted
Acapulco's mid-twentieth-century
reputation as a swinging destination. Today the city is known in
Mexico as a weekend getaway
for residents of the capital. Internationally, it is best known for
spring break excesses and drug war
violence.

Elvis, playing a lifeguard and
hotel singer, performs such unfor-
gettable songs as *Margarita, The
Bullfighter Was a Lady,* and the incomparable *No Room to Rhumba
in a Sports Car.* Elvis's scenes were
shot on a Hollywood lot. He never
visited Acapulco.

the nineteenth century another French visitor complained
of the "frightful" climate and judged it "the most paltry
village ... a desolate picture.... The whole aspect is somber
and wild and inspires a profound melancholy," while a German explorer called it "savage ... dismal and romantic" and
rated it "one of the most unhealthy places of the New Continent.... The unfortunate inhabitants breathe a burning air,
full of insects." Then, in the middle of the twentieth century,
it briefly became a playground of the jet set.

The site took its name — Acapulco — from a Nahuatl
phrase thought to mean "place of broken reeds," but to Spanish ears it sounded like "agua pulcra" — clean water — and
this seemed to make sense because of the bay's great depths.
But after a night of hard drinking it probably sounded more
like "agua pulque," or pulque water. Pulque is an alcoholic
drink made from the fermented sap of the maguey plant. Popular in Mexico at least since Aztec times, it is thick, opaque,
and slightly foamy, like the waters of the bay, or the drinkers'
tongues and brains. But whatever you called it, this forlorn
spot was one of the most important places in the world. Through it passed
much of the world's silver, the default currency of the new global economy.

In January 1616 the China Road was flooded with thousands of travelers
of every description, all on their way to the bay. Among them were government officials, wealthy gentry or their representatives, soldiers, miners, friars,
merchants, peddlers, craftsmen, sailors, adventurers, caulkers, carpenters,
blacksmiths, sail makers, porters, gold panners, gamblers, prostitutes, beggars, healers and herbalists, fortune tellers, actors, clowns, and cutpurses.
Caravans of mules were prodded forward by professional muleteers and
their assistants and slaves.

A Dutch engineer named Adrian Boot would likely have been among
the throngs descending the China Road. As he wound his way down to the
bay the engineer observed the progress on the fortress that he had recently
designed, called the Castilo San Diego de Acapulco, now under hurried
construction. Beyond the fort, and the town it overlooked, he saw resting
in the harbor two enormous galleons, each weighing in at between a thousand and two thousand tons (a law limiting their size to three hundred
tons was routinely ignored). The residents of New Spain called these the
naos de China, the China ships. They were the richest vessels in the world,
and their presence would transform the town. The giant ships had set sail
from Manila, nine thousand miles away (and substantially farther by the

routes they had taken), half a year before, in the summer of 1615, taking advantage of that season's monsoon winds. Happily, each had arrived safely in Acapulco, one on Christmas Eve, the other on January 1.

It was never an easy journey. While the westward voyage was a not-too-hazardous straight shot lasting about four months, the return trip was much longer — sometimes taking as many as nine months — and considerably more difficult. To catch favorable winds the galleons would first sail north, in the early years sometimes stopping in Japan, and then cross at a latitude of about 40 degrees — about as far north as New York City. Had they continued on that course they would have reached land near the present Eureka, California, but since some early galleons had been wrecked off Cape Mendocino they instead angled south as soon as they saw seaweed, shorebirds, and other indications of approaching landfall. The galleon voyages continued regularly for 250 years, from the first crossing in 1565 until 1815, when the Mexican War of Independence brought them to an end; yet, because of their far northern route, the ships never discovered the Hawaiian islands, which would have made a most welcome midway resting point.

Even leaving aside the *arribadas* — ships that were forced to return to port (all four of the ships departing Manila in 1616 and 1617 would fall into this category) — and other ships that were destroyed by storms or simply vanished (in the first decade of the 1600s six galleons were lost), the trip was perilous. The voyage was "the longest and most dreadful of any in the world," a seventeenth-century traveler wrote without exaggeration, "as well because of the vast ocean to be crossed, being about one half of the terraqueous globe, with the wind always ahead, as for the terrible tempests that happen there, one upon the back of another, and for the desperate diseases that seize people in seven or eight months, lying sometimes near the line of the equator, sometimes cold, sometimes temperate, and sometimes hot, enough to destroy a man of steel, much less flesh and blood."

Scurvy was always a problem on the eastward trips, and thousands of sailors and passengers perished during the journey over the long history of the voyages. "When it returns from that climate," gloated a French buccaneer, "all the crew are so sick and moribund, that of four hundred men who may compose it not a quarter are in condition to defend her, for the malady known as scurvy never fails on the way from the Philippines." (The Frenchman never took one of the huge, heavily armed ships, however; nor did anyone else except the English, who captured four, in 1585, 1709, 1743, and 1762.) Eighty people perished on a 1606 voyage, ninety-nine in 1620, one hundred five in 1629, one hundred fourteen in 1643. Around midcentury a ghost galleon was discovered drifting near Acapulco on which every person on board lay dead.

Those voyagers who survived the trip found it anything but pleasant. An Italian who made the crossing toward the end of the century reported that "there is hunger, thirst, sickness, cold, continual wakefulness, and other sufferings; besides the terrible shocks from side to side, caused by the furious beating of the waves... the ship swarms with little vermin the Spaniards call *gorgojos* [weevils], bred in the biscuit; so swift that in a short time they not only run over cabins, beds, and the very dishes the men eat on, but insensibly fasten upon the body.... There are several other sorts of vermin of sundry colors, that suck the blood. A multitude of flies fall into the dishes of broth, in which there also swim worms of several sorts.... On fish days the common diet was old rank fish boiled in fair water and salt; at noon we had mangos, something like kidney beans, in which there were so many maggots, that they swam at top of the broth, and the quantity was so great, that besides the loathing they caused, I doubted whether the dinner was fish or flesh."

Small wonder that when the first signs of land were spotted the ships often erupted in a saturnalia called the *fiesta de las señas,* the festival of the signs. A law requiring such festivities to be kept within the bounds of "decency and modesty" must have been difficult to enforce. For the occasion the seamen, "clad after a ridiculous manner," formed a mock court and sentenced the officers and passengers for all manner of transgressions. The thought of land cast away much of the gloom, despite everyone's weakened state.

As a galleon followed the coastline south it would eventually be spotted from land. Often the first sighting would occur off Baja California. Messengers in small swift boats would spread the word, which would be taken up by horsemen and long-distance runners, so that by the time the galleon pulled into the bay it seemed the whole world knew of its arrival. It would not be long before it would be joined at harbor by smaller trade ships that had made the trip up the coast from Peru, along with a few from Central America and Chile.

On the approach of the galleon an escort boat was sent out to guide the big ship into the bay. The escort was charged with preventing any contact with the galleon before it was turned over to court officials. This was the first of several steps intended to ensure that imperial regulations were observed and all taxes paid. The shipping industry was highly regulated. Acapulco had had an officially authorized monopoly on the trans-Pacific trade since 1579 — there was no other legal landing port anywhere in the Americas — and trade between Mexico and Peru was limited in an effort to keep it from cutting into the trans-Atlantic trade with Spain itself. But the elaborate regulations were to a large degree a universally agreed-upon fiction, and all parties routinely conspired on violations of many of them.

The official bills of lading typically omitted large portions of the ships' cargoes. These might be offloaded up the coast before the ships reached Acapulco, or the arrival might be arranged at nightfall, when the ships were not allowed to enter the bay. Then the contraband goods would be lowered over the side during the night onto boats waiting to receive them.

Arrival into the bay itself would be celebrated with a firing of all of the galleon's guns. Before anyone could disembark, the keeper of the fort and the treasury officials would come aboard for an inspection. It was understood by everyone that the inspection would consist of accepting the sworn statements of the shippers as accurate without actually checking the cargo. In 1636 one inspector violated this understanding and opened some packages to determine their contents, thereby becoming the most hated figure in the history of the galleons — in response a new decree was quickly made prohibiting officials from "any innovation in the opening of packages."

When the statements were accepted by the inspector they were sent by couriers to the capital, where the duties for the cargo were calculated and then conveyed back to the coast to be applied. By traveling around the clock the couriers could make the trip in three or four days each way. At this point, notes William Lytle Schurz, whose book *The Manila Galleon* (published in 1939 and now unfortunately out of print) is still the foremost reference on the galleon trade, "when the letter of the law had been complied with in this fashion and health drunk all around, both parties proceeded to the real business of the occasion — the making of arrangements for the landing of the illegal merchandise," that is, such of it as hadn't already been offloaded. Then, finally, the sick were transported to the hospital and the comparatively healthy to the church to give thanks for their good fortune. The cargo was taken to secured warehouses to await the opening of the fair, although if not enough palms were greased an unfortunate shipper might find his merchandise seized, removed to the royal warehouse, and sold off to enrich the king's accounts.

Despite the hellish conditions of the voyage, in a few months many of the sailors would be back. The westward-bound ships usually departed between late February and the end of April. "Notwithstanding the dreadful suffering in this prodigious voyage," one traveler reported, "the desire of gain prevails upon many to do it four, six, or even ten times. The sailors, though they foreswear the voyage when out at sea, yet when they come to Acapulco, for the love of 275 pesos, never remember past sufferings, like women after their labor."

As the engineer Adrian Boot made his way down the China Road to the bay he could make out a multitude of creatures moving around like bugs over the burning sands — on closer view these would reveal themselves to be visitors to the Acapulco Fair, which despite the wretchedness of the town and the grimness of the Pacific crossing was one of the most famous and liveliest in the world. They were a diverse group, bedecked in all the costumes of the globe. They came from inland Mexico, from Peru, from the shores of the Caribbean, from Europe, Asia, and the far-flung world. They would swell the town to five times its normal population. Unfortunately, there was not a single hotel or inn in the town until 1698, so everyone vied for the right to a corner in the few available hovels; for the majority the beach would serve as home for the duration of their visit. Food, drink, and hospitality in Acapulco were notorious for high prices and low quality.

The trade fairs would last about two months. When the fair was on, the indolent village became a restless place. Food and water had to be brought in regularly from the interior. Stevedores loaded and unloaded merchandise; new warehouses would need to be constructed to store it. Soldiers, their numbers swollen from a few dozen in the off-season to two hundred or more when the galleons were in port, enforced the peace and guarded the warehouses in which the precious cargo was stored. Entertainers, prostitutes, and con men did their best to redistribute the wealth. Ship workers were kept busy making repairs for the long return voyage, for which crews would need to be assembled and passengers recruited. Not all of the passengers were volunteers — a trip to Manila was an effective way to get rid of troublemakers. Servants sometimes found themselves sold as slaves at the end of their journey.

Boot, arriving from his home in Mexico City, was in the employ of the Spanish crown. He had been recruited in Paris by the Spanish ambassador in 1612 and had sailed to New Spain two years later. His assignment was to review and, if necessary, repair or redesign an ambitious drainage system that was being constructed to relieve flooding in Mexico City. As a consequence of the destruction of Aztec dikes during the Bloody Night when Cortés and his allied native armies overthrew the central Mexican empire, the city — located on a island and landfill in the lowest of five valley lakes — had been subject to regular flooding. The problem was exacerbated by the Spaniards'

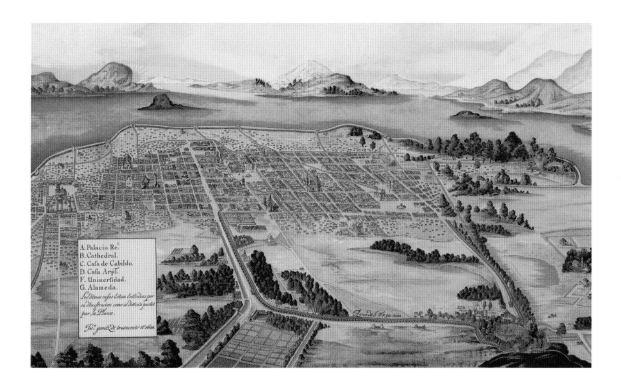

A. Palacio Re.
B. Cathedral.
C. Casa de Cabildo.
D. Casa Arpl.
F. Uniuersidad.
G. Alameda.

removal of surrounding trees in order to plow the land and graze livestock. On several occasions houses simply washed away; at other times residents were confined to the upper stories, and streets were navigated by boat.

One solution would have been to move the city, but occupying the Aztec capital was a powerful symbolic gesture that the conquerors, whose control was reliant on alliances with native peoples hostile to the old empire, were reluctant to abandon. Cortés had personally written to the king, arguing that centering New Spain on this location would legitimize it. It was the foremost city of the Americas. When goods from Asia arrived by way of the China Road from Acapulco, if they were bound for Europe, they would continue down the Europe Road to Veracruz, where they would be loaded onto vessels bound for Seville in Spain.

Another engineer, named Enrico Martinez, had been given the lead in fixing the capital's flooding problem prior to Boot's arrival. Born Heinrich Martin, he was a German who had converted to Catholicism in Spain (some sources say he was a Frenchman named Henri Martin, but this seems unlikely since in addition to his work as an engineer, he served as an interpreter of Flemish and German for the Inquisition). Martinez was one of the first printers of the Americas, specializing in the publishing of didactic books and pamphlets. He was Mexico's official cartographer and cosmographer, in which capacity he charted the movements of celestial bodies.

Mexico City, 1628, color lithograph from a watercolor probably by Johannes Vingboons based on a drawing by Juan Gómez de Trasmonte.

Flooding was a persistent problem in Mexico City, which was built on a site of lakes and swamps. The engineers Enrico Martinez and Adrian Boot were involved in a dispute that lasted for decades about how to address the problem. In 1628 Boot commissioned architect Juan Gómez de Trasmonte to produce this map of the city showing his plan at work. It is one of the few surviving representations of the city in the seventeenth century.

He also taught mathematics. He was in thick with influential people — the grand inquisitor Torquemada put his personal stamp of approval on one of Martinez's books, a sweeping survey of cosmology and the natural history of New Spain. He was, in short, a personage of importance — one twentieth-century scholar claimed that he "had brought to the intellectual atmosphere of Mexico the first feeble intimations of the dawning age of science and technology."

Applying his advanced skills in engineering and mathematics, Martinez had an enormous canal and tunnel excavated to drain the city. The tunnel was dug as much as 150 feet under the earth. It was eleven feet high and ran for more than eight miles. Nearly five thousand native workers were employed in its construction. It was one of the biggest projects of its type since the days of ancient Rome. It had only one flaw — it didn't work. The soft soil of the marshy valley was not well suited to tunneling, and the drain frequently became clogged and backed up. It was also built at too steep a slope, so that running water created great pressure against its walls, causing the tunnel to collapse.

On inspecting the canal Boot immediately dismissed the entire project as unworkable. He proposed instead a system of dikes similar to those used in his homeland (and not unlike the old Aztec system that the Spaniards had destroyed). Unsurprisingly, his opposition to Martinez's pet project did not win him a friend. Martinez claimed that Boot "does not seem to be an engineer nor to have been one in any part of the world in peace or war. He does not know any arithmetic, geometry, architecture…which it is necessary for an engineer to know. And thus it may well be doubted that he is the person sent by the King, since the tasks which he has had here are of…hardly any skill. The cleaning of canals, diversion of rivers, and building of dikes are very simple works, which even the Indians used to do."

The impasse between the two engineers was never fully resolved, as the city officials wavered back and forth between one plan and the other (along with an occasional oddball notion from some other quarter), all the while pleading for friendly cooperation between the engineers, Martinez and Boot. Finally, in the summer of 1616, the Viceroy of New Spain, after weighing the countless and widely varying opinions, contentious argumentation, and lengthy reviews, would give the go-ahead to Martinez to attempt to repair and make functional his work, overruling Boot's objections. Still, Boot would continue to work on and off on the vexing Mexico City drainage problem until 1827.

Under the circumstances, Boot was probably relieved to spend 1616 devoting his attention to expanding the fortifications in Acapulco, an assignment he had been given the previous year. What had alarmed Mexican officials at that time was an event involving another Netherlander, the Dutch pirate (as the Spanish thought him) Joris van Spilbergen. Spilbergen was a veteran of expeditions to Africa and around the Cape of Good Hope to Southeast Asia, and was acclaimed as a hero of the Battle of Gibraltar where the Spanish had been defeated in 1607.

It was not the first time enhanced fortifications had been proposed at Acapulco. Following the entry of Francis Drake into the Pacific through the Straits of Magellan in 1578 a proposal was advanced in 1582. Following raids by Thomas Cavendish in 1587 the proposal was repeated in 1593. Following Dutch expeditions in 1599 and 1600 it was repeated yet again in 1600. But nothing had come of any of these, because no one was willing to pick up the expense of building a formidable fort.

Sponsored by the powerful Dutch East India Company, Spilbergen was in command of eight hundred men, equally divided between sailors and soldiers, on a fleet of four warships, each nearly as large as the Spanish galleons, along with two swift, smaller *jachts* (one of which deserted off the coast of Chile). The Dutch East India Company (Vereenigde Oost-Indische Compagnie), founded in 1602, was known throughout the world as the VOC thanks to its logo featuring those initials, which became the first global corporate brand. The VOC was the world's first large joint-stock company, thanks to a decision by the States-General of the Netherlands to consolidate the country's commercial operations. Because most previous commercial ventures had been one-offs, for any given project new money had to be raised, insurance obtained, and participants recruited. The Dutch government, which was getting a later start on the Asia trade than the Portuguese and Spanish, was afraid that piecemeal efforts would be ineffectual and result in Dutch interests competing against each other. To correct this, it asked the various companies to merge into one corporation, which would be given a monopoly on the Asia trade; failure to participate would mean companies would not be allowed to trade there. In exchange, the corporation, governed by seventeen board members representing "chambers" from various cities and provinces, would be allowed limitless profits, less a small tax. Hundred of investors contributed funds to capitalize the company's operations. Before long it would centralize its Asian presence in Batavia (modern Jakarta) in Indonesia.

The new Dutch empire that would result from the operations of the VOC was fundamentally different from the Spanish and Portuguese

Logo of the Dutch East India Company (Vereenigde Oost-Indische Compagnie).

In the early seventeenth century the logo of the Dutch East India Company was one of the most widely recognized symbols in the world.

Aquapolque (Acapulco), 1619, by Nicolaes van Geelkercken, engraving, from *East and West Indian Mirror,* which combines accounts of the navigations of Joris van Spilbergen and Jacob le Maire.

The Dutch sea captain Joris van Spilbergen threatened Acapulco in 1615, causing the Spanish to hastily erect a fort to protect the city the following year (under the direction of another Netherlander, Adrian Boot). The engravings in van Spilbergen's book, apparently by the publisher Nicolaes van Geelkercken, are accompanied by text that is less polished than that of the main account by van Spilbergen himself. The author of the key to this engraving exaggerates in calling the town's fortifications a castle, as the fort was not constructed until the following year. The key reads as follows:

Aquapolque

With its explanation in what manner the Spanish prisoners were ransomed.

A. Is our fleet, consisting of five ships and a small Spanish vessel, which is lying on guard outside the bay.
B. Is the first meeting, each holding a small white flag as a sign of peace.
C. Are our boats, with the Spanish prisoners, who are released and set at liberty.
D. Are a number of asses, bringing our men victuals from the Spaniards.
E. Are a number of sheep, oxen, and other animals being shipped.
F. Is a castle occupied by Spaniards, and well provided with cannon.
G. Is the church or monastery.
H. Is the hamlet or town of Aquapolque.
I. Is a wonderful fish that is caught off the coast there.
K. Are some horsemen we saw with some more victuals that are being brought to us.

Aquapolque.

Nº 14

G

F

K

A

A

A

I

Indians had a long acquaintance
with Europeans. When Vasco da
Gama arrived at Calicut he was
readily identified as an Iberian.

By the early seventeenth century
Europeans had been established in
India for more than a century. In
1510 the Portuguese had defeated
the regional sultanate of Goa and
made it the hub for their Asian
operations.

Now Northern European
powers were appearing on the
scene — the English established
a trading post at Surat, further
up the West Indian coast. They
were beginning to penetrate more
deeply into the interior than had
the Portuguese, who for the most
part had been content with coastal
trading outposts.

This European appears before a
backdrop of religious symbols, but
his long sword is the most prominent of his attributes.

empires. Rather than being managed directly by the crown (by means of an
often inefficient bureaucracy), it was a private venture, little encumbered
by government oversight. The VOC was an audacious capitalist enterprise — the company had authority to govern territory, negotiate treaties,
and wage war, virtually independent of the Dutch government. In forming
the corporation the Dutch recognized that economic power was an essential component of political power. While this seems obvious today, it was
less so at the time; with the success of the VOC economics would emerge
as an increasingly important consideration in world politics.

VOC profits would increase the prosperity of the Netherlands (at the
expense of exploited peoples elsewhere); the company would pay investors an 18 percent dividend for two hundred years, before being dissolved
in 1800. England would quickly follow the same model. In fact, its East
India Trading Company had actually been formed earlier, in 1600, but was
slower to gain traction, in part because of crises at home, such as the problem of Elizabeth's succession, and in part because England's monarchical
political system was less supportive of such Dutch financial developments
as the futures market (setting prices in advance) and permanent invest-
ments that eliminated the need to recapitalize new ventures. Although initially formed to compete in the lucrative Southeast Asian trade, the English company would establish its strongest presence in India and China.

Officially a trading mission, Spilbergen's Pacific expedition was authorized by the VOC to use force on the pretext of the Spanish refusing the
Dutch the right to trade freely, and the fleet was heavily armed, each of the
ships carrying twenty-eight guns. In reality Spilbergen was charged with disrupting the Pacific trade in order to bring pressure to bear on the Philippines.
The Dutch, Spanish, and Portuguese had been struggling over the Southeast
Asian spice trade for decades. The Dutch were especially motivated because,
following their secession from the Spanish Habsburg empire in 1581, they no
longer enjoyed free access to the spice markets of Lisbon. If possible, Spilbergen would seize a galleon, but his main object was the vulnerable Spanish
outpost in Manila. He had stated that "the best and only means of reestab-
lishing our affairs in the Indies and of making ourselves entirely masters of
the Moluccas is, in my opinion, to dispatch a fleet and armada direct to the
Philippines, in order to attack the Spaniards there, and to overpower all the
places and strongholds it may be possible to conquer."

In support of this objective, his raids on the Pacific coast of the Americas were opportunistic, aimed at weakening the Spanish economically,
disrupting communications, and diverting resources that could otherwise be used in defense of Manila. The fleet passed through the Straits of

Magellan in May 1615. Alerted to its presence, the Spanish assembled a powerful armada, which engaged the fleet off the coast of Peru in July. In a twenty-four-hour battle the Dutch emerged virtually unscathed, while the Spanish lost two warships and some four hundred men and were forced to retreat. This was the most alarming development for Spain ever in the South Sea, or "Spanish Lake." There remained few armed vessels to confront the Dutch fleet in the north, where Spilbergen next headed. Inflicting damage as the opportunity presented itself along the way, the fleet arrived at Acapulco on October 11, 1615, though in a weakened state as a result of having encountered a hurricane off the coast of Guatemala, and of the long time at sea — the great difficulty of reaching the Pacific coast of the Americas from Europe was the main thing that had always protected the Spanish settlements there.

Spilbergen politely let it be known that he was prepared to annihilate the town. What he left unsaid was that there was one problem with this plan, which was, ironically, caused by the pathetic state of the hamlet he was threatening. His sailors were weak with scurvy, and his ships desperately needed provisions. The town had so few resources that it was scarcely worth destroying, and to do so would have left his fleet as weakened as before with no new prey at hand. As a result, he offered to spare Acapulco, and release about twenty Spanish prisoners (who were a nuisance to maintain), in exchange for casks of fresh water, thirty head of cattle, fifty sheep, chickens, vegetables, oranges, and lemons. Outmanned, the Acapulco officials meekly agreed to the exchange.

A strange week followed in which the Dutch and Spanish mingled with elaborate exchanges of courtesies. The town's elite were invited aboard the Dutch ships, where they inspected the armaments that were poised for their destruction. For a visit from the Spanish commander the Dutch soldiers made an appearance in full parade uniforms; meanwhile, Spilbergen's young son spent the day being entertained by the town's mayor.

Upon the completion of the exchange, Spilbergen hung around along the north Pacific coast for a while hoping to grab a galleon — and making the Mexicans extremely nervous. Chancing upon a pearling vessel, the Dutch forces captured it and added it to their fleet. Once when they made landfall they were surprised by Spanish forces waiting in ambush. The resulting battle was indecisive; the Dutch retreated to the sea and the Spanish to the woods. Both sides claimed victory. The Spanish commander, to support his claim, enclosed with a letter to the viceroy the ears of one of the Dutchmen. Finally, around the beginning of December, Spilbergen tired of these diversions and set off across the Pacific, arriving in time to harass

Manila and then join the main Dutch fleet in the Moluccas on March 31, 1616; consequently, he missed by days the arrival of the galleon that would dock at Acapulco on Christmas Eve.

The released Spanish prisoners had reported their impression that if Spilbergen did not capture a galleon along the coast he intended to return to Acapulco and wait there for the next one to show up. As a result, within a few weeks of the encounter at Acapulco, while he was still lurking about the coast, the decision had at last been made in Mexico City to construct enhanced permanent fortifications to protect the bay — and now, after years of procrastination, the job had become a rush. Three hundred soldiers were to be stationed there and two batteries of cannon installed without delay. To cover the cost of building the fort it was decided to impose a duty of 2 percent on all merchandise entering Acapulco, and 1 percent on allowable silver bullion from Peru. The fees were to be collected for six years. Meanwhile, eight cannon were to be removed from galleons and mounted over the town.

With the completion of Boot's fortress, Mexico would feel prepared to withstand the assault from the Dutch VOC. How did that private enterprise become so influential as to require such measures? In England Francis Bacon, the statesman and scientist, attributed northern Europe's new capability for global financial operations to three new "mechanical discoveries," or technologies, that, he said, had "changed the whole face and state of things throughout the world." These three inventions were paper, the compass, and gunpowder. Though Bacon didn't realize it, all three were Chinese inventions.

In the fourth century BCE, two millennia before Bacon enthused over what he thought were Europe's new technologies, a Chinese philosopher named Xun Zi had posed a riddle:

> There is a thing: its body is naked but can transform itself many times, like a god. It can clothe and ornament everything under heaven to the ten thousandth generation. Because of this thing, rites and music are performed, and the noble are distinguished from the base.... When its merit is established its body is destroyed. When its work is completed its house is overthrown — its elders are thrown out and its posterity seized. Men profit from it but birds hate it.

The answer to Xun Zi's riddle was the caterpillar of the *Bombyx mori,* a large, pale, blind moth that is incapable of flight. In its larval stage it prefers to feed on the leaves of the white mulberry tree. It molts several times during its life cycle, at one point in the process spinning a cocoon that will protect it while it is in the pupal state. That cocoon is raw silk.

In China mulberry trees had been cultivated since ancient times to feed the silkworms, and elaborate procedures established to maximize the yield of silk. Mulberry trees and silks are mentioned numerous times in the *Book of Songs* (Shi jing), one of the primary Chinese literary classics and the earliest existing collection of Chinese poems, assembled perhaps as much as a millennium before the beginning of the common era. The songs collected in the ancient classic evoke the rustic, agricultural origins of Chinese civilization. They suggest that harvesting mulberry leaves for feeding the silkworms was a task for farm girls:

> Days grow warm in spring
> Orioles sing
> Girls take beautiful baskets
> Along narrow paths
> And pick soft mulberry leaves

The mulberry groves must have been pleasant places, and convenient locations for the girls to meet their lovers.

> Oh, Zhongzi, don't jump over our wall
> Don't break our mulberry trees
> It's not that I mind about the mulberries
> But I'm afraid of my brothers.
> You I would embrace
> But my brothers' words —
> Those I dread

Who knew where such assignations might lead?

> When the mulberry shed its leaves
> They lay yellow on the ground
> Since I went away with you
> For three years I have shared your poverty

Promoting the cultivation of mulberry trees and the production of silk was state policy at least by the time Xun Zi posed his riddle; his contemporary Mencius wrote that hemp or silk textiles, grain, and personal service were the three primary forms of taxation during that period. The amount of silk rendered to the emperor was extraordinary. By the fourteenth century, imperial records indicate, more than 650 tons of silk fibers were paid to the government as household taxes in a single year, a figure that does not even count silk in the form of textiles.

The Chinese developed a form of mulberry that was produced by grafting a large-leaved variety onto a wilder variety with a robust root and trunk. The result was a large bush with dense foliage that that could be conveniently picked. China's advanced silk textile technologies, and the sheer volume of silk that it produced, were an inducement to international trade from early times. Starting in earnest roughly around Xun Zi's era, such trade was predominantly along the east-west route known as the Silk Road, a name given by a nineteenth-century German scholar to a collection of trade routes extending from the eastern Mediterranean through present Afghanistan and into China, with connections to India and elsewhere. The Silk Road was not a road but rather a series of trading posts and caravan watering holes. Few traders traveled the entire route; instead, each trading post passed goods on along to the next, like racers in a relay passing a baton. Because of difficulties involved in trade along the Silk Road — its northern and southern branches encircled the world's second-largest desert, the Taklamakan — goods that traveled long distances were likely to be of light weight and high value. During the route's heyday, precious metals, coins, glass, and semiprecious stones traveled to China, while silk textiles, lacquered bowls, and other luxury goods traveled from China to the west.

The most significant import along the Silk Road into China would turn out to be Buddhism, which was brought to China from India. Silk scroll paintings discovered in the Dunhuang caves in 1907 depict the seventh-century pilgrim Xuanzang returning to China with sacred Buddhist texts, and being welcomed by officials wearing silk robes. Religious texts were often written on silk: versions of the *Daode Jing* and *Yi Jing* dating from the second century BCE, written on silk and still largely legible, were discovered at Mawangdui in 1973.

Having developed the world's most advanced silk technology, China naturally sought to maintain a monopoly by prohibiting its spread to other cultures. But it proved difficult to control mulberry seeds and minuscule moth eggs, and the technology soon passed to Korea and Japan. Silkworms were said to have been carried to Central Asia by a woman who hid moth eggs in her headband; eastern Christian monks supposedly brought eggs to Turkey hidden in their long walking staffs. India was also producing silk quite early, but may have developed the capability independently; it used a different silk-producing moth. Mulberries and silkworms were not suitable to all climates, but eventually some sort of silk production spread to many locations around the world. In Europe the Lake Como region became a prime silk center. By the seventeenth century silk was even being produced at Mexico City (despite the enormous lengths that were taken to bring it in from Asia on the galleons). James I introduced silk-growing to England's American colonies as an alternative to the tobacco he despised. But China continued to produce silk of the highest quality.

By the Ming dynasty (1368–1644), Chinese silk production had become highly industrialized. Refinement of mulberry trees had continued, and they could now be planted closer together than ever before; farmers had to devote a percentage of their land to mulberry production or pay a punitive tax. Ming inventors had also created a "complete silk-reeling" frame that integrated many of the phases of silk production in one device. This machine was said to dramatically increase a laborer's output of silk; at least it regularized silk production and made the finished product more uniform. A silk weavers' strike in Suzhou in 1601 was one indication of the degree to which silk production had become industrialized. The weavers, protesting a proposed tax on looms, brought production to a halt for three days.

Much silk was now produced in imperial workshops in Beijing and the old capital of Nanjing and nearby Suzhou. In one year the Wanli emperor ordered 180,000 bolts of silk from his workshops. The silks were sometimes lavish productions that made extensive use of gold thread. (They also relied more heavily on strong color for their effects than in the past, and these bold colors are one way that Ming silks can often be recognized.) Because many garments, bed covers, and hangings were made for Western markets, European-influenced motifs were sometimes incorporated. Production of carpets, which had not been a major tradition in China previously, was also stepped up, often incorporating West Asian designs and colors.

The best silks, however, were made for the personal use of the emperor and his family. The Wanli Emperor's elaborate tomb, excavated in the mid-twentieth century, was found to contain great quantities of silk. A silk throne cover in the Amy S. Clague Collection of Chinese Textiles incorporates not only dyed polychrome silk yarns but gold threads and peacock feather filaments. A lady's court vest in the Asian Art Museum in San Francisco is embroidered with gold threads on silk gauze and padded with silk floss. Both textiles incorporate the motif of dragons chasing flaming pearls. This motif was associated with the emperor and expressed the idea that his dominion encompassed the entire universe. The pearl lives at the bottom of the ocean and the flames represent it ascending to the heavens. The dragon

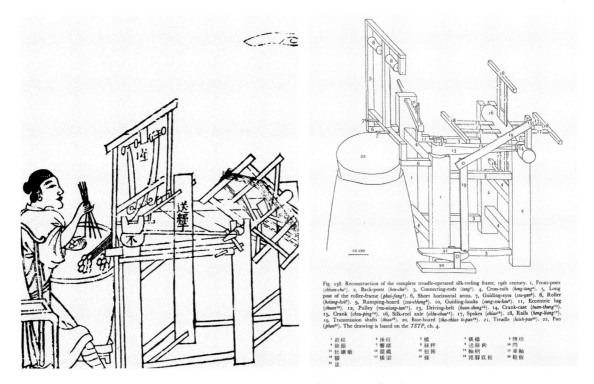

Fig. 238. Reconstruction of the complete treadle-operated silk-reeling frame, 19th century. 1, Front-posts (*chhien-chu*). 2, Back-posts (*hou-chu*). 3, Connecting-rods (*tang*). 4, Cross-rails (*heng-tang*). 5, Long post of the roller-frame (*phai-fang*). 6, Short horizontal arms. 7, Guiding-eyes (*ssu-yen*). 8, Roller (*hsiang-hsü*). 9, Ramping-board (*ssu-chheng*). 10, Guiding-hooks (*sung-ssu-kou*). 11, Eccentric lug (*shuan*). 12, Pulley (*mu-niang-tun*). 13, Driving-belt (*huan-sheng*). 14, Crank-case (*tuan-thung*). 15, Crank (*chou-ping*). 16, Silk-reel axle (*chhe-chou*). 17, Spokes (*chiao*). 18, Rails (*heng-liang*). 19, Transmission shafts (*thiao*). 20, Base-board (*tha-chiao ti-pan*). 21, Treadle (*kieh-pan*). 22, Pan (*phen*). The drawing is based on the *TSTP*, ch. 4.

¹ 前柱	² 後柱	³ 檔	⁴ 横檔
⁵ 牌坊	⁶	⁷ 絲眼	⁸ 絲桿
⁹ 送絲鈎	¹⁰ 閂		
¹¹ 壯囊墩	¹² 環鑾	¹³ 短筒	¹⁴ 軸柄
¹⁵ 車軸			
¹⁶ 軸	¹⁷ 横梁	¹⁸ 條	¹⁹ 踏鑾底板
²⁰ 鞋板			
²¹ 盆			

flies through the skies but he descends to the bottom of the ocean for the pearl. The motif announces the emperor's vast, all-encompassing power.

Zhu Yijun, the Wanli emperor, came to the throne at the age of nine in 1572 after the death of his father, the Longqing emperor, when he was only thirty-five. Just as English aristocracy could be referred to by their family name or their title — King James's favorite George Villiers, Duke of Buckingham, might be called either Villiers or Buckingham, for example — so Chinese emperors had a variety of names. During the Ming dynasty they were commonly known by their reign, or era, names, which were chosen by the emperors themselves. Because the emperor was no ordinary person, it was considered disrespectful to refer to him by his birth name — even for his own mother, who would call him "emperor," or sometimes "son." Most contemporaneous documents referring to the emperor employ his reign name, and as a result these are the names emperors are usually known by even today. The name "Wanli" means "10,000 calendars," and the Wanli emperor had, as his choice of name forecast, a long reign — his forty-eight years of rule were the most of any emperor of the 276-year Ming dynasty.

With the benefit of hindsight Chinese writers have traditionally blamed the Wanli emperor for the decline of the Ming dynasty and its fall to the Manchurians who would rule from 1644 until the Republican Revolution of 1911. He was depicted as selfish, lazy, and irresponsible. Ann

Left: Complete Silk-Reeling Frame, 1637.

Right: Reconstruction of the Complete Treadle-Operated Silk-Reeling Frame, 19th century.

These images depict the Ming dynasty silk-reeling machine that facilitated industrialized silk production. The complicated device combined several operations in one machine and standardized production.

The images are taken from Joseph Needham's *Science and Civilization in China* (vol. V:9), which contains, characteristically for Needham, an exhaustive account of Chinese silk production.

Imperial Coat Overvest, 1595. Ming dynasty, reign of the Wanli emperor. Silk satin embroidered in canvas stich and satin stich, and overembroidered in silver and gold couching, length 109 cm. Asian Art Museum, Museum purchase, City Arts Trust Fund, 1990.214.

Sumptuous silk garments like this woman's court overvest were produced for the Chinese emperor and his court. This example is embroidered with gold threads on silk gauze and padded with silk floss. The large cloud-clutching dragons chasing flaming pearls, the imperial red color, and the lucky swastikas and characters suggesting the expression "ten thousand longevities" indicate that this was a garment for the empress, and an inscription confirms that it was made for the Empress Dowager Li, the mother of the Wanli emperor, on the occasion of her fiftieth birthday. She was likely the only woman in China powerful enough at the time to wear this vest.

Ogival Throne Cover with Decoration of a Dragon Coiled about a Flaming Pearl amidst Scrolling Clouds (detail), 1600–1644. Ming dynasty. Silk *kesi* tapestry; silk, gold, and peacock feathers, 94 (max. width) x 84 cm. Collection of Phoenix Art Museum, Gift of Amy S. Clague. Photo by Ken Howie.

The image of a dragon coiled around a flaming pearl amid clouds suggests that this textile belonged to the emperor himself; these symbols conveyed his wide-ranging supremacy. The textile was originally used in a robe and at some point it was repurposed as a throne cover. The bright, complex colors — in addition to more traditional colors there are several shades of blue, as well as browns, khakis, lavendars, and pinks — combined with gold thread and peacock feather filaments date this opulent piece to the late Ming.

Paludan's characterization, in *The Imperial Ming Tombs,* of the Wanli emperor as "a thoroughly degenerate and bloated creature who dissipated his strength in rich living and lost not only the will-power but also the interest to govern" echoes this point of view. In recent years, however, scholars have sought to adjust and qualify this picture. A new portrayal views the emperor as an intelligent and, at least initially, well-intentioned ruler who was stymied by the ossified Ming bureaucracy. These revisionist scholars note that our image of the Wanli emperor is largely based on the writings of civil scholars who became his enemies. In his 2010 book *The Troubled Empire: China in the Yuan and Ming Dynasties,* Timothy Brook corrects the correction: "It would be ludicrous to cast the emperor as the tragic victim of his own autocracy," he writes. "It might be better to think of the politics of the Ming court as a matter of bargains, not tragic flaws.... The heroes in this drama — the phoenixes rising into the air — are not the emperors, in fact, but the scholars." However we apportion the blame, it is hard to view the Wanli emperor's reign as on balance a successful one.

Ming rulers, like those of the dynasties that preceded them, were thought to govern by the mandate of heaven. That mandate, once granted, could also be withdrawn (this notion caused Chinese scholars to be critical of rulers who reigned at the end of dynasties, for why would the mandate of heaven be transferred elsewhere if not through some failing of the emperor?). The best means of retaining the favor of heaven was for the emperor to maintain himself as a person of scrupulous integrity, in order to avoid any offenses that might cause the mandate to be withdrawn. For this reason, the Wanli emperor, who assumed the throne as a child of nine, was raised in an environment where his every gesture was scrutinized and judged, and the scrutiny would continue throughout his life. "What is embarrassing about working through the records of the Ming dynasty," Ray Huang, one of the most interesting writers in English on the late Ming, has confessed, "is that the trifling detours are endless. Sometimes the account of a whole decade consists of nothing but fribbles." The child monarch was not allowed many normal childhood diversions. Every day he was made to study literature and practice calligraphy (at which he excelled from a young age).

The emperor's tutor was a man named Zhang Juzheng, a powerful figure in the Ming government. Zhang rigorously enforced the dreary discipline and relative austerity (for a Chinese emperor) of his pupil's childhood. The child emperor looked up to his tutor as the embodiment of knowledge and wisdom. But after Zhang died the emperor discovered that his tutor had, unknown to him, been living in a lavish and decadent style all the while he had been exercising discipline on his pupil. This revelation

Polonaise carpets are remarkable for their rich silk pile, here highlighted with gold- and silver-colored brocading. It was once assumed that carpets of this type were made in Poland on account of the coats of arms that are sometimes interwoven into the pattern. It is now known that they were made in Safavid Persia, often for use as diplomatic gifts. There was a vigorous trade between Muslim West Asia and Christian Europe throughout the Renaissance and early modern period.

European visitors to Persia often referred to Polonaise carpets as "carpets of silk and gold." The gold effect was actually created by wrapping strips of silver around yellow silk; the silver provided a rich metallic effect, but the gold color came from the silk. Such carpets did not wear well, and this example from the Metropolitan Museum is in unusually good condition.

turned the emperor cynical, and he too began to hoard the luxuries of the world. He grew so grotesquely obese that he required assistance even to stand up. His behavior alarmed the civil officials, who foresaw the mandate of heaven slipping away; they commented openly on every detail of what they saw as failings in the emperor's personal life. His slightest gesture was subject to criticism. It was an unbearable situation. The emperor withdrew into the seclusion of his inner palace, where he fatalistically dealt with mountains of paperwork that were brought to him every day and rarely emerged into the company of his courtiers. Analysis of his remains in 1958 suggested that he was a heavy user of opium.

Though the emperor's life might not have been a happy one — he was a victim of the role prescribed for him, bound by endless ceremonial duties and obligations — it was luxurious. The luxuries of the court depended on concerted labor throughout the empire. In the year 1600 kilns in Jiangxi province produced 230,000 porcelain items for the court, from rice bowls and tea cups to ritual objects for offerings. Distant provinces sent tens of thousands of hardwood trees for construction in the imperial city. China scholar David M. Robinson offers a sample of ingredients used in the imperial kitchen during one month: "ground squirrels from beyond the Great Wall, Manchurian pine nuts, Shangxi apples, Jiangxi sugar, Zhang-zhou oranges...Mount Wutai mushrooms, Jiangnan black mushrooms, Beijing potatoes, Nanjing 'hawk-beak' bamboo sprouts from Mount Wu-dang...and Lu'an tea." The emperor paid special attention to the presentation of these delicacies, which were served up in treasures of porcelain, jade, metalwork, enamel, horn, gold, silver, and precious stones. Sumptuous silks surrounded the emperor at all times, and a special bureaucracy was set up to handle the textile needs of the imperial family.

A recluse in the inner palace of the Forbidden City, the Wanli emperor must have had difficulty understanding the contentions of his empire and its borderlands. There China continued to dip into its enormous reserves of high-quality silk to make gifts to troublesome kingdoms, buying in this manner a momentary peace. Other powers also used silks as a component of their foreign policies. By 1616 Persia had become China's most formidable competitor. (The Ottomans produced silk to a lesser degree within the Topkapi Palace complex in Istanbul, where unwanted princes were strangled with silk cords.) The Persian trade was promoted by Shah Abbas, who recruited Armenian merchants to sell silk goods. A fine collection of Persian silk textiles in the Kremlin is a result of trade exchanges with the Muscovites.

Around the beginning of the seventeenth century, silk workers in the new Persian capital of Isfahan developed a style of carpet in which silver

threads were brocaded in a rich silk pile. These carpets — called "Polonaise" because some, made for recipients in Poland, contain Polish coats of arms within the design — do not seem to have been intended for the commercial market but were designated from the outset as elite diplomatic gifts; such gifts did, however, attract merchants to Persia where they then traded for other luxury items. The Polonaise carpets' complex patterns, rendered in pastel colors (probably originally a result of the silks not taking dye in the same way as wools), appealed to European Baroque tastes.

More and more, however, the ancient land routes were being supplanted by sea trade. In China such trade had surged during the Tang dynasty (618–906), when Chinese traders carried silks from ports on the southeast coast of China to Vietnam, India, and other locations in South and Southeast Asia. From there they were sometimes transferred to ships bound for the west. Yet by the middle of the Ming dynasty (1368–1644) China had become at best a reluctant participant in the competition on the seas.

 The founder of the dynasty had already voiced doubts about the value of overseas trade in the fourteenth century. Confident that China — the "Middle Kingdom" — was central to all matters of importance, he had de-

Plan of Macau by Barreto de Resende, from Antonio Bocarro, *Book of East India Fortresses*, 1635. Public Library of Évora.

The Portuguese settlement at Macau was the only European post authorized by the Chinese on their mainland. It was an essential link in the Portuguese trade network that also included Melaka in Malaysia and Goa in India. In the seventeenth century Macau's importance would diminish as a result of the loss of the Japan trade after the closing of that country to outsiders and the loss of the trade link with Melaka after its conquest by the Dutch in 1641.

clared that "overseas foreign countries are separated from us by mountains and seas, and are far away in the corners of the world. Their lands do not produce enough for us to maintain them, and their people would not usefully serve us if we annexed them."

Still, by the fourteenth century China could not resist experimenting in sea travel — in a big way. But the ambitious project backfired, putting an end to the country's maritime ambitions for centuries. The emperor had decided to send out large fleets under the command of the eunuch Zheng He, a Muslim who had been captured in southwest China near Burma and castrated at the age of eleven.

Zheng's voyages were the greatest maritime explorations in history to that time. One expedition comprised 62 large vessels and 255 smaller ones, manned by 27,870 men, mostly from Fujian province; there were six voyages in all. The largest vessels were said to be 444 by 186 feet — bigger (by far) than a football field. Perhaps because of his background and religious affiliation, Zheng tended to follow established Muslim trade routes. The fleet sailed to Southeast Asia, India, Persia, and the east coast of Africa. Its ships carried vast quantities of silks, along with porcelains and other luxury items, which were exchanged for spices, gemstones, and exotic animals such as ostriches, rhinoceroses, giraffes, and lions for the emperor's amusement. But to the Chinese this was not a trade mission. The Ming government prohibited, or severely limited, foreign trade. To get around this, everyone agreed that any goods exchanged were to be viewed as diplomatic gifts and the goods received as tribute. Such tribute helped to reaffirm the mandate of heaven by which authority the emperor ruled the world.

But the emperor had overextended the country. The sea voyages — expensive undertakings, lacking a clear purpose — were not sustainable. China needed to devote resources to confronting the threat on its eastern border from the Mongols, led until 1405 by Tamerlane, whose legacy would include the Mughal empire in India; it was also recovering from an expensive failed attempt to conquer Vietnam, and continuing to devote resources to finishing the Great Wall. The treasure fleets were seen as a frivolous expense. Zheng He's ships were disposed of and his records and maritime charts burned to ensure that no recurrence of such follies would ever occur. Shipbuilding was banned. It was the beginning of the drawing inward of Ming China, which would no longer be as forceful with outsiders as it once had been. The great ocean voyages became a dim memory, and the new European sea powers now patrolled the Asian seas China had once commanded.

By the time of the Wanli emperor the government had become so paralyzed that decisive action on the seas seemed inconceivable. The Forbidden City, from which the emperor ruled in the new capital of Beijing, had swollen into an enormous and unwieldy bureaucracy. It has been estimated that the city held around a million people and supported as many as sixty thousand imperial family members.

Despite the prohibition on trade, many Chinese longed for foreign goods and foreign markets. An illegal sea trade grew up that was centered in Fujiang province and the nearby island of Taiwan. Without effective policing by the government, fishermen there sometimes turned to smuggling, and smugglers sometimes turned to piracy, and pirates sometimes organized themselves into virtual navies. The widening gap between rich and poor during the later Ming helped drive farmers, laborers, and fishermen to desperate measures. Around the time the first galleons sailed to Acapulco, a pirate named Lin Feng (or Limahong) assembled a large fleet carrying more than a thousand men, with which he nearly captured Manila. Had he been successful it would have been a major setback for Spain's efforts to maintain a foothold in Asia. Chinese and Spanish forces joined together against the pirate band, but the Spaniards' stock fell in the Chinese estimation when it came out that they had trapped Lin Feng but carelessly allowed him to escape. This was a blow to Spain's hopes to be granted a post on the Chinese mainland.

The Portuguese had got there first. They discovered that trade restrictions were not being enforced in Canton. They were allowed to establish a trading post in Macau, which grew into a walled city that was an important link in Portugal's Asian trade network. (The walls were a mixed blessing: they provided defense but also cut off the colony from the rest of the mainland, rendering it dependent on China for its subsistence; Portuguese were not allowed to pass beyond the walls into the interior.) From Macau the Portugues acted as middlemen, facilitating an exchange of silver and silk between the hostile powers of Japan and China. This situation was complicated when the Dutch entered the arena around the beginning of the seventeenth century, insisting as ever on open trade as a basic right (except for goods on which they claimed a monopoly), to be secured with force if necessary. They made an even more unfavorable impression than the Spaniards had on the Chinese, who regarded trade as an embarrassing secret. China was insistent about keeping the Dutch "red-haired barbarians" out of Canton Bay, labeling them "people with filthy hearts." Consequently the Dutch hovered ominously around the island of Taiwan, where they mingled with the pirates who had holed up there. They spent the next few decades trying, without a great deal of success, to break into the China trade. At one point they even attempted to organize a multinational pirate armada to attack China and force the trade concessions they were after. These wild ambitions were frustrated, but by the mid-seventeenth century they would succeed in winning some grudging concessions.

Among Chinese merchants and workers imperial restrictions and taxes were increasingly resented, and some of the pirates were viewed as Robin Hood–like figures. A colorful Taiwan-based pirate known as Yan Siqi was a subject of legend, together with his sidekicks the strongman Iron Zhang-hong and the clever and resourceful Deep Mountain Monkey. In addition to the Chinese pirates, seafaring Japanese freebooters were supported by daimyo (regional warlords) who resented the shutdown of Chinese markets. Japanese pirates made daring raids not just on shipping but on the mainland as well, and they sometimes collaborated with Chinese or other renegades.

Early in the Wanli emperor's reign China had relaxed its restrictions on trade, but it had excepted Japan. The restrictions proved difficult to enforce, as it was hard to secure thousands of miles of coastline without a navy. An illegal trade in silk and silver that was a precursor to the Manila–Acapulco trade flourished between the two countries. But as hostilities became more overt and the East Asian powers went to war in the 1590s this illegal trade became increasingly difficult to maintain without the aid of Portuguese intermediaries. This was some of the action the Spanish, latecomers to the arena, tried to muscle in on by way of Manila.

On their westward route to Manila, the galleons sometimes paused at Guam in the Mariana Islands. The Spaniards called that archipelago the Islas de los Ladrones, or Islands of the Thieves — the Ladrones for short. The name expressed the first of many cultural misunderstandings that would result from the European entry into the Pacific.

The Portuguese navigator Magellan, in command of an international crew in the service of Spain, had made the first European landfall in Asia by way of the Pacific in March 1521. Spain had been unable to reach Asia by the eastward route around Africa because of Portugal's prior claim and established presence. So it was forced to sail west. As the Spanish ships had drawn in to the island of Guam, native people swarmed around them in *proas,* or small outrigger canoes. Audaciously, they clambered onto the big ships and, before the sailors' eyes, helped themselves to anything that wasn't nailed down. The sailors, enfeebled by scurvy, barely managed to drive them off with crossbows. Less than two months later Magellan would die in a similar clash in the Philippines.

The natives of the Marianas Islands were communal people who did

O Leilai que se Faz cada dia pola menhã na Rua direita na Cidade de Goa Feita Pelo natural por Ioan de Linschoten framengo

not have the same concept of private property as the Europeans. Again and again the Spanish would be perplexed and frustrated by the way the people of the Marianas seemed to simultaneously engage in friendly trade and violent warfare — they seem never to have realized they were dealing with multiple clans, each with its own sense of relations with the intruders. As a result of these early encounters, the islands would continue to be known as the Ladrones for more than three centuries.

The handful of Magellan's crew who made it back to Europe achieved the first circumnavigation of the globe, and their cargo of thirty tons of cloves and other spices proved valuable enough that both Spain and Portugal immediately made plans for new expeditions in search of more spices. After Columbus's first voyage, Pope Alexander VI had drawn a vertical line across the globe establishing the separate domains available to the Spanish and Portuguese for new territorial claims. Soon the two powers quarreled over rights to the "Spice Islands," normally understood to refer to the part of the Southeast Asian archipelago known as the Moluccas but sometimes used in a broader sense to refer to spice-producing regions of the South Pacific and Southeast Asia generally.

It was not clear to anyone where the line would continue on the far side of a globe whose expanse was only beginning to be known, particularly since there was no reliable way at that time of measuring longitude. Spanish maps conveniently exaggerated the size of Asia, moving the islands east into their domain. In 1529, a few years after Magellan's ships had arrived home, the two powers negotiated a treaty that redrew the line. Spain ceded its claim to the Spice Islands but retained rights to the Philippines, while in the Atlantic the treaty gave Portugal a large part of

Rua Direita, Goa, 1596, engraving after a drawing by Jan Huygen Van Linschoten, from his book *Travel account of the voyage of the sailor Jan Huyghen van Linschoten to the Portuguese East India 1579–1592*.

The Dutch merchant van Linschoten (1562–1611) lived in Goa between 1583 and 1588 as secretary to the Portuguese archbishop there. On his return to Europe in 1592 he collaborated with the scholar Bernardus Paludanus (Berent ten Broecke) on books about his travels.

The *Itinerario* was the most popular of his books; it was frequently reissued and translated during the early seventeenth century. It describes all of maritime Asia from Mozambique to Japan. This engraving shows the Rue Direita ("straight street"), the main drag of Goa. Located on the central western coast of India, the city was notorious among Europeans for its hot and humid climate and its summer monsoon rains.

Brazil. The division continued to be observed, for the most part, even during the uneasy merger of Spain and Portugal from 1580 to 1640.

Because of the preexisting relations between the Chinese and Portuguese, Spain had little choice but to rely on Manila as its base of operations for the Asia trade. Having won the support of the Chinese, the Portuguese at Macau successfully turned back efforts by the Spanish in 1598 and the Dutch in 1601 to establish their own trade operations in the Canton region. Spain was unable to venture further west, because Portugal had secured important bases at Goa on the western coast of India and Melaka on the Malaysian peninsula.

The main hub of Portuguese undertakings in Asia was Goa. Portuguese activities there are well known, thanks to the work of its Chronicler and Keeper of the Archives from 1631 to 1643, Antonio Bocarro. Bocarro was a Portuguese Jew, born in 1594, who arrived in India in late 1615 or early 1616 and spent nearly a decade as a soldier in Cochin. His *Decades XIII* is a detailed account of Portuguese activities in India from 1612 through 1617. He was also the author of a helpful book with the formidable title of *Book Containing Designs of All the Forts, Towns, And Settlements in the Oriental State of India along with Descriptions of Their Situation and of All They Contain, Such as Artillery, Garrisons, Population, Income and Expenditure, Depths of the Sea Approaches, Neighboring Princes in the Hinterland, Their Strength and Our Relations with Them, and Whatever Else That Is Subject to the Crown of Spain.*

Bocarro describes a lively trade involving about a dozen main trade routes connected to Goa. Ships traveled back and forth to Lisbon, Mozambique and Mombassa in East Africa, Muscat and Basra on the Persian Gulf, Sind in current Pakistan and Diu in northern India, Kanara and Cochin in southwestern India, Celon, Manila and Macau, Malacca, and the Maldives and Laccadives off southern India. Bocarro notes, however, that by the time he arrived in Goa trade with Malacca and Manila had greatly declined, because Dutch boats lay in wait to attack ships traveling through the Straits of Singapore.

Antonio Bocarro might have been related to Gaspar Bocarro, whose story he tells in his *Decades*. In 1616 Gaspar Bocarro became the first European to reach Malawi, inland from Mozambique in Africa; it would be another 250 years before the Scottish explorer David Livingstone would reach the same region in a more famous journey. Bocarro made a difficult journey from Tete on the Zambesi River through the Shire Valley to Lake Chilwa near Lake Malawi, the great inland lake in central Africa, then through the south of Tanzania and back into Mozambique. The

Manila, **1619, by Nicolaes van Geelkercken, engraving, from** *East and West Indian Mirror,* **combining accounts of the navigations of Joris van Spilbergen and Jacob le Maire.**

Portuguese wanted to slow the spread of Islam in eastern Africa; later they became engaged in gold trade in the region, which ultimately had the result of disrupting ancient eastern African trade networks. In exchange for beads and textiles they acquired ivory and took slaves to work on plantations in Mozambique and Brazil.

Chinese traders were already active in the Philippines when Magellan made the first Western contact there. That trade was one incentive for the Spanish to conquer Manila in 1870. From that time on the Spanish presence in the Philippines was always precarious. While Jesuit proselytizers made good progress in converting peoples of the archipelago, Spanish settlers and traders failed to successfully colonize much of the islands and were largely restricted to the area around Manila, where they depended to some extent on the forbearance of powers such as China and Japan for their survival.

The Spanish colony in the Philippines was, technically, a viceroyalty of Mexico. In practice, because of their vast distance from both the Americas and Europe, the Philippines were mostly self-governing. Because the Spanish could not exercise control over all the islands of the Philippines

Joris van Spilbergen's fleet cruised around Manila Bay for about a month in early 1616, harassing shipping and generally creating havoc. He withdrew when the Spanish governor of Manila, Juan de Silva, put together a large armada with the plan of attacking the Dutch headquarters in Indonesia; after de Silva's death the expedition collapsed in failure.

(of which there are several dozen large ones and some seven thousand in all), and because they made little effort to exploit the natural resources of the region or to develop its agricultural potential, they were reduced to operating what was essentially a trading post. The economy of the Spanish Philippines was overwhelmingly dependent on the profits from the galleon trade. In the years when the galleons failed — both the ships that turned back and those that were lost were calamities for their investors — the small, fragile community was hard-pressed to survive.

While the China trade was always the most important, there was a good variety of products from different regions. A Jesuit historian wrote in the mid-1600s about the importance of Manila as a trading post:

> Manila is the equal of any other emporium of our monarchy, for it is the center to which flow the riches of the Orient and the Occident, the silver of Peru and New Spain, the pearls and precious stones of India, the diamonds of Narsinga and Goa, the rubies, sapphires and topazes, and the cinnamon of Ceylon, the pepper of Sumatra and Java, the cloves, nutmegs and other spices of the Moluccas and Banda, the fine Persian silks and wool and carpets from Ormuz and Malabar, rich hangings and bed coverings of Bengal, fine camphor of Borneo, balsam and ivory of Abada and Cambodia, the civet of the Lequios, and from Great China silks of all kinds, raw and woven in velvets and figured damasks, taffetas and other cloths of every texture, design and colors, linens, and cotton mantles, gilt-decorated articles, embroideries and porcelains, and other riches and curiosities of great value and esteem, from Japan, amber, vari-colored silks, escritoires, boxes and desks of precious woods, lacquered and with curious decorations, and very fine silverware.

Spaniards in the Philippines did not follow the American model. In the Americas the Spanish, after looting its treasures, had sought to fashion themselves wealthy gentlemen landowners on the model of the gentry of their native Castile. They made themselves into managers of large *enco-miendas,* on which they grazed cattle and grew wheat, conscripting native laborers to exploit the wealth of the land. But the Philippine islands were not as well suited to Castilian-style ranching. One Spaniard described the climate as *cuatro meses de polvo, cuatro meses de lodo, y cuatro meses de todo* ("four months of dirt, four months of mud, four months of every kind of crud"). Hardly any effort was made to farm or to take advantage of the region's natural resources. As late as 1600 there were no more than five or six Spanish farmers in the Manila area.

The Spaniards of Manila depended on Chinese labor for the business of everyday life. "From China come those who supply every sort of service," said a Jesuit located in Manila near the turn of the century, "all dexterous, prompt, and cheap, from physicians and barbers to carriers and porters. They are the tailors and the shoemakers, metalworkers, silversmiths, sculptors, locksmiths, painters, masons, weavers, and every sort of service worker." The Chinese population was by far the largest in Manila; it was said to be the first large Chinese colony outside China. In 1586 it numbered more than ten thousand, compared to only eight hundred Spanish and mestizos. The Chinese were consigned to a special district called the Parian ("marketplace"), which was initially located within the city walls. But the population disparity made the Spanish anxious, and they moved the Parian to a nearby swamp. "They rapidly turned this area into a thriving town of orderly streets with a large pond at its center," according to Ray Huang. "The pond was accessible to substantial ships and had an island in its center where punishments were administered to Chinese criminals."

Facing this bustling city outside the gates of their small, precarious settlement, the Spanirds lived in constant fear that the Chinese would rise up against them. They interpreted a visit from mainland Chinese officials in 1603 as a spy mission — a precursor to such an uprising. To preempt this, they abruptly massacred more than twenty thousand Chinese. Most of those who weren't killed fled, leaving behind a hapless population of only about 500. Almost at once, however, the Spaniards faced the realization that they were helpless without Chinese labor. One reported that in the absence of the Chinese "there was nothing to eat and no shoes to wear." Reversing themselves, they now encouraged Chinese immigration, and by 1616 the population was on its way back to twenty thousand. Trade with China — as necessary for Manila's survival as the industry of local farmers and tradesmen— also continued; the five years ending in 1610 recorded the highest volume in the history of the trade.

The governor of the Philippines was a man named Juan de Silva. He had been born in Spain and had arrived to take charge in Manila on Easter 1609; within a few months he would be besieged by a Dutch fleet of some thirteen vessels bearing nearly 28,000 men. The siege lasted for several months until it was finally broken in April 1610, when a dozen Spanish ships surprised and killed the Dutch commander. In subsequent years De Silva sought to seize the initiative, sending expeditions to the Moluccas to eradicate the Dutch presence there, but all of these failed for a variety of reasons. Finally he put together a huge armada carrying five thousand men, including a unit of Japa-

Western-Style Bell, approx. 1602. Japan, Momoyama period (1573–1615). Cast bronze. Eisei-Bunko Museum, 7271.

This large Western-style bell, weighing nearly five hundred pounds, was cast in honor of Hosokawa Gracia, a Christian convert who was the wife of a daimyo. The church for which the bell was intended was destroyed in a wave of anti-Christian repression. The bell was placed in hiding and resurfaced in the twentieth century.

nese samurai, and, taking personal command, set sail—not for Indonesia but for the Strait of Malacca. It was the largest European armada ever seen in those waters but, just to make sure, de Silva was headed up the strait to join forces with the Portuguese (allied with Spain since 1580) in order to launch a massive and decisive joint attack on the Dutch.

In February 1616, as the fleet entered the strait, de Silva's already poor health grew worse. Racked with fever and dysentery, he died in Malacca in April. The rendezvous with the Portuguese fleet never happened—the fleet had been surprised and defeated, and the surviving Portuguese had burned their galleons to avoid their being captured. In Malacca a deadly fever spread among the men of the armada as they waited for the fleet that would never come. In June the ships limped back to Manila, defeated without ever reaching Indonesia to encounter the enemy. De Silva's disastrous expedition put an end to efforts to combine Portuguese and Spanish forces in Asia, and to Spain's efforts to gain the initiative there. Subsequently it would be reduced to defending its lonely outpost at Manila, and the VOC would be conceded a virtual monopoly on the spice trade.

Thanks to the lucrative galleon trade, the Spanish no longer worried quite so much about the loss of the spice trade as they once had. From China streamed in silk, porcelains, iron, ink and paper, livestock, sugar, grains, and fruits. To China went mainly silver—and Jesuits. While there is little indication of Chinese efforts to convert Spaniards to Buddhism or the related beliefs of the followers of Wang Yangming (somewhat misleadingly labeled "neo-Confucianism" in the West), proselytizing was always fundamental to Spain's overseas program. But its absolutist and teleological religion found only a limited reception in China, where ancient traditions of Taoism and folk belief had laid the foundations for a worldview that was fluid, cyclical, manifold, situational, and relativistic.

In 1616 the Society of Jesus had been around for just seventy-seven years, having been founded by Ignacio de Loyola, a Basque soldier turned priest, in 1539. In *Rules for Thinking with the Church* Loyola wrote, "I will believe that the white that I see is black if the hierarchical Church so defines it." More than previous orders, the Jesuits sought to regularize Christian belief, an impulse that contributed on the one hand to the founding of colleges and universities and on the other to the excesses of the Spanish Inquisition. They were also a missionary order. The best-known of the Jesuit missionaries in China was an Italian, Matteo Ricci. Ricci achieved some success by dressing in the Chinese fashion and educating himself about Chinese philosophy and culture. He shared Western knowledge in mathematics, map making, and other areas, and won a following among the Chinese literati. Among the Chinese he was perceived as the champion of an interesting and exotic, though minor, school of philosophy called the Learning from Heaven. But he died in 1610 at the age of fifty-eight, and his successors did not effectively follow his example.

In 1616 Ricci's work bore fruit in the West with the publication of *De Christiana Expeditione apud Sinas Suscepta ab Societate Jesu* ("About Christian Expeditions to China Undertaken by the Society of Jesus"); the book was published in Germany in 1615 but became better known through a French edition published the following year), which brought the teachings of Confucius to European scholars. But that same year his legacy suffered setbacks in China. The head of the order's China operations reversed Ricci's policy of presenting the faith as a branch of learning, prohibiting the teaching of mathematics and calendar reform and restricting the missionaries' activities to preaching. At the same time, a Chinese official named Shen Jue, who had been appointed minister of rites the previous year, began a campaign of suppression of the Jesuits. In 1616 Shen repeatedly denounced the missionaries. He pointed out that they called their country Great West Ocean, which seemed to challenge the dynasty name Great Ming. Their claim that they were spreading the teaching of the Lord of Heaven conflicted with the official representation of the emperor as Heaven's King and the Son of Heaven. Shen's concern seems to have been that the missionaries' activities could potentially be subversive. He might have had a point.

Until Japan closed its borders, it supplied Manila with most of its metalware and some weaponry — swords and gunpowder. There was a regular commerce between the countries, with ships arriving every year, often carrying missionaries as well as goods. In Japan the missionaries, first from Portugal and then from Spain, seemed to be making great strides, and some notable figures were converted. Among these was Hosokawa Gracia, the wife of a daimyo whose castle was besieged by a rival in 1600 while he was away at battle. In order

to keep from being used as a hostage, she ordered herself killed by a servant. When her husband returned from his campaign and discovered her sacrifice, he ordered a Western-style church bell cast in her honor. But the church for which the bell was intended was destroyed following the shogun's crackdown on Christianity. The bell, hidden in a castle turret, only came to light three hundred years later; it was rediscovered in the early twentieth century.

The Jesuit missionaries were seen as a wild card that could potentially upset the fragile equilibrium achieved through the recent unification of Japan after its bloody civil wars. The priests were suspected of preparing the way for military invasion. Dutch and English traders made sure to feed these fears, but at times the Spanish were their own worst enemies. In 1596 a galleon bound for Acapulco was blown onto the coast of Japan. Its crew was seized on suspicion of spying and its cargo was carried off (which required eighty-three boats). In an attempt to impress his interrogators, a loose-lipped sailor boasted about the extent of Spain's world empire. Pulling out a map of the world, he pointed out the nation's many possessions. But how was it possible for Spain to have conquered so many nations? he was asked. "Nothing is easier," he assured his questioners. "Our kings begin by sending into countries which they desire to conquer some friars, who engage in the work of converting people to our religion. When they have made considerable progress, troops are sent in who are joined by the new Christians. They then have little difficulty in settling the rest."

The conversation was reported to the shogun, who ordered more than two dozen missionaries, to be known among the Spanish as "the martyrs of Nagasaki," executed. But repression of Christians in the following years was inconsistent and sporadic, and more evangelists took their places. They were fueled by apocalyptic zeal. Now that the extent of the globe was known, surely the whole world would soon be converted. The end times were at hand. "The world shows great signs of ending," wrote the author of the first European book on China, "and the scriptures are about to be fulfilled." In 1614 the first shogun of the Edo era, Ieyasu, ordered more rigorous anti-Christian measures, and in 1616, after his death, his successor, Hidetoda, proved even more intransigent. Christianity was almost entirely expunged, and it ceased to be a significant factor in Japanese society.

The exchanges with Japan left a mark across the Pacific. Some Japanese artists were apparently among those who made the trip to Acapulco; at the very least, Japanese style influenced American artists. Carved, inlaid desks made in Colombia have the same proportions and dimensions as their counterparts in Japan. A large seventeenth-century screen now in the collections of the Museo de Americas, Madrid, depicts a dynamic street

Opposite top: Arrival of a Portuguese Ship, early seventeenth century. Japan. Folding screen, one of a pair; ink, colors, and gold on paper, 333 x 173 cm. (overall). Asian Art Museum, The Avery Brundage Collection, B60D77+.

Opposite bottom: The Palace of the Viceroys, seventeenth century. Mexico. Folding screen; oil on canvas. *Museo de América, Madrid,* 00207.

The top screen shows a Japanese artist's depiction of the arrival of Portuguese traders in Japan. The influence of such Japanese screens is apparent in the Mexican screen, below, particularly in the gold-leaf cloud forms.

scene backed by gold-leaf clouds in a Japanese style, but the scene depicts life in Mexico City and was made for a palace there.

The Manila–Acapulco galleons were the final piece in the connection of the Americas, Europe, Africa, and Asia — they marked the beginning of globalization. International trade and exchange had occurred throughout history, but now, for the first time, two brothers, one traveling east and the other west, could meet halfway around the world. The rise of companies like the Dutch East India Company and British East India Trading Company, which developed a model for sharing the risk and rewards of coordinated global ventures, helped to fuel the new global economy and promote capitalism as a state-sponsored philosophy. Within a few years Francis Bacon would argue that economics should be the first priority of the state and that the best remedy for all problems was the promotion of economic well-being. "The first remedy or prevention is to remove, by all means possible," he would write, "that material cause of sedition...which is, want and poverty in the estate. To which purpose serveth the opening, and well-balancing of trade; the cherishing of manufactures; the banishing of idleness; the repressing of waste, and excess, by sumptuary laws; the improvement and husbanding of the soil; the regulating of prices of things vendible; the moderating of taxes and tributes; and the like."

Silver was the standard on which the new global economy was built, and would remain so into the nineteenth century. During the later years of the Ming dynasty the social and economic structure of China changed in profound ways, and these changes were associated with the shift from an agriculture-based economy to one based on the use of silver as currency — during the sixteenth century considerable quantities of silver were imported from Japan until relations with the Japanese deteriorated; silver from the Americas filled the gap thereafter. The silver currency–based economy was tied to a large, unskilled peasant labor class newly displaced from its rural origins, the collapse of land prices, the growth of urban centers, the rise of mercantilism and trade, the increased specialization of skilled craft labor, the expansion of industrialized systems of production, and increased regional and agricultural specialization. Besides the industrialization of silk, the manufacturing of goods such as porcelain, iron, and steel was also industrialized. There was a great growth in printed materials, not unlike that of post-Gutenberg Europe. Despite restrictions on sea trade, maritime exchange increased not just along the China coast but throughout Asia (and indeed the world). China's attempts to contain the sea trade actually increased its value, much as today's prohibitions on drugs such as marijuana increase their value to distributors

Spanish Dollar, 1598–1621. Mexico. Silver.

Coins such as this, usually mined and minted in Mexico or Peru, were favored as currency not only in Europe and the Americas but in other parts of the world as well. China's shift to an economy based on such coins had profound effects on its society.

and cost to consumers, and this, together with the rise of a displaced underclass, caused piracy to be rampant. Diplomatic relations during this period
were difficult because official vessels were always suspected of carrying spies
or pirates.

The silver-based economy had even more devastating consequences for
the Americas. In the early sixteenth century silver mined in Joachimsthal,
Germany, was fashioned into a coin called the Joachimsthaler, or *thaler* for
short; the word was brought into English as *dollar* (it already appears in
the works of Shakespeare). The thaler was roughly equivalent to the Spanish peso ("weight"), another silver coin, which was equal to eight reales,
and consequently known among the English as "pieces of eight" (a name
made famous in Robert Louis Stevenson's *Treasure Island*) or the "Spanish
dollar." Because the peso was more uniform than the thaler, it was preferred in world markets. Since the value of the silver coin was determined
by its weight, it could be physically divided into eight parts.

In the eighteenth century, during the American War of Independence,
the Continental Congress elected to standardize on the model of the Spanish coin (rather than the British system of pounds, shillings, and pence),
which resulted in the current American dollar. The first American paper
bills were printed by Benjamin Franklin and bore the legend "This bill en-
titles the Bearer to receive ___ Spanish milled Dollars, or the Value thereof
in Gold or Silver, according to the Resolutions of the Congress held at Philadelphia, on the 10th day of May, A.D. 1775." The Americans called each of
the eight parts of the dollar a "bit," so that a quarter dollar was known as
"two bits." Only when revolutions in Latin America disrupted the production of Spanish coins and lowered their quality did the silver standard start
to decline. The Spanish peso remained legal tender in America until just before the Civil War. China remained on the silver standard until 1935.

In 1616 the most populous city in the Americas was located in an unlikely
place, a barren mountain peak high above the Andean tree line. A motto
on its coat of arms announced:

> I am rich Potosí,
> Treasure of the world,
> The king of all mountains
> And the envy of all kings

The Andes had been associated with treasure in European minds ever
since the conquest, when conquistadors led by Francisco Pizarro promised

Vessel in the Form of a Panpipe
Player, 1300–1500. Peru, Andean
region, Chimu culture. Silver
and malachite, 7 x 11 x 21 cm.
Metropolitan Museum of Art,
New York, The Michael C. Rockefeller Memorial Collection, Gift
of Nelson A. Rockefeller, 1969,
1978.412.219. Image copyright
© The Metropolitan Museum of
Art / Art Resource, NY.

Andean artists used silver in works
such as this vessel depicting a musician playing a panpipe, but they
did not value silver as currency.
The tunic, loincloth, cap, earrings,
and bag on the figure show typical
Andean dress, and the design motifs on the clothing match those of
surviving textiles. Among Andean
people music played an important
role in both ritual and daily life.
The panpipe, a traditional Andean
instrument, is often combined today with string instruments, which
were introduced by Europeans.

Andean Americans were forcibly
conscripted to work in the silver
mines at Potosí, in present-day
Bolivia. Conditions in the mines
were atrocious. Especially after the
application of extraction methods
involving mercury in the 1570s,
labor in the mines often resulted
in death. To ensure a steady supply
of labor, slaves were brought to
Potosí from Africa.

Acosta's *Natural and Moral
History of the Indies* was one of
the first realistic accounts of the
history and natural world of the
Americas. De Bry's engravings
were reprinted often during the
early seventeenth century, in Acosta's work and many other titles.

Potosí's main silver lode was in
a mountain called the Cerro Rico.
"In contrast to pictures showing
the grand Cerro Rico from the
outside," scholar Jane E. Mangan
has written, "de Bry's engraving
opened up the view to indigenous
workers laboring inside. For those
who know Potosí's grand, conical
shape, and the slope of the mine
entrances, it would appear that de
Bry, who had never seen Potosí,
had it all wrong. His image became legendary, however, because
it portrayed the Indians' victimization by the Spanish. In this aspect
de Bry could not be accused of
misrepresentation."

the hostage Inca Atahualpa his freedom if he would order his subjects to fill
a large room with gold. The room was filled, but Atahualpa was killed.

Before long the conquerors were hungry for more treasure. They demanded to be told the sources of the precious minerals from which the Inca
made their beautiful objects, which the Spaniards melted down into pure
metal, some to adorn altarpieces glorifying their god. The Inca had known
about the Potosí lode, but they valued silver only as ornamentation and not
as currency, and they had more convenient sources that were sufficient for
their limited needs. They kept their knowledge of the Potosí silver veins to
themselves — native peoples throughout the Americas quickly learned that
revealing the sources of the minerals the Europeans coveted tended to turn
out badly for them.

The secret was kept until 1545. Even after the Spaniards got wind of the
rich source of silver, they had difficulty extracting the prize. Native smelt-
ers knew how to mix silver with lead in portable wind ovens to facilitate its
melting, a skill the Spanish were slow to master. The colonizers found themselves in the disagreeable position of being forced to pay for silver that was
mined and smelted by natives. It upset their sense of the order of things to
watch some of their conquered subjects grow rich before their eyes. Consequently, in 1570 a special commission determined that forced conscription
of native labor (called the mita) was justifiable on the basis of the greater
public good. Henceforth the people of the Andes would be forced to labor
not for themselves but on behalf of the Spanish. In 1589 Philip II of Spain
formally approved this decision, provided that the native miners be given
the consolation of religion, along with wages, food, and medical care.

Around the same time, a new method of extracting silver that involved
the chemical application of mercury was put into effect. The new method
vastly increased the yields of silver, at the expense of subjecting the workers
to grave environmental hazards. As a measure of the increase, in the decade
of the 1570s, during the early years of the galleon trade, China imported
about 1200 tons of silver from the New World; by the turn of the century
the quantity was 3000 tons. Being made to work in the mines had now become a virtual death sentence. This was considered an acceptable trade-off
since the mines made everyone rich, except for the region's original inhabitants, or the African slaves who were brought in to take their places after so
many had perished that production began to slacken.

"He who has not seen Potosí," said an early seventeenth century visitor,
"has not seen the Indies." Called by many the eighth wonder of the world,
the city rivaled London in size. It was larger than Madrid, Paris, or Rome.
Matteo Ricci made certain to include it on the world map he produced for

the Chinese imperial court. The city's wealth was legendary: "To compen-
sate you as you deserve," Don Quixote told Sancho Panza, "even the mines
of Potosí would not suffice." A seventeenth-century French traveler oberved
that in Potosí "even the common people live comfortably, all very proud and
haughty, and go about well dressed in gold- and silver-embroidered clothing of scarlet silk, adorned with a lot of gold and silver jewelry." A Spanish
writer from the same period remarked on on clear nights in Peru one could
see a "white stain" in the sky that resembled a a cloud. This white cloud was
believed to have settled over the Cerro Rico—the "Rich Mountain"—of Potosí as a sign of God's favor.

But the labor in the mines was a different kind of stain on the city. It is estimated that over the years the mines were in operation around eight million
men died working in them. One-seventh of the population of sixteen dis-
tricts stretching from Potosí north to the old Inca capital of Cuzo was conscripted to work in the mines. The workers were organized into three shifts
of more than four thousand men each, so that one group could be working
at all times, day and night.

After their mina service was completed, many mine workers found it difficult to return to their home areas and resume their former lives. As a result,
a large urban underclass was created in the city. Volutary laborers at minimal
wages consequently added to the pool of workers, though those conscripted
through the mina system were forced to do the most onerous tasks. The Bol-
vian writer Eduardo Galeano has described a priest newly arrived in the city
who was disturbed by the sight of miners with lash scars on their backs filing
by like ghosts. Told to simply shut his eyes he replied that he couldn't. "With
my eyes shut," he said, "I see more."

A seventeenth-century writer of native Andean descent, Guaman Poma,
tells a similar story:

> At the mercury mines of Huancavelica the Indian workers are pun-
> ished and ill treated to such an extent that they die like flies and our
> whole race is threatened with extermination. Even the chiefs are tor-
> tured by being suspended by their feet. Conditions in the silver mines
> of Potosí and Choclloccocha, or at the gold mines of Carabaya, are
> little better. The managers and supervisors, who are either Spaniards
> or half-castes, have virtually absolute power. There is no reason for
> them to fear justice, since they are never brought before the courts....
> Beatings are incessant. The victims are mounted for this purpose on a
> llama's back, tied naked to a round pillar, or put in the stocks.

s[i]vsi
DEFIELVDADELESPAÑOLA
su yra
drelos pobres yndios

soberbia y luxuria   q̃ los

882

298

In *Memory of Fire: Genesis,* in which he described the priest haunted by a vision of oppressed miners, Eduardo Galeano also offered a moving account of a defiant Guaman Poma, who "curses the invader in the invader's tongue and makes it explode." According to Galeano (who dates his scene 1615), "Today, Guaman finishes his letter. He has lived for it. It has taken him half a century to write and draw. It runs to nearly 1200 pages. Today, Guaman finishes his letter and dies. Neither Philip the III nor any other king will ever see it. For three centuries it will roam the earth, lost."

Galeano has slightly fictionalized his story — there is no evidence that Guaman Poma died shortly after finishing his letter to Philip, and certainly not on the day he completed it. The latest datable incident referred to in Poma's text occurred in the latter half of December 1615. Current scholarship suggests that he finished his book in the early months of 1616; nothing is known of his death. Who can say when a project like Poma's began? Galeano's "half a century" supposes that Poma had begun his work as a young man, and indeed he had poured his life into it, so in a sense he had always been composing it. But based on the evidence of the text itself, it appears that he began writing sometime after 1600 and then spent several years intensively writing and drawing.

There is a reason Poma began his book around 1600. In that year he lost a protracted legal battle, with catastrophic results. Poma's full name was Felipe Guaman Poma de Ayala. Guaman Poma is a name of Quechua origin that means "Falcon Puma"; de Ayala was the name of a Spanish conquistador whose line became entangled with that of the native family in ways that are not clear. "From their beginnings," historian John E. Wills, Jr., has observed, "there was a great deal of ethnic mixing in the colonies, as Native American women bore the children of Spanish men." Poma's Quechua origins were at the center of his identity as well as of his name, but he moved in both worlds. He was fluent in several Andean dialects and was literate in Spanish, having been educated by Catholic priests in childhood. In the latter half of the sixteenth century he worked for the Spanish as a translator from Quechua and served as a minor functionary in the colonial and church administrations.

Poma was from a region in the central Andes, where he insisted that his family had hereditary land rights. The lands were also claimed by another clan, the Chupas. The dispute was the subject of multiple lawsuits, beginning in the 1590s, in which Poma generally prevailed. Finally his antagonists tried a roundabout approach—they claimed that Poma had falsified his identity. Calamitously for Poma, this time they were victorious. In 1600 a colonial court publicly proclaimed its finding that Poma was nothing but a "poor Indian" named Lazaro who "always behaved and sought offices with malicious intentions and is an Indian of evil inclination." He was condemned to be publicly lashed, stripped of his property, and exiled from his home city for two years; he was also liable for the court costs.

Poma was forced to relocate to an area farther south in the Andes, where he began obsessively writing his extraordinary book, *El Primer Nueva Coronica y Buen Gobierno* ("The First New Chronicle and Good Government"). The book was influenced by Fray Martín de Murúa's *Historia General del Piru* ("General History of Peru") which was published in 1616 but begun before Poma's work. There are indications that Poma assisted Murua as a translator, source of information, and illustrator, and that he saw Murua's work in manuscript. Poma seems to have felt that Murua presented a one-sided view of Peruvian history. In Poma's book Murúa appears in an illustration kicking a woman working at a loom over the caption "The Mercedarian friar Martín de Murúa abuses his parishioners and takes justice into his own hands."

A Spanish Traveler Mistreats His Native Bearer, drawing 215 from *El Primer Nueva Coronica y Buen Gobierno* ("The First New Chronicle and Good Government"), 1615–1616, by Guaman Poma. Bound book; ink and colors on paper, 119 x 205 cm. Det Kongelige Bibliotek, Copenhagen, Denmark.

Poma's book is 1189 pages long and is as remarkable for its 398 full-page line drawings as for the text itself, which is divided into two parts as indicated by the title. The first part broadly chronicles the history of the Andes, beginning with biblical history and including a detailed portrait of the Inca empire. The second is a denunciation of the Spanish government of Peru, which Poma insists was inferior in many respects to that of the Inca. The entire work is presented as a letter to King Philip III of Spain in which Poma pleads for the king to curtail abuses by placing indigenous people in positions of authority.

The *Coronica* is the longest and most thorough critique of Spanish colonial rule by a native American of the period. Poma piles detail upon detail in his relentless documentation of the abuses of the Spaniards. He is outspoken and direct in his criticisms, his energy never flagging, up to his sly concluding sentences: "There is no god and there is no king. They are in Rome and Castile."

Poma's manuscript reached Spain but was probably never seen by the king. It entered the library of a Danish diplomat as an intriguing curiosity, and was lost in the Danish Royal Library from the 1660s until 1908, when a German researcher chanced upon it. Today, with the support of Rolena Adorno, the leading authority on Poma, the library has made the entire work available in facsimile on the Internet, its illustrations electronically enhanced to be truer to the original than the print reproductions of the twentieth century. Although Poma's appeal was not heard during his lifetime, his voice now thunders across the centuries.

Mining disrupted the lives not just of those who worked in the mines but also of the wider Latin American society. In the mid-1500s silver was discovered in the arid mountains of the states of Zacatecas and Durango in northwestern Mexico; these lodes would become the largest producers of silver after Potosí, and eventually they would even exceed its output. The Spanish called this region La Gran Chichimeca, after the Aztec name for the seminomadic peoples who inhabited the area. For both the Aztecs and the Spanish the name Chichimeca had pejorative overtones somewhat equivalent to the term "barbarian" (the Aztecs were probably peeved because they had never managed to conquer the Chichimecans). The Spanish believed that they had pacified the region, but in 1616 they learned otherwise.

After the discovery of silver Zacatecas had almost overnight become Mexico's third-largest city. The explosive growth not only of mining communities but of the ranching and commerce that came with them brought pressure to bear on the region's native peoples. Among these were the Tepehuans, a formerly warlike and fiercely independent people who had settled into a peaceful coexistence with the Spanish during the colonial period. Some Tepehuans worked in the mines, but it was not the mining itself that affected them as much as the intrusions into their territories that followed in the mines' wake. In 1615 the Tepehuans were devastated by an epidemic whose spread was facilitated by the region's population growth. Tepehuan elders feared that their traditional ways of life were threatened with extinction. Secretly they plotted a carefully coordinated rebellion.

On November 16, 1616, the Tepehuans simultaneously attacked multiple targets, including a wagon train traveling to Mexico city, a mission, and several estancias, killing scores of people. Their single most damaging attack, which would become notorious among the Spanish, was on a church in Zape, where about a hundred people were killed — the shocking news was reported by the lone survivor, a teenage boy. The attack on the church was not random: the Tepehuans knew that an altar and a statue of the Virgin would be dedicated on that day, and they took advantage of the fact that many people would gather there for the ceremony.

The Spaniards of New Spain were astonished and mystified by the uprising. They could not comprehend how the Tepehuans could be so ungrateful after having been given the gift of the faith. The only explanation was that treacherous Tepehuanes had engaged in "familiar intercourse with the devil." The attack on the church and the killing of Jesuit priests were pointed to in support of this explanation.

Completely unprepared for the assault, the Spaniards could offer little resistance. Without the assistance of native allies they would likely have been overrun. Instead, the warfare ground on for four years, over which the Spaniards were forced to summon more and more resources in order to finally prevail. A seventeenth-century historian called the revolt "one of the greatest outbreaks of disorder, upheaval, and destruction that had been seen in New Spain... since the Conquest." A provincial governor reported in 1618 that the region had been "destroyed and devastated, almost depopulated of Spaniards. The churches of the faith were burned. The silver mines and their machinery were also burned." In the end hundreds of Spaniards, along with countless of their native allies and African slaves, were killed, as well as more than a thousand Tepehuans. Mining was disrupted, and towns and ranches were destroyed.

The attribution of diabolical origins to the revolt was used to help win assistance from other parts of Mexico and beyond. After the cessation of hostilities most of the remaining Tepehuans withdrew into isolated areas of the mountains. New waves of Jesuit missionaries were brought in to ensure against further satanic eruptions; to be on the safe side they were supported by a beefed-up military presence. "The Viceroy and the governor... desired that the Jesuits, who had founded the [Tepehuan] mission, rebuild it, and the land returned to peace, so the Spanish could do business as before," the historian reported, "and the miners return to working the mines."

The exchange of silk and silver between China and the West required an enormous investment of energy on both sides. As silk was produced in greater and greater quantities in imperial workshops, China accelerated its movement from an agricultural to an industrial economy. Thousands of peasant farmers were displaced to urban centers where they were subsumed into an anonymous labor mass. Each year dozens of junks carried the silks to

Manila. Spain sailed its massive galleons from there every year across the vast Pacific, enduring, as we have seen, great hardships. It conscripted thousands of native laborers to serve out death sentences in the black depths of its silver mines, and it transported slaves from Africa to assist in the labor. Pirates from the South China Sea to the Pacific coast of America strove to cut in on the action. Armadas were assembled and defeated and reassembled.

It was all a passing vanity. It was all for momentary gain. Neither China nor Spain would derive much lasting benefit from all this striving. Within just a few decades both powers would collapse. China would fall in 1644 to invaders from its northern frontier who were no longer satisfied to be bought off with gifts of silk and porcelain. Its Great Wall proved powerless to stave off the outside world. Never again would a native Chinese dynasty bask in the mandate of heaven. Spain's empire by the same time would be exposed as a chimera, a fleeting illusion. The riches of the Americas had been but a stopgap that disguised Spain's need to streamline its bureaucracy, develop its resources, and restructure its economy. Spain's armadas against England, Joris van Spilbergen, and the VOC base in the Moluccas had all failed. It had proven unable to suppress revolt in the Netherlands or prevent the rise of Protestantism in Germany. By the time of the fall of the Ming dynasty, Spain was incapable even of holding on to Portugal on its own peninsula. Never again would it be perceived as a supreme force in Europe.

As the new fort of San Diego rose up in Acapulco over the year 1616, the Dutch engineer Adrian Boot must have watched with pride. Shaped like a five-pointed star, it was placed on a hill overlooking the bay, called El Morro (The Nose); there it was defensible to attack from any direction. In a nod to the traditional hierarchies of Spanish society, the five protruding sides were known by names such as King, Duke, and so on. On the interior it consisted of a number of domed rooms arranged around a central courtyard, providing ample space for provisions, ammunition, and soldiers. The fort was intended to be large enough to provide shelter for residents and soldiers if necessary, while also training powerful cannons upon the bay. Signal fires would warn the town of an impending attack.

While the Acapulco trade fair was in full swing, the construction was well underway and several of the heavy artillery pieces had been cast. In May the supervisor in charge of the construction wrote that it was a triumph of military architecture. Well constructed and architecturally advanced, the fort would be substantially finished by the end of the year; the archbishop of Mexico reported that it was complete when he visited in

January 1617. It would be one of the three strongest fortresses in Spanish America (the others are located at Veracruz, Acapulco's Gulf Coast counterpart, and at Cartagena, Colombia, the Caribbean slave trade port). Under its protection Acapulco would never again be taken.

Boot made his final report on the project on February 4, 1617. He then resumed work on the Mexico City drainage problem, and later on fortifications in Veracruz. Yet twenty years later he would be imprisoned by the Inquisition. What occasioned the trouble? A letter sent from the king to the viceroy of Mexico reports that many of Boot's colleagues, jealous of his salary of a hundred ducats a month, were his bitter enemies. Enrico Martinez, in his role as interpreter for the Inquisition, no doubt had fed the resentment before his death in 1632. Boot's origins in the Low Countries could have brought him under suspicion, yet he had lived and worked in Mexico for twenty-three years. It is hard to escape the suspicion that, after nearly a quarter century in New Spain, the engineer was done in by office politics.

Fortification at Veracruz, 1628. Color lithograph from a watercolor probably by Johannes Vingboons based on a drawing by Adrian Boot. Benson Latin American Collection, University of Texas at Austin.

In 1621 Boot would be called upon again for work on fortifications, this time at Veracruz on the Gulf coast. Boot's representation of the fortifications, while capturing the tropical light and ambience, is laid out on a grid-like plan suggesting an orderly and systematic mind.

2   Shakespeare's Sisters

In June 1616 a desk clerk in a London hotel checked in a party of travelers that was remarkable even to his jaded eyes. The lodgers were a mixed group of about ten or twelve men, women, and children. The most startling was a shaman named Uttamatomakkin. His face was boldly painted in bright colors. His hair was shaved on one side of his head and braided to a length of several feet on the other. He wore a breechcloth and carried a long, notched stick, on which he had tried for a time to record an estimate of England's population before giving up the attempt as hopeless. He was probably traveling in the company of his wife, a daughter of the *mamanatowick,* his people's paramount chief, Powhatan. The clerk must have eyed him nervously, because Uttamatomakkin was in a foul mood — he found everything about London annoying, especially the condescension of its citizens. He would be unimpressed with its King James, about whom he had heard so much, for when English colonists had given Powhatan a white dog the chief himself had fed it. But after Uttamatomakkin had crossed the ocean the English king had given him nothing, proving that he was ignorant of the standards of diplomacy of civilized people. "I am better," he said, "than a white dog!"

Also among the party was a Virginia tobacco farmer named John Rolfe. He was traveling with his young son, Thomas, and his nineteen-year-old wife, whose name prior to her marriage was Matoaka but who would be known in London by her Christian name, as "the Lady Rebecca." She was Uttamatomakkin's wife's half-sister; both were daughters of Powhatan. The group, led by firebrand Virginia governor Sir Thomas Dale — who had hanged a man on board ship during the ocean crossing — had been assembled as a promotion on behalf of the managers of the Virginia Company, a joint business venture financed by a group of London shareholders who were increasingly impatient to see a return on their investment. But it was Matoaka, whose childhood name had been Pocahontas ("Mischief"), who was to be the celebrity of the party.

It is said that the inn the travelers checked into was the Bell Savage, which was located on London's Ludgate Hill, not far from St. Paul's Cathedral; the site is now mostly a parking lot. The inn had doubled as a playhouse since about the 1560s, making it one of the first stages of the Shakespearean era, and one of the few that somehow managed to operate within the city walls, despite prohibitions against such entertainments. The inn

Opposite: A conventionalizing twentieth-century representation of the Basque hell-raiser Catalina de Erauso featuring Mexican film star Maria Félix in *The Lieutenant Nun* (1944). Movie viewers were supposed to believe that the starlet's female identity could not be discerned beneath her male disguise. The true story of early-seventeenth-century women is richer and more interesting than such reductionist renderings.

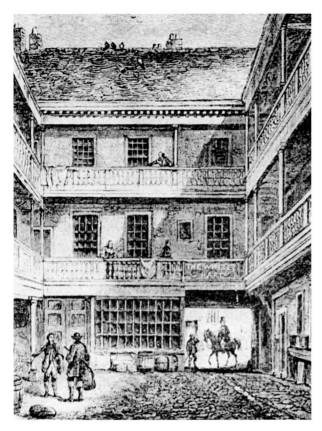

An early inn and playhouse, the White Hart at Southwark. From Joseph Quincy Adams, *Shakespearean Playhouses* (1917).

The Virginia Company's delegation to London, including the Powhatan maiden Matoaka (Pocahontas), probably stayed in an inn similar to this one — a long tradition maintains that it was the Bell Savage in London's Ludgate Hill. The arrangement of such inns made them suitable for performances: the yard served as a stage and the stables as dressing rooms for the actors. Lower classes craned for a view from the outer edges of the yard while the more privileged looked down from the upper levels.

could not have offered the most tranquil lodging experience, as the playhouse had presented martial arts exhibitions by the London Company of the Masters of Defense along with such entertainments as bear baiting and demonstrations of song and wit by actors such as Richard Tarlton. Theatrical "enterludes" were also part of the fare. In 1579 a writer critical of theatrical entertainments made an exception of "the twoo prose Bookes plaied at the Bel-Sauage" (whose name derived from that of an early owner of the establishment), "where you shall finde neuer a woorde without wit, neuer a line without pith, neuer a letter placed in vaine." By the turn of the century, however, the entertainments had been suppressed. Yet the alien, noisy, and aromatic London setting must still have made sleep difficult for the American visitors accustomed to the green forests of the Chesapeake Bay river drainage.

The party's stay at the Bell Savage is presented as fact in many sources, including P. L. Barbour's *The Three Worlds of Captain John Smith;* Anthony Parr's *Ben Jonson, The Staple of News;* Camilla Townsend's *Pocahontas and the Powhatan Dilemma;* Alden Vaughan's *Transatlantic Encounters: American Indians in Britain, 1500–1776;* Ben Weinreb's *The London Encyclopaedia;* Grace Steele Woodward's *Pocahontas;* and many more. Yet not a single comment exists from the time of her visit that mentions Pocahontas staying there. Rather, the story's persistence reflects an enduring association that was deeply held among the colonizing powers.

Europeans had long viewed America as a "belle savage." The word *America* is a feminized version of the name of the Italian explorer and cartographer Amerigo Vespucci. The feminization was not inadvertent. On early maps the continent is often represented by a naked native woman. Columbus had set the tone at the outset, when he claimed to have discovered the Garden of Eden on the Caribbean coast of South America — it was shaped, he said, like a nipple on a woman's breast. Much later, when England entered the Caribbean, Walter Raleigh still saw the region as a woman ripe for taking: "Guayana," he said, "is a country that hath yet her maidenhead." The travel writer Sam Purchas, an active cheerleader for the

Virginia Company, saw Virginia in similar terms, as "a virgin … not yet polluted with Spaniards' lust"; the name *Virginia* (honoring England's Virgin Queen) encapsulates this point of view. The role of the colonizers, Purchas advised, was to woo her and make her "not a wanton minion, but an honest and Christian wife." Needless to say, as a wife she would serve in a subordinate position. If the early returns from the Virginia colony were not impressive, William Crashaw, in a sermon to "Adventurers and Planters of the Virginia Company," advised, the suitors should not lose heart. Crashaw urged the "adventurers" (investors) to be patient with the results of the "planters" (settlers), on the grounds that even great leaders were once infants "carried in the arms of sillie women."

In an elegy entitled "To His Mistress Going to Bed," John Donne inverted the conceit of colonialism as sexual conquest, comparing his mistress to the continent:

> Licence my roving hands, and let them go
> Before, behind, between, above, below.
> O, my America, my Newfoundland,
> My kingdom, safest when with one man mann'd,
> My mine of precious stones, my empery;
> How am I blest in thus discovering thee!
> To enter in these bonds, is to be free;
> Then, where my hand is set, my soul shall be.

Elsewhere, however, the poet's imperious conceit breaks down, and his lover appears a more treacherous continent:

> The hair a forest of ambushes,
> Of springes, snares, fetters and manacles;
> The brown becalms us when 'tis smooth and plain,
> And when 'tis wrinkled shipwrecks us again.

For Londoners, Matoaka — the Indian "princess" who as a naked girl had once turned cartwheels on the quad in Jamestown but now was making the rounds as a Christian lady bedecked in London finery — embodied and validated their paternalistic vision. Matoaka herself addressed John Smith, the man she was to become famous for rescuing from execution by her father, on this theme. According to Smith, he visited her with several other people in the country home outside London where she and her son and husband had relocated. Upon seeing him "she turned about" and "obscured her face, as not seeming well contented." She was left alone to cool off. When — hours later — she had collected herself and returned to the group, she confronted Smith, telling him, "You did promise Powhatan what was yours should be his, and he the like to you; you called him father being in his land a stranger, and by the same reason so must I do you." Smith replied smoothly that it would not be right for her to call him "father" because she was nobility, the daughter of Powhatan, a king. To this Matoaka answered that Smith was "not afraid to come into my father's country, and cause fear in him and all his people (but me)." Yet, she said, "you fear you here I should call you father. I tell you then I will, and you shall call me child …"

The encounter between Matoaka and John Smith in England is one of history's palimpsests. Virtually all of the many writers on the Pocahontas story mention it, and all interpret it according to their perceptions of the participants, particularly of Smith. He is the only source for this incident, which nonetheless has the flavor of authenticity and is one of the few times we hear Matoaka speak.

Smith's admirers tend to believe that Matoaka was flustered by a surprise encounter with a man she had loved, when she had thought him dead. Smith encouraged this reading. Over the years he gradually upped her age in retelling the story, presumably to make a romance more plausible, or less prurient; in fact she was no more than ten or eleven years old when Smith was held captive by Powhatan. Throughout his writings Smith tells of admiring women coming to his assistance when he is in tight spots. He reports that as a slave in Turkey he was protected by a young Muslim princess named Charatza Tragabigzanda. On his escape, Callamata, the wife of a Cossack chief, came to his aid. After he was shipwrecked in France a Madame Chanoie befriended and tended to him. In Virginia, Smith reported, "thirty young women came naked out of the woods (only covered behind and before with a few green leaves), their bodies all painted, some white, some red, some black, some parti-colored" and danced a ring around a fire, offering themselves to him, each in turn crying "Love you not me?"

Despite this suspect pattern in his narrative, Smith has many champions, especially among those who think of him as one of the founding fathers of America. In historian J. A. Leo Lemay's assessment, for example, Smith was "energetic, disciplined, assertive, brave, independent … practical yet idealistic, studious and learned as well as a man of action, a social visionary as well as a pragmatist, and a kindly humanitarian … [with] nearly universal competence." Lemay and others tend to have faith in the veracity of Smith's stories, many of which have indeed been substantiated from other sources.

There are problems, however, with Smith's account of his rescue by

Pocahontas. According to Smith, in December 1607 he and two companions were exploring (or perhaps trying to extort corn from the Indians — his story varies) upriver from the English settlement at Jamestown when they were attacked by Powhatan Indians. Smith was captured and taken to the confederacy's leader, Powhatan, father of Pocahontas (somewhat confusingly he was known by a throne name that was the same as the name of his people, and not by his regular name, Wahunsenacawh). As Smith told and retold this story, his part in it swelled with the passage of time — and the passing of witnesses to his Virginia adventures. In a 1608 account of his capture, for example, Smith reported that he held off a small group of Indians with a pistol until being overwhelmed by a force of two hundred men. In 1612 he revised the story and now held off two hundred men until getting mired in a bog. By 1624 the party had grown to three hundred men, with Smith suffering several wounds not previously mentioned. In this version he singlehandedly held off the warriors even after falling into the bog, being captured only after he had become too numb with cold to continue.

Powhatan, believing Smith to be a leader of the English colony, tried to coopt him into his confederacy, as he had done with other vassal chiefs. The two men shared a banquet, and then Smith was released back to Jamestown. The entire legend of Pocahontas's rescue of Smith while he was Powhatan's prisoner stems from this brief passage from his *Generall Historie of Virginia, New England, and the Summer Isles, 1624* (Smith refers to himself in the third person):

> At last they brought him to Meronocomoco, where was Powhatan their Emperor. Here more then two hundred of those grim Courtiers stood wondering at him, as he had beene a monster; till Powhatan and his trayne had put themselues in their greatest braveries. Before a fire vpon a seat like a bedsted, he sat covered with a great robe, made of Rarowcun [raccoon] skinnes, and all the tayles hanging by. On either hand did sit a young wench of 16 to 18 yeares, and along on each side the house, two rowes of men, and behind them as many women, with all their heads and shoulders painted red; many of their heads bedecked with the white downe of Birds; but every one with something: and a great chayne of white beads about their necks. At his entrance before the King, all the people gaue a great shout. The Queene of Appamatuck was appointed to bring him water to wash his hands, and another brought him a bunch of

The Portraictuer of Captayne Iohn Smith, Admirall of New England, seventeenth century, after Simon Van de Passe. Engraving.

The rousing tales of John Smith, such as his report of beheading three Turks in combat, gave rise to a satirical poem by David Lloyd, a Welsh clergyman, entitled "The Legend of Captain Iones." Published in 1631, the year of Smith's death, it parodied his autobiography. The poem proved popular and went through six printings. According to Lloyd, "Nor need we stir our brains for glorious stuff / To paint his praise, himself hath done enough."

feathers, in stead of a Towell to dry them: having feasted him after their best barbarous manner they could, a long consultation was held, but the conclusion was, two great stones were brought before Powhatan: then as many as could layd hands on him, dragged him to them, and thereon laid his head, and being ready with their clubs, to beate out his braines, Pocahontas the Kings dearest daughter, when no intreaty could prevaile, got his head in her armes, and laid her owne vpon his to saue him from death: whereat the Emperour was contented he should liue to make him hatchets, and her bells, beads, and copper; for they thought him as well of all occupations as themselues.

The only source for the legend is again Smith himself, and whether it happened at all has been the subject of lively debate since the nineteenth century. Because the story is difficult to prove or disprove, the debate will doubtless continue. But it is hard to reconcile Smith's romantic tale of rescue with what is known of Powhatan practices, and it promotes a ten- or eleven-year-old girl to a position of power that has no precedent in this context. Anthropologist Helen Rountree, the leading researcher on Virginia Indians and an honorary member of the Nansemond and Upper Mattaponi tribes, has written that "the 'rescue' is part of a sequence of events that would be farcical if so many people did not take it seriously as 'Virginia history.'... Pocahontas did not rescue John Smith. Even if she had been inside the house at the time, he would not have needed rescuing from anything other than overeating."

Smith also reported a conversation with Powhatan that curiously echoes one of the themes of his exchange with Matoaka in London. As was so often the case, the occasion was a meeting where Smith attempted to coerce Powhatan into providing the colony with corn, as the settlers had proven unable to survive without native assistance. Smith told Powhatan he was acting as an emissary from Captain Christopher Newport. He pointedly reminded Powhatan that the English had a great advantage in arms, but assured him that they would not use them because of the fellowship they felt with Powhatan. To this the chief cogently replied,

> Captain Newport you call father, and so you call me. But I see, for all us both, you will do what you list, and we must both seek to content you. But if you intend so friendly as you say, send hence your arms, that I may believe you.

All of this talk of fathers reminds us that the history of Virginia comes down to us from the Englishmen who recorded it. The paternalistic English society typically spoke of both religious and civil leaders as fathers. James I said, "Kings are compared to fathers in families: for a king is truly *parens patriae,* the political father of his people." The position of women was distinctly subordinate; often, as with John Rolfe's first wife, who died during the couple's passage to Virginia, we do not even know their names. While the native Virginians also esteemed fathers, their society was matrilineal, and this led to confusion and misunderstanding. Friends of Smith, for example, proposed that "he would have made himself a king by marrying Pocahontas, Powhatan's daughter," but this was not the case. The English were mistaken in thinking her a princess. Upon Powhatan's death his "kingdom" would fall first to his brothers and then to his sisters (the society was matrilineal not matriarchal — inheritance passed through the mother's line, but it went to the sons before the daughters). Thereafter his nephews and nieces would be next in line. Since the mother of Pocahontas was not one of Powhatan's important wives, neither she nor her brothers would ever be in the line of succession, despite his having been their father — in fact, with each succession her proximity to power would grow more distant. She was just an ordinary girl, though one whose bold and inquisitive personality found favor both with her father and with the newcomers to Powhatan lands.

Still the settlers persisted in their notion that the girl was a princess of the highest value. It appears that Powhatan played along with the idea, often sending his daughter along with messengers to the fort at Jamestown in a show of good will. Finally the colonists seized their chance and kidnapped her for use as a diplomatic pawn, though they rationalized the action as bringing her the benefit of the Christian religion. Kidnapping children was an explicit strategy of the English. Biblical precedents were cited in sermons in London, and the Virginia Company had issued a directive to the settlers "to procure from them some of their Children to be brought up in our language and manners if you think it necessary … by a surprise of them and detaining them prisoners and in case they shall be willful and obstinate, then to send us some 3 or 4 of them into England, we may endeavor their conversion here." It is conceivable that the kidnapping was not unforeseen by Powhatan, who still hoped to convert the newcomers into vassals of his confederacy. Marriage of women into outsider groups was as much a component of diplomacy for the American natives as it was for the Europeans. Powhatan himself was reported to have had a hundred wives, and this created many kinship ties that enabled him to secure his base of power.

The Americans' matrilineal system of succession helped to ensure that rule would not pass to an underage child. An entire set of siblings — including

Opposite: Lady Mary Wroth
with a Theorbo, ca. 1615–1620,
possibly by John de Critz (1555–
1641). Pemhurst Place, Kent.

Lady Mary Wroth is pictured here
with a long-necked lute. The instrument has often been identified
as an archlute, but this appears to
be a larger instrument, developed
around the end of the seventeenth
century, called a theorbo. The
theorbo's strong bass register made
it useful in the emerging art form
known as opera; some scholars
consider Florentine composer
Domenico Belli's *L'Orfeo Dolente*
(1616) the first true opera.

Lady Wroth's choice of instrument expresses her rounded
sensitivities, her familiarity with
current cultural trends, and also
her ability simply to afford such
a refined and elegant large-scale
instrument.

women — would be in line before succession passed to the next generation. This prevented governance by wards and counselors of child rulers,
as had been the case with Powhatan's contemporaries James I of England,
Louis XIII of France, Michael Romanov of Russia, the Ottoman sultan
Ahmed I, and the Wanli emperor of China.

A crisis that occurred in 1616 in the circumstances of Mary Wroth, a
lady in Queen Anne's circle, exemplified the consequences of the preference shown to male heirs by the Europeans. At the time of the Powhatans'
visit to London, she was working on a sequence of sonnets that she would
include in the first published work of fiction by an English woman. One of
the sonnets begins like this:

> Like to the Indians, scortched with the sunne,
> The sunn which they doe as theyr God adore
> Soe ame I us'd by love, for ever more
> I worship him, less favors have I wunn . . .

The book would be read in its time as a *roman à clef.* Wroth came from a
distinguished aristocratic family. Her mother was a cousin of Walter Raleigh
and her father the younger brother of Philip Sidney, the courtier poet. Her
aunt Mary Sidney, Countess of Pembroke, was an important patron of the
arts, as well as a poet and translator. In the Banqueting Hall of Whitehall on
Twelfth Night (January 6), 1605, Wroth danced — together with the queen
herself — in Ben Jonson and Inigo Jones's *Masque of Blackness;* she played
the part of Baryte, an Ethiopian maiden. The masque, created at the queen's
request, was the first of many on which Jonson and Jones would collaborate.
The queen and ladies, representing the twelve daughters of Niger, all performed in blackface — that they had painted their faces rather than worn
masks occasioned criticism. Wearing pearls and feathers in their hair, they
made a dramatic entrance on a giant seashell. They were accompanied by
torchbearers representing nymphs, whose faces, hands, and hair were dyed
blue. The performance created a stir. One scandalized observer complained
that the ladies' costumes were "too light and curtizan-like for such great
ones." But the performance ushered in a new era of spectacle for the court of
James and Anne, and Lady Mary Wroth seemed well positioned for a central
role among the queen's circle.

Only a few months before this performance she had been married (by
James himself) to Sir Robert Wroth; the marriage was the culmination of
negotiations that had begun when she was twelve. Her husband shared with
the king an interest in hunting, and James promoted him to the position of

Riding Forester, responsible for flushing out game. An avid keeper of hounds and spaniels, he had few literary interests. While many men in his position, because of their roles as patrons of the arts, could boast of several books dedicated to them, Wroth had but one — a study of mad dogs. He seems to have led a dissolute life, and it was soon apparent that neither party was happy with the marriage. Robert may have nursed some grudge about the nature of the dowry (a concept that would have seemed strange to the Powhatans, who instead paid "brideswealth" to the wife's family), while Mary must have watched in alarm as he burned through their resources. Ben Jonson (who boasted that he preferred love affairs with married women to those with unmarried women) observed that "my Lady Wroth is unworthily married on a Jealous husband." He dedicated his play *The Alchemist* to her — his only First Folio play dedicated to a woman — but no one seems to have suggested anything beyond a literary relationship between them.

Jonson also took an interest in Mary Wroth's cousin Elizabeth, Countess of Rutland, for whom he wrote several poems, and whose writing he also praised. One writer reported a scene in the Rutland household: "Ben one day being at table with my Lady Rutland, her husband coming in, accused her that she kept table with poets, of which she wrott a letter to him which he answered. My Lord intercepted the letter, but never challenged him." Jonson was a dangerous man to challenge, having once slain a theatrical associate with a sword during a quarrel on a London street.

Jonson praised Wroth's skill as a love poet in a sonnet (one of only five in his collected works, it pays homage to her preference for the form):

> A Sonnet,
> to the noble Lady, the Lady
> MARY WROTH
>
> I that have been a lover, and could shew it,
> Though not in these, in rithmes not wholly dumbe,
> Since I exscribe your Sonnets, am become
> A better lover, and much better Poet.
> Nor is my Muse, or I asham'd to owe it
> To those true numerous Graces; whereof some,
> But charme the Senses, others over-come
> Both braines and hearts; and mine now best doe know it:
> For in your verse all *Cupids* Armorie,
> His flames, his shafts, his Quiver, and his Bow,
> His very eyes are yours to overthrow.

But then his Mothers sweets you so apply,
Her joyes, her smiles, her loves, as readers take
For *Venus Ceston,* every line you make.

In 1614, after ten years of marriage, Wroth gave birth to a son; one month later her husband died of gangrene, leaving her with the staggering sum of £23,000 of debt. Catastrophically, when her son died, in 1616, the Wroth estate passed not to Mary (because of her gender) but to her husband's nearest male relative, his uncle John Wroth. For the rest of her life Wroth would struggle with debt, constantly responding to a never-ending barrage of demands from creditors. This fate would continue to befall women into the nineteenth century — a similar case of distant male inheritance is a key story element in Jane Austen's *Pride and Prejudice.*

Around this time Mary consummated a relationship with her first cousin William Herbert, with whom she had two illegitimate children. A dashing figure, and a womanizer (but not, apparently, one who shared Jonson's preference for married women), Herbert had been imprisoned by Elizabeth in 1601 for refusing to marry one of her ladies-in-waiting whom he had gotten pregnant. He nonetheless became a favorite of Queen Anne. In her long romance *The Countesse of Mountgomeries Urania,* the first published work of fiction by an Englishwoman, Wroth describes a queen who exiles a rival from her court in order to obtain her lover. Wroth seems herself to have been, if not exactly banished from the court, at least much reduced in prominence following the downturn in her fortunes.

Wroth published her book in the large folio format, which asserted its importance in a way that underlined her subversion of the conventional prescription that women should be silent and self-effacing. Book formats were determined by how many times a sheet of paper — most often about 19 x 25 inches — was folded. One fold produced a folio, two a quarto, three an octavo, and so on. The quarto — about 9.5 x 12.5 inches — was the most common size; sizes smaller than octavo were intended for pockets and purses. The folio format (sometimes known as foolscap, from a watermark sometimes used that showed a fool's cap and bells) was expensive and, at about 8.5 by 13.5 inches after trimming a large folded sheet, awkward to carry. Such books — Bibles, songbooks, publications by monarchs and the upper nobility — were generally intended for display in large rooms or public places. Ben Jonson's publication of his *Collected Workes* in the folio format in 1616 was a gesture expressing an elevated estimation of the literary value of drama; the First Folio of Shakespeare's plays would not be published until seven years later. By the same token, Wroth's book, which preceded the First Folio by a couple of years and was the first publication in this format by a single woman author (contributions by women had occasionally appeared in anthologies), asserted her right to be raken as seriously as an male writer.

The forms in which Wroth worked, the pastoral romance and the sonnet sequence, were falling out of favor at the time she was writing, but both were associated with her uncle Philip Sidney; her authorship as a woman and her female characters give them a fresh twist. The romance's title character is a woman raised by shepherds, who, she learns, are not her biological parents (she is actually the daughter of the king of Naples). This discovery initiates a kind of quest for self-discovery — "to know my own selfe" — that some have seen as a search for feminine identity. Along the way she forms female friendships that, in the words of scholar Naomi J. Miller, are "not cut off by the traditional terminus of romantic couplings so common to the works of many of her predecessors." The sonnet sequence *Pamphilia to Amphilanthus,* part of *Urania,* expresses the emotions of a faithful woman in love with an inconstant man. Pamphilia (Greek for "all loving"), a character usually seen as modeled on Wroth herself, loves the unfaithful Amphilanthus (Greek for "having multiple loves").

In the estimation of Germaine Greer and the other editors of *Kissing the Rod: An Anthology of Seventeenth-Century Women's Verse,* "the intensity of her poetry comes from its casting and recasting of several key concepts, as if it were writhing in the bonds of the rigid forms she chooses." For example:

> Griefe, killing griefe: have nott my torments binn
> Allreddy great, and strong enough: butt still
> Thou dost increase, nay glory in mine ill,
> And woes new past afresh new woes beeginn!
> Am I the only purchase thou canst winn?
> Was I ordain'd to give dispaire her fill
> Or fittest I should mounte misfortunes hill
> Who in the plaine of joy can-nott live in?
> If itt bee soe: Griefe come as welcome ghest
> Since I must suffer, for an others rest:
> Yett this good griefe, lett mee intreat of thee,
> Use still thy force, butt nott from those I love
> Let mee all paines and lasting torments prove
> So I miss these, lay all they waits on mee.

Ben Jonson notwithstanding, many in the established community of male authors did not approve of Wroth's publication. One writer, perceiving an unflattering portrayal of himself in the work, accused her of slander and tarred her with the labels "hermaphrodite" and "monster"—confirming Virginia Woolf's assertion that if Shakespeare had had a talented sister who had sought to become a playwright she would have been called a monster. Wroth was compelled to withdraw *Urania* from circulation by the end of the year, and a follow-up volume would go unpublished until the late twentieth century.

Not until 1630 would another woman publish in the folio format, when Elizabeth Cary's translation *The Reply of the Most Illustrious Cardinall of Perron* appeared. It too would be suppressed.

To publish books was for a woman an indiscretion suggestive of immodesty. From John Knox's mid-sixteenth-century *The First Blast of the Trumpet Against the Monstrous Regiment of Women,* through the advice of the Earl of Morton, chancellor of Scotland under Mary Queen of Scots, that it is "a thing against nature that the hen should crow before the cock; yea against the commandment of the eternal God, that a man should be subject to his wife, the man being the image of God," women were urged to be chaste, silent, and obedient. Around 1616 a preacher named William Whately preached a wedding sermon that advised:

> The whole duty of the wife is referred to two heads. The first is to acknowledge her inferiority, the next to carry herself as inferior. First then, the wife's judgement must be convinced that she is not her husband's equal, yea that her husband is her better by far: else there can be no contentment, either in her heart or in her house. If she stand upon terms of equality, much more of being better than he is, the very root of good carriage is withered, and the fountain thereof is dried up.... If ever thou propose to be a good wife, and to live comfortably, set down this with thy self. *Mine husband is my superior, my better:* he hath authority and rule over me: nature hath given it him....

Around the same time, in France, Jacques Olivier published *An Alphabet of Women's Imperfections,* a popular book that would see seventeen reprintings over the next hundred years. A brief excerpt will suffice. Addressing women, he writes: "You live here on earth as the world's most imperfect creature: the scum of nature, the cause of misfortune, the source of quarrels, the toy of the foolish, the plague of the wise, the stirrer of Hell, the tinder of vice, the guardian of excrement, a monster in nature, an evil necessity, a multiple chimera, a sorry pleasure, Devil's bait, the enemy of angels ..." and so on, and on, and on. The reason for women's imperfec-

Lady Frances Howard (1590–1632)
was already notorious as a woman
of purportedly less than sterling
virtue when she determined to an-
nul her marriage to her husband,
Robert Devereux, Third Earl of
Essex, and marry instead Robert
Carr, King James's favorite.

A farcical trial ensued after she
petitioned for annulment on the
grounds that the marriage had not
been consummated and she was
still a virgin — a claim regarded
by many as preposterous. A team
of matrons and midwives was
presented with a woman who was
veiled "for modesty's sake," and
they confirmed her virginity. It
was commonly believed the veiled
woman a substitute, as expressed
in a popular verse:

> The dame was inspected but fraud
> interjected
> A maid of more perfection
> Whom the midwives did handle
> While the knight held the candle
> O there was a clear inspection!

Friends of her husband, meanwhile, to demonstrate that he was
sexually capable, reported that
once during a chat he had lifted
his nightshirt to show off a fine
erection.

(cont'd facing page)

tion could be found in medical theory, according to Helkiah Crooke in his book on the human body, *Microcosmographia*, published in 1618. "Nature ever intendeth the generation of a male, and ... the female is procreated by accident out of a weaker seed which is not able to attain the perfection of the male," he explained. "That females are more wanton and petulant than males, we think happeneth because of the impotency of their minds: for the imaginations of lustful women are like the imaginations of brute beasts which have no repugnancy or contradiction of reason to restrain them."

Who would want to marry the scum of nature? Thomas Overbury thought it a bad idea. Overbury, a poet and essayist, was an intimate friend of King James's early favorite, Robert Carr. In 1612 Carr began an affair with a married woman, Frances Howard, Countess of Essex. Motivated in part by jealousy and in part by political considerations, Overbury sought to turn his companion away from the affair, arguing that the woman was "noted for her injury and immodesty." Nonetheless, she secured an annulment by the king of her marriage, and the two made plans to marry. In response Overbury wrote a poem called "A Wife," which detailed the virtues that he believed were to be sought in a woman. Among his advice:

> As good and wise; so be she fit for me,
> That is, to will, and not to will, the same:
> My wife is my adopted selfe, and she
> As me, so what I love, to love must frame:
> For when by mariage both in one concurre,
> Woman converts to man, not man to her.

Despite Overbury's efforts, the pair were married. John Donne wrote a verse for the occasion.

Overbury had made a powerful enemy in the countess, who persuaded James to send him off to Russia as ambassador to the court of Michael Romanov — a prospect that, as it happened, suited James, as his fancy was already turning to a new favorite. Sensing his influence slipping away, Overbury refused the assignment, and James, furious, imprisoned him in the Tower of London. There, with the help of some of his jailers, he was fatally poisoned by one or both of the newlyweds, creating the biggest scandal of James's reign. Following a high-profile trial, the couple were found guilty in 1616 (but later released).

How could a man be certain that his beloved was not concealing a latent harlot beneath her petticoats? Author Banabe Rich, in *My Lady's*

Looking Glass, another work published in 1616, offered a helpful guide containing "rules how to distinguish between a good woman and a bad." The bad woman, he advised, "is impudent, she is shameless, she cannot blush: and she that hath lost all these virtues, hath lost her evidence of honesty; for the ornaments of a good woman is temperance in her mind, silence in her tongue, and bashfulness in her countenance.... The woman that is impudent, immodest, shameless, insolent, audacious, a nightwalker, a company-keeper, a gadder from place to place, a reveler, a ramper, a roister, a rioter: she that hath these properties hath the certain signs and marks of an harlot."

A good woman was, above all, a mother. Martin Luther had said that birthing children was a woman's obligation. "Even if they bear themselves weary, or bear themselves out," he said. "This is the purpose for which they exist." Often women had a great many children, in part because many did not survive childhood (a fifteenth-century woman in Florence had thirty-nine children before dying at the age of fifty-seven). Aristocratic women had more children than did the lower classes, partly to preserve wealth in the family line but also because they did not nurse their own children. Lower-class women served as wet-nurses for the rich. The result was a cycle in which some women were constantly birthing and others constantly suckling. (A wet-nurse in Ming China was so mortified to find herself pregnant before the end of her three-year nursing contract that she committed suicide by drinking mercury. Her case comes down to us through an account by a member of the employing family, who wished to make it clear that they did not pressure her into the act.) Births were viewed as the most heroic moments in women's lives, when, briefly, they were lauded and cheered. Madonna and Child images expressed the Renaissance esteem for motherhood (while depictions of the Immaculate Conception were a way of overcoming the seemingly contradictory valuation of virginity).

The reverence for motherhood provided an opening for some women to break the proscription against speaking up. One of the best-selling

(cont'd from facing page)

In defense of his marriage, Devereux further asserted that he had managed sex with several other women. Finally the king personally put an end to the proceedings by annulling the marriage himself.

A friend of Carr's, Thomas Overbury, wrote a pedantic poem called "A Wife," which implied that Lady Howard possessed none of a wife's desired virtues. He soon ended up in the Tower of London, where he was murdered by the newlyweds with poisoned drinks and enemas.

titles of the seventeenth century was written by Dorothy Leigh on her deathbed and published in 1616. In format it was at the opposite end of the spectrum from Mary Wroth's folio: it was a tenpenny duodecimo edition — one of the cheapest books available, the equivalent of today's mass market newsrack paperback. By 1674 it had gone through twenty-three reprintings, making it far and away the most reprinted text by a woman of the period.

Leigh, born Dorothy Kempe, was a gentlewoman from a distinguished family. Her maternal grandfather had been an influential minister during the reign of Queen Elizabeth. The Kempe family was notably pious, and family members often left bequests for the funding of sermons in their wills. The origins of her husband, Ralph Leigh, are much less clear, with the implication that she married (remarried actually: she was widowed by her first husband) beneath her station. It has been suggested that for Leigh her husband's spiritual integrity was more important than his worldly position; certainly this would be consistent with the content of her book.

Today Leigh's best-seller, *The Mothers Blessing,* would come across to most readers as a litany of conventional pieties, but by the standards of its time it was seen as opinionated and outspoken. Leigh addressed the text to her three sons, thereby fulfilling the legacy of her second husband that the boys be brought up "godily." Aware of her own impending death and cognizant of her sons' young ages, she chose to put her motherly advice into print. In this way she defended herself against the injunction against women speaking up — she was only fulfilling her husband's wishes and preparing her sons for the world. But in fact she made clear that she intended the work for a wider audience. Indeed, the title page explicitly advises that the book would be "profitable for all Parents to leaue as a Legacy to their Children."

Leigh claimed that if she left the book in manuscript "should it be left with the eldest, it is likely the youngest should haue but little part in it. Wherefore setting aside all fear, I have adventured to shew my imperfections to the view of the world." It's a thin pretext for a sizeable printing, but one that suggests an erosion of conventional hierarchies in Leigh's worldview. Just as she appears to have been relatively unconcerned with social station in her marriage, so she implies in this argument a lessened regard for the traditional priority of the firstborn. Although she advises women to "giue men the first and chiefe place," she seems less conventional in other views. She always adopts a tone of grave piety, advising her sons regarding their "choyse of wiues" that "a little with a godly woman is better than great riches with the wicked." For Leigh spiritual salvation was to be found through individual communion with God rather than through rituals and social systems, and she is especially scathing on the subject of "Catholic superstitions." She also dedicated the book to King James's daughter Elizabeth, a champion of the Protestant cause who married Frederick V — the Calvinist monarch ruled a portion of the Holy Roman Empire around the Rhine River, known as the Palatinate; he would soon be at the center of the devastating religious conflict known as the Thirty Years War. In counter-reaction to attempts to standardize religious belief by means of confessional practice during the sixteenth and seventeenth centuries, some Christians had begun to place greater emphasis on interior piety and personal spiritual communion (a development paralleled by kabbalah in Judaism and Sufism in Islam).

As a result of her belief in individual salvation, Leigh was a champion of female literacy at all levels of society. The main point of literacy, in her view, was the ability to read the Bible. This view, which was most common in Protestant communities, had sometimes been outweighed by a concern that if young women were literate they would use the skill to write love notes — a sixteenth-century Spanish Jesuit had for this reason proposed that women should be taught to read but not to write. But Leigh urged her sons (and her wider readership) to begin teaching their children to read at the age of four and continue teaching until the age of ten. She even advised "witnesses" (a Puritan word for "godparent") at baptisms to refuse to participate unless the parents promised to teach the child to read. Leigh's book helped to fuel a craze for mothers' advice books, and to advance the cause of female literacy beyond the privileged classes.

Throughout much of the early modern world family relations were a key to status and power. At the highest level, rule itself was most often hereditary. An unexpected death in the royal line could alter the political map to the benefit of sometimes quite distant rivals — this was how the Habsburg dynasty came to dominate the political map of Europe. It was

---

THE
MOTHERS
BLESSING.
OR
The godly counsaile of a *Gentle-woman not long since deceased, left behind her for her* CHILDREN:

Containing many good exhortations, and godly admonitions, profi-*table for all Parents to leaue as a Legacy to their Children, but especially* for those, who by reason of their young yeeres stand most in need of Instruction.[1]

By M^ris. DOROTHY LEIGH.

PROVERB. 1. 8. My sonne, heare the instruction of thy father, and forsake not the lawe of thy mother.

Printed at *London* for *Iohn Budge*, and are to be sold at the great South-dore of Paules, and at Brittaines Burse. 1616.

Title Page from *The Mothers Blessing,* 1616, by Dorothy Leigh.

Leigh's book was one of the best-selling titles of the seventeenth century. It started a vogue for advice books and helped forge a path into print for women writers. Leigh was an advocate for universal literacy. Rising rates of female literacy resulted both in a bigger pool of women authors and in larger potential audiences for their work.

important to produce healthy heirs. Consequently, royal midwives were persons of importance.

Henri IV of France, who ruled from 1589 until his death by assassination in 1610, had been the king of Navarre since 1572. Navarre today is a region in northern Spain, but at the time it was an independent kingdom uncomfortably situated between hostile powers, France and Spain. ("Spain" was really a loose confederacy of bickering states, which often seemed to share little beyond a king. France too was far from homogenous, with even its linguistic unification still incomplete — in fact, as late as 1794 a report showed that the majority of people in France did not speak French.) Succession to the French throne fell to Henri IV on the death of the brother of Henri III in 1584. Henri IV assumed titular rule when that king (his ninth cousin) was assassinated five years later — French law disinherited all of the king's sisters and those descended from the mother's line. But, unfortunately for France, Henri was a Protestant, and the powers of Paris recoiled at the prospect of Protestant rule; this ratcheted up the drawn-out Wars of Religion that ravaged the country throughout the second half of the sixteenth century. Henri attempted for years to secure his birthright by force but only succeeded in entering Paris and assuming the throne after he converted to Catholicism — history ascribes to him the wry comment that "Paris is well worth a mass." Whether he actually uttered those words is questionable, but he must have thought them.

Among those who found their lives disrupted by the Wars of Religion were Martin Bousier, a barber-surgeon, and his wife, Louise Bourgeois. The young couple (Bourgeois was born in 1563) were living comfortably in Saint-Germain, then a rural suburb of Paris, when Henri IV's troops attacked the area in 1589; Henri would use Saint-Germain as a staging area for a siege of the city, before resorting to the more convenient and effective expedient of religious conversion. As a barber-surgeon Martin was called away with the army, and Louise, years later, recalled those times. "We paid a high price," she wrote. "My mother and I along with my three children went into the city with a few pieces of furniture. . . . Anything of value was pillaged." The soldiers "finished off everything, right down to the straw."

The family fled to Paris with only a few possessions, which they gradually sold off in order to survive. Now living in desperate conditions and in dire need of a livelihood, Bourgeois turned first to stitching, weaving, and embroidery but soon began to get work as a midwife, passing the examinations for a license in 1598. The city was dense with refugees from the war, and there was no shortage of babies to be delivered, especially in the Latin Quarter, where she lived in proximity to the colleges, which

Opposite: *The Apotheosis of Henri IV and the Proclamation of the Regency of Marie de Medicis* (detail), 1621–1625, by Peter Paul Rubens. Oil on canvas, 394 x 727 cm. Louvre, 1779.

In the early 1620s Rubens painted a series of twenty-four monumental canvases exalting Marie de Medicis. A reconciliation between the queen and her son Louis XIII had been arranged by the future Cardinal Richelieu, who had been appointed prime minister in 1616.

This painting represents the key moment when power passed to the queen regent. On the left (not shown here) Henri IV is carried into heaven by Jupiter while his assassin is depicted as a snake pierced by an arrow. On the right, in the detail shown here, the queen is surrounded by mythological figures heralding her coming reign. Divine Providence hands over the helm of state, the queen is advised by Prudence and Minerva the warrior goddess, and a helmeted figure representing France kneels before her with the globe of government.

seem to have been nearly as randy at that time as they are today.

By then Henri IV was established as king, but as yet had no heir. His strained first marriage was childless, though he had three children with a favored mistress, whom he hoped to make his queen by annulling his marriage; but the mistress died in giving birth prematurely to a stillborn son. Succeeding in annulling his first marriage, he then married Marie de Medicis in 1600, but this marriage too would be an unhappy one. The new queen had an unseemly propensity to quarrel publicly with the king's paramours. When she became regent of France following Henri's assassination in 1610, she quickly banished his chief mistress.

Meanwhile Louise Bourgeois's client list was moving up the social ladder, and among her many satisfied mothers were women among the circle of the queen.

She won the support of the queen's favorite, Leonora Galigai, and secured the position of royal midwife in 1601. Like most important positions it had been the subject of factional wrangling, and by succeeding in choosing Bourgeois over the king's own preference, a Mme. Dupuis (who had delivered his mistress's children), the queen asserted her independence and authority. The future of France would now be in Bourgeois's hands, and she successfully delivered the future king Louis XIII in September of the same year, living among the court for a month before and after the birth before returning home.

The birth of the future king was a public spectacle. Bourgeois estimated that there were about two hundred people in the antechamber and the birthing room. Characteristically unafraid to speak up, Bourgeois complained that this might be too many for the new mother, to which the king responded "Hush, hush, midwife, do not be angry, this child is everyone's, everyone must rejoice." Bourgeois noticed that the infant was weak, and asked permission to blow some wine into his mouth, as she would do with other infants in the same condition. "Do as you would do onto another," the king replied, and the baby revived. The next day, when the midwife came to visit the queen, the king publicly commended her, saying "I have known many people, but I have never seen one, either a man or a woman, with such resolve — not at war or anywhere — as this woman." Such, at least, was Bourgeois's own account of the birth. One of the king's physicians left a very different version, in which she serves only a subordinate role as an assistant to the physicians. Already Bourgeois was locked in rivalry with the king's physicians. It would take another quarter century before they would prevail. A power struggle between the queen and the future king Louis XIII that came to a head in 1616–1617 would contribute to their triumph.

During the subsequent decade Bourgeois and Martin Boursier lived well in a house on the Left Bank. Each royal birth paid 900 livres, compared to an average midwife's income of 50 livres a year, and she received additional payments as well, such as a lump sum of 6,000 livres in 1608. She also continued to work for other clients, and a book she published in 1609 suggests that by that time she had delivered about two thousand babies.

Bourgeois continued as midwife to the royal court for twenty-six years. After the future Louis XIII, she delivered five more children of Marie de Medici (among them future queens of Spain and England), including one breech birth. On that occasion a male midwife was kept in reserve in an anteroom in case the problem proved beyond the skill of a woman. Bourgeois scorned this help and delivered the child successfully. Over her career she dealt with many difficult situations and complications, and performed minor surgeries. She was the first midwife to write extensively of her work, issuing several substantial publications between 1609 and 1635; German, Dutch, and English translations of her writings popularized her level-headed advice. She was a woman of great confidence: as she advised in her first book, "Never seem to be at a loss; for there is nothing so unpleasant to witness as those households all at sixes and sevens. Never be surprised if something does not go well, because fear troubles the senses. Someone who is self-contained and does not become upset is able to set important matters right."

In 1627, when she was sixty-four, Bourgeois served as midwife to an aristocratic woman who died of the inflammatory condition now called puerperal peritonitis. An autopsy was performed and signed by no fewer than five physicians and five surgeons. The report left the cause of death open but implied that Bourgeois might have been partly at fault. Bourgeois responded fiercely, publishing an *Apology of Louise Bourgeois* that defended her actions and competence. "I have practiced my profession now for fully thirty-four years, faithfully, diligently, and honorably, and acquired not only a good certificate, after various examinations, but have also written books and published several editions that were translated into foreign languages, for which trouble many noted physicians have rendered me thanks and have gladly confessed that they were of great use to humanity," she said. She flatly called the physicians and surgeons unethical and ignorant — a bold attack on a professional fraternity of men from a woman. The problem, she said, was that they knew nothing about women's bodies. "Based on your report you make it clear," she insisted, "that you have no knowledge of the placenta and the womb of a woman, either before or after her delivery."

Unfortunately for Bourgeois, the court had changed considerably since she had first earned the position of royal midwife. Most of her original supporters were dead or no longer in positions of influence. The king was no longer Henri IV but the icy young Louis XIII; the queen mother, Marie de Medicis, had been sent into exile. She had served as regent for Louis since 1610 when he was not yet nine years old. Marie was from Florence, and she had fallen increasingly under the influence of an Italian couple, the foppish Concino Concini and his wife Leonora Galigai, Bourgeois's champion. Even after Louis reached majority at age thirteen, Concini and Galigai, through Marie, continued to exert control over the young king. In 1616, supporters urged Louis to assert himself. Concini was assassinated the following spring — the citizens of Paris expressed their loathing for the foreign schemer by digging up his body, tearing it apart, and eating it. Galigai was arrested and put in the Bastille. Hebrew texts found in her apartment were taken as proof at least of black magic if not outright Judaism. Witchcraft would explain her hold over the queen, though Galigai claimed, "My spell was the power of a strong mind over a weak one." Taking no chances, the authorities beheaded her and then burned her body at the stake.

In this way Louise Bourgeois had lost an important champion, and she was forced to defend herself to the dramatically changed court. The male doctors fired back against Bourgeois's charges, attacking not just her conclusions but also her presumption in overstepping her place as a midwife

Louise Bourgeois at Age Forty-Five, 1608. Engraving from *Observations diverses sur la sterilité, perte de fruict, foecondité, accouchements ey maladies des Femmes et Enfants nouveaux naix* (Various Observations on Sterility, Loss of the Ovum after Fecundation, Fecundity, and Childbirth, Diseases of Women and of Newborn Infants; 2nd ed., 1626). Medical Library, University of California, San Francisco.

The royal midwife's "wide pratice, she claimed, would show up the mistakes of Physicians and Surgeons," writes Natalie Zemon Davis in *Society and Culture in Early Modern France*. "She looks out with poise from her engraving at the reader, this skilled woman who corrected men, publicly and in print."

and a woman in criticizing male doctors. "You should rather have passed the rest of your life without speaking," the response read, "than to suggest . . . that the great princess had not been helped as well as she should have been.... Contain yourself within the limits of your duty. No longer involve yourself in responding to doctors, because ... you are not capable of judging them.... All learned men who have seen your book and practice know and reject them, and it would be very good and useful if France never again felt the effects, as the princess has."

No one came to Bourgeois's defense in the face of this onslaught, and she was forced to withdraw from service to the court. Five years later Martin died, and Louise followed in 1636. She had had a long and distinguished career, and through her prominent service and her publications had helped to raise the profile of midwives and promote the role of women in medicine. But, at the same time, her fall from favor contributed to the marginalization of midwives, who were to be constrained to a more limited role, as France became one of the first European countries to insist on the regulation of midwives by male authorities.

It was difficult for women to compete in struggles of power as independent players. Most built instead upon their roles as wives, mothers, daughters, or consorts (the most notable exception was Elizabeth of England). One of these was a woman whose birth name was Mihrunnisa ("Sun of Women"). In March 1616 she acquired a new name — henceforth she would be known, and become famous, as Nur Jahan ("Light of the World"). The name was given to her by her husband, Jahangir, ruler of the Mughal empire. Jahangir left much of the day-to-day governance of the empire to his favorite wife. A Dutch observer at the Mughal court went so far as to claim that Jahangir was "King in name only" and that "misunderstandings result, for the King's orders or grants of appointments, etc, are not certainties, being of no value until they have been approved by the Queen." Another Dutch observer, no better friend of the queen, claimed that Jahangir "suffered in his mind because he found himself too much in the power of his wife, and the thing had gone so far that there were no means of escaping from the position. She did with him as she liked, his daily reward being pretended love and sweet words, for which he had to pay dearly."

Jahangir was not someone to take lightly, and Nur Jahan had to have possessed considerable resources of courage and cunning to gain such control over him. Normally mild, and often accused of passivity, the Mughal ruler was capable of erupting in flashes of cruelty. He had men

killed for breaking a china dish. He killed servants who he thought had got in the way of a good hunt. He order the thumbs of a man cut off who had taken down some trees he happened to like. He had a woman who had been caught kissing a eunuch buried up to her armpits and kept without water in the hot sun (she died in less than a day). When his first-born son, Khusrau, unsuccessfully attempted to overthrow him, Jahangir had the leaders of Khusrau's revolt beheaded or impaled. Then he placed their heads on stakes on either side of a road and personally led his son, strapped to an elephant, between them, "introducing" each head to him in turn.

Nur Jahan was one of the most powerful women of premodern India. She had coins minted in her own name, collected duties and tariffs, and engaged in international trade. She owned a line of ships that carried pilgrims and cargo to Mecca. Her patronage was often sought and often needed. She amassed considerable private wealth and ruled with a firm hand.

She was a Persian, born in Kandahar, now the second-largest city in Afghanistan but at that time a trading town on the border between Persia and the Mughal empire. Her parents were on their way to India, fleeing difficult economic circumstances in Persia and hoping to gain favor at the Mughal court, where Persian learning and sophistication were held in high esteem. The family lost most of their possessions to thieves during the

The Decapitation of Leonora Galigai, 17th c. Engraving. France. Bibliotheque Nationale, Paris.

Leonora Galigai, the queen regent's favorite, and her husband, Concino Concini, were, like the queen herself, originally from Florence. They were resented by the citizens of Paris as rapacious outsiders who were mainly interested in converting assets of state to personal wealth. Galigai's influence over the queen was attributed to witchcraft. In 1617, after Louis XIII had at last asserted himself and taken over rule from his mother, Galigai was decapitated and her body burnt.

journey, but were favorably received in Jahangir's court. They prospered, and Nur Jahan's father rose to a position of prominence.

Nur Jahan's story has fascinated many people in South Asia and elsewhere, and as a result a great deal of legend has surrounded her; it is difficult to be certain of the historical truth of many aspects of her life. A story has it that Jahangir and Nur Jahan fell in love as teenagers. Unfortunately, she was to be wedded to another man, and only after his death, when she was in her thirties, would she and Jahangir finally marry. How might the young lovers have met? Jahangir, then merely Prince Saleem, was walking, so the story goes, through a garden. As ruler he would be famous for his fondness for beautiful things, and already he displayed his aesthetic inclinations. He was carrying two pigeons as he walked, when he noticed some beautiful flowers that he wished to pick. As chance would have it, the young Nur Jahan — herself celebrated for her beauty — was passing by just then, and Jahangir asked her to hold the pigeons so that he could pick the flowers. But when he returned to the girl he found her with only one of the birds. "How did that happen?" he demanded. "Like this!" she replied, releasing the second pigeon into the air, and Jahangir was captivated by the young woman's wit and charm.

All such stories probably belong to the realm of legend. In 1594, when she was seventeen, Nur Jahan was married to a young man of the Persian community, and it is doubtful that she had had significant contact with Jahangir before that time. Many of the expatriate Persians, including most of Nur Jahan's family, were then viewed with suspicion as a result of having placed their bets on the wrong horse in the inevitable conflicts that always seemed to rise up over issues of succession among the Mughals. Nur Jahan's husband was given an undesirable post in Bengal. Not long after ascending the throne in 1605, Jahangir became suspicious of him and sent a delegation to check up on him. Somehow a melee resulted in which Nur Jahan's husband killed the leader of Jahangir's party and was himself killed in response.

Some say that Jahangir had arranged Nur Jahan's husband's death because he was already in love with her, but there is no evidence for this among documents of the period. Now a widow with a young child, she returned to the Mughal court (then in Agra) and entered the *zanana,* the community of the harem, as a lady-in-waiting to one of Jahangir's stepmothers. It was the custom of the Mughals to care for the widows of courtiers, and they were often adopted by women of influence.

It is unclear how many women were resident in Jahangir's zanana; the likeliest guess seems to be a thousand or more. Besides his wives and con-

Jahangir and Prince Khurram with Nur Jahan, ca. 1624. India, Mughal dynasty. Opaque watercolor and gold on paper, 14.2 x 25.2 cm. Freer Gallery of Art, Gift of Charles Lang Freer, F1907.258.

This scene is probably set in the Ram Bagh garden, which the empress Nur Jahan, a great patron of gardens, had remodeled in 1621, not long before the painting was made. According the the Freer Gallery of Art, "The Ram Bagh epitomizes the imperial Mughal (1526–1858) garden aesthetic that thoroughly integrated nature and architecture. Carpets like fields of flowers, wall paintings of cypresses, open porches with blossom-adorned columns, and water channels that ran from exterior to interior contributed to a fluid, delightful whole. Delicately scented breezes and burbling fountains further set the stage for royal pastimes."

The idyllic setting, however, disguises underlying tensions. The power of Nur Jahan, wife of the Mughal ruler Jahangir, is indicated by her position as the second most prominent figure in the painting. Waiting in the wings, however, is Prince Khurram (later Shah Jahan, famous for building the Taj Mahal), who was not Nur Jahan's choice to succeed his father. With his accession Nur Jahan would be stripped of power and effectively kept under house arrest for the remainder of her life.

cubines there were the female members of his family and their children, as well as ladies-in-waiting, servants, guards, entertainers, and many other women, from all ethnic groups and levels of society. The community was in effect a largely self-governing city. It was guarded by women armed with daggers and bows and arrows; the guards were changed every twenty-four hours to maintain vigilance and protect against intrigues. (Nur Jahan herself was said to be the most accomplished archer of Jahangir's court; she was equally adept with firearms, once, it is said, bringing down four tigers with just six bullets.) Because of the practice of *parda,* or seclusion of women, very few men were ever allowed inside, although the higher-ranking women would have two or more eunuchs as attendants. The main exceptions to the exclusion of men were visits from husbands, who could also sometimes bring fathers and brothers with them. After his marriage to Nur Jahan, Jahangir would grant the extraordinary privilege of access to the zanana without the women being veiled to her father, a clear sign of the powerful role she wielded.

As a woman of the zanana, Nur Jahan met Jahangir at the Nouroz festival of 1611. Nouroz is the traditional Persian (originally Zoroastrian) festival of the new year, which occurs on the first day of spring by the solar calendar. It was also one of the two main festivals observed by the Mughal court (the other being the emperor's birthday). Nouroz was a particularly festive time for the women of the zanana, for a bazaar was then set up in the emperor's palace compound where they were allowed to shop at stalls, almost as if they were out free in the world. The stalls were operated by the wives of the merchants. The emperor would also go from stall to stall, chatting and flirting with the women. As he made his rounds during the 1611 Nouroz, he chanced upon Nur Jahan and was startled by the beauty of her unveiled face. The two were married two months later, in May 1611. She was the last of the emperor's wives.

Jahangir's line was vulnerable to alcoholism. Two of his brothers died at an early age from the disease. Jahangir compounded the effects of heavy alcohol use through the addition of opium, which he also consumed in large quantities on a daily basis. In this stupefied (and probably constipated) condition, he became disinterested in, and perhaps incapable of, tending to the details of governance. It was Nur Jahan who triumphed in the struggle to fill this vacuum, and who became in many respects the de facto ruler of the Mughal empire.

Nur Jahan was thirty-four or thirty-five years old when she married Jahangir (who then called her Nur Mahal, "light of the palace"). Women over thirty were considered in the Mughal court to be of advanced years, and the Mughal emperor rarely had sexual relations with them. An English visitor reported that the nobles of the court never "came near their wives or women, after they exceed the age of thirty years" and such women were never "much regarded by those great ones, after the very first and prime of their youth is past." Nur Jahan had no children by Jahangir — nor did any other woman of the zanana after their marriage — and it is possible that his heavy consumption of alcohol and opium rendered him impotent. Although there is little doubt that it was her beauty that first inflamed the emperor's passions, her relation to him seems quickly to have become mostly maternal in character.

The mother-son relationship was particularly valued among the Mughals, according to Nur Jahan biographer Ellison Banks Findly. "Given the structure of Mughal households, where religious custom obligated providing shelter for any older unattached women and where 'multiple mothers' (wet-nurses, barren aunts and foster mothers of all types) were the norm, Jahangir found it easy to feel strongly for the older women around him." Jahangir had observed of a couple such women that they were as dear to him as his own mother, and he seems easily to have projected a maternal role onto his final wife. His reverence for mothers caused him to collect Western Madonna-and-child paintings. Thomas Roe, who established the first official English embassy to the Mughal court in 1616, was constantly writing home for more and better paintings on this theme, and images of the Madonna appear in the Mughal court paintings sponsored by Jahangir.

Jahangir was aware that his drug use was affecting his health, but he could not control it. Only Nur Jahan was able to instill a degree of moderation, reducing his intake by degrees and then rationing his usage at a still high but somewhat less excessive level. By controlling Jahangir she effectively held the reins of power, although, because of the practice of *parda,* she was often forced to govern from behind a screen. Visitors would hear a whispered voice giving directives to Jahangir during their audiences. Her father and brother completed the ruling junta, and after her father died she teamed up effectively for a time with her brother. But as Jahangir's health continued to decline, the empire's attention turned increasingly to the troubling matter of succession.

The Mughals did not subscribe to the practice of royal inheritance by birth order. The eldest son had no automatic priority over other male descendents. Jahangir's father, Akbar, had for a time favored his grandson Khusrau over Jahangir, and Jahangir had led an army against his father's forces before reconciling with him. Jahangir later had Khusrau blinded (some say with an herbal concoction, some with a glass held to the sun, some by sewing patches over his eyes, some by puncture with a wire — the last is unlikely, since physicians later sought to restore his sight). Unrestrained by the mediation of their father, Nur Jahan and her brother began to vie with each other for power, and a complicated tangle of deceptions and treacheries ensued, as each promoted a different candidate to succeed Jahangir.

It was a long struggle well fought, but one that Nur Jahan finally lost, and her brother's candidate, Jahangir's third son, assumed the crown as Shah Jahan. He would be best known in the West for building the Taj Mahal in honor of his wife, a niece of Nur Jahan. Despite Nur Jahan's years of effective governance, as a woman her power was still in some sense by proxy, and without her husband she could not hold on to it. She was forced to retire to Lahore where she lived under guard on a pension provided by her triumphant brother. It was said that she "never went to parties of amusement of her own accord, but lived in private and in sorrow" for the next eighteen years until her death in 1645.

Then as ever it was a world of suffering and illusion, as the Buddha had long ago observed. The Japanese called this *ukiyo,* or "sad world." But in the seventeenth century the phrase *ukiyo* got rebranded. Cessation of warfare had brought with it a new spirit of optimism. Now it would be written with characters that were pronounced the same but meant "floating world." Around the middle of the century a popular writer, who happened also to be a Buddhist monk, explained what he understood as the "floating world": "Living only for the moment, devoting our attention to the pleasures of the moon, snow, cherry blossoms, and maple leaves; singing songs, drinking wine, diverting ourselves by merely floating, floating, unconcerned at the prospect of poverty, never losing heart, floating like a gourd on the river currents — that is what we call the floating world." The concept of the floating world is strongly associated with the pleasure district of Edo, called the Yoshiwara. It was formalized as a government-sponsored district as one of the final decisions of the shogun Ieyasu, founder of the long-lived Tokugawa shogunate, who died in 1616.

Through most of the sixteenth century Japan was torn apart by devastating warfare among its regional warlords, or daimyo, and many women were displaced as a result. Some of these were "wandering shrine maidens" and nuns who had been driven from shrines and temples and forced into prostitution. In the mid-sixteenth century a Bureau of Prostitution was created in order to capitalize on this development in the form of tax revenue, a first step toward full government regulation. When Japan was unified under Toyotomi Hideyoshi a walled pleasure quarter was constructed in Kyoto; it would be the model for the Yoshiwara, the "floating world" of pleasure in Edo (present Tokyo).

Under the Tokugawa shogunate Edo would house the government of the shogun, Japan's military and civil leader, until well into the nineteenth century (the emperor, still residing in Kyoto, was limited to a more ceremonial function). Hideyoshi's successor Ieyasu took the first steps toward instituting the practice of alternate-year residence, by which daimyo would be forced to leave their home regions and live every other year in Edo. Lower-ranking vassals and samurai, usually without wives, also gathered in Edo, along with merchants who, at least initially, considered other towns to be their true homes and tended not to bring their families with them. The result was a class of men without women companions, ensuring steady business for the Yoshiwara. Eventually, operating with government protection, the Yoshiwara would become a world onto itself, with its own customs, rules, and fashions.

The impetus for the district began in 1612 when a brothel owner named Shoji Jinemon called a meeting of his fellows. His two main concerns were the proliferation of houses of prostitution and the need for security. He proposed petitioning the government for exclusive rights to operate brothels in a defined, restricted area. The idea had a kind of precedent in the trade guilds related to specific types of merchandise that had flourished in Japan for centuries, but now women were the merchandise being handled. Over some dissent Shoji's proposal prevailed among the owners of the houses, but the petitioners had to wait years for a response.

In 1616, before his death, the shogun Ieyasu set the policy on the path to approval, and official approval came the following year. Ieyasu had long been liberal on the issue of prostitution, and putting the district under government control fit with his overall plan of centralizing power. There was also widespread concern about homosexuality, since the congregation of warriors and their attendants in large all-male companies over the previous century had been accompanied by an increase in homosexual relations, and in pederasty. The ready availability of women as sexual objects would, the government felt, provide a check against this.

In March 1617 the brothel owners led by Jinemon were called to the Edo court where they were awarded about twelve acres of land on the outskirts of the city. No brothels were to be permitted outside this area. Besides brothels the district would be populated with tea houses and kabuki theaters. It would be surrounded by a river and moat, and there would be only one way in and out. To prevent dangerous *ronin* (masterless samurai) from hiding out in the district, no client would be allowed

to stay there longer than twenty-four hours. In addition, unknown persons would be required to provide proof of their identity or they would be reported to the police. Even the architectural standards of the district were strictly regulated, much as they are in the gated communities of today. Near the end of 1618 the district opened for business, and it was an immediate hit. (It would burn down in 1657 and be rebuilt in a different location.)

The Yoshiwara flourished for centuries. In its heyday its revenues approached the equivalent of a million dollars a day. By the end of the seventeenth century two thousand or more women might work in the district at any time, a figure that later rose to three thousand. The women were strictly ranked, and priced accordingly. A high-level courtesan established in a personal suite cost more than $400 a day, a lower-level courtesan with just a single room about half that amount; the lowest-level sex workers cost from about $50 to as little as $18. High-level courtesans were expected to be accomplished conversationalists and skilled in music and the arts. *Ukiyo-e,* or images of the floating world (which featured higher-level courtesans), became a popular painting genre. One of the pioneers of the genre (though the range of his painting was actually quite wide) was Iwasa Matabei, who began painting images of worldly-wise women in the first quarter of the seventeenth century. "Beauty paintings" became a popular genre, and they promoted an image of the pleasure quarter as a place of glittering elegance and sophistication.

For many of the women who worked in the quarter, the reality was different. Some were sold as children to the brothels, where they would work as apprentices before coming of age. Most sex workers were bound by ten-year contracts, and few of the women ever acquired the means to escape the district, so becoming a worker there was usually a lifelong fate. A courtesan's best chance at release was to beguile a wealthy client into buying out her contract, and women in general were dependent on men. Even a free woman was expected to respect the "three obediences": as a child she had to obey her father, as a married woman she had to obey her husband, and as a widow she had to obey her eldest son. Would a comparatively comfortable high-level courtesan position be in some respects preferable to that of a toiling wife? Unfortunately, the women of the Yoshiwara left little record of their private feelings, and we can only imagine how they regarded their situations.

One of the great writers of the European Renaissance may have been a courtesan. She was Gaspara Stampa, who lived in the mid-sixteenth century. Born in Padua to a dealer in gold and precious gems, she enjoyed a privileged childhood and was trained in music, Greek and Latin language and literature, and the arts. After the death of her father the family moved to Venice, where she later found herself left to her own devices by the death of more members of her family. In Venice a long, unsatisfactory love affair with a count inspired her verses (later praised by Rilke, among others) — and led her, many say, to become a *cortigiana onesta* (a "reputable courtesan"). Her name, along with that of another noted poet, Veronica Frano, appears in a directory of courtesans, although this was published after her death.

The *cortigiana onesta* was an established figure in Venetian society. Serving men from the highest levels of society, she was expected to be beautiful, artistic, cultivated, and skilled in the art of conversation. Sustained by patronage, she chose her own lovers based on mutual attraction and generally maintained her affairs over long periods of time. The work of Gaspara Stampa, directly or indirectly, may have influenced Mary Wroth. Like Wroth she wrote sonnets from the perspective of an abandoned lover and favored pastoral themes and settings.

The cultivated courtesan continued to be a fixture of European society through the sixteenth and seventeenth centuries. A woman named Ninon de Lenclos, who was born in Paris in 1616, would become famous as the "Queen of Courtesans." Molière was among those who visited her popular salon. She founded an institution called the School of the Love Arts, which offered advice on seduction and lovemaking (men paid a fee but women attended lectures and classes free of charge).

But the privileged classes — nobility, gentry, wealthy merchants, and yeoman farmers — made up only a small fraction of society. Faced with increasing urbanization, crop failures and resulting high food prices caused by the "Little Ice Age," infectious diseases causing the evacuation of entire regions, and frequent warfare, many persons suffered severe economic stresses (this was one cause of overseas adventurism and migration). These stresses usually hit women harder than men, and women had a shorter life expectancy, not just in Europe but throughout the world. Somewhere between 2.5 and 10 percent of women died in childbirth (a much higher percentage than in subsequent centuries).

Opposite: Court Ladies Viewing Chrysanthemums, early seventeenth century, by Iwasa Matabei. Hanging scroll, ink and colors on paper, 55 x 132 cm. Yamatane Museum of Art, Tokyo.

Iwasa Matabei was initially influenced by classical traditions that looked to the literati of China as models, but he lived through a time of great social change and became one of the first painters of beautiful women in a style that would later become associated with ukiyo-e: images of the "floating world." The eighteenth-century poet-painter Yosa Buson contributed to the identification of Matabei with, in the words of Sandy Kita, author of a book on the artist, "the courtesans, actors, playboys, rich merchants, and panderers of Edo." Though lacking the bright colors seen in other of Matabei's paintings, this charming painting of traveling court ladies pausing to enjoy a bed of chrysanthemums captures something of the spirit of the floating world.

Opposite: Ladies of Venice, ca. 1490, by Vittore Carpaccio, oil on wood, 61 x 94 cm. Museo Correr, Venice.

This painting was long thought to document the Venetian tradition of the *cortigiana oneste:* the refined courtesans who charmed their elite clients with their elegance, sophistication, and artistic skills. That presumption is probably the legacy of the Victorian writer John Ruskin, who dubbed the painting *The Courtesans.* Thanks to the discovery of a companion painting, it now seems likely that these women are not courtesans at all, but that the point was argued for nearly a century indicates the degree to which some European courtesans adopted the style of upper-class ladies.

Although this image was painted long before the period that is the subject of this book, the association of Venice with courtesans in the minds of many Europeans had not dimmed over the intervening century. The English traveler Thomas Coryate described a visit to such a courtesan (though not, he assured his readers, as a client) in his entertaining book of travels called *Coryate's Crudities* (p. 343).

The ladies might not be courtesans, but the pomegranate on the balastrade by a dove is a symbol of love, as is the kerchief the younger woman dangles. And the stylish but uncomfortable looking shoes in front of the peacock might bring to mind Leonard Michaels's maxim that "bad girls have the coolest shoes."

Fewer than half of all children survived to adulthood — children were particularly vulnerable to plague — and women were often advised not to get overly emotionally invested in their offspring for that reason. Widowhood and abandonment were leading causes of destitution. Unmarried mothers were another vulnerable group — women in this situation were often the victims of rape or had been promised marriage and then abandoned. Such women often lacked the means of providing for infants, and were forced to resort to infanticide or to abandonment — children "found" on upper-class doorsteps might, if fortunate, be raised as servants. Foundling "hospitals" were created where wet-nurses were available for abandoned infants, but the survival rate in them could be as little as 10 percent. Girls were given up more often than boys because of the dowry system that made daughters a financial liability. Even married women were often left to manage on their own for long stretches; both Cervantes and Shakespeare spent much more time living away from their wives than they did living with them.

In his eye-opening study of illicit sex in early seventeenth-century England, based on data from court records, G. R. Quaife claims that "the promiscuous/prostitute activity of many wives, widows and experienced spinsters was widespread and regarded with much less opprobrium than Puritan publicists would like us to believe." At the lowest level were "vagrant whores," who wandered from town to town. Better situated were those who operated out of inns and bawdy houses. There were also private whores, some of whom, Quaife believes, may have operated "as part of a circuit servicing the clergy of the diocese." Some husbands encouraged their wives in prostitution; marriage was, after all, largely an economic partnership. One court case relates how a wife of an innkeeper was the subject of complaints from many drinkers that she "put her hand into his breeches to feel what he had," several of the witnesses complaining that this same wife "indecently would force an honest man to occupy her, spreading of her legs abroad and showing her commodity." Another case concerned a man who invited a lodger to join him and his wife "all three in one bed," a practice that became habitual for the threesome; this case landed in court not because of the sex but because the wife encouraged her lovers to steal things from their masters in order to continue the relationship.

Some writers felt that such behavior reflected a general worsening of standards of morality. It had formerly been traditional for family and servants to share a common bed. According to a French noble this practice did not present problems. He wrote:

**Mary Frith, the "Roaring Girl,"
1611, from the title page of a play
by Thomas Dekker and Thomas
Middleton. Woodblock print.**

Mary Frith — "Moll Cutpurse" or
the "Roaring Girl" — was a notorious transvestite carouser whose
exploits were to some degree street
theater. To Londoners she was a
source of both entertainment and
scandal.

Do you remember those big beds in which everyone slept together without difficulty? All the people, married or unmarried, slept together in a big bed made for the purpose, three fathoms long and nine feet wide, without fear or danger of any unseemly thought or serious consequence; for in those days men did not become arroused at the sight of naked women. However, since the world has become badly behaved, each has his own separate bed, and with good reason.

By the early seventeenth century, servants tended to have separate quarters, and houses were increasingly compartmentalized by rooms fitted with doors that closed.

Thomas Middleton and Thomas Dekker's play *The Roaring Girl* also suggests that rowdiness at the lower levels of society may have been more common than the decorous silence of women implied by sermons and respectable texts. In a prologue, the authors claimed that there were many kinds of "roaring girls":

... One is she
That roars at midnight in deep tavern bowls,
That beats the watch, and constables controls;
Another roars i' th' daytime, swears, stabs, gives braves,
Yet sells her soul to the lust of fools and slaves.
Both these are suburb roarers.
Then there's beside
A civil city roaring girl, whose pride,
Feasting, and riding, shakes her husband's state,
And leaves him roaring through an iron grate.

The particular Roaring Girl of the play is modeled on a woman named Mary Frith — better known as Moll Cutpurse. In his *Book of Scoundrels* (1897), Charles Whibley (a mentor of T. S. Eliot) introduced her with a richly textured paragraph that is worth quoting:

The most illustrious woman of an illustrious age, Moll Cutpurse has never lacked the recognition due to her genius. She was scarce of age when the town devoured in greedy admiration the first record of her pranks and exploits. A year later Middleton made her the heroine of a sparkling comedy. Thereafter she became the favourite of the rufflers, the commonplace of the poets. Newgate knew her, and Fleet Street; her manly figure was as familiar in the Bear Garden as at the Devil Tavern; courted alike by the thief and his victim, for fifty years she lived a life brilliant as sunlight, many-coloured as a rainbow. And she is remembered, after the lapse of centuries, not only as the Queen-Regent of Misrule, the benevolent tyrant of cly-filers and heavers, of hacks and blades, but as the incomparable Roaring Girl, free of the playhouse, who perchance presided with Ben Jonson over the Parliament of Wits.

The Roaring Girl was most likely written in 1611, with the two authors, who had previously collaborated on *The Patient Man and the Honest Whore,* working as a team on most scenes. The story concerns a young man who tries to persuade his reluctant father to approve a marriage with the woman he loves by pretending to be in love with the disturbingly butch Moll Cutpurse — "a scurvy woman . . . nature hath brought forth to mock the sex of woman. . . . woman more than man, man more than woman . . . a monster" — hoping by this means that his father will view the real object of his affection as a less undesirable alternative.

The name "The Roaring Girl" comes from the carousing and brawling young gentlemen known as roaring boys, upon whom Frith seems to have modeled herself. She dressed in men's clothes and smoked a pipe (her cross-dressing was considered the most scandalous of her actions; dressing in men's clothes was thought to signify sexual looseness). She is said to have earned a living as a fence and a pimp. She first appears in the court records in 1600 and shows up there from time to time for the next quarter century.

An epilogue promises that "the Roaring Girl herself, some few days hence, / Shall on this stage give larger recompense." Apparently her performance took place as promised, for shortly afterward Moll was brought to court, where she confessed that she had appeared on the stage of the Fortune Theatre. She testified "that she had long frequented all or most of the disorderly & licentious places in this Cittie as namely she hath vsually in the habite of a man resorted to alehowses Tavernes Tobacco shops & also to play howses there to see plaies & pryses & namely being at a playe about 3 quarters of a yeare since at the ffortune in mans apparell & in her bootes & wth a sword by her syde, she told the company there p[re]sent that she

ALFEREZ DOÑA CATALINA DE HERAVSO N DN̄SĒHASTI...

Catalina de Erauso, 1630, by Francisco Pacheco. Oil on canvas.

Upon the revelation of her identity as a woman Catalina de Erauso had her portrait painted twice. Francesco Crescenzio's version is lost; this image was done by Francisco Pacheco, who was the great court painter Diego Velázquez's father-in-law.

thought many of them were of the opinion that she was a man, but if any of them would come to her lodging they should finde that she is a woman & some other immodest & lascivious speaches she also vsed at that time."

Because she "sat there vppon the stage in the publique viewe of all the people there p[rese]nte in mans apparrell & playd vppon her lute & sange a songe," Moll Cutpurse was duly sentenced to serve time in Bridewell Prison.

Moll had a reputation as a formidable street fighter, suggesting the aptness of lines written half a century before by Isabella Whitney, the first professional English woman writer: "When we women, too, are armed and trained / We'll be able to stand up to any man." Several women writers, like the later sixteenth-century French poet Catherine des Roches, imagined a world of Amazons who would subjugate men by force: "We hold men prisoner / In the places where we rule," she wrote, "And force them to spin." But few women would wish to emulate the macho qualities of pride, aggression, and violence exemplified by a Spanish soldier known as Alonzo Díaz Ramírez de Guzmán, who fought during this period against native peoples in Chile and Peru. Although Ramírez de Guzmán was in about the same Andean area as the native author Guaman Poma in 1616, there is no record of their paths having crossed — which was fortunate for Poma. The hot-blooded swordsman's own memoirs boast of the "trampling and killing and slaughtering of more Indians than there are numbers," as well as the slaying of some fifteen Spaniards in bar arguments, street brawls, and duels over twenty years in the region.

In the early 1620s, one such confrontation would reveal this hell-raiser to be anything but a typical soldier. While it, like so many of the other of the swordfights, left Ramírez de Guzmán's opponent dead, it also left the brawling soldier with an apparently fatal injury. When a priest was called for last rites, the injured warrior revealed her identity as Catalina de Erauso, a Basque woman from Spain. (The rites proved unnecessary, and she fully recovered.)

De Erauso's military service, quick temper, propensity for violence, and prowess with the sword are documented in historical records. Her baptismal certificate and convent fees are a matter of record. High-ranking eyewitnesses formally testified to her service in the Americas. Petitions made by Erauso after she returned to Europe for compensation for her services and against a loss to robbery still exist. A portrait has survived. And at least five accounts of her life were published by different authors while she was still alive, though these already incorporate mythologizing elements that resulted from her brief (except in the Basque region, where she remains a local hero) celebrity status as a woman warrior; such mythologizing makes it difficult to separate fact from fiction in Erauso's story.

The fullest source of information is her memoirs, but their authorship must be considered an open question. They did not see print until 1829, and although a complicated provenance involving at least two copyings was claimed for them it cannot be confirmed. On stylistic grounds the text does appear to date from the period of Erauso's lifetime. But, while she was literate, there is little in her life that would suggest serious literary interests. Certainly the memoir does not depict her in the favorable light that would have been required to win the concessions she sought from king and pope.

The text falls more or less within the genre of the picaresque novel, which in the early seventeenth century was near the high point of its popularity. But it is more transgressive than most picaresque novels, since Erauso makes no attempt to conceal her sexual indifference to men and her attraction to women, not to mention her persistent thievery, violence, iconoclasm, and insolence, for which she shows little remorse. It is conceivable that the core of the story was dictated by her to some other person who added embellishments, and that it circulated privately as a titillating underground document before finally surfacing, but this is speculation. In any case, much of the content of the book has clearly been fictionalized.

Modern discussion of de Erauso has been so focused on gender issues that there has been comparatively little effort to clarify the chronology of her life. A recent English translation of her memoirs, for example, and its accompanying critical essays and translators' note, never address the question of the memoir's authenticity. "When Catalina de Erauso fights duels, steals money, leads soldiers into battle, rescues a woman in distress, evades the marriage plans of hopeful widows and their daughters, and marches across league upon league of uncharted Peruvian terrain, it is tempting to see in her tale an allegory of early modern woman's emergent subjectivity," says the scholar Marjorie Garber, who emphasizes that most readings of de Erauso's life have been allegorical — "as *exempla,* as indications of deeper or higher truths."

A case could be made for referring to Erauso with male pronouns, but no solution is entirely satisfactory, and I will follow precedent and refer to her in the feminine. There are many variant stories of Erauso's life, but it is usually told something like this: She was born to a family of minor nobility in a town in the Basque region of Spain and was sent as a young child to a convent there. Her father and four brothers pursued military careers — like Catalina, the brothers would end their lives in Latin America, but she would outlive them all — while three sisters took their vows in the same convent to which she had been sent.

Shortly before she was to take her own vows, when she was about fifteen, Catalina abruptly departed from the family script and ran away from the convent — in response, her memoirs claim, to having been beaten by one of the nuns. Historical records, however, show that the woman she identified as her abuser did not become a nun until some years later.

According to her memoirs, after fleeing the convent she hid in the woods for about a week. She cut her hair short and fashioned herself a boy's outfit from her convent garments, and set off on her extraordinary journeys. Being literate, she served first as an apprentice to a tutor but rebelled against the boredom of Latin lessons and became a muleteer's assistant. One story says that she spent a month in jail during this period for throwing stones at a boy who had insulted her.

After three years of wanderings in the Basque region, during which, like all *pícaros,* she served a variety of masters, Erauso booked as an apprentice sailor on a ship bound for Mexico. The story is told that an uncle on the same ship failed to recognize her, and that Erauso stole 500 dollars from him and jumped ship with the loot in Panama.

From Panama she made her way to Peru, where she worked briefly as a storekeeper. This, it is said, is where she learned to use a sword. Following a dispute with a man who was blocking her view in a theater, Erauso armed herself with a sword and, a few days later, confronted him and a companion; she killed the companion and took refuge in a church. She moved on to another town, where the same man confronted her again with a new companion, whom she also slew, again taking refuge in a church.

Moving down the coast, Erauso continued cutting a swath of terror, eventually reaching Chile, where she signed on as a soldier under the command of one of her own brothers (this service is apparently factual — it is confirmed by her petition to the king). For three years she worked as his right-hand man without being recognized. Needless to say, the two shared a similar background, and Basques tended to form tight-knit communities in the Americas. Eventually — following, it is said, an argument over a woman — the two came to blows, and Erauso was transferred to one of the most heated zones of conflict. Here she proved her valor by recapturing, together with two companions, the company flag during a battle. Both of her companions were killed and she was seriously injured. For this she was promoted to the rank of second lieutenant, and this promotion is also documented in historical records. As a result, she would later enjoy celebrity in Europe as "the lieutenant nun."

The memoirs would next have us believe that Erauso was selected by a companion to serve as his second in a duel. When both the principals in the duel fell dead, Erauso, never overly troubled by niceties of protocol, began fighting with the other second. It was a pitch black night, so her opponent was hard to make out, but she succeeded in vanquishing him. On hearing his dying words she realized he was her brother.

Only after the confrontation that left her with what appeared to be a fatal injury did the veteran soldier reveal her identity as a woman to a bishop in Guamanga, Peru. The bishop had her examined by two elderly women, who confirmed her to be not only a woman but also a virgin.

Now perceived as female, she was forced, after her recovery from her wounds, to dress in women's clothing (an eyewitness reports seeing her dressed as a woman in Lima), which surely must have galled her. But it was necessary to wait for confirmation from Spain that she had never taken vows, because that would have condemned her to spend the rest of her life in a convent, an unimaginable prospect.

In 1624 Erauso returned to Spain, where her combination of masculine valor and female purity (having maintained her virginity in a camp of soldiers) won her acclaim as a modern Amazon. She traveled to Rome for an audience with the pope, who granted her a special dispensation to wear men's clothes. King Philip of Spain granted her request for an annual pension. She had her portrait rendered by two painters in Italy, where she met with the traveler Pietro della Valle. Della Valle described her as "tall and strong of frame, rather masculine in appearance." He thought she resembled the eunuchs he had seen in Persia. "She wears men's clothing in the Spanish style," he noted, and "she bears her sword with as much bravado as her life."

In 1629 Erauso formally signed her portion of the family inheritance over to a fourth sister, who had escaped the convent fate of her other sisters by getting married. In exchange Erauso received a cash sum of one thousand reales, and with this seed money she returned to America. She spent the remainder of her days as a muleteer (and slave owner) in Veracruz. Around 1650, when she would probably have been sixty-five years old, she was found dead along the mule road that led from Veracruz to Mexico City.

In her petition to Philip IV for a pension based on her military service — which has the flavor of having been drafted by a lawyer or some other person experienced in such matters — Erauso plays up her dual identities as a man and as a woman. On the one hand she requests recognition for her "inclination to take up arms in defense of the Catholic faith and in the service of Your Majesty" in which capacity "she distinguished herself with great courage and valor, suffering wounds, particularly in the battle of Peru." Yet she also alludes to "the uniqueness and prodigiousness of her story, mindful that she is the daughter of noble and illustrious parents."

Erauso seems to have won general acceptance of her male identity as Antonio de Erauso, the identity in which she lived out the last decades of her life. Several witnesses testified, in connection with a claim related to the family estate, that they had seen her on a visit to her home town in 1629. All refer to her in her male identity, as "Lieutenant D. Antonio de Erauso."

In Florence on July 1616, another woman was also moving in a man's world. She was a twenty-three-year-old painter named Artemisia Gentileschi, who was being admitted at this time to the Academie del Disegno, the professional artists' association of Florence. She was the first woman so honored: among the obstacles women painters faced were that they were not allowed to paint male nudes or frescos and other works that had to be done in public. Gentileschi's achievement was probably facilitated by her patron, a member of the prominent Medici family. Her talent was hard to dispute, but her virtue was, for some, a point of contention. She was, first of all, a woman working in a man's profession. Additionally, she had been the center of attention in a scandalous trial (despite being the victim) that had gripped the attention of the city of Rome. A month after the trial concluded, in November 1612, she had hurriedly married and moved to Florence, but she would later separate from her husband and lose track of him. She would have another child after the separation.

She was the daughter of Orazio Gentileschi, a painter originally from Tuscany who was based in Rome, working in a studio not far from the Spanish Steps. He was a follower of the dramatic Baroque style of Caravaggio, an influence that would also appear in his daughter's more naturalistic painting. Her mother died when she was twelve, and within a few years she joined her brothers in the painting studio, where she quickly outshone them. Her training was that of an artisan — she did not learn to read and write until she reached adulthood.

Seeing her artistic promise, her father hired a fellow painter, Agostino Tassi of Florence, with whom he was collaborating at the time, to instruct her in the art of perspective. She was eighteen years old. Assisted by a hanger-on named Cosimo Quorlis, Tassi trapped Artemisia in her room and raped her; to complete the violation the men also stole one of her paintings. According to Artemisia, Tassi entered her bedroom on the pretext of looking at a painting, threw her on the bed, and put his hand over her mouth so she couldn't scream. She scratched his face and cut his chest. Afterward, he promised to marry her. The Gentileschis hoped that he would do as he promised, and so she continued to have sexual relations with him. Only when it was apparent that a marriage was not in the offing did Orazio sue.

Workplace rape was common during the Renaissance, and not necessarily considered an especially grave offense, though by the early seventeenth century it was increasingly frowned upon. Servants were especially vulnerable. One man in the early Renaissance sent a maid along to his nephew with the comment "Because you writ me word that you were in love with Dirty Sluts, I took great care to fit you with a Joan that may be as good as my Lady in the dark." Women working in male-dominated trades were another often victimized group, in part because the men they came in contact with often lacked the wherewithal for marriage. Gang rape was not uncommon; it was usually justified by the imputation of a lack of chastity to the victim. In such cases the woman might be forced to take a small sum of money as proof of her harlotry. Despite its nonconsensual character, rape still resulted in a loss of honor to the woman. In this situation the father could seek compensation, as Orazio did; such compensation could increase the woman's dowry. That was important, for the rape victim's loss of honor could be corrected through marriage. In many cases the rapist would marry the victim himself rather than make a cash payment that would end up in the hands of another man.

The trial that followed Artemisia's rape lasted seven months. The transcript of the trial survives. Tassi's main line of defense was that Artemisia was "an insatiable whore" and consequently could not be raped as she had no virtue to defend. The household, he claimed, was really a bordello — her late mother, aunts, and sisters were also whores, he said, and Orazio had sold Artemisia for a loaf of bread. He claimed that she had written erotic

Above: *Judith Slaying Holofernes,* 1598–1599, by Michelangelo Merisi da Caravaggio. Oil on canvas, 144 x 192 cm. Galleria Nazionale d'Arte Antica, Barberini, Rome.

Right: *Judith Slaying Holofernes,* 1620, by Artemisia Gentileschi. Oil on canvas, 162 x 199 cm. Uffizi, Florence.

In the Book of Judith Holofernes laid seige to the town of Bethulia. The town was saved by Judith, who seduced and then slew him while he was drunk. While Caravaggio's Judith appears to recoil from the gory scene, Gentileschi's Judith attacks her victim with vigor.

Gentileschi depicts the blood from Holofernes's neck spurting along parabolic paths. This may have been a contribution from her friend Galileo, who helped her obtain payment for the painting — by this time he had discovered the parabolic law of projectiles.

letters to various men, apparently not realizing that she was illiterate. She was subjected to a gynecological exam that was supposed to determine how long she had been sexually active. She was also tortured with thumbscrews, on the theory that if enough pain was applied the truth would come out. This must have been doubly painful for the young artist, whose work depended on the use of her hands. A painting of Artemisia's hand exists — it was made by the artist Pierre Dumonstier le Neveu in 1625.

Tassi brought forth several witnesses to support his position. His credibility suffered, however, when it came out that he had had sexual relations with his sister-in-law and had conspired to murder his wife, who was missing and presumed dead. That wife he had acquired by first raping her. Artemisia learned of the marriage in the course of the trial. A witness further testified that Tassi had boasted about his attack on Artemisia. He was convicted and exiled from Rome, but was back within months. Strangely, he was later invited by Orazio back into the Gentileschi household. There are hints that Artemisia's relationship with her father cooled for a time, perhaps in part as a result, but they appear later to have reconciled, working on projects together near the end of his life.

Around the time of the trial — perhaps even while it was in progress — Artemisia painted *Judith Slaying Holofernes.* Now in the Museo di Capolodimonte in Naples, the painting is remarkable for, among other things, being a particularly graphic expression of female anger and violence. Among the few works to rival it was another version of the same scene that Artemisia painted in 1620; it is now in the Uffizi Gallery in Florence. Caravaggio painted the same bloody scene years before Artemisia's trial, but his Judith shows nothing of the purpose and passion of Gentileschi's version.

Within a month of the trial Artemisia was married to a Florentine artist named Pietro Antonio di Vincenzo Stiattesi. He was presumably a relative of the main witness in Artemisia's defense, a man named Giovanni Stiattesi, who testified that Tassi had been rejected by Artemisia, became obsessed with her, and stalked her. One can only speculate what sorts of dealings led to the marriage that restored Artemisia's honor, but in any case payment to the husband was the essence of the dowry system. The two were not, however, to live long together as husband and wife.

After the notoriety of the trial Rome was too hot for Artemisia, and the newlyweds made their way to Florence, where she gave birth to two sons who did not survive infancy and a daughter named Prudentia. There Artemisia won the patronage of Grand Duke Cosimo II de Medici and of the Grand Duchess Cristina. She made the acquaintance of influential people like Galileo Galilei, with whom she kept up a correspondence; later she would meet and be celebrated by notable artists from many parts of Europe, such as the Flemish painter Anthony Van Dyck. Among her substantial works from this period is her *Allegory of Inclination,* probably painted in 1615 or 1616, in which a young woman embodies natural talent or affinity with art. The painting was commissioned by Michelangelo Buonarroti the Younger, a grandson of the great Florentine artist. It was said that the figure in the painting resembled Gentileschi. Even for late Renaissance Florence the large female nude was a bit in-your-face as a ceiling decoration, and a few decades later a descendant of Buonarroti had it covered with a mass of unfortunate drapery.

In Florence Gentileschi's husband, Stiattesi, apparently lived large and racked up debts well beyond the young couple's means. After another daughter was born (she did not survive), and Gentileschi painted her second *Judith Slaying Holofernes,* they were forced to flee their creditors. They separated, never, it seems, to meet again. With her daughter Prudentia, Gentileschi returned to Rome.

The remainder of Gentileschi's life was spent in a perpetual quest for lucrative patronage for her painting. She probably traveled to Genoa, and certainly to Venice. In Rome she gave birth to another daughter in 1627, but nothing is known of the circumstances. Her most sustained residence was in Naples, then the largest city of southern Europe and part of the Habsburg empire of Spain. She lived there for about a decade before traveling to London in 1638 to paint for King Charles I, the son of King James and Queen Anne. With her father she painted ceilings for the Queen's House in Greenwich, which had been designed by Inigo Jones; the canvases were later moved to Marlborough House in Westminster. But when civil war broke out in England in 1641 she returned to Naples, where she remained until her death, around 1656. Her later works are graceful but less forceful and original than the paintings of her youth.

Opposite: *Allegory of Inclination,* 1615–1616, by Artemisia Gentileschi. Oil on canvas, 61 x 152 cm. Casa Buonarroti, Florence.

Above: *The Right Hand of Artemisia Gentileschi Holding a Brush,* 1625, by Pierre Dumonstier le Neveu. Black and red chalk, with charcoal. British Museum, AN92210.

Gentileschi's painting is thought to be a self-portrait. The figure as painted by her was nude, and the drapery was added later.

The French artist Pierre Dumonstier le Neveu said that the hand holding a paintbrush in his chalk and charcoal drawing was that of "the excellent and wise noble woman of Rome, Artemisia."

The well-known phenomenon whereby hostages feel sympathy with their captors is called the Stockholm syndrome, after a 1973 bank robbery in Sweden. FBI data suggests that such sympathy is felt by more than a quarter of hostages. It is most common where the aggressor holds power over a victim who feels grateful for the occasional small kindness. Something similar must have affected some of the women who, to restore their honor, became the wives of men who had raped them. It may also have affected the Powhatan maiden Matoaka, who was kidnapped and subsequently married to John Rolfe, a member of the colony that abducted her. Consistent with Stockholm syndrome behavior, she complained that her father Powhatan would not exchange her for weapons (he did pay part of the ransom the colonists requested but felt he could not in good conscience give up the weapons and tools requested of him), and she was reported to have been reluctant to leave England and return to Virginia after her visit. In the broadest sense, a large percentage of the female population of the early modern period, essentially held subject by their brothers, fathers, and sons, may have experienced aspects of something like the Stockholm syndrome. Some women exhibited the feelings of shame, self-blame, subjugation, paradoxical gratitude, and resignation that have been identified as symptoms of a victimization syndrome that may be thought of as a subset of posttraumatic stress disorder. (Reading the above, my daughter Ellen suggests it could be argued that "attitudes that

Illustration for The Tempest **from Rowe's Shakespeare, 1709.**

John Rolfe and his first wife were among the passengers on the *Sea Venture,* a merchant ship bound for Virginia. Caught in a hurricane, the ship was wrecked off the coast of Bermuda. Rolfe survived and continued to Bermuda, but his wife and a daughter born on the island died. Survivors' descriptions of the storm that wrecked the ship probably inspired Shakespeare's play *The Tempest.*

seem to be gratitude and indebtedness were carefully crafted written and public expressions in line with social mores of the time, rather than innermost feelings." She says I should grant women more "subtle autonomy" than the passage might imply.)

More is known about John Rolfe than about his wives, as is typical of the time. Matoaka is, to a degree, an exception, but even in her case we have only a few remarks in her own voice, whereas we have extended texts from her husband. Her brief moment of celebrity in London was in a sense artificially generated as an aspect of the public relations efforts of the Virginia Company, whose directors wanted to show a reformed heathen as an example of their work. Apart from that moment, she does not often appear in contemporaneous writings related to the Virginia Colony, and does not become a prominent part of its history until John Smith's romanticized story about her became popular in later centuries.

Matoaka was the second of John Rolfe's three wives. The first was a woman known to history only as "Mistress Rolfe." In 1609 Rolfe, then in his mid-twenties, decided to take passage to Virginia on a newly built 300-ton armed merchant ship called the *Sea Venture.* One hundred forty men were aboard, along with ten women, among them Mistress Rolfe, who was with child. The expedition, funded by the Virginia Society, was intended to bring resources of people and supplies to the new, struggling Jamestown colony. In July the vessel was hit by a hurricane. The ship took water and everyone aboard patched cracks with anything they could find, cast off possessions and cargo, and bailed furiously for thirty-six hours. Just as the travelers had reached the end of their strength and were preparing for death, the ship crashed on a reef off the coast of Bermuda. Everyone aboard was able to reach the island in the ship's boats; there the castaways happily discovered a population of hogs left by early explorers.

Among the travelers was William Strachey, who left an account of the voyage. "The storm in a restless tumult had blown so exceedingly as we could not apprehend in our imaginations any possibility of greater violence; yet did we still find it not only more terrible but more constant, fury added to fury.... Winds and seas were as mad as fury and rage could make them," Strachey wrote. "The sea swelled above the clouds and gave battle unto Heaven.... I had been in some storms before.... Yet all that I had ever suffered gathered together might not hold comparison with this: there was not a moment in which the sudden splitting or instant oversetting of the ship was not expected." Although the Virginia Society tried to suppress his account as bad press, it probably inspired Shakespeare's *Tempest*, which was first performed in 1611.

The Rolfes' daughter, christened Bermuda, was born on the island but died shortly after. Over the following months the enterprising colonists constructed two pinnaces, which they called the *Deliverance* and the *Patience*. The Rolfes took ship for Virginia on one of these vessels, but Mistress Rolfe died on the way, or soon after arriving. Women's lives were short, so marriages seldom lasted more than a couple of decades.

In Virginia Rolfe now found himself without a family, and Matoaka caught his eye. When she was captured, she was a married woman. What became of her husband, a man named Kocoum, is unknown. Among the Powhatans separation could dissolve marriage bonds, but it is curious that little was made of her first marriage by the English. Possibly they considered it nonbinding because of its non-Christian nature, or maybe they just chose to ignore it because it did not suit the message of native conversion that they were trying to convey back to England in order to garner additional support for the colony.

Matoaka was kept captive for more than a year. She was placed in the care of the women of the colony, who dressed her in the English fashion and instructed her in appropriate female behavior. A clergyman named Alexander Whitaker was charged with making her literate and teaching her the Christian religion. She learned the Lord's Prayer, the Ten Commandments, the Apostles' Creed, and the Catechism. Whitaker baptized her with the name Rebecca. Around this time she attracted the attention of Rolfe, who was beginning to make tobacco farming in Virginia a viable business (his breakthrough had come when he imported *Nicotiana tabacum* seeds from Trinidad to replace the harsher native strain; how he obtained the seeds is not known). Rolfe wrote a long, anguished letter to the governor of the colony in which he struggled with his apparent guilt at feeling lust for a heathen but concluded that his religious duty justified marrying the captive woman. "What should I doe?" he wrote. "Shall I be

Pocahontas, 1616, by Simon Van de Passe. Copper engraving.

The inscription under this portrait made from life reads *Ætatis suæ 21 A. 1616,* Latin for "at the age of 21 in the year 1616." In fact Matoaka, better known as Pocahontas, was only nineteen at the time. The Virginia Company exaggerated her age because they wanted to show off a convert to Christianity beyond what was considered the age of consent.

of so untoward a disposition, as to refuse to leade the blind into the right way? Shall I be so unnaturall, as not to give bread to the hungrie? or uncharitable, as not to cover the naked? Shall I despise to actuate these pious dueties of a Christian? Shall the base feare of displeasing the world, overpower and with holde mee from revealing unto man these spirituall workes of the Lord, which in my meditations and praiers, I have daily made knowne unto him? God forbid."

God forbid indeed. There is no record of Matoaka's feelings for Rolfe, but he need not have been so troubled. The marriage fit perfectly with the Virginia Company's public relations plans, and was approved. The couple were married in April 1614 (the discovery of the remains of the wooden church where they were wed was called one of the top archaeological discoveries of 2010), and Matoaka gave birth to a son, Thomas, nine months later. In London in 1616 Matoaka was exhibited as a princess and made the rounds as American royalty. Her portrait was done by a young Dutchman, Simon Van de Passe. Latin and English inscriptions on the engraving he produced identify her as the "Matoaks als Rebecka," princess, daughter of Powhatani, emperor of Virginia, "converted and baptized in the Christian faith, and wife to the worthy Mr. Joh Rolff." Not everyone, however, bought the Virginia Company's line. One Londoner sent a copy of the engraving to a friend with the bitter comment, "Here is a fine picture of no fayre Lady and yet with her tricking up and high stile and titles you might thincke her and her worshipfull husband to be sombody, yf you do not know that the poore companie of Virginia out of theyre povertie are faine to allow her fowre pound a weeke for her maintenance."

As a visiting princess Matoaka attended the royal Twelfth Night masque in the Banqueting House at Whitehall Palace in January 1617. An observer reported that "The Virginian woman Poca-huntas, with her father counsaillor hath been with the King and graciously used, and both she and her assistant well placed at the maske." Although the English regarded Uttamatomakkin as Matoaka's assistant, from the Powhatan point of view it was he who should have been regarded as the visiting dignitary.

The masque, by Jonson and Jones, was called *The Vision of Delight*. Like all royal masques it exalted the king. *The Vision* celebrated the advent of spring in his kingdom, with dancers representing Delight, Harmony, Grace, Love, Laughter, Revel, Sport, and Wonder. The antimasque figures were comical pantaloons and phantasms, drawn from the Italian commedia dell'arte, who represented vices of gluttony and lechery. To begin the concluding dance, courtiers descended from a Bower of Spring; the featured dancer was George Villiers, the king's new favorite (he of the famously shapely legs), who had recently been named Earl of Buckingham.

What might Matoaka have thought of this spectacle? Again, she leaves no record of her feelings. But shortly after the performance the Rolfes prepared to return to Virginia — "sore against her will," according to an observer. She did not get far. Many of the visitors from Virginia had most likely been infected with a form of dysentery known as the "bloody flux" (some sources say their affliction was a lung disease, pneumonia or tuberculosis). The ship had to stop before it had exited the Thames. Matoaka was taken ashore. There she died within hours and was buried in an unmarked grave in a churchyard in the town of Gravesend.

Having lost his second wife Rolfe prepared to continue to Virginia with their son. But Thomas too was ill. Rolfe left the boy on shore to be retrieved by a relative and went on alone. He would never see his son again, but Thomas survived. After his father's death he would return as an adult for the first time to his birthplace, where he would fight against his mother's people and become a person of influence.

After his return to Virginia John Rolfe married for a third time, to a daughter of original Virginia colonists. His tobacco enterprise prospered, and he became a large landowner. In his lifetime he was highly regarded, while Matoaka, like most women of her age, had been thought of little consequence — except as a pawn, first in the interplay between the colonists and the Powhatans and then as a public relations symbol for the Virginia Company in London. But by 1995, when Disney Studios made an animated film of her story (presenting her, one critic said, as a "buckskin Barbie"), the situation had become reversed. The film company wrote Rolfe entirely out of the story.

3 Creative Imitation

In 1939 the Argentine writer Jorge Luis Borges published a story called "Pierre Menard, Author of the *Quixote*." What if a twentieth-century author were to write a book exactly the same as the one written by Cervantes, Borges wondered — not a copy, but an original (though identical) work. What new meanings would such a book acquire? In the opinion of Borges's narrator, Menard's *Quixote* surpassed Cervantes's.

Borges's story addresses a paradox of imitation and originality. Around the turn of the seventeenth century a group of Chinese writers known as the Seven Late Masters were grappling with similar issues. They observed that to imitate the ancients would be to adopt their form but depart from their spirit, because the ancients had not been mere imitators of others. And yet, to go off in entirely new directions would be to fail to respect the achievements of the ancestors. The leader of the group, a man named Wang Shijen, argued for a middle way. With reference to the ancients, he said, "If one's own method corresponds to theirs, one must attempt to express oneself; if one's method departs, one must attempt to return. When there is departure in correspondence and correspondence in departure, there shall be awakening."

As Chinese visual artists were exposed to new influences from Western art they struggled with the relationship between current artistic practice and the examples of ancient masters. The leading painter and art theorist of the late Ming, Dong Qichang, proposed that artists could resolve this problem through a principle that he called *fang*, or "creative imitation," by which entirely new works were to be built from structural elements borrowed from the past. The artist would pay homage to past masters by studying their techniques and constructing works from them that would be fresh and new, and would manifest a comparable spirit.

But in 1616 the angry mob that gathered at Dong's estate in Huating (now a part of Shanghai) cared little for the theoretical issues preoccupying the scholar. Already enraged, they had been rallied by a series of handbills and public denunciations of him. Shouting and carrying torches, their number swollen to at least ten thousand people (some say as many as a million), they stormed Dong's home, smashing his collection of antiquities. They did not care about his paintings, widely acclaimed by the educated elite as the best of the age, or those of the ancients that he had collected. They rushed into his home and looted it,

Opposite: Piled Snow on Cold Cliffs, 1616, by Zhao Zuo. Hanging scroll, ink and colors on paper. 76 x 211 cm. *National Palace Museum, Taipei.*

Zhao Zuo renders the isolation of a forested mountain landscape blanketed by snow. Like many Western painters of the period, he plays with contrasts of light and dark, rendering snow through areas untouched by ink.

Zhao was a friend of the art theorist Dong Qichang, and like Dong he sought precedents in past traditions of Chinese painting, often alluding to such masters such as the late Yuan painter Ni Zan. But this painting, with its volumetric molding of forms (see p. 141 for a reproduction of the entire painting) appears to show the influence of Western artistic styles.

Although Dong Qichang did not himself paint snow scenes, many other Chinese artists of his time did. The winter of the year this picture was painted, 1616, was, according to a Chinese art collector's diary, the harshest in years. Timothy Brook has suggested that the increase in winter scenes may respond to the Little Ice Age, which by one reckoning lasted from about 1550 to about 1700.

Not only in China but throughout the early modern world, artists were rethinking their connections to ancient traditions, experimenting with fresh directions suggested by exposure to new styles, and documenting the changing world in which they lived.

not only destroying his paintings but burning the house to the ground for good measure. They also destroyed a retreat Dong owned outside of town, the homes of two of his sons, and the home of his principal servant; they beat the servant's wife and flung her into the roaring flames of the burning house. Dong, however, managed to slip away with a few paintings, which he later had to sell off for funds.

There are various explanations for the mob's anger, but common to them all is a picture of Dong as an arrogant man and an oppressive landlord. Dong, then sixty years old, had taken a fancy to a beautiful young maidservant who had been adopted by the family of one of his servants. Her own parents were still alive, however, and when she learned that her mother was seriously ill she went to visit her. One of Dong Qichang's sons became suspicious that she was evading his father's attentions. Taking with him more than two hundred of the family's slaves, he went to retrieve her. The men broke into the house and trashed it, and carried her off by force.

This outrage did not sit well with the community, and someone composed a satirical ballad about the incident, which reached the ears of the artist. Dong thought he knew who had composed the song, and he had that man — who happened to be his own brother-in-law — seized and humiliated. Soon after, the songwriter died mysteriously.

The brother-in-law's wife and mother came with some maidservants to Dong's estate to complain. Dong's son had their clothes torn off, and they were bound and brutally beaten. One or more of the maidservants was probably raped. They were thrown into the street "their faces covered with mud; above, without clothing to cover their bodies," it was written, "the blood running down to their feet; and below, lacking even cloth enough to conceal their shame."

That Dong was later officially exonerated might not mean a lot, since power favors power. Three hundred fifty years later many people in China were still angry at him. During the Cultural Revolution his tomb was vandalized. His works were not exhibited or published, and he was presented as an object lesson of the abuses of the landlord class.

Contemporary art historians are more inclined to gloss over the issue, which received little attention in an international symposium devoted to the artist, held at the Nelson Atkins Museum in 1992. Which is perhaps as it should be: whatever his failings as a person, Dong, it cannot be denied, was the foremost art historian, collector of antiquities, and painter of his day. He was a driven man who had worked his way up from genteel poverty. At eighteen he was devastated by taking only second place in an exam on account of his unexceptional calligraphy. He then applied himself to the art with such dedication that he became famous as a master of it. In his twenties he took a job as a tutor in the household of the foremost art collector of that time, which trained his eye as an antiquarian. In his mid-thirties he was elected to China's most prestigious scholarly academy and served off and on in the 1590s in the imperial court in Beijing. He was a tutor to one of the Wanli emperor's sons, his unfortunate successor the Taichang emperor, who was a pawn in court intrigues and ruled for only a month before dying, likely of poisoning.

Dong Qichang, by Zeng Jing, frontispiece to the album *Eight Views of Autumn Moods,* 1620, by Dong Qichang. *Shanghai Museum.*

The future Taichang emperor was not the Wanli emperor's preference as his successor (his choice was a later son by his favorite consort), and the imperial family, the emperor's wives and concubines, the court eunuchs, and the civil officials all engaged in political maneuvers and intrigues backing one candidate or another. Dong seems to have fallen victim to this poisonous environment, and in 1599 he was assigned to be transferred to another region; he refused the post and returned home. The remaining thirty-seven years of his life would be characterized by long periods of retreat to his personal estate punctuated by short terms of government service. Through this "advance and retreat" strategy he mostly steered clear of the often fatal political intrigues of the time (in the 1620s, for example, hundreds of scholar officials were executed in a systematic purge).

Somewhere along the way Dong became a practitioner of Chan Buddhism (the Chinese counterpart to Japanese Zen). Toward the end of the sixteenth century he fell under the sway of Li Zhi, the prominent advocate of "Mad Chan." Inspired by the "Neo-Confucianism" of Wang Yangming, Li rebelled against convention. He advocated a kind of moral relativism and promoted an ideal of "sudden enlightenment." Although Dong later distanced himself from Li's philosophy, he developed a theory of painting that reflects Chan Buddhist influence. Traditionally, in Chan Buddhist practice, students study with established masters. Only the master can determine when the student has "graduated" and become qualified to become a master in turn. Because of this practice, Chan was extremely focused on the concept of lineage. Since the practice was not based on holy books, the lineages reflected its established traditions. Chan temples often contained a "Hall of Patriarchs" filled with portraits representing the lineage of the temple.

Dong adopted this concept of lineage and applied it to the traditions

Two works made in 1617 reflect Dong Qichang's mid-career painting style. Forced to flee his home by rioting tenant farmers and villagers, Dong painted prolifically in the years that followed.

The paintings reflect both Dong's study of ancient predecessors and his fundamental belief that paintings should represent the spirit of a landscape rather than its exterior form. Of the Cleveland landscape he wrote:

> Zhao Mengfu and Wang Meng both painted depictions of the Bian Mountains. I have traveled to those mountains and moored my boat beneath them. There I realized that the paintings by the two masters transmitted the spirit of the place. But the soul of those mountains and streams is inexhaustible. I went beyond the work of the others to fashion another scene of my own that is not without merit.

of painting. He distinguished two main schools, or lineages, which he called the "northern school" and the "southern school," a terminology that would take hold and become the orthodox approach to Chinese painting for centuries. It would drive generations of students of Chinese painting to distraction, because the terms "northern" and "southern" had nothing to do with geography. They were metaphors based on two traditions of Chan Buddhism. The northern school of Chan was based on long periods of chanting, study, and personal austerity. It viewed the achievement of enlightenment as a long, gradual process. The southern school of Chan, by contrast, emphasized internal examination of the self in order to achieve sudden enlightenment.

Applying this distinction to painting, Dong promoted a "southern school" that was based on amateurism as superior to a "northern school" of professional painters. For Dong, professional painting was about the acquisition of technique in order to produce pretty surfaces. But amateurs — the Confucian literati — were supposed to cultivate the self. They were expected to be accomplished in all cultural refinements, such as poetry, calligraphy, and philosophy. By cultivating the self, the amateur painter could produce works that would be more meaningful and soulful than the hollow technical achievements of the professionals, which were mere surface displays of proficiency. While professional painters might capture the outward essence of a landscape, for example, the literati painters of the southern school, because of their personal refinement, would convey the essence hidden beneath the surface.

Dong believed he embodied the virtues of the Southern School; indeed, he was the very culmination of its lineage. A cynic, however, might see his "amateurism" as a kind of professionalism in disguise, played for higher stakes. (Analogy could be made to the official Ming line that international trade was mostly not economic in nature but merely the exchange of gifts and tributes.) Northern school professionals might carry their paintings with them to market and sell them to wealthy merchants and traders like any common vendor. Southern school painters did not sell their paintings so blatantly (or so cheaply), but used them to promote themselves as scholars in order to rise in the civil bureaucracy. They also exchanged paintings as gifts, which resulted not in direct payments but in favors that were potentially more valuable.

So it was that after the torching of his estate Dong stayed with friends or traveled in a boat on the river, feverishly painting. By exchanging these paintings with other members of the educated elite he was able after a few years to reestablish his personal fortune and position in society. "A num-

青卉圖依北苑意
丁巳夏五晦。審

陳惟其世文
董玄宰

橫嶺千尋旦紫雲
雲端杻尖見郁塔
秋光月雪坏淸日
流沼亭中趣若出

晉陵

歲在丁巳夏五作於靜寄軒
王時敏并題時觀之意
右臣

ber of Dong Qichang's best works are dated to the years immediately after 1616," scholar James Cahill has observed, "when the terrible losses of the riot and fire forced him to paint and write prolifically." As Cahill has noted, two paintings made in 1617, now in the collections of the National Gallery of Victoria, Melbourne, and the Cleveland Museum of Art, are representative of his work from this period (p. 137).

The Melbourne landscape, painted around November, was an example of the works Dong made as gifts for a friends following the riot on this estate. It exemplifies his theories of "divide and unite" and "substance and void." The painting, almost ten feet tall, consists of a foreground scene of trees and rocks and a background scene of lightly wooded mountains. An empty section devoid of ink that meanders through the center of the painting represents a river separating the foreground and background. Writhing trees in the foreground lean left as if straining toward the mountains, while the mountains themselves curl to the right in counterpoint to the foreground trees. A house on the far shore is sketched in with a few light strokes, surrounded by dark trees and landscape features rendered in tones of gray. Dong judiciously balances areas of ink and blank paper.

The Cleveland painting, nearly seven and a half feet high, was made in the summer of the same year. According to its inscription, it depicts the Qianbian mountains, made famous by representations in paintings from the tenth and fourteenth centuries — the mere choice of the subject underscores Dong's scholarly bent. This mountain is part of a low range located near the Yangzi river delta, but a viewer would be hard pressed to identify the subject from Dong's rendering of it. In contrast to the other painting, this one connects the foreground and background through a peculiar mass of forms that suggest a particularly contorted mountain. It is impossible to reconcile the various shapes into any coherent set of relations. While the right side of the painting is fairly conventional, a twisted mass of shapes in the center of the painting looks like some sort of giant lichen, or perhaps a diseased kidney. It stands in

different relation to each area — foreground, background, and right and left — with which it connects.

Yet the painting succeeds as a kind of semiabstract landscape. For Dong, painting was more an expression of inner reality than of external form, and his rendering of the mountain could be thought to capture its essence without the distraction of its actual shape. According to James Cahill the painting's "ambiguities and spacial disjunctures occur as warps within an imposing, absorbing landscape that can stand on its own as a major work of art." Is it possible that such paintings reflect the dissolving of the old Confucian certainties in the newly commercialized late Ming society? "For a culture in which landscape paintings had always embodied concepts of natural order," Cahill says, such works "must have had an impact that we can only partly understand and feel.... A painting like [Dong's 'Qingbian Mountain'] must have represented, for late Ming viewers, whether or not they recognized it consciously as such, an analogue in forms to their uneasy sense of irrationality and disorder pervading established institutions." However that may be, "our perception of what constitutes 'Chinese art,'" says Timothy Brook, "derives from Dong Qichang."

"As a rule I never paint snow," Dong Qichong said. "I let winter scenery take its place." The reasons for Dong's aversion to snow scenes are unclear — it could be that he simply wasn't good at them, but Dong would probably say that including snow in a winter scene is a cheap trick: the true artist would convey the essence of the winter landscape without relying on simple surface appearances. At least one fellow painter, however, was unimpressed. He considered Dong's winter landscapes indistinguishable from his autumn landscapes — they are only winter scenes, he said, "by definition." To judge from the painting of "Clearing after Snow on Mountain Passes" that Dong made in 1635, the last year of his life, the criticism was not without merit.

There was no lack of snow and cold to inspire the painters. During the time he was in China, Matteo Ricci reported, "Once winter sets in,

Opposite and above: *Clearing after Snow on Mountain Passes,* 1635 (details), by Dong Qichang. Handscroll, ink on paper, 143 x 13 cm. Palace Museum, Beijing.

Dong Qichang painted this landscape in the year of his death. According to his inscription, the painting is based on one by a tenth-century painter. In Dong's version, however, the "forms respond to the distinctly non-physical forces of intellect and imagination," according to scholar Howard Rogers. How easy is it to tell this is a winter and not an autumn landscape?

all the rivers in northern China are frozen over so hard that navigation on them is impossible, and a wagon may pass over them." Timothy Brook has sought to correlate climatic changes to political and social developments in China. Cold winters and drought during the late spring contributed to crop failures that resulted in widespread famine and death. The crop crisis undermined confidence in the government, and the population decline left China undermanned to defend itself against the Manchu invaders who would overthrow the dynasty before midcentury.

Brook calls the period from 1615–1617 "The Second Wanli Slough," a period of extreme environmental stress, characterized by cold, drought, famine, locusts, and — so the Chinese chroniclers report — unsettling encounters with dragons. It must have been a particularly uncomfortable time for Dong Qichong to be fleeing an irate mob of villagers.

One of Dong's greatest successes was in elaborating a theory of art based on the notion that his own technical limitations were precisely the indicators of a nobility of spirit that elevated such works above those of the merely competent. Generations of Chinese scholars would follow his lead. Yet, in the estimation of James Cahill, "Aside from Dong Qichang himself, none of the literati painter-critics who assert so forcibly the virtues of amateurism was himself a painter of any real stature."

Whether amateur or professional, few late Ming painters seemed to share Dong's aversion to snow scenes. Several within his own circle tried their hand at the subject. Dong's closest friend was the critic and calligrapher Chen Jiru, who was famous for having burnt his scholars' robes after failing his examinations. Dong praised him for embodying amateur virtues, saying his paintings "do not fall into the realm of the professional painters … with their sweet, vulgar, and pernicious character." The two men boated together, and Dong probably relied on Chen's hospitality following the riot of 1616. After completing *Clearing after Snow on Mountain Passes,* Dong made preparations for his funeral and sent a final message to Chen. Chen too was interested in managing his end — his autobiography included an imagined account of his death. A snowy landscape in the Seattle Art Museum attributed to Chen is evidently a fake, but his inscriptions do appear on snow scenes by others. In China's Xixi National Wetland Park there is an island with a building that retains the name Chen gave it. He called it the "Autumn Snow Hut."

Intense cold covered much of the globe. On a typical day in a small town in the Netherlands, sometime in the summer of 1616, the sun was hidden in haze. Pale light entering the Mute of Kampen's studio cast few shadows. Kampen, located near where the river IJssel empties into the IJsselmeer (the "Zuiderzee"), was once a bustling commercial and agricultural town, but by 1616 it had been supplanted by Amsterdam, about sixty miles to its west.

The artist Hendrick Avercamp — who everyone simply called "the Mute" — rummaged through his collection of ink and watercolor drawings of stock characters drawn from the works of Flemish and Northern Dutch artists, such as Pieter Bruegel the Elder, Hans Bol, and David Vinckboons, along with his own sketches from life. He was looking for figures for a painting featuring people from all levels of society enjoying a day on the ice. He would need a lot of them to complete his plan — a single one of his paintings could show more than a hundred people, and even as many as two hundred, each engaged in some particular activity on the ice. Many were skating. Some were playing a popular club-and-ball game called colf. Others were sailing ice yachts or pulling carts or selling goods from tents or ice fishing or simply falling down in a comical manner.

It is impossible to know which of his paintings Avercamp was working on in 1616, because he rarely dated his works. A few can be roughly dated by costumery or architectural and landscape elements or just by stylistic considerations, but of many all that can be said is that they date from around 1610 to 1620. This was an active period for the artist, and he was certainly working on some ice scene in 1616, as such scenes make up the overwhelming preponderance of his work. One possibility is that he was

Hendrick Avercamp (1585–1634) painted this scene in his home town of Kampen, about sixty miles east of Amsterdam, during the "Little Ice Age," a prolonged period of global cooling.

painting the winter scene on a frozen canal that is currently among the collections of the Los Angeles County Museum of Art. The painting was a partial gift from collector Hannah Carter, and the LACMA curators so esteemed it that in January 2010 they sold off seventeen European paintings and a terracotta sculpture in part to help fund its full acquisition. There are several other surviving paintings that could date from 1616, but the LACMA painting (which, for all we know, could be slightly earlier or later) can represent them all. Extraordinary as it is, in many ways it is typical of Avercamp's work from this period.

By this time Avercamp, in order to better concentrate on his figures, was playing down the framing buildings and trees that formerly appeared on either side of his canvases. The Bruegel-like high horizons that had characterized his earlier work were moving lower, giving a less distant and more immediate perspective on the ice activities. Increasingly the viewer feels a part of the activities rather than a distant spectator to them, a trend that culminates around 1625, with a painting of colf players on the ice, in which the viewer feels almost a part of the game. In the LACMA painting, figures in the front row are strongly detailed while those more in the distance are more sketchily drawn in more muted colors. A laborer looks on at the activity from the left while a man and two women load goods in an ice cart and a horse pulls a sleigh. A gentleman fastens his skates next to a bird hunter who is accompanied by his dog. A gypsy carrying a baby on her back reads the palm of a stylishly dressed woman. Fashionable skaters sashay toward the viewer hand in hand. A lady (it has been suggested that she may represent Elizabeth Stuart, the daughter of King James of England, who visited around this time, but this is questionable) wears a mask as protection against the cold. Behind her a bearded old man trudges forward carrying a basket. More distant figures fall down, play colf, fish, sit in sleds and propel themselves with poles, and engage in many other activities. As is typical of Avercamp's work, the painting is a secular one. Avercamp was not interested in the classical and religious themes that dominate the work of Southern European contemporaries such as Artemsia Gentileschi. Instead, even though the scene does not depict any specific place, it is meant to capture the everyday life of Northern Europe.

Because he lived in an artistic backwater outside the main centers of artistic activity, only the general outlines of Avercamp's life are known. He was the son of educated parents. His father was a schoolmaster in Amsterdam when Hendrick was born in 1585, but that gig did not last long. He moved to Kampen the next year to become an apothecary and doctor. The fam-

**Colf Players on the Ice (detail),
ca. 1620–1625, by Hendrick Avercamp. Oil on panel. Edmund and
Sally Speelman Collection.**

A gentleman plays colf while a
man carrying an axe for cutting
through the ice looks on. Colf
was enormously popular in the
Netherlands, and it was depicted
in most of Hendrick Avercamp's
paintings. Players struck a sheep-
skin, or sometimes wooden, ball
with a metal-headed club. In the
most common variation of the
game, players tried to hit a post in
the fewest number of strokes; in
another version they competed to
achieve the greatest distance in a
set number of strokes.

ily briefly returned to Amsterdam, but his services were missed in Kampen and he reesumed
his medical practice there. One reason he was
needed was that the town was experiencing
an outbreak of plague. It was a fatal decision:
in 1602 the doctor himself became one of the
plague's casualties. Avercamp and his siblings
were left in the care of his mother, who seems to
have been clever and resourceful and who took
over her husband's business before passing it on
to one of Avercamp's brothers.

Probably deaf as well as mute, Avercamp
was taught to read and write, and he was sent
to study in Amsterdam with the artist Pieter
Isaacsz. Isaacz was a mannerist history and portrait painter whose influence is nowhere seen
in his pupil's work; instead Avercamp shows
affinities with other artists who were students
around the same time and with Bruegel and
other Flemish and Dutch predecessors. Some
elements in his paintings, such as a bird trap
made from an old door, are directly drawn
from Breugel's own winter scenes. Around 1613
Avercamp returned to Kampen, where he apparently lived for the remainder of his life, producing an endless stream of charming, lively depictions
of amusements on ice; they were popular and sold well. Some critics have
the impression that he continued to live with his mother, but there is no
hard evidence for this. In 1633, however, shortly before her death, she produced a document that requested an additional allowance for Avercamp
of one hundred guilders a year beyond his regular portion of the family
inheritance on the grounds of his "mute and wretched" condition. While
many critics think that this indicates he had difficulty functioning in society, this conclusion is hardly supported by the evidence of his paintings (in
which the artist himself sometimes appears). It is possible that his mother's
comment alludes instead to an illness. Just five months later, at the age of
forty-nine, Avercamp followed her in death.

The paintings of Avercamp and others who focused on winter scenes document the period of intensely cold winters from about 1550 to 1700, when
the climate cooled worldwide (in a broader view the "Little Ice Age" could

be thought to extend from about 1300 to 1850, and any of a number of alternate start and end years have been proposed). During one year in the fifteenth century so heavy a snow fell in Florence, for example, that Piero de Medici ordered Michelangelo to make a snowman in the courtyard of his palace (we don't know what it looked like, except that Giorgio Vasari, who recorded the lives of Renaissance painters, said that it was "very beautiful"). The cooling is remarkable because, while climactic temperature fluctuations are common, this is the only period in recorded history where such cooling occurred across much of the globe rather than in restricted regions. The northern hemisphere experienced a period of particularly cold winters from about 1600 to 1616.

Huaynaputina Volcano, drawing from *El Primer Coronica y Buen Gobierno* ("The First New Chronicle and Good Government"), 1615–1616, by Guaman Poma. Bound book; ink and colors on paper, 119 x 205 cm. Det Kongelige Bibliotek, Copenhagen, Denmark.

The massive eruption of Huaynaputina volcano, near the present Peru/Chile border, spewed large amounts of ash that contributed to global cooling in the early seventeenth century.

The causes of this cooling are a subject of debate. Ash from volcanic eruptions was certainly a contributing factor. The eruption on February 19, 1616, of Mayon Volcano, the first recorded eruption of the Philippines' most active volcano, was only the latest of a series of volcanic activity. Toward the end of the sixteenth century one of the largest volcanic discharges in history occurred in New Guinea. Yet even it was outdone by the enormous eruption of Peru's Huaynaputina Volcano in 1600 (also, strangely, on February 19). The Huaynaputina eruption was likely the largest in historical times, on a similar scale to the 1883 eruption of Krakatoa. The sixteen-day blowout — Guaman Poma produced a drawing of the event — destroyed several villages. Lava flowed to the Pacific Ocean, some seventy-five miles distant. Volcanic ash was dispersed for great distances; it was so thick that it collapsed roofs in Arequipa, about forty-five miles away. The ash spread globally — the distinctive Huaynaputina ash has been detected in high levels at the South Pole and as far north as Greenland. Such ash can block incoming solar radiation, leading to worldwide cooling that can last for years. Following the eruption the winter of 1601 was the coldest in six centuries. The haze was so thick that it was reported there were no shadows. Famine was widespread, especially in Russia, where more than two million people died.

Volcanic activity is not the only possible cause of the cooling. Normal

"Icarus," 1588, from the series *The Four Disgracers* by Hendrik Goltzius. Engraving, 13 x 13⅛ in. Los Angeles County Museum of Art, Mary Stansbury Ruiz Bequest, M.88.91.104.

Goltzius's strongly foreshortened Icarus demonstrates his skill as an engraver. His study of anatomy is apparent, yet the figure is individualized and expressive. Above all, Goltzius possessed a highly sophisticated understanding of tonality that helps to give his engravings a seemingly three-dimensional quality.

fluctuations in solar activity have an effect on climate, as can changes in the flow of ocean currents (perhaps caused by melt from the Medieval Warm Period). Changes in forestation and land use may have affected climate in ways that are not fully understood. Migration of peoples and changes in agriculture practices caused widespread deforestation (Japan, which had a reforestation policy, was the most notable exception). Adaptation of American crops such as corn and potatoes allowed farming at elevations unsuitable for rice. Yet population was declining. Urbanization caused squalid conditions that helped to spread plague and made large populations susceptible to disease. Smallpox and other European diseases decimated the population of the Americas.

Spread of the plague was facilitated by the new globalism. During the fourteenth century the Mongol empire — the largest empire geographically that the world has ever seen — stretched from East Asia to Europe. Rats, probably from the Gobi Desert region, attached themselves to Mongol supply trains, and fleas attached themselves to the rats. The fleas transmitted the bacteria that caused the bubonic plague. The plague reached India and China by the mid-1300s, and Europe soon afterward. As just one example of its devastation, by the late 1400s the population of Paris was only a third of what it had been a hundred and fifty years before. The plague continued to reappear frequently for some time thereafter. But the rats the fleas hitchhiked on were black rats, *Rattus rattus*. In recent centuries those rats were largely driven out by the larger and more aggressive brown or Norway rat, *Rattus norvegicus*. The brown rat is more resistant to the disease and this, together with better practices of quarantine and disinfection, much reduced the threat of plague by the eighteenth century. Next time you come across a sewer rat you can blame it for, among its other disagreeable doings, the world's present overpopulation.

Another artist named Hendrick, based near Amsterdam in Haarlem — an open-minded town that welcomed both Catholics and Protestants and attracted immigrants from the Catholic southern Netherlands, France, and elsewhere — exemplified the mannerist mode of painting that looked to the later works of Michelangelo as a model. A generation older than Avercamp, Hendrick Goltzius was a virtuoso who excelled in just the sorts of mythological scenes that failed to interest the Mute of Kampen.

Goltzius had come to painting late, having first won international renown as a printmaker and engraver. He was born in Germany, in a town near the Dutch border, of a long line of workers in the arts trades: his great-grandfather and grandfather were painters, his father a stained-glass worker, a cousin an engraver and publisher. When Goltzius was about a year old he fell into the family's hearth — especially needed for heat during the cold weather of the Little Ice Age — and was severely burned. The worst damage was to his hands, especially his right hand. The pain must have been excruciating. A neighbor wrapped the toddler's hands tightly with cloth. The burn caused tendons to fuse in his right hand. He was never able to fully open its fingers. Nonetheless, he remained right-handed, and that was the hand he used in producing his engravings and paintings. He was forced to hold the engraver's burin, and later the brush, in an unconventional way and to propel the movements of his hand with his arm, which may have contributed to the characteristic exuberance of his compositions. He did several images of his damaged hand. A 1588 pen drawing is a sort of self portrait — it was not done with a mirror; instead, the same hand that produced the drawing was its subject.

When he was sixteen Goltzius began to study with an engraver named Dirck Volckertsz Coornhert, who was a refugee from Holland. Coornhert had fallen afoul of both the Spanish and hard-line Dutch Protestants in his war-torn homeland by having made an appeal for tolerance and rationality, which offended both sides. Under Coornhert Goltzius learned the engraver's trade and was exposed to forward-thinking humanist ideals of the Italian Renaissance. After the liberation of Haarlem from Spain in 1577 Coornhert returned there, and Goltzius soon joined him. His teacher arranged for him to get assignments producing engravings for publishers in Antwerp. He began to develop a reputation. When he was twenty-one he married a thirty-year-old widow whose inheritance from her first marriage bankrolled his business; this became so successful that he succeeded in breaking the

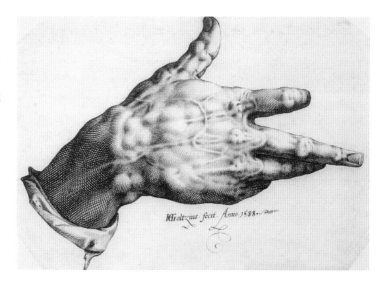

Right Hand of the Artist, dated 1588, by Hendrick Goltzius. Pen with brown ink, 32 x 23 cm. Signed "H Goltzius fecit. Anno 1588."

This closely observed drawing of Goltzius's injured hand was analyzed by the plastic surgeon F. Groenevelt, author of *The Burned Hand,* who wrote that "The person in question probably fell into the fire with the side of the hand striking the coals, after which the hand was twisted outwards so that the back of the fingers was also burnt."

The artist's hand became, appropriately, something of a personal brand. He did a number of images of it, and on at least one occasion he presented his hand while traveling to prove his identity.

Compare this to the hand of Artemisia Gentileschi shown on p. 127.

monopoly previously exercised by the printers of Antwerp. (One prominent
engraver in Antwerp was Crispijn Van de Passe, father of the young man
who produced the engraving of Pocohontas during her visit to London.)

But Goltzius was troubled by ill health and severe depression. He was
chronically consumptive. He is said to have vomited blood almost daily
for three years. The cause of these problems is unknown, and doctors
were unable to find a cure. Could they have been related to Goltzius's
alchemical researches? A Haarlem poet wrote of the artist, "a seeker after
the Philosopher's Stone, he was deemed to be above many alchemists."
His work with minerals may have developed from an interest in improving paint pigments, but one source claims that Goltzius's alchemical experiments cost him a fortune, and an eye. Records of a lawsuit suggest
that he was defrauded by another alchemist who lived for a time in his
house while searching for a means of making gold.

In part to seek relief from these troubles, or at least to view the works
of the Italian masters before dying, Goltzius traveled to Italy in 1590 with
a servant. Unlike other prominent Northern European artists who made
the Italy trip, Goltzius traveled incognito, under the guise of a Dutch
cheese merchant and other invented identities. The reason for this is unclear, though it has been attributed to his sense of humor. On at least
one occasion Goltzius's servant was entertained as a visiting dignitary
while the artist was left to his own devices. This may have been his objective, for he industriously sketched a wide range of artworks during his
trip — a friend later claimed that "of all the Netherlanders who visited
Rome... there are none who made so many excellent drawings there." He
also visited places where his own prints were being sold in order to hear
candid assessments of them.

On his return to Haarlem following a year in Italy, Goltzius was re-
invigorated: he produced his best pen and ink drawings, among other
works. But his health continued to decline, and by the end of the century
friends again feared for his life. But in 1600 he made an abrupt change
in his life. At the age of forty-two, he abandoned engraving and took up
painting for the first time. Scholars (who tend to favor the engravings)
have long speculated on the reason for this change, but all of their theories remain speculation: no written records offer an explanation. My
guess is that Goltzius's interest in symbology led him to consider the year
1600 a significant moment for a break (the vision that inspired the German mystic Jacob Boehme also occurred in 1600; p. 223): he had reached
the highest rank in engraving, and painting was increasingly regarded as
the most prestigious (and potentially profitable, as the young Antwerp

Lot and His Daughters, dated and signed 1616 by Hendrick Groltzius. Oil on canvas, 204 x 140 cm. Rijksmuseum, SK-A-4866.

painter Peter Paul Rubens — who Goltzius entertained in 1612 — would demonstrate) of the visual arts.

Goltzius became regarded as the foremost Dutch painter of his day. Between the turn of the century and his death on New Year's Day, 1617, he worked with characteristic industry on his paintings, producing about a hundred, of which around half survive. The last years of his life in particular saw a great burst of productivity: nearly half of his extant paintings date from his final three years. In his last year, 1616, he produced several important paintings. He seems to have been especially inspired by the theme of seduction. A depiction of *Lot and His Daughters* shows Lot being seduced by his daughters following the destruction of the city of Sodom, which is ablaze in the upper right (with the patriarch's wife as a pillar of salt in front of it). The leering Lot reclines with a bowl of wine. Behind the figures is a fox, symbolic of the daughter's cunning in seducing their father (believing themselves to be the last survivors on earth). A dog looks out at the viewer, its paw on a stone, symbolic of resolve; Lot's foot, by contrast, is about to slip from the stone on which it is set. Goltzius brings a raw sensuality to the subject, also seen in his *The Fall of Man* (p. 151), which shows Adam being seduced by Eve, as the serpent, depicted with the head of a woman, looks on. The first couple are surrounded by goats and a cat, symbols of carnality. (Cats were associated with sexuality and witchcraft; persecution of them contributed to the spread of plague.) The sensuality and seductive content of Goltzius's painting is in marked contrast to traditional paintings on the theme, which focused on the punishment and shame of the first couple. The artist's erotic interests are also evident in his *Jupiter and Antiope* (p. 151), in which the god, having taken the form of a satyr, and apparently abetted by Cupid, leers at the reclining maenad whom he will soon ravish.

Goltzius's international eminence would be short-lived, since he would be followed by a golden age of Dutch painting that would feature such household names as Rubens and Rembrandt. Their fame would cause him to fade from public awareness until the second half of the twentieth century. A 1958 exhibition of his work organized by a Goltzius enthusiast named Emil Resnicek initiated a new interest in the artist. By January 2010 his stock had risen to new heights: a 1612 version of *Jupiter and Antiope* sold at auction for $6.8 million.

The two Hendricks' periods of peak painting production happened to coincide with a rare peaceful interlude in the life of Northern Europe. From the mid-sixteenth century through the end of the seventeenth, some part of Europe was almost always at war — there were only a couple dozen years of peace over that entire span, and there were around a hundred when most of the major states were engaged in combat. The Dutch war of secession from the Spanish Habsburg empire was a particularly devastating and drawn-out conflict. The southern provinces of the Netherlands (roughly the current Belgium) remained loyal to Spain, while the northern provinces became an independent nation, the Dutch Republic, sometimes referred to as Holland after its most affluent province. The endless fighting took an extremely heavy toll on both sides, and from 1609 to 1621 a truce was called. Avercamp's charming scenes of diversions on the ice reflected the fact that at last people could venture outside city walls without being attacked by armies of marauding mercenaries. The soldiers, often slow to be paid, were frequently disgruntled, or even in open revolt, and so they tended to forage and pillage as the opportunity presented itself. Now the conflict moved to the colonial realm (especially Southeast Asia, where Joris van Spilbergen and Juan de Silva were currently contending), while Northern Europe enjoyed what would turn out to be only a temporary cessation of hostilities.

A visitor in the Rubens House in Antwerp, now a museum. Rubens designed the house on the model of an Italian villa with an interior courtyard. He built up a significant collection of classical statuary through connections made over the course of his international diplomatic work.

The port city of Antwerp, located near the northern border of the Spanish Netherlands, had been hard hit by the war. Once the home of the great printer Plantin, it now boasted one of the most esteemed artists of the European baroque, Peter Paul Rubens. Rubens himself had produced a large *Adoration of the Magi* to celebrate the signing of the Twelve Years' Truce; after the truce fell apart the painting would make its way into the royal collections of Spain. Commercial activity in the city, formally a major trade center, would now be brought to a halt. Fighting would again rage throughout the region. With neither side able to achieve victory the situation would drag on interminably. "Our city is going step by step to ruin and lives only on its savings," Rubens would write in 1627. "There remains not the slightest bit of trade to support it."

Rubens was not only a painter, one whose commercial success was as great as his artistic accomplishments. He was also a political agent, charged by his chief patron, the Infanta Isabella of the Spanish Netherlands, to conduct high-level negotiations with foreign powers in a desperate effort to resolve the stalemate. Isabella was the daughter of Philip II of Spain. With her husband, Albert of Austria, she ruled the Spanish Netherlands as part of the Habsburg empire until Albert's death in 1621; thereafter she served as its de facto governor on behalf of Spain. Her territory was caught in the middle of the struggles in which Spain, France, England, the Dutch Republic, Denmark, the German republics, and other nations all played parts.

In 1616 (coincidentally the same year that he took into his workroom his most talented assistant, Anthony Van Dyck), Rubens was engaged in activities that would bear fruit in both the artistic and the political realms. In that year he began negotiations with Dudley Carleton, the English ambassador to the Dutch Republic, concerning a collection of antiquities in the ambassador's possession. The contact with Carleton would subsequently open doors for Rubens to attempt to arrange terms of peace between Spain and England; by supporting (first tacitly and later, under Charles II, more actively) the Dutch rebels, England, made a peaceful solution to the conflict more difficult, Rubens felt. Peace between England and Spain would help to relieve the pressure on Antwerp in particular, and the Spanish Netherlands in general.

Carleton, who had recently arrived in the Netherlands, wanted to purchase one of Rubens's hunting scenes, but he was short of cash and ended up trading a diamond necklace for a smaller painting than he had hoped for. The necklace was one of many decorative and art objects in his possession. Thanks to his previous position as England's ambassador to Venice (where he had hosted a visiting Inigo Jones), Carleton had been charged by King James's favorite Robert Carr, Earl of Somerset, with putting together a substantial collection of Italian antiquities. James had given his favorite the sizeable country estate of Walter Raleigh. It was not really his to give, but James felt that Raleigh would not have need of it since he had been keeping the aging adventurer imprisoned in the Tower of London since assuming the throne in 1603. Carr intended to transform the estate into a grand villa in the Italian style — a plan that fell apart when he was himself transported to the Tower after his role in the poisoning of Thomas Overbury was exposed.

Carleton was left holding the goods, which were hard to move, literally and figuratively. Over the next two years he negotiated an exchange with Rubens, who finally purchased the lot at the price of eight of his paintings along with a collection of tapestries. Thanks to the rage for his work among the royalty and aristocracy of Europe, Rubens had grown wealthy. He had established himself in a property in Antwerp that he had converted to resemble the fine Italian homes he had known during his residence as a young man in Mantua, with a courtyard in the interior. The property also housed his sizeable workshop, where a crew of assistants helped Rubens crank out work at a high volume. Carleton's collection of sculptures would help to give the property a suitably classical flavor. (Ever the capable businessman, Rubens would pay Carleton the equivalent of about 6,000 florins and later resell the collection to James's subsequent favorite, George Villiers, Duke of Buckingham, for 100,000 florins, an astonishing sum.) The reconstructed Rubens House is now a public museum.

Rubens was working at the time on a large cycle of paintings on the subject of the Roman consul Decius Mus. The paintings would serve as tapestry designs for a wealthy Genoese patron. (Rubens was the descendant of a tapestry manufacturer, and his second wife was the daughter of a tapestry dealer.) In the fourth century BCE Decius Mus fought to put down a Southern Italian revolt against Rome. During the fighting he was visited near Naples by an apparition who prophesied that one of the armies would lose its commander but emerge victorious. Based on that prophesy, Decius Mus decided to place himself in a position where he would be killed in battle, in order to ensure victory.

The Decius Mus series was the first of several epic cycles of images that

Rubens would undertake in his career. He liked to work on a large scale. "I confess that an inborn gift has called me to execute large works rather than little curios," he said. "To each his own way. My talent is of a kind that no undertaking, however great and multiform the object, can overcome my self-confidence." The series was unusual in that Rubens worked in oil on canvas rather than the more traditional medium of tempera on paper that was commonly used for such cartoons, or designs for transfer to other mediums: the tapestry workers must have scratched their heads trying to reproduce the colors of Rubens's oils.

Decius Mus represented the height of heroism, and Rubens expressed this in a series of dynamic compositions that exalt the world of the warrior. He had begun his career in this very tone. His first great work was a portrait commissioned by the Duke of Lerma, Philip III's *valido,* or favorite. His roughly nine-by-seven-foot painting unabashedly glorified martial accomplishment. The duke, impeccably groomed and finely dressed, is pictured astride a magnificent steed while vast armies clash in the background and smoke rises to fill the sky. Framed by tree branches and windswept clouds, the duke is the very image of the noble warrior.

By 1616, however, though still glorifying heroism for his high-class patrons, Rubens was starting to show the violence of battle more graphically. In the painting depicting the death of Decius Mus, the consul's horse rears up majestically. As Decius Mus falls from his horse while receiving the fatal blow he gazes heavenward like the Christian martyrs of Renaissance paintings. But the gore of the battle is brought forward — beneath the consul bright blood flows from the heads and chests of the fallen.

Rubens's international clientele provided a perfect cover for his statework on behalf of the Infanta Isabella. Many of his negotiations were done in secret, using a variety of ciphers and codes. But over the course of his diplomatic endeavors Rubens grew increasingly frustrated with the European powers. On one occasion he gathered together, at some personal risk, representatives from Savoy, England, and, indirectly, the Dutch Republic in the person of Carleton, the English ambassador. The group assembled in Dutch territory and awaited an envoy from Spain, who was delayed, it was said, due to illness. It later emerged that he was in France, having arranged a secret alliance against England between the two traditional enemies. As, in effect, a representative of Spain, Rubens was embarrassed by the secret double game, and the peace party fell apart in recriminations.

The Spaniards were never comfortable with Rubens as a political representative. Philip IV wrote to his aunt, the infanta, "I am displeased at your mixing up a painter in affairs of such importance. You can easily understand how gravely it compromises the dignity of my kingdom, for our prestige must necessarily be lessened if we make so insignificant a person the representative with whom foreign envoys are to discuss affairs of such great importance." Beyond the slight to the painter, the comment suggests that the king was more concerned with keeping up appearances than with finding a remedy for the vast suffering that was engulfing nearly all of Europe. (Ironically, England's representative in the peace talks was also a Netherlander painter, Buckingham's aide-de-camp Balthasar Gerbier.)

Rubens grew increasingly disenchanted with the old values of martial heroism. He was part of a new antiwar attitude that had until recently been largely unthinkable among Europe's educated elite. For historian Theodore K. Rabb, "the decisive turn, the pivot around which all else resolves, was the long moment ... when the Renaissance came to an end." For Rabb one of the "most profound indicators" of this transformation was a revolution in attitudes to warfare, exemplified by Rubens. "It has been argued," Rabb notes, "that Rubens's thoughts turned to peace partly because he had served as a diplomat for the Habsburgs, and also because peace in his eyes meant the achievement of hegemony by his Spanish masters. Neither influence, however, can have generated the real antipathy to armed conflict that now surfaced in his work; it cannot be interpreted as just another means of advancing his patrons' interests. Far more plausible as a motive was his abhorrence for the violence, intensifying all around him."

The new attitude can be seen in *Minerva Protects Pax from Mars,* a painting currently in the National Gallery of Art in Washington, DC. Made for King Charles I and probably executed in England in 1629–1630, the painting is also known as "Peace and War" or "The Allegory of Peace." The central figure is Peace (Pax) who is identified with Ceres, goddess of the earth. Above her head a winged child holds an olive wreath and a caduceus, symbols of peace. The composition is on a diago-

Above: *Equestrian Portrait of the Duke of Lerma,* 1603, by Peter Paul Rubens. Oil on canvas, 283 x 201 cm. Museo del Prado, Madrid.

First overleaf: *Victory and Death of Decius Mus,* 1616–1617, by Peter Paul Rubens. Oil on canvas, 510 x 288 cm. Collection of the Prince of Liechtenstein.

Second overleaf: *Minerva Protects Pax from Mars* ("Peace and War"), 1629–1630, by Peter Paul Rubens. Oil on canvas, 298 x 203 cm. National Gallery, Washington, presented by the Duke of Sutherland, 1828, NG46.

These paintings shows the artist's progression from traditional glorification of militarism to an antiwar point of view.

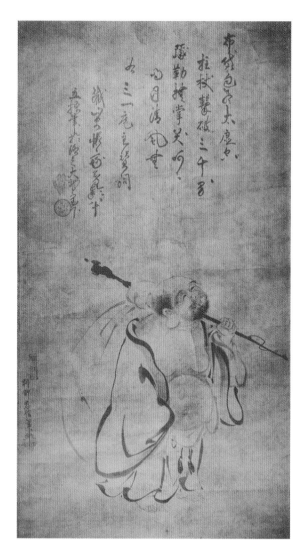

Hotei, 1616, by Kano Takanobu (Japanese, 1571–1618). Japan, Edo period (1615–1868). Hanging scroll; ink and light color on paper, 38 x 70 cm. Metropolitan Museum of Art, funds from various donors, 2006, 2006.115.

Kano Takanobu was the brother of Kano Mitsunobu (p. 164), the leader of the dominant school of Japanese painting. This depiction of the "laughing Buddha" Hotei (Chinese: Budai) reflects the school's interest in Chinese and Buddhist subjects.

nal, with the brightly lit fruits of peace in the left foreground and the dark landscape of war in the upper right. Pax expresses milk into the mouth of an infant Plutus, the god of wealth. A cupid and the young god of marriage, Hymen, welcome children (portraits of Gerbier's family) to a cornucopia of delightful fruits held up by a satyr; a leopard lolls on its back, stretching like a kitten. The satyr and the leopard are associated with Dionysus, and represent earthly pleasures. At the left a bacchante dances while another bears riches. Mars, the god of war, looks wistfully at the idyllic scene as he is driven away from it by a helmeted Minerva and is led on by a wrathful fury.

While some of the symbolism of the allegory may be obscure to modern viewers (Rubens himself reported that he could not always remember the meanings of some of his symbols when viewing his allegorical paintings in later years), the central message could not be clearer: happiness, wealth, prosperity, pleasure, and family life are all the gifts of peace. For Rubens, who had begun his career exalting martial virtues, war was now nothing but a horror.

The kinds of martial images that Rubens lost enthusiasm for were carried to East Asia by merchants and missionaries, usually in the form of engravings but sometimes as colored artworks. Some Japanese artists embraced the Western sculptural approach to form and use of perspective in composition. A large folding screen depicting foreign emperors and kings on horseback is firmly in the European style (the huge figures — the screen is six feet tall — were based on illustrations on a Dutch map). The screen appears to be an oil painting, but testing has revealed that it was made using traditional Japanese pigments. With the persecution of Christian missionaries, expulsion of foreigners, and closing of Japan to most outside contact, such overt adoption of Western styles lost favor, but more subtle influences would continue to play a role in the evolution of Japanese visual art.

During the seemingly tenuous period of peace of the early seventeenth

century, many Japanese were drawn in a different direction. They welcomed the security of understated, cautious works like those by Kano Mitsunobu, the current head of the Kano school of painting.

Painting in Japan as elsewhere required long years of training. Such training usually took the form of lengthy apprenticeship with established masters. Over many years the apprentice would slowly learn the secret methods and techniques of the master's art. These apprenticeships formed patterns of lineage that could be traced back many generations. Some schools of painting, such as the Rimpa school, were nonhereditary, but others were family based. The Kano school was one of these. It traced its painting lineage back for centuries. The earliest Kano painters were influenced by Chinese styles, and particularly by the ink paintings brought to Japan by Zen Buddhist monks. The Kano painters, whose primary patrons were members of the samurai class, gradually began to use more color and stylized effects than their Chinese models.

In the sixteenth century a brilliant Kano master exploded on the scene. Kano Eitoku, who died in 1590, produced bold, dynamic paintings appropriate for the tumultuous, violent time in which he lived. His large, colorful works featured strong, sure lines. At the turn of the seventeenth century, if you thought of Kano painting you thought of Eitoku.

Most family-based schools of art died out within a few generations, since it is difficult to sustain a high artistic level through a single family over a long period of time. For a while it seemed this could be the case with the Kano school, since Eitoku's sons did not rise to his level. Instead, just as the Tokugawa shogunate would establish itself and endure, so the Kano school would turn out to be the most influential and enduring school of painting in Japanese history. It was the closest thing to an official academy of art during Japan's years of warrior rule.

When Eitoku died unexpectedly at the age of forty-eight the school's

Foreign emperors and kings on horseback, 1610–1620. Artist unknown. Four-panel screen, ink, colors, and gold on paper, 462 x 166 cm. Kobe City Museum.

Although the gold foil background of this folding screen derives from the Japanese tradition, the emperors and kings are in a Western artistic style and were more or less copied from a European engraving. From left to right the figures are traditionally identified as Rudolf II of the Holy Roman Empire; an Ottoman sultan, probably Ahmed I; a Muscovite leader; and a Mongolian Tatar.

The large screen was originally part of a set owned by the Tokugawa shogun family. It may have been intended as a primer in world politics: the Habsburgs and Ottomans were warring, and the Muscovites and Tartars also frequently engaged in skirmishes.

A similar screen (discussed on p. 4) is reproduced on this book's endsheets.

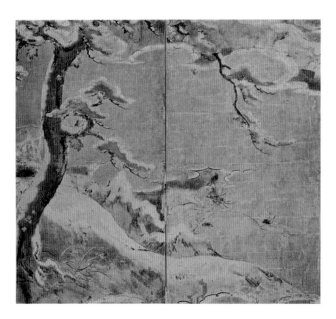

Snowy Pine (detail), early seventeenth century, attrib. to Kano Mitsunobu. Folding screen, one of a pair. Ink and colors on gold-leaf ground. 171 x 154 cm. Honen-in, Kyoto.

Though not the most talented painter in the Kano family (compare this painting to one by his adoptive brother on the opposite page), Kano Mitsunobu deserves credit for managing the Kano family workshop and positioning it for future glory.

The subject of this painting may reflect the prevalence of extreme winters during the Little Ice Age.

prospects did not look promising. Leadership of the family workshop passed to his eldest son, Kano Mitsunobu, who had been designated his father's successor when he was around ten years old. In his twenties at the time of Eitoku's death, he was not yet fully prepared for the responsibility that now fell on him. He is said to have had to do a crash course on Kano techniques, relying on relatives and pupils of the master. He did not have a reputation as a top-level painter. In his youth he was one of several painters who took the name Ukyo. Tradition has it that he was distinguished from the others by being called *heta Ukyo:* "unskilled Ukyo."

Eitoku's second son showed some promise, but he clearly lacked Eitoku's drive. Perhaps for this reason Eitoku adopted one of his pupils, who took the name Kano Sanraku. Artistically, Mitsunobu was overshadowed by his father; his brother Kano Naizen; his nephew Kano Tanyu (who would become one of the greatest Kano painters); his own pupil Kano Koi (who would train Kano Tanyu); his father's adopted son, Kano Sanraku; and Sanraku's adopted son, Sansetsu, among others. All of these painters would help to ensure the continuance of the Kano school, their lineages branching out wider and wider in a pyramidal family tree.

But Mitsunobu was not so inferior a painter as posterity has sometimes made him out to be. Unlike his father, he was a cautious and conservative painter, so he suffered by the comparison. But that was probably exactly the kind of work his age demanded. Not only did he give his patrons what they wanted, he also proved a capable manager. He steered the family atelier through a precarious period and left it stronger than ever.

Family workshops helped to stabilize the system of artistic patronage and production. It was difficult to be an independent artist without a support network. One who succeeded was Iwasa Matabei, who was the artistic equivalent of a *ronin,* or wandering masterless samurai. Iwasa's father, Araki Murashige, had plotted the overthrow of his daimyo. After the revolt failed, Matabei took his mother's name of Iwasa. Though he was trained in the traditions of the Tosa school, which looked to ancient Japan rather than China for models, he seems also to have studied with Kano Mitsunobu's brother, Kano Naizan. He drifted to Edo, where he

hung around the Yoshiwara pleasure quarter and painted its residents. His highly individualistic style, notable for women with oblong heads, plump cheeks, and delicate features (p. 112), is thought to have laid the foundations for the development of *ukiyo-e,* pictures of the "floating world."

Ukiyo-e pictures were popular with commoners, but the warrior elite wanted grand, large-scale paintings that would testify to their wealth and influence. Mitsunobu secured commissions for large paintings to decorate the imperial palace and Osaka Castle even before the death of Eitoku. Hideyoshi called on him to decorate the Nagoya Castle that he had erected as a staging area for his invasion of Korea. He also painted the Shokoku-ji and Kodai-ji temples. He wisely arranged for his talented nephew Tanyu to be tutored by his prize student, Kano Koi. And he began to shift the Kano workshop to the new shogunate capital of Edo (present-day Tokyo).

Mitsunobu's work is more delicate and restrained than his father's. At their best his paintings are subtle, graceful, sinuous, and balanced. Other times they just seem a bit dull, at least by comparison to the Kano masters who preceded and followed him. Nonetheless, Mitsunobu served admirably as a bridge between those greater artists, and he played an essential role in the development of what would come to be the dominant school of Japanese painting.

Nowhere were artists as eclectic, ecumenical, and forward-looking as in the royal Mughal workshops. The Mughal emperor Akbar had been

Peonies, early seventeenth century, by Kano Sanraku. Fusama (sliding doors), Shinden Building, Daikaku-ji Temple, Kyoto.

Kano Sanraku was the adopted son of the great sixteenth-century painter, Kano Eitoku. By adopting his talented pupil Eitoku helped to ensure the continuance of the family workshop. The Kano school would go on to dominate Japanese painting for generations.

keenly interested in art since childhood, and he had assembled a workshop of elite artists at his court. His son Jahangir became a connoisseur of painting. He selectively promoted or dismissed artists from the atelier until its ranks rivaled any group of artists in the world. Jahangir took a keen interest in their activities, and he reported that he was able to identify the painter of a work merely on the basis of its style:

> My liking for painting and my practice in judging it have arrived at such a point that when any work is brought before me, either of deceased artists or those of the present day, without the name being told me, I say on the spur of the moment that it is the work of such and such a man. And if there be a picture containing many portraits, and each face be the work of a different master, I can discover which face is the work of each of them. If any other person has put in the eye and eyebrow of a face, I can perceive whose work the original face is, and who has painted the eye and eyebrows.

Jahangir did not restrict his workshop to Muslims. More than half of his artists were Hindus. He was tolerant of different religious traditions and took an active interest in them — for example, he asked his nobles to acquire copies of the *Razmnama,* a Persian translation of the Mahabharata, in order to expose them to traditional Indian culture (p. 6). His artists illustrated classical Indian works and Hindu epics, and they assimilated influences from other cultures: first from Persia and later from Europe and East Asia.

Thomas Roe, the English ambassador to Jahangir's court, often brought him Western paintings. On one occasion, he obtained a painting that he "esteemed very much, and was for curiositye rare," which he decided would make a good gift for the emperor. Jahangir, Roe says,

> tooke extreme content, showing it to everie man neare him; at last he sent for his cheefe paynter, demanding his opinion. The foole answered he could makes as good, wherat the King turned to me, saying my man sayth he can do the like and as well as this: what say yow? I replyed: I knew the contrarie ... for I know non in Europe but the same master can performe it.

Opposite: Squirrels in a Plane Tree, 1605-1606, by Abul Hasan. Opaque watercolor on paper, 22 x 36 cm. British Library, Johnson Collection, Album 1. 30.

Above: Saint John, after Albrecht Durer, 1600-1601, by Abul Hasan. Opaque watercolor on paper, 5 x 10 cm. Ashmolean Museum, Oxford.

These early works by Mughal painter Abul Hasan reflect the influences of Persian and Western artistic traditions.

Above: Jahangir and Jesus, 1615–1620, by Hashim (Jahangir) and Abul Hasan (Jesus).

Opposite: Jahangir Preferring a Shaykh to Kings, 1615–1618, by Bichitr. Opaque watercolor, ink, and gold on paper, 18 x 25 cm. Freer Gallery of Art, Smithsonian Institution, Purchase, F1942.15a.

In these images the head of the Mughal emperor Jahangir, whose many titles included The Light of Religion, is surrounded by a halo.

The exchange resulted in a wager between the emperor and the ambassador, and the painter went off to copy the painting. He completed several versions the same day. Jahangir summoned Roe:

> At night he sent for mee, being hastie to triumph in his workman, and shewed me six pictures, five made by his man, all pasted on one table, so like that I was by candle light troubled to discerne which was which....

Who was the "cheefe paynter" who directed the production of several copies of Roe's painting? He may have been the atelier manager, and the five copies might have been made by different artists despite Roe's impression that they were all produced "by his man." If they were indeed the work of a single painter, the likeliest candidate is an artist named Abul Hasan. Not only was he well versed in Western painting techniques, he was also highest in the esteem of Jahangir. The emperor had conferred on the painter the title of Nadir-uz Zaman, "Wonder of the Age."

In contrast to much traditional Indian practice, painters in the royal Mughal workshop were recognized as individual artists, who often signed and inscribed their works. As a result we have an artistic record of the production of several prominent painters, although in most cases we have meager biographical detail about their lives. One of the main sources of information is Jahangir's reign diary, the *Jahangirnama,* but he is mainly concerned with commissions and rewards rather than details of the painters' personal lives.

In 1616 Hasan was only seventeen years old but he had already risen to a high rank among the painters of the royal Mughal workshop. His father was a painter named Aqa Riza, who had moved to India from Persia during the reign of Akbar to serve under Jahangir when he was still merely Prince Salim. Jahangir considered Abul Hasan to be a much greater painter than his father, who worked in the stylized Safavid style, with calligraphic lines and flat expanses of color and pattern. There was "no comparison between his work and that of his father," he wrote. "One cannot put them in the same category."

As a boy Hasan mastered his father's Persian style of painting, but he was also exposed to the work of Western artists. At the age of twelve he made a drawing of Saint John copied from an engraving by Albrecht Durer. This early work shows a mastery of shading and volume, combined with a sensitive treatment of face and expression. It would be a remarkable achievement for a twelve-year-old in any context.

In one of the artist's first mature works, *Squirrels in a Plane Tree,* made when he was about seventeen, he reveals the influence of his father's Persian

Dipper and Other Birds, ca. 1620, by Mansur. Ink, opaque watercolor, and gold on paper. Metropolitan Museum of Art, Purchase, Rogers Fund and the Kevorkian Foundation Gift, 1955, 55.121.10.16.

style. The flat gold sky and decorative pattern of gold and green leaves are similar to Safavid painting. The craggy rocks may reflect a Chinese influence passing through Persia. But the trunk of the tree is shaped and rounded, and the man posed to climb it is three-dimensional and naturalistic. The posture and movement of the dozen squirrels in the tree are realistic and must have derived from observation of squirrels in Jahangir's zoo, since European squirrels are not native to India.

Jahangir used his atelier to document the events and personages of his reign, as well as the curious objects and creatures that made their way to his court. At some point he also began documenting his dreams and desires. Abul Hasan was the artist in whom he most confided on such matters. A prime example is his painting of Jahangir shooting an arrow through the decapitated head of Malik Ambar (cover and p. 21), which he painted in 1616. The same year he painted *The Presentation of a Book by Sadi,* in which a thirteenth-century mystical dervish returns to give a gift to Jahangir, while the Ottoman Sultan and Persian Shah are relegated to inferior positions.

A couple of years later he did another painting in which the symbolism is even more obvious. Known as *Jahangir's Dream of the Visit of Shah Abbas* (p. 304), it expressed Jahangir's anxiety over developments on the Persian border. Shah Abbas had seized the fortress of Kandahar, which had been in Mughal possession for the better part of a century. Ostensibly the painting shows the embracing monarchs expressing deep amity. But Jahangir towers over Abbas. A golden halo seems to emanate from his head. His face is molded and well defined, while Abbas's is flat and a bit vague. (Hasan had never seen Abbas and probably relied on Persian representations of him.) He stands on a lion, while the diminutive Abbas stands on a lamb. The lion and lamb lying together are a symbol of peace, but should hostilities erupt it is clear which would be more powerful. The animals lie on a globe that recalls Jahangir's moniker Conqueror of the World, the lion stretching from India to Persia, and the lamb nestled in West Asia. According to an inscription, the painting represents a dream in which Jahangir saw Shah Abbas appear before him in a well of light. It is a masterpiece of political propaganda.

Part of the reason Jahangir was anxious about Abbas was that he was dealing with a rebellion by his son Khurram, the future Shah Jahan. Upon the death of Jahangir in 1627, Abul Hasan made a couple of paintings of the new emperor's enthronement, and then is not heard from again. Perhaps after his years of intimate collaboration with Jahangir he could not adapt to serving his once rebellious son.

It has sometimes been claimed that *Squirrels in a Plane Tree* was a collaboration between Abul Hasan and another painter of the Mughal atelier, named Ustad Mansur ("Ustad" is an honorific meaning "Master"), mainly on the basis of a notation added to the painting in the eighteenth century. Although this is probably untrue, it is understandable. Mansur was the greatest Mughal painter of natural history subjects.

North American Turkey, ca. 1612, by Mansur. Victoria and Albert Museum, IM 135-1921.

It was an area in which Jahangir was deeply interested. A world in motion brought to his court many strange and curious creatures — including the European squirrels — which he invariably directed his painters to document. In 1612, when a large number of birds and animals were brought to his court from Goa, he wrote, "As these animals appeared to me to be very strange, I ... ordered that painters should draw them in the *Jahangir-nama,* so that the amazement that arose from hearing of them might be increased."

Among the birds brought from Goa was an American turkey, which was painted by Mansur. Like Abul Hasan, Mansur ranked high in Jahangir's esteem, and the ruler gave him the title of *Nadir-ul-asr,* "Unique of the Age." "In the art of drawing," he said, Mansur "is unique in his generation." He ranked him together with Abul Hasan, saying, "In the time of my father's reign and my own, these two had no third."

Jahangir was proud of such creatures in his menagerie as flying mice, tailless monkeys, zebras, yaks, cheetahs, West Asian goats, Himalayan pheasants, dodos, ducks, and partridges. He had many of the foreign animals bred

in captivity. When he received a strange animal he typically would record a verbal description of it before having its likeness painted. In 1616 he was presented with an Abyssinian elephant, noting that "Its ears are larger than the elephants of this place, and its trunk and tail are longer." His concern for accuracy and completeness of documentation led to a naturalistic approach to paintings of natural history, of which Mansur was the foremost proponent.

Of the turkeycock he wrote that its body was "larger than a peahen and smaller than a peacock":

> When it is in heat and displays itself, it spreads out its feathers like the peacock and dances about. Its beak and legs are like those of a cock. Its head and neck and the part under the throat are every minute of a different color. When it is in heat it is quite red — one might say it had adorned itself with red coral — and after a while it becomes white in the same places, and it looks like cotton. It sometimes looks of a turquoise color. Like a chameleon it constantly changes color. Two pieces of flesh it has on its head look like the comb of a cock. A strange thing is this, that when it is in heat the aforesaid piece of flesh hangs down to the length of a span from the top of its head like an elephant's trunk, and again when he raises it up it appears on its head like the horn of a rhinoceros, to the extent of two finger-breadths.

Dodo and Other Birds, ca. 1625, probably by Mansur. Hermitage Museum, St. Petersburg.

Surrounding the dodo are, clockwise from upper left: Blue-Crowned Hanging Parrot (*Loriculus galgulus*), native to Southeast Asia; Western Tragopan (*Tragopan melanocephalus*), native to the Himalayas; Painted Sandgrouse (*Pterocles indicus*), native to South Asia; and Bar-Headed Goose (*Anser indicus*), native to Central Asia.

The new globalism was presenting people around the world with a look at aspects of foreign worlds that could seem exceptionally strange — no wonder that it was sometimes difficult to tell truth from fantasy.

Nothing is known of Mansur's life. His depiction of the turkeycock is signed "work of the slave of the court Mansur Nadir-ul-asr": such expressions of deference were common among the court painters. The painting effectively complements Jahangir's description. Mansur scrupulously details the bird's color and markings at the same time that he captures something

of its rather comical swagger. Just as Jahangir confided intimately with Abul Hasan in his dream pictures, so he worked closely with Mansur to document the natural world: he could be regarded not just as a patron but as an active collaborator on much of the artistic production of his workshop.

Mansur places his turkey against a minimalist background. In general his work features strong, lively lines with light fills of color, set against plain backgrounds, sometimes embellished with a few grasses or shrubs to suggest a context. An exception is his painting of a dipper (p. 170), which appears with other birds in a mountain landscape. In this case Jahangir probably wanted to document the setting as well as the bird itself.

He observed it while visiting the Kashmir valley. He was impressed by the abundance of wildflowers there, which he had Mansur document. "The flowers that are seen in the department of Kashmir are beyond all calculation," he enthused. "Those that Nadir-ul-asr has painted number more than a hundred." It was here that he encountered the dipper:

> The waterfall is in the middle of a valley. It descends from a lofty height. There was still ice around it.... In the stream I saw a bird like a *saj*. A saj is black in color with white spots, but this bird was the color of a bulbul with white spots. It dives and remains underwater for a long time, and then it comes back up in a different place. I ordered two or three of these birds to be caught, so that I could see whether they

were waterfowl and were web-footed, or if they had open feet like land birds. Two were caught and brought back. One died immediately, and the other lived for a day. Its feet were not webbed. I ordered Nadir-ul-asr Ustad Mansur to draw its likeness.

Jahangir had brought Mansur with him on his trip, which enabled the artist to see the live bird in action in its natural habitat. No doubt this helped him to capture its lively spirit. The bird perches beside a flowing stream in a rocky landscape, corresponding to Jahangir's written description.

To depict a Mauritius dodo that a merchant had presented to the emperor, Mansur had to study the bird in Jahangir's menagerie. It remains one of the most accurate surviving representations of the live bird, which went extinct later the same century.

Mansur was not a portrait painter — only a small number of surviving portraits are attributable to him. For portraits Jahangir often relied on a painter named Bishandas. It was Bishandas whom Jahangir sent with his embassy to Persia to bring back a true likeness of Shah Abbas so that Jahangir could better understand his counterpart and sometime adversary (p. 292). On his return from Persia Bishandas was rewarded by the emperor with an elephant, a lavish gift for a painter.

An elephant as a symbol of the emperor's magnaminity appears in a painting held within a painting by Bichitr, an artist who combined skills at portraiture and allegory. The painting is held by Bichitr himself in a self-portrait in the painting *Jahangir Preferrring a Shaykh to Kings* (p. 169). Bichitr appears in the lowest position among the figures, wearing a red turban. He looks to be around thirty, which would make him about the same age or a little older than Abul Hasan, but he does not seem to have been a prodigy, since his first paintings only appear around 1615.

Above Bichitr, in the next lowest position, is James I of England, copied from a painting by John de Critz given to Jahangir by Thomas Roe, the English ambassador. Next appears an Ottoman sultan who, unlike James, gazes at Jahangir, who is surrounded by a halo of light. An inscription identifies him as "Light of the Faith." He sits on an hourglass throne, on which Western-style angels are recording a wish for his long life. Jahangir does not return the Turk's look but instead faces a Sufi shaykh. The message is clear that Jahangir values eternal spiritual matters above those of the transitory world. Though charming and effective, the painting is a little more dogmatic and less mysterious and evocative than similar symbolic works by Abul Hasan.

Bichitr's 1615 portrait of Asaf Khan, the influential brother of Nur

Opposite: Asaf Khan, ca. 1615, ascribed to Bichitr. Opaque watercolor on paper, 20 x 27 cm. Minto (A), VA, IM, 27-1925.

Left: Inayat Khan, 1610, attributed to Daulat. Opaque watercolor on paper, 6 x 14 cm. Metropolitan Museum of Art, Purchase, Rogers Fund and the Kevorkian Foundation, 55.121.10.295.

Right: Inayat Khan Dying, ca. 1618, by Balchand. Opaque watercolor on paper, 15 x 12 cm. Bodleian Library, Oxford, Ouseley add. 171 b 4r.

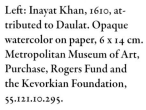

Jahan, who received one of the first copies of the *Nahagirnama,* exemplifies his skill at blending portraiture and allegory (I prefer it to his 1616 portrait of the same subject). Asaf Khan dwarfs the cityscape, warriors and prisoners, and an elephant bearing the Mughal flag behind him. The composition underscores the power of its subject, who holds his hands in a gesture of thanksgiving, as angels look down from the sky. Bichitr does not attempt to bring any of the figures other than Asaf Khan out from the background, but makes them recede by blending them with the surrounding colors. The viewer's eye is drawn to the subject's carefully worked face, which seems to convey an essential quality of his forceful character.

Jahangir saw portraiture as another form of documentation of his world. In the *Jahangirnama* he tells the story of a military official named Inayat Khan, whom Jahangir characterizes as "one of my closest servants and subjects." In a 1610 portrait attributed to Dawlat, Inayat Khan appeared as a robust, dashing figure. But eight years later he presented himself before Jahangir as a wasted man. "In addition to eating opium he also drank wine when he had the chance," Jahangir remarks without irony: opium and wine were the emperor's own vices.

> Little by little he became obsessed with wine, and since he had a weak frame, he drank more than his body could tolerate and was afflicted with diarrhea. While so weakened he was overcome two or three times by something like epileptic fits. By my order Hakim

Rukna treated him, but no matter what he did it was to no avail…. I ordered him brought to me to be given leave to depart. He was put in a palanquin and brought. He looked incredibly weak and thin — "skin and bones…." It was so strange that I ordered the artists to draw his likeness.

Jahangir had the dying man brought to the palace and propped up with pillows. His feet were wrapped in a shawl. The voluminous pillows and coverings contrast with the frailty of the dying man. The geometric planes of strong color, which give the painting a modern feel, again contrast with the man's lack of vitality. He died two days later.

Besides Abul Hasan, Mansur, and Bichitr, Jahangir's large workshop employed many more skilled painters, men with names like Balchand, Basawan, Daulat, Hashim, Manohar, Miskin, and Payag. The names of a few women also appear on the signatures of his workshop's paintings: Nadira Banu, Ruqiya Banu, Sahifa Banu. Through their efforts and Jahangir's own enthusiasm, discrimination, and active collaboration, the visual documentation of his world is one of the most ambitious and comprehensive ever undertaken by any monarch.

Through his father, Aqa Riza, Abul Hasan was influenced by the stylized painting of Safavid Persia. By coincidence, the greatest Persian painter of the late sixteenth and early seventeenth century was also named Aqa Riza, though he is better known as Riza-yi Abbasi. To further confuse matters, a third artist, the shah's favorite calligrapher, was named Ali Riza Abbasi.

"Abassi" was an honorary name given Riza by Shah Abbas to express his appreciation of the artist's talent. But the two did not always have an easy relationship. Like Mansur and other artists of the Mughal workshop, Riza served the emperor and often traveled with him. Appointed director of the royal library in 1598, he led a workshop of painters, calligraphers, bookbinders, gilders, and others, and he executed royal commissions. But Riza had a strong independent streak, which led him to withdraw from court life entirely for several years.

The outlines of his life are told in two brief biographies of him, one published in 1616 and the other about a decade earlier. To these can be added the evidence of his prolific output of paintings, many of which are dated. His career can be broadly divided into three stages: his lively work during the last decades of the sixteenth century, his period of retreat from

Barefoot Youth, ca. 1600, by Riza-yi Abbasi. Opaque water-color on paper. 7 x 14 cm. Art and Hisory Trust, Houston.

This painting exemplifies the "unspoiled sweetness and charm," the "irrestibile optimism, joy and youthful promise" that art historian Sheila Canby describes in Riza's early work. Compare this to Riza's later painting of a Page with Goblet (p. 301), where the youth's expression holds the suggestion of a sly smirk.

the court from about 1603 to 1610, and his more studied and complicated final period until his death in 1635.

The son of the painter Ali Asghar, Riza was probably born sometime in the 1560s, during the long reign (1524–1576) of Abbas's grandfather, Shah Tahmasp. Tahmasp neutralized the long-standing conflict between Anatolian Turkmen and native Iranian Tajiks, partly by assimilating large numbers of Circassians and Georgians (initially introduced as prisoners of war) to act as a buffer and serve as a military unattached to either party.

Tahmasp had studied painting, and he became a great patron of painters, commissioning important manuscripts illustrated by the leading artists of the time. By mid-century, however, he had got serious about religion. In 1555 he issued an Edict of Sincere Repentance, and he renounced sensual pleasures. He prohibited, among other things, gambling, prostitution, and alcohol use. He effectively dissolved his painting workshop. Many of his court artists sought employment in the Mughal court. Others resorted to peddling paintings in bazaars and markets or found nonroyal patrons. The result was a greater emphasis on one-off paintings as opposed to large projects of illustrated manuscripts employing many artists. Much of Riza's work would be in the nature of single paintings.

The ascension of the sixteen-year-old Abbas in 1587 would lead to a great flourishing of the arts. In 1598, having improved the country's political stability, Abbas moved his capital from Qasvin near the Caspian Sea (which was more vulnerable to attack from the Ottomans; the previous capital, Tabriz, had already been lost to them) south to Isfahan, which was essentially a planned city rather than one that had grown organically. Under Abbas's direction the city became internationally recognized as a marvel of bold, ambitious architecture.

Abbas reassembled the royal painting workshop and hired Ali Asghar and his son to participate in it. Riza's earliest dated works are from the early 1590s; they were followed by a great outpouring of paintings throughout the decade, most in the form of single pages (the single-page paintings were often gathered in albums called *muraqqa'*).

Riza specialized in two types of subjects: fashionable young men and women of the court, and older workmen and religious figures. Riza's youthful subjects during his early period come across as dandies, but they retain an air of innocence. Even as late as 1600, his *Barefoot Youth* (p. 177), who is depicted with an unusual, bright color palette, has a fresh and cheerful air. Riza's young men, in contrast to earlier Safavid painting, are fuller, rounder, and more sensuous. Despite his complicated pose the youth seems comfortable and relaxed, if a bit overindulged: he is surrounded by

Opposite top: Scribe, ca. 1600, by Riza-yi Abbasi. Drawing, 7 x 10 cm. British Museum, inv. no. 1920-9-17-0271 (1).

Opposite bottom: Wrestler, ca. 1607–1609, by Riza-yi Abbasi. Drawing on paper, 6 x 14 cm. L. A. Mayer Memorial Institute for Islamic Art, Jerusalem.

Left: Woman Seated in a Tree, 1616, by Riza-yi Abbasi. Opaque watercolors on paper, 10 x 20 cm. Philadelphia Free Library, Lewis Collection, inv. no. p120.

European Giving a Dog a Drink, 1634, by Riza-yi Abbasi. Opaque watercolor on paper, 14 x 19 cm. Detroit Institute of the Arts, inv. no. 58.334.

fruit on a golden dish, a golden ewer, and a golden cup full of wine. He rests on pillows brocaded with an ibex and other images.

Although elements of Riza's paintings are formulaic, he usually succeeds in conveying his subjects' personalities. A portrait of a scribe painted aroud the same time as the barefoot youth captures the calligrapher's intent, direct gaze, which contrasts with his haphazardly wrapped turban.

Around 1603, *Abbasi* ("of Abbas") began to appear in Riza's signature, signaling his favor with the shah. Yet, strangely, this is the very time that Riza chose to absent himself from the court. Was Abbas aware that Riza was thinking of retiring from official painting and seeking to retain him by bestowing the title upon him? Or, as Sheila Canby, who has written extensively about Riza and his context, speculates, was the burden of the honor too great for him? There is no way to know, but according to the biography of him written in 1616, Riza at this time descended into a life spent with "hapless people and libertines."

He became "addicted to watching wrestling and to acquiring competence and instruction in the sport." Wrestlers occupied a low rung of society, and Riza's attraction to them suggests a spirit of rebellion. Wrestlers were often associated with Sufism, which was repressed within the circle of Abbas's court. It is possible that Riza's rebellious libertinage had a religious component. During this period he concentrated more on drawing than painting, and gave up the rich colors of his earlier work. An example is a drawing of a wrestler from 1607–1609. The bare-chested wrestler, depicted with short hair, strong arms, and the suggestion of a pot belly, smiles unaffectedly. His masculinity is strongly asserted.

When Riza returned to court painting in 1610 (perhaps simply because he needed the income) his work no longer retained the innocent spirit of his early period. His paintings were now more studied and calculated, and less spontaneous — "Never again can we become giddy with wonder at his every stroke," says Sheila Canby. The *Page with a Golden Goblet* shown on p. 301 resembles the *Barefoot Youth,* but he now wears the hint of a jaded smirk.

Some of his later paintings could be seen as slyly ironic. In 1616 he painted *Woman Seated in a Tree.* She sits in a provocative pose, with her sash undone and her dress unbuttoned. But the pose emphasizes the mass of her thighs and belly, and it is possible that Riza intends an ironic effect by placing the large woman on a small tree. Nearby are fruits and wine bottles like those that appeared in his early *Barefoot Youth,* and the woman holds what looks like a pear in her hand. The symbolism of the hare depicted on a Chinese blue-and-white porcelain must intend some comment, but its meaning is no longer certain.

Riza's last dated work shows a European reclining on decorated pillows and feeding wine to a small dog — Riza's paintings of Europeans at the end of his life started a vogue for such subjects. The symbolic meaning of the bird, the man, and the heron on the pillows has been lost, and it is hard to be sure how to take the painting's inscription, which reads "Bare from head to toe my passion pursues a foreigner in that nation of youths." But the man on the pillow, who wears a pointed hat, seems to wear a foolish expression, and the overall effect is of a silly but handsome young dandy who might be at once an object of both attraction and amusement.

In contrast to the painters of the royal Mughal court, Riza-yi Abbasi struggled against the confines of court painting. In asserting his independence as an artist and retiring from the court scene for several years he signaled the beginning of the modern artist as an outsider and critic of society.

In China, European influence was strongest in the southern coastal regions where contact with foreigners had been ongoing since the early sixteenth

The Buddhist deity Samantabhadra (Puxian) on a White Elephant, 1602, by Wu Bin. Hanging scroll, ink and colors on paper. H: 65 x 128 cm. Palace Museum, Beijing.

Wu Bin's interest in Buddhism was expressed in paintings such as this, in which the celestial bodhisattva Samantabhadra receives a foreign monk while sitting on a white elephant.

The attendant figures include persons of several ethnicities. Wu Bin, himself a traveler, would have seen foreigners of many types during his childhood in the maritime trade province of Fujian. Buddhism itself was a religion of foreign origin, and the elephant seems to allude to this. The image of the deity surrounded by flowers is also unusual and suggests foreign influence.

Wu Bin modestly describes himself as a "lay Buddhist of Branch Hidden Temple" in his signature inscription.

century. An artist named Wu Bin was born there, and probably saw European engravings and paintings that influenced his use of light and dark
to mold three-dimensional forms, as well as the incorporation of some aspects of Western perspective.

Wu was a professional painter who shared Dong Qichang's fondness
for fantastic forms. But the two artists were not much alike. Dong's landscapes are spacially incoherent—often the components of the painting
cannot be resolved one to another in any plausible way. Instead, the paintings are unifed by brushstrokes and other semi-abstract elements. Wu, on
the other hand, uses the techniques of realism to create scenes that are spacially plausible, if preposterous.

In the last decade of the sixteenth century Wu moved to the old
imperial capital of Nanjing, where he became influenced by Northern
Song dynasty landscapes and worked as a painter for the imperial court.
Northern Song landscapes often captured in a single view one central
image, as opposed to many Chinese paintings that could be read as a
sequence of multiple views, one after another.

After a few years Wu took a leave from his court duties to partake in the
craze for travel, especially to mountainous regions, that took hold in the
late Ming. The craze found its highest literary expression in the travel writings of Xu Xiake (p. 347). Wu journeyed to Sichuan, where he climbed
many famous peaks. Afterward it was said that his paintings became "even
more remarkable than before."

A mountain scene that Wu painted probably around 1616 (opposite left)
is monumental in scale—it is more than ten feet tall. The painting must
have been made for one of the palatial buildings for which the southern
Ming capital was renowned. The contorted spires and twists of the painting
strain skyward, reflecting the late Ming taste for the fantastic. The mountain's verticality is emphasized by the painting's narrow width, less than a
third of its height. Yet halfway up a house perches implacably on a sheer
cliff ledge, while below a boat sails blithely by. The matter-of-factness of the
presentation adds to the painting's disorienting quality. Similarly, in a 1617
painting (opposite right) that is more than seven feet tall, buildings perch
precariously on a ledge while clouds wrap sinuously around spires and dan-
gling, distorted crags, and a waterfall plunges from an astonishing height.

For the Chinese, mountains were spiritual places where the earthly
world met the heavens. Wu's contorted mountainscapes are like the spires
of Western gothic cathedrals, stretching skyward out of spiritual yearning.
Perhaps because of the sheer power of supernatural presence contained in
them, the landscapes can appear dangerous or threatening. Yet boats sail

serenely under the towering peaks, and mountain residents go about their business without apparent concern for their perilous situations.

Wu demonstrates in these paintings what the technical prowess of a professional painter could achieve. Dong Qichang took note, but did not alter his theoretical preference for amateur painting. Instead, he paid Wu what for him was a high compliment: he said that Wu wasn't really a professional painter. He was a lay Buddhist who "painted in his leisure time."

Few of the painters of China's southeast were as original, or as eccentric, as Wu Bin. But most work from the region was informed by the traditions of earlier dynasties, as was Wu's, and like him many painters from the southeast were professionals. Often they worked anonymously, in the early years of the Ming creating many large works for public buildings such as temples and government offices. But by the late Ming patronage for such projects had declined, in part because the influx of vast quantities of silver into the economy through the pan-Pacific trade had enabled a larger number of young men to become educated, take the state examinations, and enter the literati class than in the past. The result was an excess of scholars, some of whom fell back on painting when the traditional bureaucratic positions turned out to be unavailable. The preference for literati painting championed by Dong Qichang and the enlarged pool of educated painters combined to reduce the opportunities for professional painters to produce such public works, and many turned to making smaller paintings for private individuals.

One of these was Zhao Zuo, a painter from Songjiang (now a part of Shanghai), where an atmospheric style of painting that stood in contrast to the hard, intellectual style of Dong Qichang was popular. Zhao was quiet and reserved, and impoverished; consequently, not much is known of his life. He spent his later years living with his family on the shores of a picturesque lake where he admired the scenery. But he did leave an essay on his painting, in which he extolls the virtue of "dynamic force" as a key principle. "If you capture this dynamic force in your mountains," he said, "then even when they coil and twist from top to bottom they will be strung together. If you capture it in your forests, even those that are irregular and diverse from front to back will be clearly readable."

In the cold winter of 1616, during the Little Ice Age, Zhao painted a large vertical scroll of *Piled Snow on Cold Cliffs* (p. 132, 141). To James Cahill the painting is "startling" for its use of Western techniques of "illusionistic chiaroscuro rendering"—Zhao uses contrasts of light and shadow to model three-dimensional forms in a way that was not common in traditional Chinese painting.

Zhao was a friend of Dong Qichang. One of his paintings, which shows similar modeling with light and shadow, bears the seal of Dong Qichang on it. Dong must have been aware of Western art, but he never alluded to it, acknowleged it, or showed overt evidence of having been influenced by it.

Following the riot that destroyed his home and drove him from it, Dong applied himself to painting and also sought to restore his reputation through political advancement. When the Wanli emperor died in 1620 his successor, the Taichang emperor, is said to have remembered his former tutor and summoned Dong back to court. The Taichang emperor reigned only one month, but by 1622 Dong was back in the capital, where he served in a succession of important posts, rising higher than any other artist of the Ming dynasty. But by 1525 he had again succumbed to its poisonous infighting and was impeached on a variety of charges, among them that he was "besotted by calligraphy and painting."

In his seventies Dong once more retired to the south, yet within six years he would again be back in the capital. Finally, in 1636, shortly before the fall of the Ming, he headed south for the last time. His friend and fellow painter Chen Jiru described what happened:

> When Dong returned home from the north he was eighty-one. Brilliant and vigorous, with beard and eyebrows flowing in the wind, he had the air of a far-off immortal.... He suddenly began to cough up phlegm, and not three days later he was dead. The crown of his head was hot, and his limbs were like cotton floss. Was he not what the Buddhist would call "one without pain and suffering, bound by no evil bonds"?

None of his three sons — two of whom "had earned for themselves an unsavory reputation, even before the burning of the Dong estate in 1616," according to scholar C. C. Riely — shared their father's scholarly bent. None passed the official examinations. Nor did Dong's grandchildren distinguish themselves. But his theories would form the standard approach to Chinese painting for centuries of scholars.

Dong and his wife were buried together near the city of Zuchou. The gravesite was honored with memorial arches and a temple. They no longer exist. In 1967, during the Cultural Revolution, the tomb was looted and trashed. The stele containing Dong's epitaph, now lost, was destroyed. But by the end of the twentieth century Dong's fortunes were again on the rise. Scholars from around the world assembled at the Nelson-Atkins Museum in Kansas City, Missouri, to honor Dong and argue about his theory of creative imitation.

4   Witch Hunters and Truth Seekers

On January 1, 1616 — the same date that *The Golden Age Restored* was being performed in the royal banqueting hall at Whitehall, London, and a massive galleon was pulling into the port of Acapulco in New Spain — the astronomer Johannes Kepler wrote a letter to the Senate of Leonberg, a town near the city of Stuttgart in southwest Germany, on behalf of his mother, Katharina, who stood accused of practicing witchcraft. Kepler was an exceptionally learned man, an inspired mathematician who worked out the laws of planetary motion that would lead Newton to formulate the principle of gravity; but his mother, like many women of the time, was illiterate. Now in her seventies, she was an herbalist, like her aunt, who had already been burned at the stake as a witch. While Kepler embodied the worldview of the male literati, whose ideas of the world were codified in written texts, his mother represented the old folk traditions, knowledge of which often resided in women, passed from mother to daughter. With the spread of literacy to a greater range of society, such folk knowledge became increasingly marginalized and demonized, and these women became popular targets of witch hunts. Witchcraft, not particularly gender biased during the medieval period, now became increasingly associated with women, and especially older women.

Kepler's mother's case was a typical one of petty village malice. Her accuser was another old woman, who had fallen ill after being given one of Katharina's herbal infusions. Kepler sought to discredit this woman's testimony and to use his influence at court to protect his mother. He wrote:

> There is a case before you concerning several people accused by the court, based purely on the fanciful rantings of your dear darling housewife and sister, Ursula Reinbold. Everyone knows that until this day, this woman his lived frivolously, and now, by your own account, she has become mentally ill. Caught in the middle of this depressing web of suspicion, my own dear mother, who has lived honorably into her seventieth year, has been accused by you of giving this same crazy person some silly magic potion, which you say caused her insanity....
>
> I want you to know that I will seek the help of my friends and mentors, and that I will gain favors from well-known and respected persons I am acquainted with. I intend to contest this matter and bring to bear the full extent of my powers until it is finally remedied in accordance with the written laws....

Facing page: Astronomical clock, fifteenth century. Palazzo del Capitanio, Padua, Italy.

Throughout the Renaissance and the early modern period, astronomical clocks were in vogue. These ingenious and sophisticated clocks attempted to show the conjunctions of celestial bodies as an aid in casting horoscopes. The first such clock was constructed in Padua in the fourteenth century; a rebuilt version was placed on the tower of the Palazzo del Capitanio in the fifteenth century.

Galileo Galilei would have passed under this clock often during his twelve years on the faculty of the University of Padua. Although today we think of astronomers such as Tycho Brahe, Johannes Kepler, Taqi al-Din, and Galileo as scientists, they were more broadly considered in their day to be "stargazers." Employed in this capacity by their royal and aristocratic patrons, they combined scientific observations and mathematical calculations with astrological calendars and predictions.

Johannes Kepler, copy of an original oil painting, 1610.

The artist Maira Kalman, in an image based on this portrait by an unknown painter, noted that "Kepler wrote about celestial harmony, but domestic harmony eluded him. He wrote in his diary 'My wife is fat, confused and simpleminded.'" (Kalman's work cannot be reproduced here because permission requests went unanswered.)

Despite Kepler's difficult familial relations, he defended his mother vigorously when she was accused of witchcraft.

Kepler's family background and childhood situation gave little hint that he would one day acquire the kind of clout this letter implies. His father, Heinrich, was a mercenary soldier who was by all accounts a bitter and violent man; Kepler described him as "vicious, inflexible, quarrelsome, and doomed." When he was home he beat his wife and children, and he once tried to sell Johannes's brother — his namesake, Heinrich — into slavery. (The younger Heinrich was a teenager at the time, so perhaps he had cause.) But he was usually off fighting some war, for whichever side offered the better price. When Kepler was a young child his mother left him in the care of his grandparents while she journeyed to the Netherlands — it cannot have been an easy trip for a woman presumably traveling alone. She was searching for her husband, who was fighting for the Duke of Alba of Catholic Spain. But ultimately she could not succeed in holding him within the circle of the family, and he drifted off to parts unknown, or perhaps was killed in battle; all contact with him was lost.

Born Katharina Guldensmann, Kepler's mother was the daughter of an innkeeper (her husband would also make a brief attempt at running a tavern in between his mercenary excursions). In a private document, at once narcissistic and self-excoriating as was typical of him, that Kepler wrote in his mid-twenties, he described himself and his family. His mother, he said, was "small, thin, swarthy, gossiping, and quarrelsome, of a bad disposition" (from this description she seems to have been the family member whom Kepler himself most resembled, in appearance at least, and perhaps in personality). She had been raised by the aunt who would later be burned as a witch. In Kepler's birthplace, a town of some two hundred families, thirty-eight witches were burned between 1615 and 1629. In nearby Leonberg, where his mother now lived, six witches were executed in the year that she was accused.

Katharina was nearly among them. Her trial, which would drag on until 1621, six months before her death, was among the longest in the history of the witch hunts, which reached their peak between the 1580s and the

1630s — the span of Kepler's life. Only her son's influence — along with her own stubborn refusal to confess — seems to have saved her (most of the accused confessed under torture, but Kepler's success in preventing her from being tortured enabled her to hold firm).

Katharina and Ursula Reinbold, the wife of a glazier, had been companions, but they had a falling out. On one occasion, Ursula alleged, she had fallen ill after Katharina had given her a "potion." She blamed Katharina, though others whispered that her ailments were the result of a long-ago abortion, from the time when, it was said, she had worked as a prostitute. But the Reinholds had connections with the local magistrate, and Ursula's charges against Katharina were soon acted upon. Then more witnesses came forward to testify that they too had fallen ill after accepting a drink from the old woman; that she had caused the deaths of their children merely by touching them; that she took wild midnight rides on neighbors' livestock; that cattle and pigs fell ill in her presence, or began to kick and tried to climb walls; that people merely passing her house would feel sudden sharp pains in their arms and legs; that she tried to seduce younger women to follow her devilish arts; that she questioned the idea of heaven, claiming that life terminated at death; that she had been known to pass through locked doors; that she attempted to make a drinking vessel out of her own father's skull (this one was true); and many other incriminating facts.

Kepler himself had inadvertently appeared to incriminate his mother through a story he had written called *The Dream* (Somnium). The story, sometimes called the first science fiction based on something resembling modern science, imagined a trip to the moon. Kepler had drafted an early version during his student days at Tübingen University. He had not yet seen the work through to publication, but versions of it had circulated in manuscript. In the story a student is banished by his mother, a witch, to Denmark, where he studies with the Danish astronomer Tycho Brahe (for whom Kepler himself had been an assistant). On his return she reveals that she learned the arts of witchcraft from a demon who instructed her how to travel between the earth and the moon at times of a lunar eclipse. The story began as an attempt to imagine how the universe would look from another celestial body, but, under the circumstances, the portrayal of the Kepler-like protagonist's mother as a witch cut a little close to home.

In the early seventeenth century, before the heavens had been polluted by all the lights of modern technology, the stars and the planets were a more intimate part of daily life than they are today, when some people cannot even say what phase the moon is in — unthinkable ignorance by

Opposite page: Model of the "Cosmic Cup," by Johannes Kepler, from *The Cosmographic Mystery,* 1596.

On July 9, 1595, the twenty-three-year-old math teacher Johannes Kepler had a eureka moment while diagraming a problem on the blackboard for his small, bored, and restless class. In his off hours Kepler had been working on a grand aspiration: fathoming the divine order of the universe.

What determined the orbits of the six planets, Kepler wondered. (Saturn was the most distant planet then known.) He felt certain that there must be some significant relation among the sizes of the orbits. "But I could find no order either in the numerical proportions," he lamented, "or in the deviations for such proportions." Now, in the middle of his class, it struck him: he was working in two dimensions and needed to be working in three — the orbits must be related not to the proportions of flat forms but to the five Platonic solids.

It seemed to make sense. Why were there only six planets "and not twenty or a hundred," Kepler asked. It had been known since ancient times that, while an infinite number of regular polygons can be constructed in two dimensions, there were only five kinds of perfect solids in which each side is identical to all the others (they are the tetrahedron or pyramid, the cube, the octahedron, the

(continued on facing page)

earlier standards. When Kepler was six, not long after his father abandoned the family for the final time, his mother led him to "a high place" to observe a famous astronomical phenomenon, the Great Comet of 1577; at age nine he was called outdoors to witness a lunar eclipse. These incidents suggest that his mother wanted to initiate him in the realm of heavenly mysteries; if so, the lesson took. Kepler, whom Carl Sagan called "the first astrophysicist and the last scientific astrologer," remained something of a mystic throughout his career. From his first major astronomical work, *The Cosmographic Mystery,* through the massive *Harmony of the World,* on which he was working in 1616, his writings chart an indefatigable, indeed almost a desperate, search for evidence of God's divine plan in the physical world, and especially in the heavens. "The diversity of the phenomena of nature is so great, and the treasures hidden in the heavens so rich," he wrote, "precisely in order that the human mind shall never be lacking in fresh nourishment." This quest to fathom the divine plan made him thirst for accurate astronomical data.

Today Kepler, despite his mystical leanings, has been claimed by science, and he occupies a prominent position in the pantheon of figures in the "scientific revolution" of the Renaissance and early modern period. His signal accomplishment, from the standpoint of science history, was his three laws of planetary motion: in brief, planets follow elliptical orbits around the sun, they move more rapidly when they are closer to the sun (technically, the radius vector of their orbits covers equal areas in equal times), and the square of their orbital periods is proportional to the cube of their mean distance from the sun. The first two laws appeared in *New Astronomy* in 1609, the third in *The Harmony of the World,* which was published in 1618. The discovery of these laws was doubly remarkable since Kepler did not have calculus as part of his mathematical arsenal (in fact, he didn't even have decimals) and had to derive his results by arduous trial and error, using traditional geometry.

He had achieved these results by working from data compiled by the Danish astronomer Tycho Brahe, whom he served as an assistant at Prague. Tycho had taken a position there as imperial astronomer to the eccentric Bohemian king Rudolf II, the Austrian Habsburg emperor. Rudolf had moved his court to Prague from Vienna in in 1583, and he had become a great supporter not only of science but of the arts as well; he was also deeply interested in the occult and the arcane. Some say Rudolf was mad, others that he was just deeply melancholic; certainly he was not as disturbed as his son Don Giulio Cesare, who dismembered his mistress and flung the parts out the windows of Frumlow Castle. Rudolf ruled what was called the Holy Roman Empire but was really a loose confederation of cities, duchies, and principalities mainly located in modern Austria, Germany, and central Europe. (Control of the eastern Habsburg lands had gradually ceded to Rudolf's grandfather, Ferdinand I, from his brother Charles V of Spain in the first half of the sixteenth century, and the two branches had become became effectively autonomous.) The political and religious strains of the early seventeenth century brought the two astronomers together. Tycho had been forced to abandon his home, where he had built the most elaborate astronomical observatory up to that time, located on the island of Hven in the Oresund strait between the Swedish region of Scania and Danish Zealand. (Historically a part of Denmark, the island has been part of Sweden since the second half of the seventeenth century.) The observatory, which Tycho called Uraniborg, doubled as a research institute, housing some hundred students, scholars, and workers. King Freder-

(continued from facing page)

dodecahedron, and the icosahedron). The five solids, he suddenly realized, would fit (more or less) in the intervals between the orbits of the six planets.

This revelation was the guiding inspiration of Kepler's life. All his subsequent astronomical work derived from it. It was, unfortunately, wrong. Kepler's own later work with Tycho Brahe's data proved this, but he never completely abandoned the notion that he was on the verge of decoding God's master plan. "Seldom in history," said the historian of science Owen Gingerich, "has so wrong a book been so seminal in directing the future course of science."

Young Kepler was so taken with his revelation that through sheer enthusiam he managed to convince Frederick, Duke of Wuerttemberg, to construct his model of the universe in the form of a drinking cup. It would be "a true and genuine likeness of the world and model of the creation." Each part, he advised, should be made by a different metal worker, so that the cosmic secret would not leak out. The solids, each representing a planet, would be cut with different stones: diamonds for Saturn, jacinth for Jupiter, and so on. The cup would serve various beverages: Mercury would be brandy, Mars would be Vermouth, Jupiter a white wine. The project dragged on for several years before petering out, as the royal metal workers proved unequal, finally, to the task of replicating God's design for the universe.

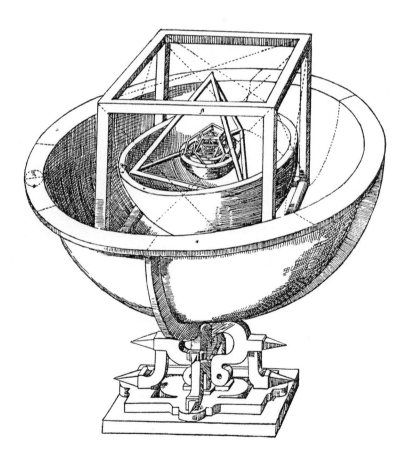

Rudolf II, Holy Roman Emperor, as Vertumnus, the Roman God of the Seasons, about 1590, by Giuseppe Arcimboldo. Oil on panel, 57 x 70 cm. *Skokloster Castle, Sweden.*

Tycho Brahe and Johannes Kepler each served as imperial mathematician to Rudolf II of Bavaria. Rudolf, renowned as a patron of the arts and the occult sciences, was also famous for such eccentricities as withdrawing from contact with his court for weeks on end and speaking at an inaudible volume. This portrait of him by Giuseppe Arcimboldo was among his favorites. It was acquired by Sweden when the Swedish army sacked Prague during the Thirty Years War.

ick II of Denmark (whose daughter Anne would marry James and become queen of England and Scotland) had been so pleased with Tycho's international fame that he had supported him with an amount equal to a full percent of the country's total wealth, but after Frederick's death in 1588, the situation changed dramatically. The new king, Christian IV, wanted to reduce the political power of the small but influential Danish aristocratic elite of which Tycho was a part; he seems also to have held some personal animus against Tycho. Tycho was forced to find a new location for his observation and a new patron; this turned out to be Rudolf of Bohemia.

At about the same time, Kepler too had to flee from his home. He had been living in Gratz, in Eastern Austria, where he was employed as a teacher of mathematics at subsistence pay. (He was not an exceptional teacher. His mind tended to wander. In his first year a few students signed up for mathematics; in his second year not a single one took the course.) A crackdown on Protestants in the region forced him to look for a new situation, as he refused to renounce Lutheranism and convert to Catholicism. A similar stubbornness later in his life, when he rejected the concept of "ubiquity" — the idea that God's *body* is ubiquitous in the world and not just his spirit, as Kepler held — caused him to be excommunicated from the Lutheran church. From the distance of the twenty-first century it can be difficult to understand how such distinctions could be so important as to expel a person who subscribed to all of the other official church doctrines from its community, or why it was so important to Kepler to maintain this position despite the serious consequences, but within a few years, in the Thirty Years War, a great many people would die for just such fine distinctions (ironically, the Lutheran church itself would abandon the doctrine of ubiquity within a few years).

Kepler and Tycho had corresponded, and the result was his moving to Prague to serve as Tycho's assistant. The two were an odd couple. Tycho was aristocratic, rich, outgoing, and robust. He loved banquets and celebrations; Danes at this time had a reputation as the heaviest drinkers in Europe and Tycho was no exception. (He had been raised by an uncle who had kidnapped him as a young boy from his parents; the uncle died of pneumonia after fishing the drunken King Frederick out of the icy Copenhagen waters into which he had toppled.) Kepler, on the other hand, could barely tolerate alcohol because of his perpetual poor health. Something of a tortured soul, he was solitary and inward-looking, and he shrank from social situations. Secretly believing himself the better astronomer, Kepler resented Tycho's wealth and popularity. He also coveted Tycho's data, which he needed to figure out why the planetary orbits refused to properly conform to his theories, but Tycho was not ready to share the information in more than a limited way. He had previously had his work stolen — a man calling himself Ursus ("Bear") had obtained some of his work and passed it off as his own; in fact, this is the man Tycho had now replaced as Rudolf's royal astronomer.

Brahe was a flamboyant figure, who combined his astronomical observations with alchemical experiments. Having lost part of his nose in a duel, he wore a prosthetic metal one. He is said to have kept a pet moose that died when it got drunk on beer and fell down the stairs. Among his household was a dwarf who was supposed to be clairvoyant: he would make portentous pronouncements from a position underneath the dining table during parties. Despite his personal eccentricities Tycho had compiled decades of data from his celestial observations that were far more meticulous and precise than anything previously available. His elevation of observation over speculation was one of the key developments leading to the modern concept of inductive scientific investigation. Kepler, though appreciative of the benefit of accurate data, was less capable of obtaining it directly. A bout of smallpox in childhood had left him frail and sickly, with a severe visual handicap: he was short-sighted and had double vision in one eye. Nor did he have the means to construct a large observatory like Tycho's Uraniborg. So he depended on Tycho for the data he needed to elaborate his theories of celestial harmony. How far would he go to obtain that data? In an odd echo of the case against his mother, Kepler was accused, nearly four hundred years after the fact, in a 2004 book by Joshua and Anne-Lee Gilder, of poisoning his mentor.

Traditionally, Tycho was said to have died of bladder failure after a banquet, because etiquette required him not to leave the table in the presence of royalty. Even today some Czechs who need to leave the table for a bathroom break may say "Excuse me, please. I don't want to end up like Tycho Brahe." This explanation never made much sense: Tycho was completely at ease with royalty and could have found some means of handling the situation. The Gilders' attempt to build a case against Kepler was based on then-recent forensic analysis of Tycho Brahe's hair that suggested he had ingested a potent dose of mercury shortly before his sudden, unexpected death in Prague in 1601. From this they deduce that he was murdered, and they go on to paint Kepler as a sociopath who would stop at nothing to obtain Tycho's data. With the case gone more than four hundred years cold, Kepler, like a number of others, cannot be ruled out as a suspect in the murder, if there was one. But the Guilders' case is speculative in the

Tycho Brahe, 19th century engraving by Johann-Leonhard Appold (1809–1858) after portraits by Jacob de Gheyn (1565–1629).

Tycho's prosthetic nose is evident in this portrait.

extreme. The mercury could have been administered as a form of euthanasia, or it could have been taken inadvertently. Mercury was used to treat various diseases, and an accidental overdose is a possibility championed by, among others, an archaeologist who exhumed Tycho's remains and a historian of science at Johns Hopkins University. The mercury could have been taken by Tycho himself or administered by his wife or any number of people other than Kepler.

A Danish scholar, Peter Andersen, has proposed that Tycho was killed by a visiting cousin in a plot concocted by the Danish king Christian IV. (Contentious cousins bedeviled Tycho — it was another cousin who had removed the bridge of his nose in a duel. Four more of his cousins died in other duels, one killed by yet another cousin.) This particular cousin arrived in Prague from Denmark not long before the alleged murder, and Andersen says his diaries tend to implicate him. He also suggests that Christian resented Tycho for having had an affair with his mother, Queen Sophie. And, to add a bizarre Oedipal complication to the theory, he goes on to suggest that Christian could have been Tycho's son, and he has called for DNA testing of the king's remains to test this theory.

Finally, the conclusion reached by the forensic analysis has itself been challenged by a professor of pharmacy and medicine at the University of Toronto. This point at least should soon be settled. In November 2010 Tycho's body was once again exhumed, and new tests were made; the results of those tests are unknown at this writing — perhaps they will shed some light on the Danish astronomer's death, although whether he was murdered and, if so, by whom, will almost certainly remain a mystery.

Kepler may not have been a murderer, but he was in many respects an unpleasant personality. Despite his talents he suffered from feelings of inadequacy, which made him by turns resentful, suspicious, calculating, fawning, and obsequious; he was opportunistic, duplicitous, and deceitful. As a young man he kept an enemies list, on which it seemed nearly everyone he associated with appeared — he never forgot slights but would not hesitate to shower praise on the offending party when it was beneficial to him to do so (while criticizing him behind his back). His correspondence with Tycho is marked by alternating fits of rage and cringing apologies. He did not believe in washing and bathing, and perhaps as a result complained constantly about boils and sores, as well as a variety of other ailments and afflictions; sitting was painful for him, so that he would often walk in preference to riding a horse. In a horoscope he cast for himself as a young man he compared himself to an annoying little dog that imitates the behavior of others, fawns on its masters but snaps at everyone else, and snarls when things are taken from it; like a dog, he liked to gnaw on bones and hard dry bread. "He is malicious," wrote Kepler of himself, "and bites people with his sarcasms."

And yet, he was more generous with the results of his work than were Tycho or Galileo with theirs. He would not bend his religious principles, even when faced with excommunication. He was inspired by beauty and motivated by the desire to understand the workings of God. He was relentless in pursuing a problem to its final solution. He combined brilliant intuition with a willingness for inexhaustible labor when needed.

When the published version of *The Cosmographic Mystery* appeared, Kepler was still convinced that his connection of the planetary orbits to the five regular solids was a fundamental breakthrough toward discovering God's plan for the universe. With great enthusiasm he mailed copies to all of the influential people he could think of who had an interest in astronomical topics or might assist him in his career, but the results of these mailings would be disappointing. Still, among the recipients was a thirty-three-year-old professor of mathematics at the University of Padua, who wrote back to confess that he too was a Copernican, subscribing to the radical notion that the earth orbited around the sun. But he was afraid, he said, to state that belief publicly. Kepler responded by urging him to speak out, but Galileo did not acknowledge this second letter — in fact, he would not be in touch with Kepler again for thirteen years. The reason, according to Albert Einstein, was vanity, which he considered a failing of many great scientists. "It has always hurt me to think," he wrote in a letter to a friend, "that Galileo did not acknowledge the work of Kepler."

Galileo was the son of a musician, Vicenzo Galilei, who was an early advocate of what is called "equal temperament" in music theory, in which octaves or other intervals are divided into mathematically equal steps. This idea was in the air, as it was championed around the same time by Zhu Zaiyu in China and Simon Stevin in Flanders; wherever it originated, it may have spread through East-West trade channels. Kepler took Galileo's father's book, *The Dialogue on Ancient and Modern Music,* with him in 1616 when he traveled to assist his mother's defense in her witchcraft case. In questioning traditional music theory, Vincenzo Galilei had made experiments with strings of different lengths to determine the mathematical relations among notes of varying pitch. In writing about this he said, "It appears to me that they who in proof of anything rely simply on the weight of authority, without adducing any argument in support of it, act very absurdly. I, on the contrary, wish to raise questions freely ... as becomes those who are truly in search of the truth." Rejection of authority in favor of empirical research would likewise be the hallmark of Galileo's scientific methodology. Of course, experimentation in itself was nothing spectacularly new, and to yield really innovative results it needed to be combined with thinking beyond the bounds of convention.

Galileo's mother, like Kepler's, was a source of aggravation. Galileo had taken a Venetian woman as his mistress, with whom he had three children. (One of these, Virginia, who took the apropos name Sister Maria Celeste when she entered a convent in 1616, would be a particular solace to him in his later life. Her birth, in 1600, had been announced in the parish registry as "Virginia, daughter of Marina of Venice, born of fornication.") His mother, who seems to have been difficult and disagreeable, disapproved of this relationship, and her visits to Padua from Galileo's childhood home of Florence (where the family had moved from Pisa when Galileo was ten) were known to degenerate into shrieking bouts of hair pulling.

As a student at the University of Pisa Galileo developed a reputation for questioning authority and contradicting his professors. The famous demonstration of dropping balls of different sizes from the Leaning Tower began with his questioning of the accepted idea, based on Aristotle, that the speed of falling bodies was proportional to their sizes. (Many scholars are convinced this incident is apocryphal since there is no contemporaneous documentation of it. It first appears in a biography of Galileo written by a young man who lived and studied with him in his old age. Still, the showy demonstration fits Galileo's style. His biographer may well have heard the story from him, and Galileo's own writings do contain suggestive passages on the topic of dropped objects.) Galileo may have questioned accepted wisdom about falling bodies after observing that hailstones of different sizes reach the ground around the same time: if larger bodies fell faster, shouldn't hail descend in waves of diminishing sizes?

Observation was the essence of Galileo's approach to science. His investigation of the rate of motion of falling bodies was typical. The conventional belief (odd as it seems today) was that acceleration was not at all a continuous process but rather a series of successive, uniform rates of speed, each faster than the one before — not like a continuous incline but like the series of steps of a stairway. Initially Galileo worked from that assumption, but the evidence soon led him to abandon it. To discover the truth he constructed a gently sloping ramp down which he allowed a ball to roll. Using musical beats as a timing device, he marked the position of the ball at regular intervals. He found that speed increased by odd numbers — as 1, 3, 5, 7 — and therefore distance from the beginning point by the sequence 1, 4, 9, 16 ($1+3=4$, $4+5=9$, $9+7=16$) with

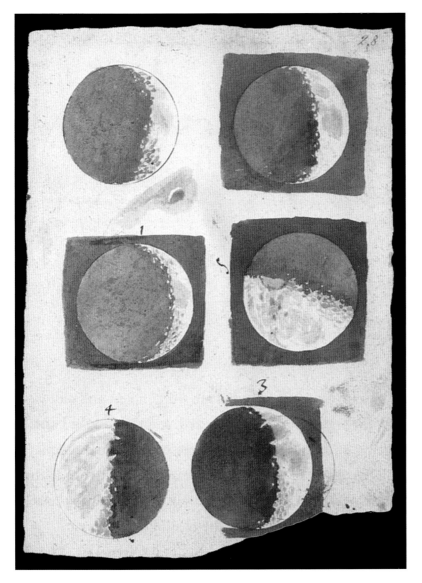

Phases of the Moon, about 1610, probably by Galileo Galilei. Watercolor or sepia ink on paper.

Two developments in the early seventeenth century enabled the gathering of highly accurate astronomical data. The first was Danish astronomer Tycho Brahe's construction of elaborate observatories and his systematic accumulation of detailed data from them. The other was Galileo's refinements of the technology of the telescope and the celestial discoveries they enabled. This depiction of the phases of the moon was pasted into a printing of *The Starry Messenger* (1610), Galileo's report on his celestial discoveries based on observations by telescope; the book caused a sensation.

Galileo was not only a scientist but also an accomplished musician and artist, and a friend of artists. It is generally supposed (though on scant evidence) that this is his own work, perhaps the original images that served as models for some of the engravings in *The Starry Messenger.*

Galileo's depictions of the moon might seem beautiful today, but they struck some at the time as an affront: surely God's heavenly objects must be perfect, they thought, not pocked and roughened with craters and protuberances like some ordinary rock of the earthly realm.

each successive beat. From this he derived the law of falling bodies, that distances from rest are as the square of the elapsed times (1, 4, 9, 16 = $1^2, 2^2, 3^2, 4^2$).

Unlike Kepler, Galileo was not trying to lay bare God's perfect plan for the universe. He did not expect observation to yield flawless results, because he knew that the conditions of experimentation were almost never ideal, measurement was accurate only to a certain level of precision, and data could be subtly corrupted by any number of real-world factors. He merely wanted scientific theory to generally correspond with actual observation. Because of this basic difference in their attitudes, Galileo was not sympathetic to some of the directions of Kepler's work.

Kepler had begun to recognize that astronomical bodies exert forces on each other. He posited a force of the earth that governs the orbit of the moon and a force of the sun that governs the orbits of the planets, in this way explaining their varying velocities by their proximity to the sun in elliptical orbits (he thought the force might be a kind of magnetism; in fact, it is gravitation). Galileo thought that all of this was hokum. He rejected the notion that heavenly bodies can influence each other, or even terrestrial phenomena such as tides, from afar. To Galileo such notions smacked of the occult. "Among the great people discussing this phenomenon of nature," he wrote, "the one who surprises me the most is Kepler, who, possessing a free and sharp mind and being quite familiar with the motions ascribed to the earth, admits a fundamental power of the moon on water, hidden properties, and such similar childishness." Galileo's skepticism is understandable but, as it turns out, Kepler was right.

Galileo was charismatic, and he won a following at Padua as a brilliant and inspiring lecturer, though he also ruffled feathers among the senior faculty. Unlike Kepler, Galileo was supremely confident and self-assured — smug and arrogant, his enemies would say. But that did not mean he was as rash and imprudent as Giordano Bruno, who had been burned at the stake in the Campo dei Fiori in Rome in February 1600 for holding heretical beliefs. (The inquisitor for Bruno's trial was Cardinal Bellarmine, who would later play a similar role in Galileo's trial; Bellarmine was canonized in 1930.) Bruno was a pantheist and a Copernican. In his audacious, inspired vision of an infinite universe, "there are innumerable suns, and an infinite number of earths revolve around these suns, just as the seven we can observe revolve around this sun that is close to us." Galileo wasn't looking for trouble, but his caustic and condescending attitude to his detractors helped fan its fires.

His life was changed by a technological breakthrough. Around 1608, a team of Dutch spectacle makers ground lenses and arranged them in a tube in such a way that they magnified objects viewed. These first devices magnified only by a power of about three or four, but this was enough to cause a good deal of excitement. In London, Thomas Harriot bought one of the instruments and, inspired by an appearance of Halley's comet in 1607, trained it on the moon; he would be the first person to produce a drawing from astronomical observation through a telescope. He was a member of the so-called School of Night, a group of reputedly atheistic freethinkers centered around Walter Raleigh. Harriot served as Raleigh's mathematics tutor and accountant, and he advised him on shipbuilding and such theoretical questions as the most efficient way to stack cannonballs. As a young man he traveled to Roanoke Island on an expedition or-

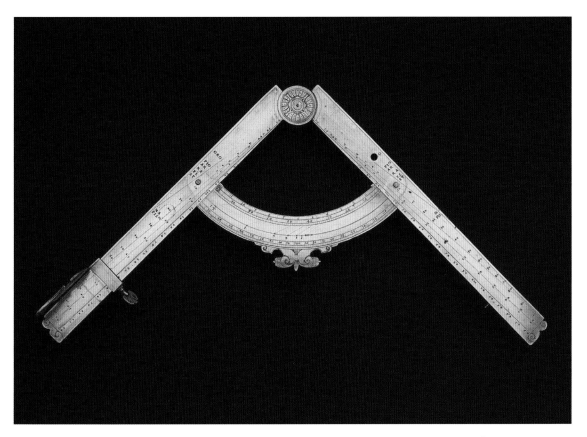

Calculating Device, about 1606, by Galileo Galilei. Brass, 26 x 36 cm. © *Museo Galileo,* inv. 2430.

ganized by Raleigh and reportedly learned the Algonquian language. He corresponded with Kepler, but his mathematical and astronomical discoveries did not become widely known because of his failure to publish.

A former pupil of Galileo's sent word to Venice about the new instrument, and Galileo immediately realized its military potential. Then, in August 1609, a Dutchman showed up in Padua proposing to sell the device to the doge of Venice. This Galileo managed to prevent with some fast talking, downplaying the Dutchman's product and assuring the Venetians that he could produce a much better version. Having bought a little time, he returned to Padua and succeeded in producing a telescope in only a day (he said), a remarkable feat of reverse engineering. More important, he continued to refine the instrument until he had achieved a magnification around the equivalent of common modern binoculars; later he would improve the optics even further. His telescope was a triumph not only of his skill at applied science but also of the glasswork and craftsmanship of the artisans of the Veneto.

Measurement and calculation were the essence of Galileo's approach to science. Near the turn of the century, pressed by debts — his sister's dowry, his brother's wedding — Galileo turned to the manufacture of a sort of super slide rule /compass of his invention, produced in collaboration with a toolmaker trained at the Arsenale in Venice. It was intially marketed as an aid to military caculations and later expanded to a variety of other uses. He further profited by offering instruction in the device's use.

Galileo demonstrated his leather-tooled, yard-long telescope — which he called a "perspicillium" — to the doge and his counselors, showing how approaching ships could be detected hours before they could be seen by the naked eye. The demonstration was a resounding success, and Galileo was rewarded with a doubled salary, a handsome bonus, and a lifetime appointment at the University of Padua. He had it made.

Like Harriot, Galileo began to turn his telescopic attentions skyward. Among his discoveries were moons orbiting Jupiter, which could be identified by the way they changed their positions from day to day relative to the planet. With unprecedented clarity this discovery gave the lie to the conventional notion that the universe was a sort of giant snow globe in which celestial objects were fixed to a crystal sphere and could not move independently. The book that he published in 1610 about his observations, *The Starry Messenger*, made him an international celebrity, though a controversial one. Kepler published an article of support and later obtained a telescope with which he was able to confirm the Jupiter observations. Galileo was hailed as a discoverer comparable to Columbus and Magellan. The Scottish poet Thomas Seggett, for example, wrote:

> Columbus gave man lands to conquer by bloodshed,
> Galileo new worlds harmful to none.
> Which is better?

But to academic philosophers whose livelihood depended on teaching the traditional Aristotelian dogma, Galileo's discoveries did not seem harmless. They claimed the moons and other celestial discoveries were optical illusions created by the telescope itself. They labeled Galileo a charlatan, an attention-seeking fraud. Some looked through his telescope but denied seeing the objects Galileo said were there. Others, like Cesare Cremonini, the leader of the Aristotelian faction at Padua, and Giulio Libri, a professor of philosophy at Pisa, simply refused to look through the glass at all. Christopher Clavius, a Jesuit mathematician in Rome, said that the apparent roughness of the moon must be an optical illusion — perhaps its apparent unevenness was smoothed over by a perfect transparent crystal.

Then the philosophers went further. Not only was Galileo's radical new astronomy erroneous and fraudulent, they began to claim, but it was also heretical. If the earth was not unique, how could the people on other planets have descended from Adam and Eve? What would be the meaning of the Flood? In Florence this faction was led by a man named Ludovico delle Colombe. Colombe means "dove," so Galileo began to dismiss his

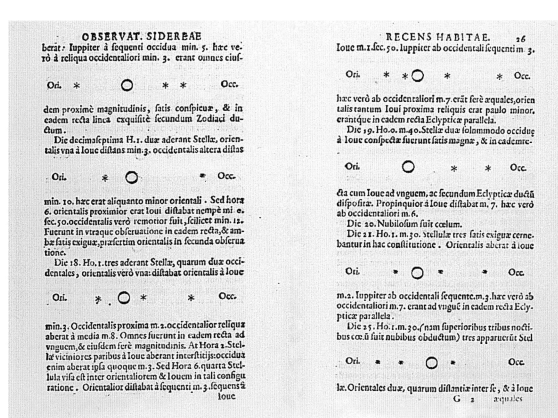

Pages from *The Starry Messenger*, 1610, by Galileo Galilei.

Galileo's telescopic observations of the movements of the moons of Jupiter made *The Starry Messenger* a sensation. The diagrams on these pages from the book chart the changing positions of the moons relative to the planet. These observations proved that some celestial objects orbited others: the heavens were not permanently affixed to a vast celestial sphere revolving day by day about the earth.

critics by referring to them as the Pigeon League. He wasn't concerned, he said: "Since the malicious league is few in number I laugh at it."

But an academic establishment doesn't become established without having influential connections. It found a receptive ear in the priests who recalled the divisions the Protestant revolution had caused in the church. The new science seemed to them to be another threat to religion. A young priest in Florence denounced Galileo — along with science in general — from the pulpit. Things continued to build until Pope Paul V himself pronounced the stability of the sun and the movement of the earth to be contrary to scripture.

It all came to a head in February 1616. A formal accusation had been lodged against Galileo, and the Inquisition was obliged to investigate it. Faced with these worrisome developments, against the advice of his friends, Galileo decided at the end of 1615 to travel to Rome and argue the matter on his own behalf. Though in poor health, he exuded confidence in his ability to set matters straight through the superiority of his reasoning and the strength of his argumentation. Arriving in Rome, he immediately set about making speeches, debating opponents, and meeting with church officials. His main argument was that religion and science should be kept separate — for the good of the church. If religious leaders took positions on science, he argued, the church itself would be damaged should observational research prove them wrong. Better to concentrate on the moral, the higher, the truer sense of the Bible than to read it literally in a misguided effort to settle issues best left to science.

To Galileo's astonishment, however, he found that this argument, which he thought the clincher, was turning out to be a hard sell. Apart from the argument's merits, his right even to advance it was questioned — if the Reformation had made one thing clear it was that issues with theological implications should be left to theologians. No matter how brilliant Galileo was and how persuasively he argued, the taint of the unorthodox was starting to hang about him, and many influential persons he tried to meet suddenly seemed always to be in meetings or out of town: perhaps he could leave a message with their assistants? Meanwhile, his case, and specifically the issue of Copernicanism, had been referred by the Inquisition to a committee of "Qualifiers," to determine whether they were contrary to the teachings of the church. In February the Qualifiers returned the following verdicts on the two main points:

1   *That the sun is in the center of the world, and totally immovable as to locomotion:* Censure. All say that the said proposition is foolish and absurd in Philosophy, and formally heretical inasmuch as it contradicts the express opinion of Holy Scriptures in many places, according to the words themselves and according to the common expositions and meanings of the Church fathers and doctors of theology.

2   *That the earth is neither in the center of the world nor immovable but moves as a whole and in daily motion:* Censure. All say this proposition receives the same censure in Philosophy, and with regard to Theological verity it is at least erroneous in the faith.

Galileo was then called to a meeting with Cardinal Bellarmine to receive this ruling. What exactly happened in this meeting has long been debated, as his later trial would hinge on it. Apparently Bellarmine had been instructed by the pope to inform Galileo that it was not permissible to "hold or defend" the offending beliefs. If Galileo resisted this directive he was to be further enjoined against teaching them — that is, of presenting them as one line of thought among others without holding or defending them; in other words, without passing judgment on their validity.

Galileo saw how things stood, and he didn't resist. In fact, he even asked for and received a document from Bellarmine specifying that he had not received any sort of personal reprimand; the ruling was not aimed specifically at him but was directed to the whole Catholic world. This document would be a major piece of evidence during his trial for heresy in 1633. Although Galileo had mostly steered clear of these controversial subjects for two decades, his investigations into such questions as the cause of tides had eventually brought him back again to the issue of heliocentrism, and he published his thoughts on the subject in a daring book called *Dialogue Concerning the Two Chief Systems of the World: Ptolemaic and Copernican*. The new pope, Urban VIII, though at one time friendly with Galileo, saw this provocation as a deliberate personal betrayal. Galileo was again teaching Copernicanism. At his trial Galileo produced the document that Bellarmine had given him, but this was countered by a document the Inquisition produced indicating that he had been enjoined not only against holding and defending the prohibited beliefs but also teaching them. Galileo denied that he had been prohibited from teaching, and the Inquisition's document was unsigned. On the weight of evidence Galileo's signed document should have trumped the other one, but he had angered the top papal authorities, and he was found guilty. Galileo prudently admitted having "gone too far," and hoped thereby for a light sentence, but these hopes were dashed. He would spend the rest of his life under house arrest, he was prohibited from all further publishing, and all of his books were placed on the Index of prohibited publications

Galileo's case had begun as a dispute with academic philosophers, for whom grand conceptualizing held more value than menial observation. Applied science, such as Galileo specialized in, was considered mere technology; true science, they felt, concerned itself with the ultimate causes of things, not the quirks of their everyday mundane expression. This was a debate that Galileo was fully capable of waging. Unfortunately for him, however, the rifts caused by Luther and others in what had once appeared (deceptively) to be a monolithic European religion had made the Catholic church extremely sensitive to deviation from doctrine. Faced with the Protestant threat — which had resulted in a considerable loss of income from northern parishes — the church was fighting back. With the establishment of the Jesuit order and the standardization of religious thought following the Council of Trent, the church was now on the offensive. The effectiveness of its Counter-Reformation depended, it felt, on standing firm against any further deviant or subversive beliefs.

Applying this line of thought to the case of Galileo resulted in a disaster for the church's public relations. Many historians of science today emphasize

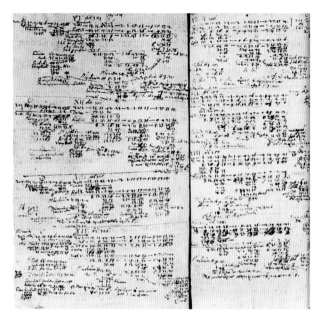

Pages from Kepler's Calculations, early seventeenth century.

In calculating the orbit of Mars, Kepler lacked advanced mathematical tools, but he was dogged in pursuing the answers he sought.

that Galileo's troubles were largely caused by his own difficult personality. They caution against the assumption that science and religion were necessarily at odds. Still, for centuries following his trial and condemnation, despite its protests to the contrary, the church would find it hard to shake the charge of being opposed to science. Not until the mid-seventeenth century did it remove Galileo's works from the Index so they could be read. Catholic schools were prohibited from teaching that the earth orbits the sun until well into the eighteenth century. As late as the mid-twentieth century the church was still censoring biographies of Galileo. Finally, in 1992, Pope John Paul II issued a statement that seemed to exonerate the scientist. But Cardinal Paul Poupard, chairman of the Galileo pardon board, in an interview with James Reston, Jr., clarified that the statement was not an apology, it was merely a "formal recognition" of error.

Kepler's working calculations on the orbit of Mars take up nine hundred pages in a minuscule hand. How many more pages would he have needed if he had had to make his calculations using Roman numerals? It is no longer possible to see the Scientific Revolution as a self-contained European phenomenon; exchange of ideas between Islamic West Asia and Christian Europe was a lively and vital component of the new scientific discoveries.

Kepler had been an enthusiastic Copernican since his student days, when his embrace of heliocentrism was probably more intuitive than rational. Galileo was a more reluctant Copernican, who tried to avoid addressing the issue until led to confront it through his astronomical observations and other research. Two other major figures of the European scientific revolution from this same period, Simon Stevin, a pioneer of hydrostatics, and William Gilbert, one of the fathers of electrical engineering, were also Copernicans. Social theorist Howard Margolis, author of *It Started With Copernicus,* has proposed that Copernicanism enabled original thinking by encouraging a similar rethinking of other established beliefs. But, in all likelihood, none of the four scientists realized that Copernicus, who had published his groundbreaking book *On the Revolutions of the Celestial Spheres* just before his death in 1543, had been significantly influenced by Islamic astronomical research made centuries before his lifetime.

In 1957 Otto Neugebauer, a scholar researching Copernicus, happened on some diagrams by the fourteenth-century astronomer Ibn al-Shatr, and he recognized that they were identical to some in Copernicus' work. Later he found that Copernicus had also relied on the work of Nasir al din al-Tusi, an even earlier astronomer, who had tried to revise traditional Ptolemaic astronomical theory to make it better conform to actual observation. (The ancient Aristotelian and Ptolemaic astronomical theory had spread east through Byzantium — the Byzantine capital of Constantinople was conquered by the Ottomans in 1453 and renamed Istanbul — into Islamic lands, as well as north and west through Europe. Even earlier, many Greek thinkers had relocated to Iran after Christians closed the Platonic academy in Athens.) It was subsequently discovered that Copernicus had even used the same letters as al-Tusi to designate the points in a key diagram, removing any lingering doubt that Copernicus had access to the work of Muslim astronomers. (Evidence for Copernicus's reliance on the work of early Islamic astronomers is summarized by George Saliba in his *Islamic Science and the Making of the European Renaissance*.) How Copernicus was exposed to these Islamic scientists' works is unknown, but the likeliest explanation is that he found either a native Arabic speaker or else a Renaissance Arabist to report their contents to him, though the exact texts he consulted remain unclear.

A remarkable Arabic publishing operation was funded by Cardinal Ferdinand de Medici, Duke of Tuscany, in Italy in the late sixteenth century. The Medici Oriental Press — relying on the library of a Turkish scholar who had fled a dispute in his homeland, arrived at Venice around 1577, and converted to Christianity — published a number of Arabic-language books. Among those publications was one based on the work of Nasir al-Din al-Tusi, one of the astronomers whose work Copernicus drew upon. There was sufficient interest in Arabic in Europe that, sometime around 1616, it was proposed that the language be taught for the benefit of medical students at Herborn Academy in Germany.

The same Turkish scholar whose library formed the foundation of the Medici Oriental Press's Arabic-language publishing program was picked by Pope Gregory XIII to serve on his committee for calendar reform. Through him the Muslim astronomical tradition must have contributed to the Gre-

An Astrologer Surrounded by His Equipment, early seventeenth century (detail). Marginal illustration from Jahangir's album, 420 x 625 cm (full page). Naprstek Museum, Prague.

Interest in astrology stimulated development of scientific instruments such as the astrolabe. The simple mariner's astrolabe measured the height of the sun above the horizon to figure latitude. More complicated planispheric astrolabes combined a fixed part, representing the sky viewed from a certain latitude, with a movable part simulating the daily apparent motion of the sky. These astrolabes work on the principle that if you know the time you can locate celestial bodies, and if you can identify celestial bodies you can determine the time. By lining up the movable part with an observed celestial object the user can consult a chart based on the angle of the object in the sky to figure the desired result.

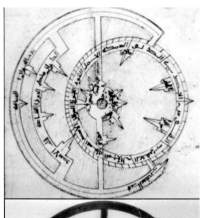

Above: Draft-paper copy by Antonio de Sangallo the Younger, early sixteenth century, perhaps Rome; and original astrolabe by Khafif Ghulam 'Ali b. 'Isa, mid-ninth century, Baghdad. Opposite: Planispheric astrolabe, seventeenth century. India. Brass with inlaid silver. The Nasser D. Khalili Collection of Islamic Art, SC153.

Antonio de Sangallo, architect of St. Peter's cathedral in Rome, apparently took an interest in Islamic scientific instruments. As George Saliba has shown, his copy of a several-hundred-year-old Arabic astrolabe is so exact that the name of the original maker can be read. European interest in such devices facilitated the exachange of scientific knowledge and reflected a desire for accurate implements of measurement.

The large (about two-foot-tall) Indian astrolabe on the facing page also demonstrates cross-cultural connections: it combines Muslim and Hindu elements with inscriptions in both Arabic and Sanskrit.

gorian calendar. Soon Jesuit scholars would carry astronomical devices and advanced calendrical calculations to the court of the Wanli emperor in China, where they would serve as examples of Western achievements and provide the missionaries with an entrée to the Ming court, which saw the need to reform its own calendar.

Despite its early brilliance, Islamic astronomy had fallen into decline by the end of the sixteenth century — perhaps in part because it had largely accomplished its goals of determining the correct time for prayers and finding the direction of Mecca — when one last great effort was made to revive it. Taqi al-Din Muhammad ibn Ma'ruf, chief astronomer to the Ottoman empire, succeeded in having a large astronomical observatory built in Istanbul in 1577, around the time that Tycho Brahe was constructing Uraniborg. He hoped to use the observatory to update existing astronomical data, but his hopes were dashed when Sultan Murad III consulted him regarding the recent appearance of a large comet. In the Muslim world as in Europe, astronomers were expected to produce horoscopes and prognostications based on celestial events. Taqi al-Din reported that the comet presaged a particularly rosy period; instead, Turkey experienced an outbreak of plague. The observatory project never regained momentum following Taqi al-Din's catastrophically errant prediction, and the observatory was torn down in 1580, only three years after it had been built.

Taqi al-Din's observatory had been stocked with all sorts of state-of-the-art scientific instruments. Along with a 6,000-entry table for timekeeping based on solar observations, a manuscript in his hand in the library of the Kandilli Observatory in Turkey contains his observations on stereographic projection and notations on observational instruments. Scientific and navigational devices, rather than the theoretical astronomy that influenced Copernicus, provided most Europeans' exposure to Islamic science. Such objects, which generally responded to a new thirst for accurate measurements in a variety of real-world contexts, were sold and traded widely; among the most common were astrolabes, quadrants, calendar scrolls, and celestial globes.

Astrolabe technology was related to that of clocks. Clocks, though not a recent invention, became more common in the early seventeenth century — Kepler said that the universe was "similar to a clock." Before clocks were in widespread usage, timekeeping was marked by rituals and by the tolling of church bells. Adaptation

of clock technology would contribute to increasing regularization of work hours and a new differentiation between work and leisure time.

Astrolabes had many uses, but chief among them was aid in the determination of time, location, and direction by reference to celestial objects. Muslims had been navigating the Indian Ocean, sometimes with the aid of sailors' astrolabes, for centuries. Zheng He, admiral of the early Ming Chinese treasure fleets, had followed the extensive network of Muslim trade routes to reach Africa; Vasco da Gama, the first European to sail to the Indian Ocean, also followed existing routes. In fact, upon reaching the east coast of Africa one of da Gama's first objectives was to obtain the services of a Muslim navigator. Initially he had attempted to recruit a Swahili navigator but they all declined, "even though they were put to torture" (the torture was double because it involved dropping on the victims' skins boiling oil from pork fat). Finally he found a "Moor of Gujarat" who was well familiar with those waters, and who provided his own navigational instruments and sea charts. India in those years was known for producing high-quality instruments; a Mughal workshop in Lahore, comprising at least four generations of one family, produced a large number of astronomical instruments during the reign of Jahangir.

When da Gama arrived at Calicut in India, it is said, he first sent ashore a convict to test the reception he might expect. To the guinea pig's relief he received a friendly welcome. "Are you Portuguese or Spanish?" the Indians wondered, and they took him to North African translators fluent in European languages. Clearly the world of the Indian Ocean was a cosmopolitan place before the Europeans' arrival.

Navigational and measuring devices had circulated widely since the late medieval period. The earliest astrolabes in Europe had apparently entered through Muslim Spain. They quickly became so popular that the famous French lovers Abélard and Héloïse named their son Astrolabe. Geoffrey Chaucer wrote a *Treatise on the Astrolabe* that owed a debt, ultimately, to West Asian sources (in particular the eighth-century Persian Jewish astronomer Masha'allah ibn Atharī). By the early seventeenth century a family of Flemish astrolabists was familiar enough with Arabic to adapt a thirteenth-century astrolabe made in Muslim Spain for use in northern lattitudes (which required identifying celestial objects through their Arabic labels). The designs of this family's astrolabes also show Arabic influence.

In 1616 maritime globalism stimulated demand for mariners' instruments. A French astrolabe in the collection of the Naval College of Coimbra in Portugal was signed by the maker, Nicol Paternal, and dated 1616. A mariner's astrolable in the collection of the University of Saint Andrews was also signed, by Elias Allen, and dated 1616 — in the estimation of Robert Gunther, former curator of the Lewis Evans Collection at the Ashmolean Museum in Oxford, "in point of completeness it is the premier English Mariner's Astrolabe in the world."

Although Islamic science was in decline by the seventeenth century, leading intellectuals in Iran were pushing philosophical explorations to new heights. Foremost among these was the man known as Mulla Sadra, who is usually accounted the preeminent Islamic philosopher of the past several hundred years. In 1616, at the age of forty-six, he was probably living in the holy city of Qom, a center of Shi'a scholarship (his second daughter had been born there in 1615), where he was beginning to compose a series of innovative philosophical treatises.

Mulla Sadra had been born to an aristocratic family in Shiraz in southwest Iran. He seems to have been an only child, and his father indulged his interest in philosophy. He studied with notable philosophers in Shah Abbas's capital city of Isfahan and elsewhere. He took an early interest in Sufism, a form of Islam that emphasizes denial of self and direct, personal communion with God (in this respect it is analogous to Northern European Protestantism). Sufis, so called from their *sufs,* or wool robes, are often described as mystics. They are associated with ecstatic dance, and wandering Sufi ascetics are termed dervishes.

Because of its bypassing of traditional authority, Sufism was controversial, and efforts were made to suppress it. While there is no evidence that Mulla Sadra was associated with any formal Sufi sect, his independent bent of mind antagonized leaders of the faith in Shiraz, and he was forced to relocate to a village called Kahak in northern Iran, where he spent several years in reflection and meditation and began his philosophical writing. In 1612 he was called back to Shiraz to inaugurate a new madrassa, or religious school, but within a few years he returned to Qom, which was near the place of his earlier retreat. In subsequent years he appears to have led an itinerant life, dividing his time between Qom, Istafan, and Shiraz, before settling permanently in the latter city in 1630; he also made several pilgrimages to Mecca. He died while attempting his seventh such journey. Perhaps his frequent travel helped him to elaborate his philosophy, in which motion is a fundamental element.

Among Mulla Sadra's primary concerns was existentialism. Since ancient times philosophers influenced by Plato had argued that essence precedes existence — that there is some ideal form (called a "quiddity," or "whatness") of cat or tree or person, say, of which all earthly cats or trees or people are im-

Opposite: The Invisible College of the Rose Cross Fraternity, 1618, by Theophilius Schweighardt.

This print, one copy of which was bound into a book published in 1618 under the pen name Theophilus Schweighardt, alludes to the first Rosicrucian manifesto, the *Fama* (the word *fama* appears under the ribbon over the building's cupola). The building is winged and on wheels; it appears to hang by a thread held by a hand that emerges from a cloud where the name *Jehova* appears in Hebrew: this alludes to a passage at the conclusion of the *Fama*, "Under the shadow of thy wings, Jehova." At the sides of the door are the Rosicrucian symbols of the rose and cross. The serpent and swan at the top refer to the new stars that had recently appeared in the constellations Serpentarius and Cignus; their appearance was considered to augur the arrival of a new prophet. The building is protected by battlements where shielded warriors brandish feathers. A kneeling figure transmits a prayer directly to Jehova; inside the building another figure appears engaged in alchemical researches. A trumpet projects from the right side of the building labeled "C.R.F." — the F probably represents "frater" (brother) or "fraternitatis" (brotherhood). Opposite the trumpet is a sword labeled "Jul. de Campi"; this refers to a defense of the brotherhood by one Julianus de Campis, which was included in a 1616 edition of the manifestos.

In his masque *The Fortunate Isles, and Their Union* (the last masque of the Jacobean era, performed in 1625), Ben Jonson alluded to this print in satirizing Rosicrucianism ("outis" is Greek for "nobody"):

Know ye not Outis? then you know nobody;—
The good old hermit, that was said to dwell
Here in the forest without trees, that built
The castle in the air, where all the Brethren
Rhodostaurotic live. It flies with wings,
And runs on wheels; where Julian de Campis
Holds out the brandish'd blade....

perfect manifestations. Existence, in this view, is a kind of accident, and the world we live in is fundamentally flawed. Mulla Sadra, however, maintained that existence and reality were the same thing, and that the essences of the Platonic tradition were nothing but mental constructs derived from existence. The apparent multiplicity of the world, he said, results from different degrees or gradations of a single underlying reality. What's more, because all reality is ultimately one, it cannot be readily grasped by the intellect, which is essentially divisive and limited.

Mulla Sadra viewed existence as constantly in flux; because it is always in motion, no single intellectual construct can encompass it. Existence is renewed instant by instant, and we are not the same people now that we were at the beginning of this paragraph. Mulla Sadra went on to assert that everything in existence has a consciousness, and since these things are gradations of a single reality they all yearn for a greater intensity of existence. In this way he arrived at a transcendental philosophy that emphasized inspiration and was generally consistent with the basic impulses of Sufism. Although a philosopher and not a scientist in the modern sense, Mulla Sadra, having built his philosophy on the premise that everything is constantly in motion, had formulated a deeply considered rebuttal to the traditional notion that the stars are fixed in an unchanging sky, at the same time that Galileo was reaching the identical conclusion through the path of close observation.

One European traveler who was said to have journeyed to the lands of Islam in search of esoteric knowledge was a mysterious figure at first known only as "C.R." or "C.R.C." Born in Germany, he was said to have left his home at sixteen and traveled to Arabia, where he received instruction in arcane knowledge from Islamic adepts. After three years there he moved on to Egypt and then Morocco, where he studied the kabbalah and became skilled in North African magical arts. He continued to Spain, where his newfound esoteric wisdom met an unfriendly reception, and to various European states where it was likewise rejected. Finally, back in Germany, he settled down to a quiet and obscure life, but after a few years he recruited a small band of loyal followers with whom he established a society devoted to his "secret and manifest philosophy." The band swore an oath of agreement to a few principles such as healing the sick without charging for their services; wearing no special dress but passing as ordi-

Placing the Stone on the Mountain, 1617, probably by Matthieu Merian, engraving from *Atalanta Fugiens* by Michael Maier.

The third Rosicrucian manifesto, called *The Chemical Wedding of Christian Rosenkreutz,* by Johann Valentin Andreae, recounts the journey of an elderly hermit to attend a royal wedding in a castle atop a mountain. Engravings in *Atalanta Fugiens* by Michael Maier, formerly the physician to Rudolf II, echo the flavor of Andreae's text; both books were inspired by alchemy and Rosicrucianism. Maier uses classical mythology as symbols for alchemical processes. In a poem accompanying this engraving he writes, "If you believe mere words, your mind is weak, / For Saturn's STONE in truth is CHEMICAL." The Stone is the Philosopher's Stone, the ultimate quest of alchemists; in Greek mythology Mount Helicon was the source of springs sacred to the Muses.

The caption to the engraving reads, "The Stone that Saturn vomited up, after having devoured it in place of his son, Jupiter, has been placed on Helicon as a monument for mortals."

nary citizens; meeting once a year (or sending a letter explaining the reason for their absence); taking the initials "C. R." as "their seal, mark, and character"; and recruiting a successor to carry on after their death.

Eventually, at the age of 104, C.R. passed away, but the brotherhood continued. In 1604 — the same year that a new star appeared in the heavens, which Johannes Kepler suggested portended the appearance of a prophet who would unify and rationalize Christendom — C.R.'s tomb was miraculously discovered behind the wall of the house of a current member of the order. The seven-sided vault, which calls to mind the geometric forms that inspired Kepler, was marked with figures, symbols, and cryptic sentences, and the interior was divided in a pattern of triangles, circles, and other suggestive shapes. "Although the sun never shined in this vault," the first text describing C.R. and his secret brotherhood tells us, "nevertheless it was enlightened with another sun, which had learned this from the sun." A key belief of the brotherhood was that the macrocosm of the universe could be encapsulated within the microcosm of the human body. On an altar in the center lay the "fair and worthy body, whole and unconsumed" of C.R., who by this point had been dead 120 years, a parchment book in his hand. That book would guide further generations of the secret brotherhood, whose symbol would be the cross and rose, in their quest for esoteric wisdom.

Such is the story told in the first of three Rosicrucian "manifestos" that were published anonymously between 1614 and 1616. The mysterious tale of symbols and secrets, which may have circulated in manuscript as early as 1610, was the *Da Vinci Code* of its day, causing a sensation in Europe. The second text, published in Latin in 1615, was a more scholarly elaboration on Rosicrucian beliefs. The third, published in 1616, was a remarkable romance of alchemical spiritualism called *The Chemical Wedding of Christian Rosenkreutz;* it confirmed that "C.R." stood for Christian Rosenkreutz (sometimes also called Christian Rosy Cross). Alchemy is conventionally thought to have originated in Egypt and to have come to Europe through Arabic and Greek sources; the word *alchemy* came to European languages, through Spain, from the Arabic *al-kimiya*. The secret knowledge obtainable through chemistry that it promised was therefore associated with esoteric Arabic wisdom such as that Rosenkreutz was said to have obtained in his travels.

According to the Rosicrucian manifestos, it was possible for outsiders to win admittance to the society, but no instructions were given as to how this was to be accomplished. The French philosopher René Descartes was among those who publicly expressed a desire to join the brotherhood. Elias Ashmole, whose library would form the core of the Ashmolean Museum at the University of Oxford, wrote a letter asking to join the order, though it is not clear that it was ever delivered to anyone. So far as is known, neither they nor any of the other petitioners ever received the invitation they sought to the secret society. Still, traces of Rosicrucian influence can be detected in writings of Francis Bacon and others.

The authorship of the manifestos has been debated ever since their publication, with most attention focused on Johann Valentin Andreae, a German theologian who admitted to having written the *Chemical Wedding*, although he denied, probably truthfully, having been the author of the first two texts, the *Fama* and the *Confession*. Andreae insisted that the *Chemical Wedding* was nothing but a "ludibrium" (a joke, jest, or farce), and in his later works, he disparaged Rosicrucianism (which was prudent since he had risen to a position of some prominence in the Lutheran church). But it is likely that the earlier manifestos were written by someone in his circle of scholars associated with Tübingen University, where Kepler (who was fifteen years older than Andreae) had also studied; the manifestos show an awareness of Kepler's work, and their theme of harmonious correspondences resonates with his search for "the harmony of the world." They may also reflect the influence of the occultist scholar John Dee, who had been an advisor and astrologer to Queen Elizabeth of England, and had later spent time among Rudolf II's court and elsewhere in central Europe in the company of his somewhat sinister, reputedly clairvoyant assistant Edward Kelley, who summoned angelic messages by means of a crystal during seances. Dee had at least some familiarity with kabbalah and Arabic science, and it is possible the concept of "wisdom from the East" that is at the core of the *Fama* owes something to him.

The authors were probably responding to the crisis of faith in the Holy Roman Empire, which had become of patchwork of domains in which Catholicism and various flavors of Calvinism and Lutheranism were officially endorsed according to the preference of the local ruler, a situation that would contribute to the outbreak of the Thirty Years War in 1618. The manifestos are strongly anti-Papist and can be regarded as a reaction to the crackdown on Protestantism following the succession of Rudolf II — who had been an enthusiastic supporter of alchemical and Paracelsian scholarship — by Matthias of Austria, who became emperor in 1612. After Rudolf's death the mantle of patronage for alternative paths of knowledge passed to Frederick V, who was based in Heidelberg. Frederick was encouraged by supporters to expand his domain and carry Protestantism to more of the Empire. His marriage to Elizabeth, daughter of King James of England, was a step in this direction since he hoped England would lend its support to his cause. Frances Yates, who pioneered research into the political contexts of Rosicrucianism, argues that the manifestos express a desire for a new age of Protestant tolerance under Frederick and Elizabeth. The first manifesto appeared the year after the monarchs' wedding. But Frederick overplayed his political hand and reigned only until 1620. It is suggestive that the period of his reign coincides with the initial wave of Rosicrucian activity.

Perhaps lending support for Andreae's assertion that he composed only the third of the manifestos, the version of Christian Rosenkreutz's life given there does not match that given in the earlier pamphlets. There is no mention in it of a secret brotherhood; instead, Rosenkreutz is presented as an elderly hermit. But it was a simple matter for proponents of the Rosicrucian cause to present the narrative as symbolically rather than literally true.

The *Chemical Wedding* is the most interesting of the three so-called manifestos from a literary point of view. The narrative takes place over seven days. On the first day Rosenkreutz is invited to a royal wedding by an angelic figure bedecked with golden stars. Her wings are covered with eyes, and she bears a trumpet and a sheaf of letters in all the languages of the world. The invitation begins with these words:

> Today — Today — Today
> Is the wedding of the King.
> If you are born for this,
> Chosen by God for joy,
> You may ascend the mount
> Whereupon three temples stand
> And see the thing yourself.

On the second day, dressed in white linen and with roses in his hat, the hermit journeys eastward, arriving at sunset at the castle where the wedding is to be held; it rises into the air atop a high mountain. There he succeeds in passing through various gates and obstacles to arrive at a banquet hall. On the third day all of the guests are weighed on scales balanced against a variety of moral virtues, and Rosenkreutz is determined to be worthy. He is given a favorable place at the banquet and is shown the wonders of the castle, which include a globe of the world and a clockwork device that shows the motions of the heavens. On the fourth day a "merry comedy" in seven acts is presented before the king and queen and the guests by a troup of "artists and students." The play concerns a princess who is captured by a Moor but is freed and is married to a prince, whereupon all join in a "Song of Love." On day five Rosenkreutz discovers a secret vault covered with mysterious symbols and inscriptions. Meanwhile, three royal couples are beheaded for reasons that are unclear. On the sixth day royal alchemists succeed in creating a living bird in their laboratory. The bird is fed the blood of the beheaded royals and undergoes a series of changes of colors. Then it too is beheaded. From its ashes grow a boy and girl who are fed the bird's blood. Finally, on the seventh day, the guests are ushered into twelve ships bearing flags on which the signs of the zodiac are displayed. Rosenkreutz is told that he has become a knight of the Order of the Golden Stone, ready for "the good warfare of the faith," and he returns home.

The story is an allegory of an inner journey of the soul, colored by alchemical concepts. The royal marriage expresses an alchemical fusion, and other story elements suggest the alchemical concept of *nigredo,* or blackness, in which elements are broken down in order to be transformed and raised to a higher level. Though grounded in the traditions of alchemy, it is sufficiently obscure that each reader drawn to its puzzles could extract some personal guidance from it.

Among those who responded enthusiastically was Robert Fludd, an English physician, who published an influential defense of Rosicrucianism, called *Apologia Compendaria,* in 1616. He would go on to publish two more works on Rosicrucian topics, as well as an encyclopedia of esoteric subjects called the *History of the Macrocosm and the Microcosm.* Johannes Kepler, in an appendix to his *Harmony of the World,* contrasted his work with Fludd's and rejected the concept of macrocosm and microcosm. Fludd took offense at this and published a pamphlet attacking Kepler, in which he claimed that Kepler was only interested in the outer surface of things and not their inner nature. Inner truth, he said, remains invisible to vulgar mathematicians, who measure only the shadows that

Diagram of Perception, 1619, by Robert Fludd, from *The Metaphysical, Physical, and Technical History of the Two Worlds, Namely the Greater and the Lesser* (Utriusque Cosmi Maioris Scilicet et Minoris Metaphysica).

Fludd, along with Michael Maier, helped to promote Rosicrucianism in England and lay the groundwork for the Freemason movement that arose later in the seventeenth century.

Fludd's scientific activities included study of the circulation of the blood and the nature of perception. He divided perception into sensual, imaginable, intellectual, and sensible realms, which in turn were governed by three pairs of faculties, science and imagination, conscience and reflection, and memory and motive. He proposed that science and imagination are governed by the frontal lobe, reflection by the center of the brain, and memory by the back.

reality casts. To this Kepler (who wrote in a letter around this time "I hate all kabbalists") published his own sarcastic reply. "One sees that Fludd takes his chief pleasure in incomprehensible picture puzzles of reality, whereas I go forth from there, precisely to move into the bright light of knowledge the facts of nature, which are veiled in darkness." Elsewhere he added, "What kind of unblanced swarm of mental freaks now come flying with this *Fama Fraternitatis*.... When, by God's decree, the devil tries to play blind man's bluff with humans, then he needs such a cloak of fanatic opinion with which to cover the eyes of reason." Fludd was not one to let this rest, and he published yet another reply, but Kepler had had his say and chose not to continue the debate.

Fludd's massive work on the macrocosm / microcosm theory amounted to its last gasp as something approaching a mainstream philosophy in the West. The theory, which had appeared in classical times (though without dominating ancient philosophical discourse), had reached its apogee in the sixteenth century with the work of Paracelsus (Paracelsus is best re-membered today for his alchemical work but he could also be viewed as a pioneer of modern medical theory — he rejected the idea that disease was caused by an internal imbalance of humors and suggested that it was the result of outside influences, and that it could be chemically treated). During the medieval period, the macrocosm / microcosm theory had fig-ured, notably, in the Zohar, a key text of kabbalah, and in the *Encyclo-pedia of the Brethren of Purity* produced by an Islamic religious society based in Basra near the Persian Gulf. Classical, Jewish, and Islamic influ-ences mixed with Western theological speculations to culminate in the theories of Paracelsus. The essential forms of the universe and the human being, he said, were echoes of each other — the heavens, for example, were like the skin of the human body. Both the body and the universe were composed of the four basic elements: People eat because they are of earth, drink because they are of water, breathe because they are of air, and require warmth because they are of fire.

By Fludd's time the influence of Paracelsus was starting to wane. In-creasingly, Western physicians, building on West Asian precedents, viewed the body as a system of hydraulic and pneumatic machines; this would result in the explanation of the circulatory system by William Harvey, physician to King James of England, in the 1620s. But in China a concept not unlike the Paracelsian notion of the macrocosm and microcosm was and would continue to be a vital strain of Taoist philosophy. The Hongwu emperor, founder of the Ming dynasty, had explicitly sanctioned the coexistence of the "Three Teachings" of Confucianism, Buddhism, and Taoism (although he later took steps to limit the influence of organized religion). While subsequent Ming emperors favored one or another of the teachings, in general all three continued to thrive simultaneously. Confucian texts were the basis of the imperial examinations, and in theory they provided the moral guidance required by the educated elite. Buddhism, with its vision of release from the cycle of suffering, was popular among ordinary people, and Buddhist priests performed essential rituals such as funeral services. Taoism (which is difficult to separate from the innumerable folk beliefs embraced throughout China's immense domain) was also widely respected, although by and large it lacked something of the status of the other teachings. It was possible, and indeed common, for a person to incorporate elements from all three teachings, in effect picking and choosing as the occasion demanded. Taoists were consulted for geomancy, the determination of auspicious locations, and for astrology, the determination of auspicious dates. Alchemy also fell within the purvue of Taoism. The Jiajing emperor, who reigned in the mid-sixteenth century, was an enthusiastic supporter of Taoism who experimented with a variety of elixirs in an effort to obtain immortality. Unfortunately for him, however, the elixirs, some of which contained mercury and other toxic ingredients, had the opposite effect and were probably responsible for his death.

By the time of the Wanli emperor Taoism was enjoying a revival of influence. The emperor himself commissioned a supplement to the official canon of Taoist texts. Taoists continued their work with elixirs, but they complemented this "outer alchemy" with a corresponding "inner alchemy," the goal of which was to transform the subject's spiritual essence through meditation, breath control, and other practices in order to bring the body's internal energies into harmony with the elemental energy (qi) of the universe. In effect, the body would thereby produce its own transformative elixir within the crucible of its organs to bring about its spiritual rebirth. This inner alchemy became the basic metaphor for Taoist medicine, which sought to bring into balance the male and female principles, the *yin* and the *yang,* with the ultimate goal of achieving union with the Tao.

In China as in Europe there was a tendency to move away from the "outer alchemy" of laboratory processes and to devote more attention to the "inner alchemy" that focused on the symbolic values of the core alchemical principles of rending, uniting, and transforming. In part this may have reflected a disillusionment with the results of laboratory alchemy. In England John Donne wrote in "Loves Alchymie":

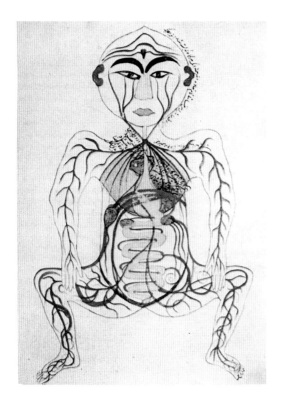

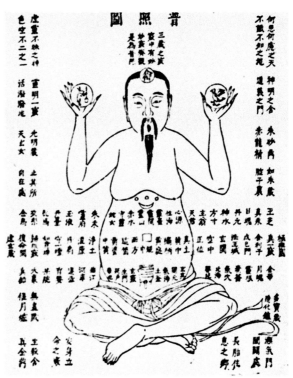

Left: From the *Tashrih-i-mansuri*, seventeenth century, by Mansur ibn Muhammed Ahmad. Persia. Majles Library, Tehran, ms. no. 5266. Right: From *Directions for Endowment and Vitality*, 1615. China. Woodblock-illustrated book. British Library, London (15113.e.6). Opposite: Illustration of Inner Circulation, 19th century. China. Richard Rosenblum Family Collection, Newton Center, Massachusetts.

While the Persian illustration is mechanical and analytical, the symbolic Chinese illustrations of "inner alchemy" concern flow of energy. The goal was to effect the "elixir within," which is represented in the diagram by a symbolic crucible in the abdomen. The inner alchemy remained popular in China for centuries as shown by the illustration opposite.

And as no chymiques yet th'Elixar got,
    But glorifies his pregnant pot,
    If by the way to him befall
Some odoriferous thing, or medicinall,
So, lovers dreame a rich and long delight,
But get a winter-seeming summers night.

In the inner alchemy of Taoism, however, alchemical concepts are not merely metaphors for spiritual development (as they often seem to be in the West) but refer to specific physical aspects of the body; inner alchemy was both medicine and regimen for hygiene and health.

The *Directions for Endowment and Vitality*, first printed in 1615 and often reprinted thereafter, is a Taoist text describing the processes of inner alchemy. The author details a variety of approaches aimed at bringing the secondary energies of the body into alignment with the primary life energy. China scholar Joseph Needham called this text "the *Summa* of physiological alchemy." The book is attributed to a certain Gaodi, said to be a disciple of "Master Yin"; both figures remain obscure. The text describes what it calls the most important of the three thousand six hundred techniques for preparing "the elixir within."

The foundation of inner alchemy was the idea that everything is made up of admixtures of yin and yang. These elements, moreover, are not stable but are always trying to change into their opposite. The adept's goal was to bring them together. As an alchemical text from the tenth century said:

> If the water is true water, and the fire is true fire,
> And if you can bring them to bed together,
> Then you will never see old age.

Speaking of bringing things to bed, sexual fulfillment was a major component of the inner alchemy. Taoist adepts prescribed a regimen of retention of bodily fluids (the teeth should be gnashed to create saliva which should not be spit out; the male sex partner should hold back from ejaculation) and frequent change of sex partners. "He who can make several dozen unions in a day and night without once emitting semen," one Taoist text said, "will be cured of all diseases, and benefit himself by augmentation of longevity." The Taoist recommendation that a man have many sexual partners should not be confused with libertinism. Rather, it reflects the practice of concubinage, which was conventional in China. Still, one Chinese writer did delve into licentiousness, at enormous length. In so doing he created a novel that is considered one of the masterworks of Chinese prose fiction.

Tang Xianzu, who died in 1616 at the age of sixty-six, was the leading playwright of the Wanli era. His major plays are sometimes called the Four Dreams, because dreaming plays a role in each. The plays are often performed as operas: one, *The Peony Pavilion,* was presented at Lincoln Center in 1999 in a six-part, nineteen-hour production that won critical acclaim. Tang retired from a low-level civil service job in 1598 and retired to his home in southern China. How did he spend his eighteen years of retirement?

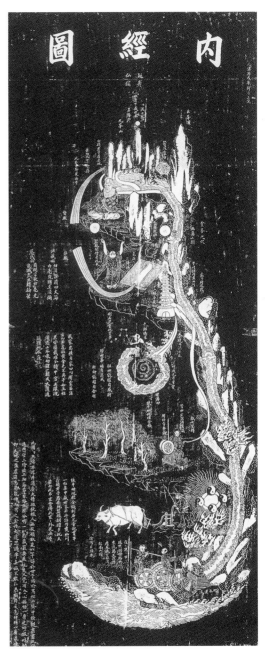

In the opinion of David Tod Roy, Tang spent much of those years composing the massive—2,923 pages in the original blockprint edition, which was printed between 1610 and 1618—classic novel *The Plum in the Golden Vase,* which Roy is translating in five volumes (the first volume was published in 1993, the fourth appeared in July 2011). The book is attributed only to "The Scoffing Scholar of Lanling," and Tang's authorship of it remains unproven. The title, *Jin Ping Mei*, which could also be translated, perhaps more conventionally, as "Plum Blossoms in a Golden Vase," is made up of the names of three of the main female characters. It is also a pun on a phrase that means something like "The Glamour of Entering the Vagina," and the book's erotic content, including more than seventy sex scenes, is the first thing that has struck many of its readers.

The story, set in the historical past during the Song dynasty, charts the rise and fall of an ambitious but decadent merchant, Ximen Qing, who has inherited a wholesale pharmaceutical business. Other primary figures are Ximen's six wives, but over the course of the novel he also beds thirteen additional women. The book comprises one hundred chapters. The plot hinges on an episode in the forty-ninth and fiftieth chapters in which Ximen obtains a powerful aphrodisiac from a mysterious Indian monk, who is presented as the personification of a penis. From that point on Ximen's excesses lead him down a path that will end with his death at the age of thirty-three.

The author uses a merchant's household in a provincial town as a microcosm of greater Chinese society. Ximen's six wives are probably meant to recall the "six traitors" who were blamed for the fall of the Song dynasty. Ends of dynasties were traditionally associated with moral failings, because they represent the loss of the mandate of heaven. By showing the effects of decadence and cupidity on Ximen, the head of the microcosmic household, the author implies a criticism of Chinese governance that he would not have been allowed to make directly. He is careful to show that Ximen's unrestrained ambition found outlets not only in the sexual but also in the economic and political spheres, the areas in which the Wanli emperor was likely to have been criticized. A key episode in the novel concerns Ximen's affair with Pan Jinlian, whose husband he would murder and whom he would then take as one of his wives. A poem describes their intercourse:

> When pleasure reaches its height passions are
> intense, and feelings know no bounds,
> as the mouth of the divine turtle
> disgorges its silvery stream.

The "divine turtle," David Tod Roy tells us in an analysis of this passage, is a euphemism for penis. The allusion to the "silver" it emits is not incidental; a following line repeats that Ximen "left behind a few pieces of loose silver." The implication is that unrestrained sexual striving could be compared to economics in the new silver-based economy of China, which produced luxuries for the indulgence of the emperor but disrupted many aspects of the conventional order. The author was probably a Neo-Confucian but, considering that aspects of Buddhism, Taoism, and Confucianism were often mixed together during the late Ming, he was likely influenced by Taoist inner alchemy in valuing retention of bodily fluids, which would suggest a parallel in moderation on the level of the larger society. One of the themes of the book, according to Roy, is that "if the resources of the human body are not adequately distributed, but are constantly being drawn upon to replenish the supply of semen in the testicles, because it is being prodigally wasted, the result will be death for the individual." Immoderate sexual activity, another scholar, Katherine Carlitz, agrees, "is destructive both of the individual self and the fabric of social relations. In this it functions exactly like the drives for wealth and power.... Immoderate drives for or exercise of sex, wealth, and power are equivalent in outcome ... they are inextricably linked throughout the book, in part by the image of the bad last ruler."

As the Wanli emperor grew increasingly estranged from the literati class, some scholars moved toward a form of Confucianism that was less inclined to tolerate alternate beliefs. In those last years of the Ming, society grew increasingly factionalized, and a sense of commonality was lost. Some scholars even moved away to join the troublesome new kingdom in Manchuria; in 1644, when the Manchus would overthrow the Ming and establish the Qing dynasty, Taoists would be subjected to increased suppression. But the cultivation of the individual through the practice of outer and inner alchemy would continue into modern times.

The author of the *Jing Ping Mei* was not the only one to associate mysterious sexual practices with India. When Pietro della Valle, an early-seventeenth-century Italian traveler through the three great Islamic empires, departed Persia for India, he carried with him a most curious manuscript. Called *The Kamarupa Seed Syllables,* it was an Indian text that had been translated into Persian and copied out for him in the southern Persian city where he had spent several months discussing science and religion with Shi'ite scholars. According to della Valle, the manuscript concerned a practice centered around spiritual exercises related to "arts of divination, secrets of herbs, and other natural things, and also in magic and enchantments." To della Valle these secrets amounted to "nothing else but correspondence with the Devil.... Sometimes they have carnal commerce with him, not believing, or at least not professing, that it is the Devil, but that there are certain immortal, spiritual, invisible women ... whom they reverence as deities, and adore in many places with strange worship."

The title of the manuscript gives a clue about its nature. Kamarupa was an early kingdom in northeastern India that was thought to be the place of origin of the esoteric tradition known as Tantra. This tradition was strongest in remote regions of India where Hinduism had not fully established itself, and it probably represents a melding of ancient shamanistic and folk beliefs and practices with Hindusim. The second part of the title, the "seed syllables," alludes to the recitation of mantras. Della Valle brought the manuscript back to Italy following his travels, and an heir donated it to the Vatican library, where it was forgotten until recently, when the scholar Carl W. Ernst examined it. Ernst described the work as "something like a large recipe-book for occultists"—at least, that is how it would have been perceived in the Islamic Persian context.

The book is a treatise on yogic breathing and divination techniques centering around devotion to the cult of the Sixty-Four Yoginis (female followers of yoga), whose leader was the fierce Tantric goddess Kamakhya Devi. According to della Valle, "Whoever is occupied with the theory and practice of this they call a *jogi* and respect him greatly." This branch of yoga tradition (called Kaula Tantra) was concerned with the purification and perfection of the body through devotion to the feminine principle. In contrast to the personal austerity and bodily denial of Indian ascetics, Tantric followers of the Sixty-Four Yoginis strove for the perfection of the body: if it could be made as immutable and incorruptible as a diamond, the result, in della Valle's words, would "lengthen life and make one nearly immortal." In some contexts devotees of Tantra were allowed to drink wine, eat meat, and indulge in sexual relations. As one Tantric text argues, "Donkeys and other animals wander about naked too. Does that make them yogins?"

Physical movements and postures (*asanas*), gestures (*mudras*), and breathing disciplines (*pranayama*) were keys to the perfection of the body. Energy points within the body, known as chakras, were identified and made a focus of physical development. Mantras were recited and mandalas employed as objects of meditation. Some practitioners of Tantra engaged in sexual rituals whose goal was union between the male principle, represented by Siva, and the primordial creative female energy known as Shakti, after one of the names of his consort. In these rituals men typically sought to delay or deny ejaculation. The goal of union of male and female principles and retention of bodily fluids resembles the Taoist practice of inner alchemy, but possible paths of cross-influence are now nearly impossible to trace. *The Kamarupa Seed Syllables,* however, takes this practice another step. It claims to offer guidance for conjuring female spirits and then engaging in sexual relations with them. Perhaps this is best taken metaphorically.

In India, as in China, devotees of so-phisticated sexual techniques were often associated with alchemical explorations, as the combining of alchemical substances was likened to the sexual act. Use of such mixtures is what struck Marco Polo about the yogins he encountered. "These people make use of a very strange beverage," he reported, "for they make a potion of sulfur and quicksilver mixed together, and this they drink every month. This, they say, gives them long life." By the seventeenth century the perception of visitors had not much changed. A French traveler of that time, François Bernier, echoed Marco Polo's words, calling yogins "strange people" who "know how to make gold and prepare mercury so admirably that one or two grains taken in the morning restore the body to perfect health and so fortify the stomach that it digests very well." Such observations do not penetrate beyond outward appearances, as for centuries travelers in non-Muslim areas of India were intrigued by yogic practices without ever achieving much understanding of them.

Alchemical theories would, in Lusatia (now Saxony), influence a twenty-five-year-old shoemaker who in 1600 would have a visionary experience. Sitting in his simple home, he was struck by a glint of sunlight reflecting off a dish. That flash of light penetrated his being and convinced him that he was seeing into the secret depths of nature. He rose and walked into the countryside. There, he later wrote, he

> saw the Being of all Beings, the Ground and the Abyss; also the birth of the Holy Trinity; the origin and first state of the world and of all creatures. I saw in myself the three worlds — the Divine or angelic world; the dark world, the original of Nature; and the external world, as a substance spoken forth out of the two spiritual worlds.... In my inner self I saw it well, as in a vast depth; for I saw right through as into a chaos where everything lay wrapped, but I could not unfold it.

The Tantric Buddhist Deity Guhyasamaja in Union with His Consort Sparshavajri, seventeenth century. Tibet. Thangka, colors and gold on cotton, 58 x 76 cm. Rubin Museum of Art, New York, F1997.31.13.

Aspects of Tantric traditions mixed with many South Asian religious currents. In its esoteric Buddhist form, it traveled to the Himalayas. Tantra emphasized the union of the male and female principles. In the visual arts of the Himalayas this took the form of a symbol known as *yab-yum* ("father-mother") in which the male deity is shown in sexual union with his female consort.

Opposite: Jacob Boehme at His Workbench, with the Tools of His Trade. Engraving from an early Dutch edition of his works.

The isolation and concentration of the shoemaker as he works on his text are conveyed by this engraving reproduced in Andrew Weeks's *Boehme: An Intellectual Biography*.

"It is certainly not impossible that Boehme wrote his first book like this," according to Weeks. "His writing has certain artisanlike qualities.... Refractory cogitations come up repeatedly, as if he were hammering out his ideas from a verbal material, widening, altering, and shaping them."

Yet from time to time it opened itself within me like a growing plant. For twelve years I carried it about within me, before I could bring it forth in any external form; till afterward it fell on me, like a bursting shower that kills where it lands as it will. Whatever I could bring into outwardness I wrote down. The work is none of mine; I am but the Lord's instrument, with which He does what He will.

The whole experience, he said, lasted about fifteen minutes. Jacob Boehme went back to his work as a shoemaker, his life outwardly little changed. Then, ten years later, he had a second experience, and around this time he began an attempt to put his thoughts into words. The result, a book that he called *Morning Glow Ascending* but that has become known by the name his followers gave it, *Aurora,* was completed in 1612.

The book did not spring full-blown from the author's fleeting mystical visions but built upon Lusatia's complicated intellectual traditions. Near the end of 1616 Lutheran clergymen throughout Europe began informing their parishioners that 1617 would mark the centenary of Luther's *Ninety-Five Theses,* and would be a Year of Jubilee. But in the century since the beginning of the Reformation Lutheranism had become increasingly rigid and authoritarian, and dissident splinter religious groups had developed and won followers. Lusatia was a hotbed of such groups, including Anabaptists, Moravian Brethren, Crypto-Calvinists, and others. The Lutheran pastor in Boehme's hometown of Gorlitz sympathized with some of these currents, and he led a study group called the Conventicle of God's Real Servants, of which Boehme was said to be a member. The pastor got into hot water with Lutheran authorities, who accused him of being a Crypto-Calvinist, a Lutheran who believed the Calvinist doctrines of the Eucharist, such as that Christ's body was present spiritually but not physically. (The same subject would get Kepler excommunicated.)

In addition to such theological currents, there were other influences that affected Boehme. The mayor of Gorlitz was an acquaintance of both Kepler and Tycho Brahe, and he corresponded with a prominent kabbalist rabbi in Prague. One of Boehme's key supporters was also a student of the kabbalah, and, like Christian Rosenkreutz, he had traveled to Arabia in search of Eastern wisdom. He was also an alchemist and a Paracelsian, and these traditions had many adherents in Gorlitz.

Prior to his first visionary experience, Boehme had accepted the idea that "the true heavens" of God were remote, miles and miles above the earth; afterward, having experienced the presence of God within himself and flowing like an electric current through the world, he felt certain that

conception must have been wrong. He distinguished between the "inner birth" of the world beyond the visible and the "outer birth" of the visible world. Although not a scientist, he arrived at Copernicanism around the same time as Galileo. His approach, like Kepler's initial attraction to the idea, was theological. For Boehme, God's animating energy penetrated the universe. The glint of light of his first visionary experience was a glimpse of that solar energy. The traditional view of the universe as a series of interlocking spheres confined human beings, he felt, to the equivalent of the cellar of creation, and this did not conform to the sensation that he had experienced. Rather, the sun represented the omnipresent energy that Boehme, influenced by alchemy, called the *salitter,* and which he viewed as a kind of higher-level saltpeter — saltpeter, or potassium nitrate, was an ingredient in gunpowder and a substance much admired by alchemists.

The Gorlitz pastor whose study group Boehme may have been a part of, and who had been accused of Crypto-Calvinism, had died by the time Boehme wrote *Aurora,* and he had been replaced with a hardliner (who, ironically, was himself said to be a Philippist, a follower of Luther's colleague Philipp Melanchthon, a lineage also accused of Crypto-Calvinism). In 1613 the new pastor obtained a copy of Boehme's book. Accused of holding unorthodox views, Boehme was imprisoned, and his master copy of *Aurora* was seized. The pastor denounced him as a heretic in a Sunday sermon. He was released after promising to desist from writing. He sold his shop in town and took up work as a traveling yarn goods salesman. This brought him into contact with persons of influence in Prague and other towns. Perhaps in 1616, during this period of wandering, he was working out the complicated theosophical vision that he would record, at the urging of his widening circle of literati friends, in his second book, which he completed in 1618–1619. With increased patronage he then began a new phase of intense writing, producing several dense works between then and his death in 1624. Probably the best-known of these is the *Signatura Rerum,* written in the early 1620s. Though largely a rehash of his earlier books, it popularized the idea of the "signature" in which "each thing manifests its mother, which thus gives the essence and the will to the form." In other words, each microcosm reflects echoing correspondences extending up to the highest macrocosm, and these correspondences manifest themselves in such things as a characteristic shape or color, which give a clue to the object's secret essence.

In his many books Boehme elaborated a complicated theory of the universe that involved seven source-spirits, three divine principles, and other arcane constructions. But it was his persona as an outsider, a shoemaker mystic who experienced God's all-infusing energy directly through nature rather than through the mediation of the church, that was ultimately most influential, rather than the details of his actual philosophy. Blake, Novalis, Schopenhauer, and Hegel were among many who were profoundly affected by him. Robert Browning contrasted Boehme as a "poet of things" with mere philosophers of thoughts. "Boehme's book and all," he wrote, "Buries us with a glory, young once more, / Pouring heaven into this poor house of life." Stephen Daedalus in Joyce's *Ulysses* thinks to himself, "Signatures of all things I am here to read." And Kenneth Rexroth, in the title poem of his third book of poetry, *The Signature of All Things,* begins and ends with these verses, which capture something of Boehme's own visionary experience:

> My head and shoulders, and my book
> In the cool shade, and my body
> Stretched bathing in the sun, I lie
> Reading beside the waterfall —
> Boehme's 'Signature of All Things.'
> ...
> I went out on my cabin porch,
> And looked up through the black forest
> At the swaying islands of stars.
> Suddenly I saw at my feet,
> Spread on the floor of night, ingots
> Of quivering phosphorescence,
> And all about were scattered chips
> Of pale cold light that was alive.

In 1621, in the midst of the Thirty Years War, Jacob Boehme was feverishly setting down his vision of God's presence; *The Signature of All Things* would appear the following year. Meanwhile, just over 350 miles to the southwest, the accused witch Katharina Kepler was being subjected to psychological torture. Kepler had prevented his mother from being physically tortured through the implied threat of reprisal from his influential friends, and through generally making himself a pain to all concerned. The court scribe at one point set into the record, "The accused appeared in court, accompanied, alas, by her son, Johannes Kepler, mathematician." The defense's 128-page Act of Conclusion was mainly written by Kepler. The case was presided over by the Tübingen Faculty of Law. The faculty decided that the mildest form of torture should decide the old woman's fate. This involved the executioner confronting the accused, presenting his instruments one by one, and describing, presumably with disturbing rel-

Ziarnko was a Polish printmaker who lived and worked in Paris. This image was made to accompany a book by Pierre de Lancre, one of the most notorious witch hunters of the early seventeenth century. De Lancre was credited with six hundred executions in just three years, although current scholarship suggests the actual number is less than one hundred.

The image was printed as an oversized fold-out sheet in de Lancre's book. It can be read as a parody or grotesque inversion of a court masque. Letter keys helpfully identify the main elements for curious readers: Satan, depicted as a five-horned goat, oversees the sabbat from his throne at the upper right. A naked witch and a demon are presenting him with a young child. For the banquet at lower right, body parts of children are served up. As flying witches arrive with more children, riotous dances take place at either side of swirling smoke rising from a diabolical brew being prepared at the center foreground.

ish, the exact methods in which they were used and their effects on the victim. Whatever satisfaction the executioner obtained from this charade, however, there would be little satisfaction for Katharina's accusers. The same stubbornness that kept her son pursuing twenty years of calculations to determine the orbit of Mars, the stubborness that had seen her follow after her husband's army for many hundreds of miles to bring him home, remained strong in her. The provost reported that

> I led her to the usual place of torture and showed her the executioner and his instruments, and reminded her earnestly of the necessity of telling the truth, and of the great grief and pain awaiting her. Regardless, however, of all earnest admonitions and reminders, she refused to admit and confess to witchcraft as charged, indicating that one should do with her as one liked, and that even if one artery after another were to be torn from her body, she would have nothing to confess; whereafter she fell on her knees and said a paternoster, and demanded that God should make a sign if she were a witch or a monster or ever had anything to do with witchcraft. She was willing to die, she said; God would reveal the truth after her death, and the injustice and violence done to her.

Katharina was freed, but others accused of witchcraft, lacking her resources, were not so lucky. In January 1616, the same month that Kepler wrote his initial letter in defense of his mother, a large number of women in Spa de Ban, in the Walloon region of what is now Belgium, were accused of witchcraft. The sorcery was manifested in illnesses and deaths of children and livestock, failed pregnancies, and other misfortunes. Fourteen persons were found guilty; at least ten were executed (the other four may not have survived their torture in order to be executed). All were women.

Women accounted for somewhere around three-quarters of all witchcraft accusations. Of those accused, women were more likely to be convicted, and of those convicted women were more likely to be executed. To a large extent this was the result of their relative lack of power. Particularly if the woman was widowed, she might lack male relatives available or willing to defend her. Despite notable exceptions, by and large victims of witchcraft trials tended to be among the poorer, less educated, and more remotely located of citizens.

The number of people accused, convicted, and executed as witches is difficult to determine. Some witch hunters claimed extraordinary results — one, Nicolas Remy, boasted of having convicted nine hundred

witches over about a decade. This number seems vastly inflated, but at the height of the witch trials, between the mid-sixteenth and the mid-seventeenth century, somewhere between fifty and one hundred thousand trials may have been held. There is a tendency among contemporary historians to question the vast numbers sometimes given, but whatever the tally the fact remains that a lot more supposed witches were killed during this period than in others, and more in Europe than elsewhere.

Not that the trials were distributed in all parts of Europe equally. About two-thirds of the cases occurred in German-speaking areas. There were few trials in Spain — the Inquisition there generally scoffed at suggestions of witchcraft and declined to prosecute them. (Still, on a visit of the inquisitor to Navarre in 1611, 1,802 people came forward to admit involvement in witchcraft; 1,384 of them were children.) In England, there were few trials, despite King James's interest in witchcraft, and torture was relatively uncommon. His *Daemonologie* was his best-selling title, and one of his acts during his first year after assuming the crown of England was to make witchcraft punishable by death. His interest probably arose from his conviction that the rough seas he experienced during his one trip outside Britain, when he had traveled to Norway to meet his bride, Anne, were the result of sorcery. On its way to Scotland Anne's royal fleet had been forced to wait out a storm for several weeks in Norway. James determined to meet her there, but his ships too were beset by storms (similar storms had saved England from the Spanish armada). On his return to Scotland — in 1590, when this occurred, he had not yet become king of England — James launched a large-scale investigation, which rounded up several dozen suspected witches, many of whom confessed under torture to having been involved in causing the storm. Particular attention was given to an unfortunate woman named Agnes Sampson, a midwife and herbalist. Examined by James himself, she confessed to having attended a witches' coven that caused the storms. Prior to this confession she had been fastened to the wall of her cell by four iron prongs forced into her mouth, kept without sleep, and held by a rope around her head, so the garrotting and burning that followed her confession at least put an end to her ordeal.

One of those accused of conspiring with witches to cause rough seas during James's voyage was Francis Stewart, the Fifth Earl of Bothwell. Stewart's father had been the chief suspect in the murder of James's father, and he had subsequently married James's mother, Mary, Queen of Scots. James and Stewart were political rivals. While most victims of accusations of witchcraft were among the poor and the vulnerable, at the highest levels of society witchcraft became politicized, as happened with Louise Bourgeois's patron, Leonora Galigai. Even Cardinal Richelieu resorted to charges of witchcraft against political rivals.

The combination of witchcraft and palace intrigue in Scotland was juicy material for a play that might please the new king. James assumed the throne of England in 1603, and not long afterward William Shakespeare produced just such a play. The dating of many Elizabethan and Jacobean plays is uncertain but current scholarship suggests that Shakespeare's original *Macbeth* was written in 1606. In the play the witches prophesize that Banquo will father a line of kings: these are the Stuarts who were James's ancestors, his claim to the throne.

But Shakespeare's witches were not the weird sisters familiar from modern texts of the play, nor was the play the one we now know. A theatergoer who attended a performance of the play describes them, rather,

A Portrait of the Artist as a She-Owl, woodcut from *The Owles Almanac,* 1618, by Thomas Middleton. Printed by Edward Griffin, sold by Lawrence Lisle.

The artist of this woodcut, no doubt executed to Middleton's instruction, is unknown. It parodies traditional images that presented authors surrounded by various symbols of arcane knowledge. Here, in front of a bookshelf and a clocklike device, the owl inscribes esoteric symbols with a quill pen.

as "women feiries or Nimphes." Those were parts that would have been played by boy actors. The current text of the play, however, takes pains to mention their beards. "You should be women," Banquo tells them, "And yet your beards forbid me to interpret / That you are so." This change would have allowed the parts to be played by men (perhaps even by the original boy actors, now grown up).

That is far from the only change in the text. The task of adapting Shakespeare's play for a "modern" audience was given to Thomas Middleton, who had recently had a success with his play *The Witch;* both the existing version of *Macbeth* — which includes enough Middleton that it is included in the recent collected edition of his works edited by Gary Taylor and John Lavagnino for Oxford University Press — and Middleton's own *The Witch* were probably produced in 1616. *The Witch* was probably performed in the spring and followed by the revival of *Macbeth* in the fall.

Another play from 1616 also concerned satanic doings. A satiric comedy by Ben Jonson called *The Devil Is an Ass,* it most likely opened at Blackfriars in October or November, after the new adaptation of *Macbeth.* It concerns a visit by one of the lesser demons of hell to London, where he inhabits a human body but finds himself outdone in devilment by the ordinary citizens

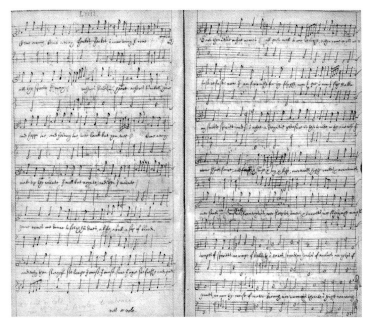

of the city and winds up in Newgate Prison. "The hurt th' hast done, to let Men know their strength," Satan upbraids the miserable imp, "And that the'are able to out-do a Devil / Put in a body, will for ever be / A scar upon our Name!"

When *The Tragedy of Macbeth* was included in the folio edition of Shakespeare's works the editors did not have the words to its songs, which had been reprised wholesale from Middleton's *Witch,* and so the text simply reads "Music and a song. Sing within: 'Come away, come away, etc.'" But the full text and music were included in a printing of *The Witch,* and a handwritten copy exists in the New York Public Library.

"Come Away, Hecate, O Come Away," ca. 1616, from Thomas Middleton's *The Witch.* Musical manuscript, hand copied by Anne Twice. New York Public Library, MS Drexel 4175, no. liiii.

This text of this song, which was performed not only in Middleton's own *The Witch* but also in his adapatation of Shakespeare's *Macbeth,* was handwritten by a woman named Anne Twice, who must have wanted to perform it. According to Gary Taylor and Andrew J. Sobel, "It is hard to resist the assumption that the female owner/creator/user of this manuscript identified in some way with the song's 'I' and its triumphant evocation of female power, pleasure, and flight."

In *The Witch* the song was sung by Hecate, witches, and a cat. For the lyrics of the song see the Source Notes, p. 366.

Macbeth is among the shortest of Shakespeare's plays (less than two-thirds the average length of his tragedies), in large part because Middleton abridged substantial parts of it. Shakespeare's original version apparently began with a battle scene, but the audience's taste for such scenes had faded by 1616. Ben Jonson satirized such scenes in *Every Man in His Humour* as "three rusty swords, and help of some few foot-and-half-foot words." Instead, the action of the battle is quickly summed up in dialogue.

In the decade between the original version and Middleton's adaptation, the King's Men had moved from the Globe to Blackfriars Theatre — in other words, from a semi-outdoors setting to an indoor one. This enabled new special effects, which the scenes of witches and ghosts made use of, but it also required the elimination of such elements as the horses that Banquo and Macbeth apparently rode in on. In all, Middleton probably cut somewhere around a quarter of the original text.

He also moved elements around and added new ones. In general, Middleton pumped up the spectacular and fantastic elements of the play, no doubt to capitalize on the popular reception to his *Witch*. The witch Hecate, subject of the song "Come Away, Hecate, Come Away," was one of his additions; she had been the title character of *The Witch*. That play, a comedy set in Italy, has an extraordinarily convoluted (and preposterous) plot, which involves a lover who had been thought dead returning on his fiance's wedding night and his efforts to prevent the wedding from being consummated; a duchess's attempts to kill her husband out of resentment at his having made a drinking vessel from the skull of her father; a young woman's secret pregnancy and delivery of the child; the comeuppances of a glutton and a courtesan; and much more. All of these plot twists are facilitated by charms and potions prepared by the 117-year-old witch, Hecate.

Hecate embodies the European notion of the witch in the early seventeenth century. We meet her as an outsider, living in a cave. She has made a pact with the devil, who has granted her 120 years of life. She is heating up a pot in which she will boil a dead child. Serpents also go into the potion. It will enable the witches to fly in the moonlight. She discusses a charm that will curse a farmer's livestock. Besides her fellow witches, cats and spirits are her companions. She rhapsodises about transforming into a guise that will enable her to have sex with young men:

Witches Roasting a Child, from *Compendium Maleficarum* **(Compendium of Witches), 1626, by Francesco Maria Guazzo. Milan. Woodcut.**

Guazzo, a priest, described ceremonies preliminary to taking a vow of allegiance to Satan and detailed varieties of demons. Here, while witches roast a child in the foreground, two others place another child in a boiling broth. Eating children to obtain supernatural powers was commonly believed to be an activity of witches, whose powers were associated with an inversion of traditional symbols of fertility.

> Here, take this unbaptised brat.
> Boil it well, preserve the fat:
> You know 'tis precious to transfer
> Our 'nointed flesh into the air
> In moonlight nights o'er steeple tops,
> Mountains and pine trees, that like pricks or stops
> Seem to our height; high towers and roofs of princes
> Like wrinkles in the earth: whole provinces
> Appear to our sight then ev'n leek
> A russet mole upon some lady's cheek.
> When hundred leagues in air, we feast, and sing.
> Dance, kiss, and coll, use everything.
> What young man can we wish to pleasure us
> But we enjoy him in an incubus?

Opposite page: Witches' Sabbat, 1606, by Frans Francken II (1581–1642). Antwerp. Oil on oak panel, 36 x 48 cm. Victoria and Albert Museum, London, bequeathed by Rev. Alexander Dyce, Dyce.3.

Frans Francken II was known for his "monkey kitchen" paintings, in which monkeys represent human vices and follies. But Francken also did a series of paintings devoted to witches and witchcraft, including this witches' sabbat taking place in a domestic interior at night. The foreground is dominated by finely dressed ladies, whose youth and beauty are juxtaposed with the grotesque appearance of older, naked or seminaked women behind them. The hectic scene is filled with winged demons, flying witches, and other creatures. There may be a suggestion that evil lurks behind female sensuality.

A variety of types of magic is represented: incantations, burning of herbs, rituals involving skulls, magic runes, the preparation of a potion in a cauldron. A burning house seen through a doorway may represent the object of the destructive power of all these magic arts.

Francken's detailed representation of witchcraft "gave the impression that he knew more about it than the popular culture allowed," a V&A curator has written, "although the reason for this remains unclear." The European witch hunts reached their height between about 1580 and 1640, just when this painting was made. Who at such a time would have been the audience for an image of this kind?

All of these elements — old age, night flight, destruction of livestock, killing and eating children, preparation of potions, companionship of cats, pacts with the devil, sex with young men — are standard attributes of the European witch. With the spread of literature and literacy following Gutenberg, and the beginnings of political consolidation of disparate villages into large states governed by literate bureaucracies, two distinct lineages of knowledge increasingly began to diverge. Knowledge from written texts, despite exceptions, was a largely male domain, and men had positions of power from which to oppress the oral, largely female tradition of folk knowledge. As a result, witches came increasingly to represent unorthodox and illicit wisdom. Where once conjurers were regarded as dangerous but potentially helpful, increasingly they were associated with evil and with the devil himself.

Witchcraft had long been a part of village-centered life. So much about the world was mysterious. Why does the object of my affections not reciprocate my feelings? Why has my cow stopped giving milk? What is causing my wheat to be covered with black mold? Faced with these kinds of questions, it only made sense to give the neighbor's potion, amulet, or spell a try. Prayers were known to produce beneficial results, so why not spells? Such white magic was distinguished from black magic. There was good reason to believe in that too, for the church insisted that the devil was real, and that he was active among us. But now, with religious leaders more concerned than ever with standardizing belief, people more and more were hearing that *all* magic, both white and black, was evil — if it didn't involve the intervention of some demon, how else could it be effective?

Emerging science left much unexplained. What caused the storms that buffeted King James's wedding ships? What caused the plagues and famines that struck at seemingly random intervals? Old women, often widows, took much of the blame. Not only were they frequently burdens on families struggling for subsistence, but they also symbolized infertility, represented by the deaths of children and livestock and the failure of crops. The union of women above child-bearing ages with young men was considered unnatural and unproductive, and consequently a likely indication of witchcraft. However old and haggard, such witches were often depicted as highly sexualized. They gathered in witches' sabbats together with younger women recruited by them into the service of evil. In these sabbats they would have sex (anal sex, it was sometimes said) with the devil, but this would result in their being infertile, or else giving birth to monsters. During such liasons the devil would leave his mark, and women

with moles and birthmarks were wise to keep them concealed if they could. Of course, the mark was not always easy to find. James I advised that "the Deuill dooth lick them with his tung in some privy part of their bodie, before he dooth receiue them to be his seruants, which marke commonly is given them vnder the haire in some part of their bodye, whereby it may not easily be found out."

Female sexuality in the person of witches was frightening to many men. A 1603 manual warned that "through their dances, their obscene kisses" female witches "contrive to send demons and evil spirits into a man's body." Those evil spirits could deprive a man of his vitality, turn him impotent, or worse. The grandfather of all witch scare books, the *Malleus Maleficarum* (Hammer of Witches), which was reprinted at least thirty times between 1487 and 1669, explained that witches

Deceitful Sorcerers and Witches, drawing 109 from *El Primer Nueva Coronica y Buen Gobierno* ("The First New Chronicle and Good Government"), 1616, by Guaman Poma.

Poma's drawing of Inca witches clearly shows the influence of European images of the devil. With new and more frequent encounters among peoples during the age of maritime globalism, cross-cultural influences were frequent and complex.

collect male organs in great numbers, as many as twenty or thirty members altogether, and put them up in a box, where they move themselves like living members, and eat oats and corn, as has been seen by many and is a matter of common report.

Among the evidence the *Malleus* provides about this practice is the case of an unfortunate man who "had lost his member" as a result of witchcraft. This man

approached a known witch to ask her to restore it to him. She told the afflicted man to climb a certain tree, and that he might take which he liked out of a nest in which there were several members. And when he tried to take a big one, the witch said: You must not take that one; adding, because it belonged to the parish priest.

A saying in Burma has it that "out of seven houses there must be one witch." Belief in witchcraft was hardly unique to Europe but was found throughout the world. (And it has been remarkably persistent. In 1977, as old women confessed on the radio to changing shape into owls and devouring babies, the postal service of the People's Republic of Benin responded with a postage stamp bearing the legend *La Lutte Contre la Sorcellerie* — The Battle against Sorcery.) What was unusual about the European witchhunts was the scale on which they were conducted and the number of victims they produced. Whereas witchcraft had traditionally been managed on the village level, in the German-speaking Empire, where the largest number of witchcraft executions occurred, some of the highest-ranking state figures took it upon themselves to oversee hunts. Village-centered religion had been based around ritual and symbol, only loosely surrounded by nebulous constellations of beliefs that had varied considerably among communities and individuals. The Reformation and Counter-Reformation had represented an attempt to codify belief on a scale beyond anything previously attempted. In this context witch trials were part of a trend toward intolerance of customs and beliefs that diverged from institutionalized standards.

The maritime globalism of the seventeenth century resulted in contact with many foreign witches. Nahualism, the belief that humans have animal souls and can change into animals, was so persistent in Mexico and Mesoamerica that church officials there had to play down the traditional symbols of the evangelists, the lion (Mark), bull (Luke), and eagle (John), because their animal symbols were overshadowing their human forms in the popular imagination. Witchcraft was sufficiently alarming there that in the middle of the century a priest named Diego de Landa ordered the burning of all Mayan texts, which, he said, contained "lies of the devil." So thorough was this auto-da-fe, which Landa said the Maya "regretted to an amazing degree, and which caused them much affliction," that only three Mayan codices are known to have survived out of what had been the richest written culture of the Americas. In Asia too strange new forms of witchcraft were encountered. When the Portuguese and Dutch first came to Indonesia they were mainly looking for valuable spices. Islands such as Bali, which were not prime spice areas, were raided for slaves. On these expeditions the Europeans are likely to have witnessed the traditional exorcistic dance drama called the Calonarang, which features the witch known as Rangda — a copy exists of a palm-leaf manuscript referring to the drama that contains a colophon dated to 1462.

The Europeans would have recognized in Rangda a figure seemingly consistent with their own concept of witches. Her name means "widow" — she is associated with a widowed eleventh-century queen who delved in magical arts. She is usually depicted as a hideous hag with matted hair, bulging eyes, sharp fangs, and a flaming tongue. She is the queen of the frightening creatures that haunt graveyards. In tourist performances today, in which she does battle with a protective lionlike creature called Barong, she appears the per-

A Witch Giving an Anal Kiss to Satan (detail), from *Compendium Maleficarum* (Compendium of Witches), 1626, by Francesco Maria Guazzo. Milan. Woodcut.

Rangda, approx. 1800–1900. Bali. Painted wood, 42 x 60 x 25 cm. Asian Art Museum, Gift of Thomas Murray in memory of his father Eugene T. Murray, 2000.37.

With her shaggy hair, bulging eyes, pendulous breasts, long fingernails, and fangs, the widow Rangda, who is associated with the warlike Hindu goddess Durga, appears the epitome of the witch. For more than five hundred years she has figured in a popular Indonesian dance drama.

In the drama Rangda does battle with a lionlike figure called Barong who attempts to protect people from Rangda's black magic. Early Western visitors to Indonesia believed that there would ultimately be a day of final reckoning. They viewed stamping out witchcraft as one step toward the ultimate binding of Satan. The Balinese held a different view. Evil and good define each other; in a sense they require each other. Both Rangda and Barong possess power that can be called upon and used under the right conditions.

At the end of the drama Rangda is driven away, but she is not killed. She will be back to cause more trouble.

sonification of evil. But in traditional Balinese culture her role was more complex.

In the Calonarang dance drama Rangda was portrayed as so feared for her black magic that no one was willing to marry her beautiful daughter. In anger, Rangda caused pestilence and crop failiures. In the end Barong defeats her, but he does not destroy her. For the Balinese good and evil could be defined only by reference to each other. And, similar to the Taoist conception of yin and yang, each contains elements of the other. Rangda — who was associated with Durga, the wrathful form of Siva's consort, and who was assisted by demonic imps, called *leyak,* that may have evolved from Tantric rituals — was capable of benevolence as well as evil. Get on her good side and she could help you. She had her own shrines, and she appeared in festivals and processions. Although she was feared, she was also respected. In her person the Dutch had actually encountered a different sort of witch. She may have been a hag, but she embraced that role. Though an old widow woman, she did not bow down but stood proud and defiant. Though defeated, she returned to do battle again. Ultimately, in her role as witch, the widow Rangda represented not debasement but female empowerment, and triumph.

Johannes Kepler's quest to uncover the secret of celestial harmony — the music of the spheres — was but the latest in a long tradition that sought to unveil the mathematical and musical secrets of the universe. It would not be the last: in the twentieth century it would bear fruit in a verse by Leonard Cohen. In his "Hallelujah" he sings of a "secret chord" that "pleased the Lord." According to a reviewer in London's *Sunday Times,* the song succeeds "through some mysterious alchemy," and to judge from the number of times it has been covered — 1818, according to one database of musical covers — it is among the most popular of the songwriter's works. In an interview, Cohen explained that "'Hallelujah' is a Hebrew word which means 'Glory to the Lord.' The song explains that many kinds of Hallelujahs do exist. I say: 'All the perfect and broken Hallelujahs have an equal value.'"

According to Cohen's lyrics, the secret chord was made up of a particular mixture of fourths and fifths and of major and minor keys. Kepler, calculating proportions among the varying velocities at which the planets orbit the sun, thought that he had discovered just such a secret chord: it was made up of intervals of a fourth, an octave, a major third, a minor third, and a fourth. For example:

The secret chord was also being sought, in 1616, by the former physician and counsellor to the Habsburg emperor Rudolf II. The physician, whose name was Michael Maier, must have been planning his *Atalanta Fugiens: That Is, New Chemical Emblems of the Secrets of Nature,* a remarkable Rosicrucian-inspired multimedia book published in 1617 that combined musical scores, poetry, and evocative imagery. The book was, its title page announced, "adapted partly for the eyes and intellect in figures engraved on copper, with legends, Epigrams and notes attached, partly for the ears and the soul's recreation with about 50 musical fugues in three voices, of which two are set to a simple melody suitable for singing the couplets, to be looked at, read, meditated, understood, weighed, sung and listened to, not without a certain pleasure."

The twentieth-century psychologist Carl Jung, who was greatly influenced by the alchemical tradition, considered himself a modern representative of the lineage Maier embodied. "I feel strongly," he said, "that I am under the influence of things or questions which were left incomplete and unanswered by my parents and grandparents and more distant ancestors." Among these ancestors he particularly counted two who were likewise named Carl Jung: his grandfather, who was a Grand Master of the Swiss Lodge of Freemasons, and

Above and opposite: Three engravings, 1617, probably by Matthieu Merian, from *Atalanta Fugiens* by Michael Maier. Left to right: The Philosopher's Egg, Alchemy and Geometry, and Following the Footprints of Nature.

In the wake of the publication of the Rosicrucian manifestos, two authors, Robert Fludd and Michael Maier, were influential in promoting the Rosicrucian philosophy in a number of publications.

Fludd was an English physican, astrologer, and mathematician. His *Apologia Compendiaria* of 1616 helped win Rosicrucianism a favorable reception in England.

Maier was the physician to Emperor Rudolf II; after Rudolf's death he lived in England until 1616. His alchemy-inspired *Atalanta Fugiens* is notable for its evocative illustrations, suggestive of esoteric wisdom; called the first multimedia work, it combined illustrations with poetry and musical scores.

a distant ancestor who, Jung says, was a follower of Michael Maier and one of the "founders" of Rosicrucianism.

In his "Preface to the Reader," Maier hailed the power of music and placed himself squarely in the Pythagorean tradition:

> Socrates was educated in Music, and Plato, too, who stated that one is not put together harmoniously who does not rejoice in Music's harmony. Most celebrated in the same was Pythagoras, who is said to have used musical symphonies morning and evening to compose the spirits of his disciples....

For the ancient Greek and Romans, Harmonia was a goddess — the Romans called her Concordia — who was the daughter of Ares and Aphrodite, of war and love; it is harmony that reconciles differences and resolves opposites. By some accounts she was also the mother of the muses. As early as Homer's *Odyssey* the word *harmonia* also meant joining or fitting together. Harmony, in sum, concerns the relations among different things, and this was the focus of the Pythagorean tradition that culminated in the work not only of Maier but of Kepler and many others.

Pythagoras, who lived in sixth-century BCE Greece, was more or less a contemporary of the historical Buddha, Confucius, Laozi, and other teachers whose followers have multiplied manifold since their lifetimes. But the Pythagoreans were a secretive, cultlike group who did not promulgate their knowledge widely: Pythagorean teachings were passed in private from adept to aspirant, and knowledge of its tradition relies largely on secondhand reports. Its fundamental teaching was that there was order to the universe,

and that order was made of numbers. All things, the Pythagoreans held, had number, without which nothing could be thought or known.

Music was essential to their philosophy, and to the Pythagoreans is owed the first mathematically formulated scientific discovery, that musical pitch was a function of the length of a vibrating harp string. A Pythagorean philosopher named Archytas proposed that sounds existed that cannot be heard by humans, "some because of the weakness of their force, some because of their great distance from us, and some because their magnitude exceeds what can fit into our hearing, as when one pours too much into narrow-mouthed vessels and nothing goes in." This led to the notion of the Music of the Spheres, the idea that proportions in the movements of celestial bodies compose a divine music that is inaudible to humans. Pythagoreans thought that this music radiated outward from the center of the universe. The secret of this divine music was the ultimate truth that Kepler, who called Pythagoras "the grandfather of all Copernicans," was seeking.

Kepler's first interest was theology. He was deeply disappointed when the University of Tübingen, where had studied, would not find him a post as a professor of divinity but instead shunted him off into the backwater position of teacher of mathematics at Gratz. Mathematics and theology were inextricably bound for him. "Geometry," he insisted, "existed before the Creation, is co-eternal with the mind of God, *is God himself.*" He explores this theme most fully in the work that he considered his magnum opus, the one he was working on even as he was defending his mother against the witch hunters, his *Harmony of the World*.

In times of disorienting and disturbing change, of turmoil and strife, there are people who are driven to search for the opposite: for signs of harmony in the world. So it was for Kepler. *Harmony* was published in 1618, while Kepler was defending his mother. He had recently been excommunicated. The daughter he had named after his mother had died. At his moment of triumph Kepler had been cut adrift — to support himself he had been forced to resume publishing and selling yearly astrological calendars after having abandoned the practice for more than a decade; the first of these had come out in 1616. Now war was breaking out.

Yet Kepler's *Harmony* unveils the hidden beauty of creation. Astronomical considerations take up only a part of the work (buried among its hundreds of pages is the revelation of the Third Law of Planetary Motion). The book's main impulse, the culmination of the inspiration that had driven him to write his early *Cosmic Mystery,* was the desire to reveal that geometrical patterns and harmonies govern all things: "Geometrical things," he wrote, "have provided the Creator with the model for decorating the whole world." The harmonies that we perceive with our human senses are echoes of the larger harmony that we are unable to hear. By attuning oneself to the correspondences among things, one's soul resonates with the cosmic harmony. In the tradition of Pythagoras, Kepler saw mathematics as the key to universal harmony, the unheard music of the universe. "The more anyone falls in love with mathematics," he said,

> the more fervent will be his dedication to God, and the more he himself will make every effort to practice gratitude, the crown of virtues, so that he will join me in prayer to the merciful God that much more sincerely: let him crush the warlike confusion, eliminate devastation, sniff out hatred, and venture forth to discover that golden harmony once again.

Der Wolff vom Auffgange/vnd der Hund vom Nidergange
kommende/haben sich vnter einander gebissen.

Atalanta fugiens.

Hinc u bi Sol ori tur lu pus
Mer gi tur inde ca nis qui du o

advenit, Ast ubi Pon to
bile tu ment, qui duo bile tu ment.

Hippom. sequens.

Hinc, ubi Sol oritur lupus advenit,ast ubi Ponto, ubi Pon to
Mer gitur inde canis,qui duo bile tument,qui duo bile tument.

Incipe in nota 11. & retrogredere.

Pomum morans.

Hinc ubi Sol oritur lupus ad-
Ponto, Ponto ubi ast venit
Mergitur inde canis,qui duo
tument,tument bile,tument bile.

XLVII. *Epigrammatis Latini versio Germanica.*

ER Wolff von Auffgang der Sonnen/aber der Hund kompt gelauffs
Vom Nidergang/diese beyd haben der Gallen ein hauffen/ sen
Der hat diesen/ vnd dieser jenen im grossen Zorn gebissen/
Vnd haben ein den andern mit Wütigkeit zerrissen/
Es seynd zween Stein/so werden vmbsonst einem jeden gegeben
An allen Orten vnd Zeit/die behalt du gar eben.

EMBLE-

Lupus ab Oriente & Canis ab Occidente venientes se
invicem momorderunt.

EPIGRAMMA XLVII.

HInc,ubi Soloritur,Lupus advenit,ast ubi Ponto
Mergitur,inde canis,qui duo bile tument:
Hunc is, & hic illum,stimulante furore momordit,
Et rabidus rictu visus uterque fuit.
Sunt gemini hi lapides,gratis qui dantur ubique,
Omnibus atque omni tempore,quos teneas.

Bb 3 Phi

Kepler completed his book the same week that the Defenestration of Prague occurred — the incident that triggered the long war that would eventually suck in all the major nations of Europe, leaving central Europe a wasteland. "I cast the die and write a book for the present time," he wrote, "or for posterity. It is all the same to me. It may wait a hundred years for its readers, as God also waited six thousand years for an onlooker."

In the end Kepler's *Harmony,* though it contains scientific discoveries of the highest order, was a work in the prophetic tradition. In his own way, a rabbi in the Jewish ghetto in Venice, struggling like Kepler with family tragedies and personal finances, was also working in that tradition. In December 1616 he had a disturbing dream. In his dream he saw a man surrounded by a crowd of people. That man was a prophet, they said. "The spirit of God is in him." The rabbi boldly stepped forward to ask the prophet how long he had left to live. "Four years, seven months," came the answer.

The rabbi, whose name was Leon Modena, was a son of the Renaissance. An accomplished musican, he had long been a cantor in his syna-

The Wolf Coming from the East and the Dog Coming from the West Have Bitten Each Other, 1617, probably by Matthieu Merian. Engraving from *Atalanta Fugiens* by Michael Maier.

Maier's remarkable multimedia book included music, pictures, prose, and poetry. Maier's emphasis on music derives from the esoteric Paracelsian tradition, which also influenced Kepler, that considered the mysteries of the universe to be revealed by music and mathematics.

A Jewish Woman Gives Birth to Two Piglets, ca. 1574, by Bernhard Jobin. Woodcut. Probably Strassburg, Germany.

As the woman who has delivered the piglets rests in bed, a caricature Jewish man stands over the newborn piglets. The same sorts of demonic and unnatural acts that were attributed to women accused of witchcraft were also applied to others whose beliefs and practices seemed outside the mainstream. A rapidly changing society and increased cross-cultural encounters vied with the segregation of groups by ethnicity and religion to create tensions that would explode in an age of religious warfare.

gogue. He was also a poet and playwright. He was well known as an interpreter of Judaism, and the number of Christians who consulted him shows the interest in Jewish wisdom at this time. He was the official translator of Hebrew to the government of Venice. Between 1614 and 1615 he wrote a treatise on Jewish rites and beliefs at the request of a nobleman who intended to give it to King James of England; this was the first book in a vernacular language that described Jewish rituals for a gentile audience. Following James's ascension to the throne, England and Venice resumed diplomatic relations after a gap of forty-five years, and English scholars working on the bible King James commissioned in 1604 visited Modena for Hebrew instruction. His most lucrative poem, written in both Hebrew and Italian versions, celebrated the birth of a son to Henry IV of France and Marie de Medicis (the boy, delivered by the midwife Louise Bourgeois, would become Louis XIII). The brother of the French king would attend one of his sermons, as would the leader of the French Huguenots.

On waking, Modena decided to test the prophecy against his horoscope. He did not doubt the prophetic power of dreams. Later, during a plague year, prophets would appear to him in another dream to teach him a prayer based on a divine name. He had the prayer made into amulets, which he sold to augment his modest salary. No house on which he had placed the amulet, he maintained, had been visited by the plague.

Rabbi Modena consulted four astrologers, two of whom were Jewish and two Christian. "From my youth I had had a passionate desire to learn from astrologers," he would write in his autobiography. All of the astrologers agreed that he would live to be fifty-two, which was close to the prediction in the dream (in fact he would live to be seventy-seven). Unhappy with the result of his horoscope, Modena regretted having it made, "for man's only proper way is to be pure before God, and he should not make such inquiries. So here I am today, pained on account of the past and anxious about the future.... Ever since I was born I have had no joy, that I should worry about lacking it; neither have I seen any good in this world, that I should have difficulty leaving it."

The year 1616 was indeed a difficult one for Modena. His favorite son, Mordecai, his eldest, was seriously ill, on the verge of death. The trouble had begun in 1614, when Mordecai had set up an alchemical laboratory, working in collaboration with a priest named Joseph Grillo. By 1615 they had succeeded in creating ten ounces of pure silver from nine ounces of lead and one ounce of silver — at least, that is what Modena thought. "This I saw done by him twice, " the rabbi wrote, adding that he "examined it and sold the silver myself for six and a half lire per ounce."

What Mordecai had actually created was copper arsenate, through a process that involved the use of arsenic: the result was a compound that, though not actually much like real silver, had a silverish patina. This was a fumious process, and one that took two and a half months to complete. After his son had been working in this manner over many months, on October 15, 1615, Modena sadly informs us, "much blood from Mordecai's head started flowing out of his mouth." Despite consultation with numerous healers and the application of every conceivable remedy, Mordecai failed to improve, and within two years he was dead.

It was not the last of Modena's trials. The youngest of his three sons would be knifed to death by a Venetian gang. The middle son, whose behavior Modena disapproved of, would run away to Brazil, only returning after the Portuguese reconquest of that country from the Dutch in 1654, six years after Modena had died; on his return he would sue his sisters, contesting Modena's will in costly legal actions they could ill afford. And, in 1634, his fourteen-year-old grandson was arrested for trying to print copies of Modena's midrashic anthology, which was prohibited by Venetian authorities.

Jews in Venice were confined to an island known as the Ghetto Nuovo, or New Ghetto. The word *ghetto,* of Italian origin, alludes to a place where a foundry is located. It became associated with places of Jewish community confinement after a law was passed at the beginning of the sixteenth century confining Jews to the island. The law established gates on each of its two bridges, which were to be locked at sunset and opened at sunrise. Jews caught away from the ghetto outside these hours were subject to hefty fines.

Easter was the time of greatest danger for Jews in Europe. Just as women were blamed for the fall of man from the garden of Eden, so Jews were blamed for the crucifixion of Christ (never mind that he was Jewish too). Jews, like witches, were sometimes thought to bear the mark of the devil, and the segregation of Jewish communities made it easier for some Christians who lacked contact with them to believe fantastic stories of their having horns or tails. In addition, Jews were urban dwellers, and it was believed at this time that groups that did not engage in agriculture were economic parasites. Their presence was tolerated, however, in certain places because their networks of bankers, traders, and merchants stretching throughout the world was necessary for the functioning of incipient capitalism. In addition, they dealt in risky goods such as jewels that were dangerous to handle because of their attractiveness to highwaymen. Prohibitions against Christian money lending meant that the resentment of debtors tended to focus not just on individuals but on Jews as a group.

One of the oldest ghettos in Europe was the Judengasse ("Jews' Alley") in Frankfurt (the district was destroyed in World War II). There Jews worked as money lenders and bankers, pawnbrokers, and small-scale merchants, paying taxes and tariffs beyond those required of the city's Christian residents. In the mid-fourteenth century, Jews had been denied the rights of citizenship, and a century later the ghetto was established. It was a crowded place because it was not allowed to expand its boundaries.

In the early seventeenth century guild workers, most of whom were Calvinists, objected to restrictions imposed by the city's Lutheran patricians. They charged the city government (rightly) with mismanagement of funds, including taxes obtained from the ghetto. A hotheaded gingerbread baker named Vincez Fettmilch (his name means "milk fat") pushed his way to a leadership position. Fettmilch demanded more guild involvement in city governance. He also demanded a reduction in the rate Jewish moneyleaders could charge, and a limit to the number of Jews allowed in the city. Economically stressed guild workers began to fantasize about their debts being wiped away by city edict.

City leaders tried to negotiate with Fettmilch, but he was dissatisfied with their response, and he declared the Town Council deposed and himself in charge. This caught the attention of the emperor, who ordered the Council reinstated. At that a crowd took to the streets. The Jews of the Judengasse were a convenient target of their anger. Rioters stormed the ghetto, and intense fighting ensued. The outmanned Jews were defeated and driven from the city. Their homes were plundered. About fourteen hundred people fled the city in small boats, seeking refuge in neighboring communities. The emperor issued a sentence against Fettmilch. He was captured, and in March 1616 he was hanged and quartered, his house razed, and his family banished. Jews then began returning to the Judengasse. They declared a day to be observed annually as Purim Vinc (after Fettmilch's first name); on this day a song was sung about the assault on the Jews and their eventual deliverance and return to the city.

The Fettmilch riots responded to economic stresses, but the special treatment of the Jews because of their religion, along with tensions between Calvinists and Lutherans, set the stage for the uprising. Despite pockets of pluralism, many people assumed that one faith would soon be shown to be the only true religion, and the others would be defeated. Then, perhaps, the End would be at hand. In Europe the looming Thirty Years War seemed to presage such a moment.

Plundering of the Judengasse, 17th century. Institut für Stadtgeschichte Frankfurt / Historisches Museum Frankfurt am Main.

The Jewish ghetto was attacked by a mob during the Fettmilch riots of 1614, and the residents were forced to flee; their houses were plundered. When they returned in 1616 they established a purim, or celebration of deliverance, to mark the occasion.

While there was comfort in looking back to the golden ages of lore in the face of a scary future that was fraught with unprecedented uncertainties, in many parts of the world there was a sense that the end of time was at hand. This sense was one of the factors that motivated Jesuits and other missionaries to carry Christianity to foreign lands. "If this is not the end of the world," wrote the Habsburg king Philip II of Spain, "I think we must be very close to it." Protestants who rejected the mediation of a church hierarchy discovered in the Book of Revelations prophecy of a coming apocalypse; some added 666, "the number of the beast," to the thousand years of the millennium to determine that 1666 would mark the end of time. Writers like Joseph Mede optimistically foresaw the devil being defeated step by step in a triumphal progression of history; others like William Gouge grimly foresaw ever-increasing "chastisements and afflictions" prior to the final reckoning. Many Jews, facing growing difficulties, looked forward to the messiah's deliverance. In parts of the Islamic world the anticipation of the final reckoning had reached its peak around 1591 and 1592, which was the year 1000 according to the Hegiran calendar. But the feeling barely lessened as predicted apocalypses passed; instead, astrologers and prophets renewed their study of the signs, attempting to formulate a new understanding of the order of the universe. This quest led to all kinds of forays into esoteric forms of knowledge, from which emerged both new scientific discoveries and new superstitions and heresies.

Shah Abbas of Safavid Persia was forty-five years old in 1616, and he had ruled for twenty-nine years. Throughout the course of his reign he had dealt with many threats and outmaneuvered many opponents and dissident factions. The threats had not always been material or military ones; ideas could be just as subversive, and indeed during the early seventeenth century wars of beliefs and wars of arms were often inextricably entangled. In the early 1590s, for example, he had had to deal with an order of Sunnis called the Nuqtavis, who objected to his Shiite notions. The Nuqtavis were not powerful enough to bring down Shah Abbas by force, but they fomented unrest by announcing that they had read signs predicting that the ruler of Persia would soon die and that one of their number would occupy the throne. The power of the prediction derived from the mounting fear that momentous matters — perhaps indeed the end of the world — were at hand. A second millennium of the Hegira calendar was just beginning. When Shah Abbas consulted his own court astrologer he was shaken to discover that he confirmed the prophecy, based on the coming conjunction of Saturn and Jupiter. But Shah Abbas was not a fatalistic man. So he acted decisively.

The shah's first maneuver was a practical one: he executed or imprisoned most of the Nuqtavis. This removed some of the threat, but it did not undo the prophecy, so he spared one young man among their number. He then abdicated the throne in favor of this unfortunate. He, Shah Abbas, would henceforth be no more than the guardian of the royal harem. Several days passed in this arrangement, until the planets moved apart. Now the young "sultan" was executed, and his body publicly displayed. The prophesies that the sultan would die and a Nuqtavi occupy the throne had both proven true.

In 1611, following a long and exhausting but ultimately indecisive war against the Ottomans, Rudolf II was forced to cede power over the Empire to his younger brother Matthias; nine months later Rudolf died at the age of sixty. With his death Kepler lost his powerful patron, and he left Prague for a position as provincial mathematician in Upper Austria. The childless Matthias reigned for only a few years. In 1617 he was succeeded by his nephew Ferdinand as king of Bohemia (the region around Prague that is now the western half of the Czech Republic). That's when all hell broke loose.

Ferdinand was an ardent Catholic who had won the support of the Spanish Habsburgs. Restive Bohemian Protestants called a diet to press the new king for guarantees of religious rights. Ferdinand forbade the diet from meeting. It assembled anyway in May 1618. A deputation marched to Hradshin Castle and confronted the king's regents, demanding an explanation for the diet having been declared illegal. Dissatisfied with the response, the delegates seized the two regents and their secretary and threw them out an upper-story window. Landing in a mound of manure, all three survived. Catholics subsequently claimed the three men had been saved by the intervention of angels, while Protestants attributed their survival to the horse dung into which they fell. This grotesque incident, known as the Defenestration of Prague, is traditionally marked as the beginning of the Thirty Years War.

Protestants gathered around Frederick, the son-in-law of James I of England, Catholics around Ferdinand. Largely because of its religious implications, the initially local conflict escalated, eventually involving the nations of Denmark, Spain, Sweden, and France, among others; the pacifistic

The Defenestration of Prague, 1618, woodblock illustration.

Angry Protestants confronted King' Ferdinand's regents in Hradshin Castle in Prague and threw them and their secretary from a window. The incident is usually considered to mark the beginning of the calamitous Thirty Years War. This illustration appeared in a pamphlet published shortly after the event.

King James was one of the few leaders with a potential stake in the outcome to hold back from military involvement.

By the time Denmark entered the conflict in 1625 the Empire's finances had been strained to an alarming degree. At that point a Bohemian Catholic convert from Lutheranism, Albrecht Wallenstein, recruited more than thirty thousand men at his own expense and led them in battle. Wallenstein, who became supreme commander of the Empire's armies, was a military strongman whom Ferdinand, wary of his ambition and fearful of his changing sides, would eventually have assassinated. This was the man to whom Johannes Kepler attached himself in the later years of his life.

Rejecting invitations from Italy and England, Kepler remained in Germany through the years of warfare. "Am I to go overseas?" he wrote of an invitation from England. "I, a German? I, who love the firm continent and who shrink at the idea of an island in narrow boundaries of which I feel the dangers in advance?" In 1624 Kepler did a ten-year forecast of the generalissimo's fortunes that concluded with a prediction of "dreadful disorders" in 1634. That February Wallenstein would be murdered. Meanwhile, in 1628, Wallenstein hired Kepler as his full-time personal astrologer and mathematician.

For Kepler these were years of painful wandering. Perhaps he recalled his father's distant wartime service during this time, or his mother's difficult journey to the Low Countries in search of her husband. Her story anticipates that of Mother Courage, a character in a tale by the greatest seventeenth-century German novelist, Hans Jakob Christoffel von Grimmelshausen. Grimmelshausen's narrator, the title character, is a camp follower who refuses to bow to the slings of fortune but schemes her way through the Thirty Years War and prospers from it. For Bertolt Brecht, who would base his play of the same name on Grimelshausen's character, Mother Courage was both complicit in and victimized by a capitalist system that profits from war. In the same way, Kepler, a committed Lutheran who had scant faith in astrology, spent his final years wandering war-torn Germany making horoscopes for the military commander of the Catholic forces.

Finally, in 1630, in a Bavarian town at the confluence of the Danube and Regen rivers that was then called Ratisbon, now Regensburg, Kepler took to bed, delirious and raging with fever. He was bled, but it didn't help. After a time he stopped raving, and in the end he spoke little, only pointing first to his head and then to the sky. Attended by Lutheran priests, he would be buried in a church cemetery. The churchyard would be desecrated by Swedish forces, and his bones scattered and lost. His epitaph, however, survives:

I measured the heavens, now I measure the shadows of the earth
My mind was of the heavens, here my body's shadow lies

It is estimated that a quarter of the population of the Holy Roman Empire — around eight million people — died over the course of the Thirty Years War, the most devastating in central Europe before World War II. More than four hundred years later, in 1939, as Europe was again descending into the madness of all-encompassing war, and new, even more ruthless and senseless witch hunts were beginning, German composer Paul Hindemith was, like Kepler before him, thinking about the harmony of the world, despite, or perhaps because of, the coming conflict. Also like Kepler, Hindemith (whose wife was Jewish) had a somewhat compromised relation to political power, accommodating the Nazi regime in small ways before fleeing Germany in 1938.

Hindemith researched Kepler's life and work for an opera that he would call *Die Harmonie der Welt* — "The Harmony of the World." Through the cataclysmic war years the music of that opera coalesced and reverberated in Hindemith's head. Finally, in 1951, he prepared a symphony based on passages from the as yet unwritten opera; the symphony was performed to acclaim by the Basel Chamber Orchestra. Then, in 1956, during the chill of the cold war, Hindemith completed the libretto of the opera, which premiered in Munich the following year. It portrays Kepler as a spiritual seeker in a violent and senseless world. Kepler's spiritual quest is contrasted with the furious efforts of General Wallenstein to impose harmony by force. Yet Kepler does not succeed in hearing the harmony of the world until, at the last moment, with death approaching, in a surreal final scene in which Hindemith pulls out all the dramatic and musical stops, he relinquishes his own striving. Then he gives himself up to the world as it truly is.

Its Nurse Is the Earth, 1617, probably by Matthieu Merian. Engraving from *Atalanta Fugiens* by Michael Maier.

The text reads:

> A she-wolf's udders nourished
>   Romulus,
>   A she-goat Jupiter, so 'tis believed:
> What wonder, if we say the tender
>   CHILD
>   Of the PHILOSOPHERS is
>   nursed by the EARTH?
> If poor beasts fed such Heroes, then
>   HOW GREAT
>   Shall be the one NURSED by the
>   GLOBE of EARTH?

5   World in Motion

Dark skin and black hair, long, arched eyebrows, eyelids made up with kohl over dark eyes with "bright, sparkling pupils" — these were among the qualities the thirty-year-old groom admired in his eighteen-year-old Baghdad bride. All in all she had "very acceptable physical beauty," he said, "not to exaggerate it, because it is not right for husbands to exaggerate the beauty of their wives, though were I otherwise, I would perhaps speak differently of her." After all, she was "in every part finely proportioned" and "of very ancient Christian blood." In December 1616, when the wedding was held, they had known each other barely a month, but theirs would be both an effective partnership and a true romance, if one with a strange, sad ending.

Her name, as he wrote it, was Maani Gioerida (in a more conventional transliteration today it would be Ma'ani Juwayri). *Ma'ani* means "reason" in Arabic. She was linguistically adept, fluent in Arabic and Turkish, and conversant in Chaldean, Armenian, Georgian, and, soon, Persian. Her husband's native language was Italian, and her ability to communicate across all sorts of cultural boundaries would prove invaluable to him in their travels together through the Ottoman and Persian empires.

There was one small point of contention — her nose ring, which to the groom recalled "those worn by our oxen in Italy." But she finally agreed to give it up, and marital bliss was restored.

Her parents were Nestorian Christians who had moved to Baghdad from southeastern Turkey, and she had grown up in the city. Baghdad was part of the Ottoman empire at this time, having first been captured in 1534, but the Turks' hold on it was tenuous. Within a few years it would be taken by Persians under Shah Abbas, though it would remain in Safavid control for only about fifteen years.

The "Church of the East," to which Maani Gioerida's family belonged, had at one time been the most geographically widespread of the branches of Christianity, reaching to China and India. Nestorius, a fifth-century patriarch of Constantinople, had claimed that Jesus had two separate natures, one as a man and one as a god. Mary had given birth, he said, to Jesus the man, not Jesus the god, and therefore she should not be called the Mother of God. Nestorius's doctrine was officially condemned, but his followers simply moved east, making Nestorianism the predominant religion of Persia until it was supplanted by Islam. During

Opposite: Foreign Ambassadors, 1616–1617, by Giovanni Lanfranco and workshop. Fresco. Sala dei Corazzieri, Quirinale Palace, Rome.

In 1616 the room in the pope's summer palace designated for receiving foreign dignitaries was adorned with frescoes. The overall plan was apparently charged to Agostino Tassi, who created an illusionistic plan in which ambassadors peer down from balconies opening onto imaginary rooms.

Giovanni Lanfranco and Carlo Saraceni were among the artists who painted the figures. Those in the center here appear to be West Asian ambassadors, the younger of whom may be Robert Sherley, an Englishman sent by Shah Abbas of Persia on an embassy to Europe.

Dark-skinned figures appear in most of the panels, one of which depicts Emanuele Ne Vunda, an ambassador sent by King Alvaro II of Kongo. Others seem intended to represent Ethiopians, South Indians, or other ethnicities. To Europeans such figures would recall the tradition that one of the wise men was supposed to have been black.

At the right in this panel is Hasekura Tsunenaga, who traveled to Rome from Japan by crossing the Pacific to the Atlantic through Mexico.

The commemoration of these notable visits was meant to emphasize the prestige of the pope. It also marks the beginning of the globalization of the world.

Sitti Maani Gioerida della Valle, 1745, by F. G. Scotin, l'aîné, from *Les Voyages de Pietro della Valle.* Engraving.

the years of Mongol rule the church had been suppressed, and it had never managed to recover its prior status. Nonetheless, there were sizable Christian communities in both the Ottoman empire and Safavid Persia, which were treated as protected minorities.

Most people of her time, like Maani Gioerida before she married, lived out their lives in just one place. So the historians, quite rightly, like to remind us: "In the world of the 1500s and 1600s," says John E. Wills, Jr., "most people never traveled more than ten miles from home." "Most Europeans never traveled very far from their home towns and villages," agrees Merry Wiesner-Hanks. According to Henry Kamen, "Most people's experience was limited to their own region. Food, tools and clothing were all normally produced within the home area."

And yet a great many people were on the move in 1616. Artists and artisans often moved to serve their patrons: Artemisia Gentileschi and her father Orazio, for example, traveled to London to complete commissions; many Persian artists relocated to the Mughal court. Traders sometimes ranged long distances: a traveling yarn salesman like Jacob Boehme might crisscross Bohemia; maritime traders might spend years traversing oceans. Diplomats like Peter Paul Rubens or Thomas Roe were sent on distant missions. Pirates and adventurers buckled swashes around the globe. Algiers was filled with corsairs from every nation. Walter Raleigh was released from the Tower of London in 1616 to search for El Dorado. Settlers like John Rolfe (though the Powhatans would call him not a settler but an invader) also crossed oceans. It was a time of warfare: soldiers like Heinrich Kepler went where the fighting was, and women like Katharina Kepler followed them; other women also followed the men, as Grimmelshausen's Mother Courage would do, to turn tricks or peddle goods. Missionaries traveled far. Vagrants and beggars rambled from town to town. Refugees fled conflicts in many parts of the world; pestilence and famine also caused migrations. Pilgrims, like Mulla Sadra, traveled long distances for religious reasons. Some people were forcibly moved: Cervantes and Malik Ambar were carried off as slaves, and a slave industry had begun that would move unprecedented numbers of sub-Saharan Africans to the Americas to harvest sugar or cotton, or to work in the mines after the native labor pool had been exhausted.

Artists and artisans; diplomats; pirates, adventurers, and explorers; migrants and settlers; soldiers and their hangers-on; traders and merchants; prostitutes; vagrants and beggars; opportunists; exiles and refugees from war, pestilence, or famine; religious and cultural pilgrims and missionaries; servants and slaves: they were all on the move. Maani Gioerida's parents were refugees. But Pietro della Valle, a nobleman from a distinguished Italian family, was none of these, exactly. He was a new breed of traveler: though he had a little of the qualities of many of those different kinds of travelers, in the end he was a tourist, wandering mainly out of curiosity and a desire for new experiences.

Or maybe he was a refugee after all — a refugee from love, from a previous love affair that had been unsuccessful. For twelve years he had courted a woman named Beatrice Boraccio (taking time out along the way to father two illegitimate children by other women), only to be rejected in favor of another man. Wallowing in romantic broodings about killing his rival and then himself, he drifted listlessly, casting about for some grand gesture that would demonstrate his exceptional qualities: he wanted, he said, to play a role on the stage of the world — *nel gran teatro di tutto l'universo*. In 1611 he participated in some skirmishes against corsairs off the coast of Africa, and this awakened in him a curiosity about the ancient world. He latched onto a leading European orientalist, Mario Schipano, a professor of medicine at Naples. Schipano inspired him to undertake a journey to the Holy Land, making observations and collecting information about literature, science, and culture along the way.

Pietro della Valle, 1745, by F. G. Scotin, l'ainé, from *Les Voyages de Pietro della Valle.* Engraving.

In June 1614, accompanied by a Flemish painter named Giovanni, an Augustinian monk called Brother Andrea, and two servants, Tomasso and Lorenzo, he set sail from Venice for Istanbul on his way to the holy land. He was, at first, to be a typical pilgrim making a journey, like many others, to a religious center of his faith; in fact, he often referred to himself, through what would turn out to be many years of wandering, as "Pietro the Pilgrim." At the outset he dressed as a traditional pilgrim, in a white robe with a horsehair belt. He strung a little gold pilgrim's staff on a chain around his neck.

Except for that amulet, which he intended to leave in the holy city of Jerusalem, he abandoned this costume when he got to Istanbul. Something of a popinjay, he delighted there in dressing in the silks of an Ottoman pasha. On his head he placed "an immense white plume to make me easily distinguishable at a distance from everybody else." Nothing pleased him more than

Above: Pietro della Valle Discovers Egyptian Mummies, 1664–1665, from *Der Voortrefelkyke Reisen van Pietro della Valle,* a Dutch translation of his travels. Engraving.

Opposite: Egyptian Mummy Portrait of a Man with a Richly Decorated Tunic. Inv. Aeg. 777. Skulpturensammlung, Staatliche Kunstsammlungen, Dresden, Germany. Photo: Elke Estel / Hans-Peter Klut. Image copyright © bpk Berlin / Skulpturensammlung / Elke Estel / Hans-Peter Klut / Art Resource, NY.

to draw a crowd as he walked down the streets of the city in his extravagant costumes. Turkish maidens, he said, would fondle his moustaches and stroke his cheeks, crying "Ghiuzel! Ghiuzel!" as he passed by: "How handsome! How handsome!" When he learned that the elite of the city soled their boots with iron to go riding, he had a pair made with silver soles — "a thing so out of the ordinary that not even the Prince himself does the like."

Della Valle didn't know it yet, but he was already hooked on exoticism. Or we might call it "orientalism," a term associated with the Palestinian-American literary theorist Edward Said, which refers to the tendency of Western writers to erect exotic, and ultimately belittling, mythologies about "oriental" peoples and cultures based on stereotypes and assumptions. Like others of his time, della Valle contributed to such mythologies, and consequently he has not fared well with some modern critics. J. D. Gurney holds him up as a prime example of "the limits of perception," objecting that in his writing there are no more than "the barest indications of escape from a thoroughly Eurocentric attitude." In Glenn Most's assessment, "Pietro's desire for great deeds, fame, and a typically Humanist form of immortality stood in a certain disproportion to his own capabilities."

I think we should cut the man some slack. Admittedly, he was not an especially deep thinker, and his writing (which he did not intend for publication in its existing form, without editing) is marred by repetition and a lack of proportion. But the early seventeenth century — the "age of religious wars" — was not an era noted for tolerance and cross-cultural understanding. Della Valle was a man of his place, time, and station. The mere fact that he resided in Islamic countries for nearly a fifth of his life is itself remarkable by the standards of his time.

In Istanbul he spent a year partying, seeing the sights, and learning Turkish, which was to be his go-to language throughout his journeys. He discovered there a strange new drink called *cahue* (coffee) and another called *sherbet,* as well as an unusual loose-weave fabric called *terry cloth* and a kind of furniture called a *sofa,* all of which he resolved to introduce into Italy. He judged coffee to be improved by the addition of sugar, cinnamon, and cloves, and he speculated that it could be made even better by brewing it with wine rather than water. He described his discoveries in a series of letters he sent to his friend Dr. Schipano. Before he was done he would send thirty-six lengthy letters back to Naples. Remarkably, all would reach their destination. They would be published after his death by his sons as *The Travels of Pietro della Valle* (Viaggi di Pietro della Valle) — Schipano had faithfully kept all of della Valle's correspondence, misplacing just one letter.

Although della Valle wrote nothing about his own wedding ceremony in Baghdad, he did describe a wedding he had attended in Istanbul. It was held in the evening. Women guests arrived with trunks full of clothes, and they changed their outfits several times during the celebration. "I have never seen women so superbly dressed and bejeweled," della Valle

enthused. A lavish meal was served at 2:00 AM. Because it was considered inauspicious for the couple to consummate their marriage before dawn, the party continued through the night, the guests dragging themselves off at daybreak.

From Istanbul he sailed for Cairo. He found the city disappointing. As a consequence of the discovery of the sea route between Europe and India, trade through Cairo had fallen off, and the city was suffering from neglect by its Turkish governors. Still, della Valle was a sociable sort who made friends easily, and he attended another wedding there, of a Coptic Christian couple. This was accompanied by singing, playing stringed instruments, and ribald pantomime. To honor the new union the guests and the groom all got falling-down drunk.

In Egypt he came across white monkeys, and arranged for one to be shipped back to India. He visited the Sphinx (at that time almost entirely buried in sand) and the pyramids. He climbed to the top of the Pyramid of Cheops, where he carved his name on the side facing Italy. He became the first European to excavate Egyptian mummies, descending into a pit where many examples were stacked on top of one another "just like cheese and macaroni." He shipped some mummies and the mummy portraits with which they were buried back to Italy. He saw Cleopatra's Needles before

In 1616 Pietro della Valle became the first European to discover the Fayum mummy portraits of Egypt's late antiquity. He sent examples back to Europe, including this portrait, which is now in the Albertinum, the state art museum in Dresden.

"On this outer casing was painted the figure of a young man, no doubt the portrait of the deceased, but fully dressed and decorated from head to foot with so many painted and gilt devices, with such a quantity of hieroglyphs, characters, and the like," della Valle wrote, "that you can well imagine that it was the prettiest thing in the world."

they were removed to erode as monuments to imperialism and capitalism in London and New York. At Mount Sinai he prayed to the patron saint of marriages to heal his broken heart.

In Cairo della Valle witnessed the departure of a caravan to Mecca. The caravan was so long that it took a full day to pass by. It seemed to della Valle to contain

> the whole body of those who in Cairo profess the holy life, bearing an infinity of different banners. These false friars marched two by two, singing in alternating choirs much as our monks do when they psalmodize. Among them was a handful of their ascetics, variously clad and posturing extravagantly, wearing theselves out with ceaseless cries of "hu!" Some, completely naked, freely displayed their nudity to proclaim their holiness.

Of the world's religious pilgrimages, none was more important than the hajj, the journey of devout Muslims to Mecca. Mecca (the birthplace of the prophet Muhammad), and the secondary pilgrimage destination of Medina (his burial place) about two hundred miles to its north, were inconveniently located in the Hejaz, the region of the Arabian peninsula along the coast of the Red Sea. Vast numbers of pilgrims nonetheless made the arduous trip to these destinations. A late-sixteenth-century Portuguese writer estimated that two hundred thousand people assembled at a prayer meeting at Mount Arafat. Pilgrims came from as far away as Central Asia, passing through the steppes to the Caspian Sea in order to avoid their Persian enemies, and from Southeast Asia, stopping over at ports in India along the way.

The hajj was unique in that it was in theory obligatory, as one of the pillars of Islamic faith, for Muslims to make the journey at least once in a lifetime, so long as the worshipper was capable financially and otherwise of undertaking it. It was also unusual in that pilgrims were required only to set eyes on the Kaaba, the cube-shaped building said to have been constructed by Abraham and his son Ishmael, and not necessarily to enter it to visit holy relics. Those who were able to enter would emulate Muhammad and kiss its holy black stone if they could, but this was also not a requirement. Those who could not reach the rock would circle the Kaaba seven times. They would cry "Here, my God, here I am," and point in its direction.

What was required was that pilgrims arrive by the time of the annual prayer on Mount Arafat on the ninth day of the twelfth lunar month. Because the Islamic lunar year was shorter than the solar year, the exact date of this event varied with respect to the solar calendar. But if the date was missed the pilgrimage would be invalid. Pilgrims were always attentive to the phases of the moon in order to measure their progress against this date. If the Day of Arafa fell on a Friday, the pilgrimage was held to be especially auspicious and effective. As a result, reports of new moon sightings always multiplied around the appropriate day. One local judge at Mecca complained of such reports that "a hair escapes from their eyelashes, they see something, and immediately they think it to be the new moon."

The need to arrive on time by the Day of Arafa meant that caravans to Mecca had to run efficiently, at a predictable rate. There were two main caravan routes: one led down the eastern coast of the Red Sea from Cairo and the other led from Istanbul through Aleppo and Damascus south to Medina and then Mecca. Sometimes there was also an east-west caravan that ran from Basra on the Persian Gulf across the Arabian Desert to Medina, but this route was complicated by tensions between the Ottomans and Persia, as well as by the predations of Bedouins. A fourth route may have led north from Yemen on the southern tip of the Arabian peninsula, but scant historical record of such a route exists, whereas the northern caravan routes are well documented as a result of the compulsive record-keeping of the Ottoman bureaucracy.

The Ottomans had to make provisions for the safety of the caravans or risk suffering a damaging loss of prestige. This was not always easy, since their control over the desert regions was partial at best, and almost nonexistent over the route from Basra. A detachment of janissaries was assigned to protect the caravans, sometimes supplemented by cavalry, especially on the vulnerable Syrian route from Damascus. In particularly dangerous times caravans were sometimes armed with cannon, which proved to be the most effective deterrent against attack. Many of the pilgrims themselves carried personal arms.

The Ottomans attempted to establish guard garrisons along the caravan routes, but these were usually undermanned and vulnerable to takeover. In 1625, for example, Bedouins gained control of one such fort by drugging its soldiers. Bedouin maidens distributed spiked sweets to the soldiers, saying they were the charitable offering of a deceased person. The Bedouins took command of the fort while its defenders snoozed.

Caravans used precious water supplies in desert regions, which Bedouins would not share without compensation. Tolls and tributes were key components of caravan expenditures. Merchants moving goods by caravan found the variable protection costs to be one of the most difficult aspects of business. Once arrived at Mecca, the travelers could face a variety of fees imposed by the local rulers there, known as sharifs. The sharifs constantly vied with the central Ottoman government in Istanbul over their degree of autonomy in governing and their authority to impose taxes and fees.

The cost of maintaining camels and horses was a major caravan expense. Spare animals had to be taken to ensure against losses. Soldiers and officials alone required more than six hundred animals, and the travelers required thousands more. If it appeared that the caravan was running behind schedule the animals would be driven hard, since making the Day of Arafa was critical. Camel entrepreneurs often complained bitterly about the way their animals were treated. In general the entrepreneurs were held responsible for replacing beasts that fell out of service. There are conflicting reports of the profitability of the camel trade but the fact that participation sometimes had to be conscripted by the Ottoman state suggests that camel entrepreneurship was at the least a chancy way to make one's fortune.

The leaders of caravans were responsible for arranging the pilgrims. Otherwise anarchy would result when crossing narrow passages or vulnerable areas. Generally the wealthiest and most heavily armed travelers were placed in the front — this was the position Pietro della Valle occupied in his caravan journeys — while poorer travelers were made to travel in the more vulnerable rear. Security had to be provided not only against outside attack but also within the caravan itself. Thirsty, tired, and anxious travelers from different parts of the world, many of them armed, could easily get into dangerous disputes, which the caravan master would have to adjudicate.

Because the requirement of the hajj was recognized by both Sunni and Shiite Muslims, safe conduct could be given to high-ranking pilgrims even from enemy nations. The system was far from foolproof. The hajj could be a pretext for spying, and travelers from hostile nations were naturally viewed with suspicion. The Ottoman government had a top Safavid official who made the journey in the late sixteenth century murdered; to prevent the outbreak of war they staged a Bedouin attack to conceal their role in his assassination.

In addition to the caravan routes, some pilgrims, especially from India, arrived by sea. The most direct route was to sail up the Red Sea, although such voyages were susceptible to piracy then as today. Sailing to the Persian Gulf required passing the Portuguese stronghold at Hormuz. This route was complicated by international maritime conflicts, and once arrived on the Gulf pilgrims would still face difficult choices for completing their journey. Nonetheless, the hajj contributed to the vitality of sea travel in the Indian Ocean region.

Ships even arrived from the distant east coast of India. Between 1610 and

Pilgrim, late sixteenth–early seventeenth century. Unknown artist. Isfahan, Persia. Ink and colors on paper, 5 x 10 cm. British Museum, ME 1920.0917.0.279.2.

Depictions of pilgrims, shaykhs, and dervishes were popular during the reign of Shah Abbas. A popular pilgrimage destination among Persians was the Shrine of Imam Riza in a region disputed with the Uzbeks. Pilgrims often endured hardships during their travels. This pilgrim is aged and stooped but retains a look of determination.

1620 a ship from Golconda successfully carried pilgrims up the Red Sea despite the contentious international maritime situation in the Indian Ocean. As ballast the ship carried rice to be distributed to the poor in Mecca.

The Mughal emperor Akbar, Jahangir's father, was at one time an enthusiastic supporter of the hajj. In the early years of his reign he subsidized the travel expenses of poor people and founded a hospice in Mecca. Perhaps feeling that his efforts were insufficiently appreciated or his people inadequately cared for, he later cooled to the pilgrimage; Jahangir's support for the hajj was likewise tepid. But many pilgrims from South and even Southeast Asia continued to make the journey.

Poorer pilgrims would sometimes run out of funds and be reduced to begging. In time a large community of poor Indians made up a slum in central Mecca. The destitute Indians were unwelcome to the Ottomans. Some degree of charity had to be provided for them, and they disrupted plans to upgrade the city center. Information is scarce, but it appears this community was forcibly relocated to the outskirts of the city around the beginning of the seventeenth century.

Maintaining an attractive city center provided an environment conducive to the sale of goods and souvenirs. Pilgrimages were not simply religious journeys but were often combined with trade. Wealthy pilgrims would carry goods for exchange in order to help finance their trips, and the large assemblies of pilgrims at Mecca provided an opportunity for a great deal of trade. Caravans and ships carrying pilgrims also brought vast numbers of merchants and peddlers, although it was often hard to draw a sharp distinction between religious and commercial travelers. Cotton garments brought along with pilgrims by ship from India made their way into Turkish and European markets where they became something of a fad in the seventeenth century.

As a result of trade disparities, silver brought to Spain from the Americas often passed through the Ottoman empire and ended up in India. By some estimates as much as a third of the silver that entered Europe in the century and a half after 1600 made its way to India. The Ottomans encouraged importation because they saw the customs imposed on imports as a source of revenue. They also tolerated non-Muslim residents in the empire in part because they were taxed at a higher rate than Muslims and thus were another source of revenue.

Della Valle's caravan from Cairo proceeded with little incident, and two years after setting out from Istanbul he reached Jerusalem. A few years before, another European traveler had made the same journey in reverse. Like della Valle, he was wandering for no better reason than restlessness and curiosity. In 1616 he was enjoying a rare moment of comfort, dining in the company of the North African corsair captain Yusuf Reis (Jack Ward). His name was William Lithgow, and he had made the journey from Damascus to Jerusalem (and then on to Cairo) in the company of "about 900 Armenians, Christian Pilgrimes, men and women: 600 Turkes trafficking for their owne businesse, and 100 souldiers, three Showsses, and sixe Janizaries." His trip had been more eventful than della Valle's,

> being oft assailed with Arabs, fatigued with rocky mountains, and sometimes in point of choaking, for lacke of water. The confusion of this multitude, was not onely grievous in regard of the extreme heate, providing of victuals at poore Villages, and scarcity of water, to fill our bottles, made of Boare-skins; but also amongst narrow and stony passages, thronging, we oft fell one over another, in great heapes; in danger to be smothered: yea; and oftentimes we that were Christians had our bodies well beaten, by our conducting Turkes.

Even after he reached Jerusalem — where he had his right forearm tatooed with the Cross of Jerusalem and the Crown of King James I in the Church of the Holy Sepulchre — Lithgow's troubles continued. He booked a tour led by Franciscan Guardians to the River Jordan and the Dead Sea (noting bitterly the fee of the equivalent of forty-two shillings sterling). Stopping by the river at the spot where Jesus was supposed to have been baptised, the party, despite an escort of a hundred soldiers, fell under attack from a band of thieves. Lithgow, who had wandered off from the others, had been bathing in the river's waters and was in danger of being left behind. Hearing gunfire, he

> ranne starke naked above a quarter of a mile amongst thistles, and sharp pointed grasse, which pitifully pricked the soles of my feete, but the feare of death for the present, expel'd the griefe of that unlooked for paine. Approaching on the safe side of my company, one of our Souldiers broke forth on horsebacke, being determined to kill mee for my staying behinde: Yea, and three times stroke at me with his halfepike; but his horse being at his speed, I prevented his cruelty, first by falling downe, next by running in amongst the thickest of the Pilgrimes, recovering the Guardians face, which when the Guardian espied, and saw my naked body, hee presently pulled off his gray gowne, and threw it to me, whereby I might hide the secrets of nature; By which meanes, (in the space of an houre) I was clothed three manner of wayes: First,

like a Turke: Secondly, like a wild Arabian: And thirdly, like a grey Frier, which was a barbarous, a savage, and a religious habit.

Lithgow was a grimly determined tourist, who by the end of his major travels estimated that his "paynefull feet traced over ... thirty-six thousand and odde miles, which draweth neare to twice the circumference of the whole Earth." Most of his travel had been on foot — and most of it in a bad mood. What drove him to wander so prolifically is not easy to make out, as he seemed to derive little pleasure from it, although as a fierce Calvinist he did receive some satisfaction from vilifying the "deceitful deepes" of the "bottomless Gulfe of Papistry." Orthodox Christians, Jews, and Muslims were also objects of his scorn, although the empire of the sultans comes off better than the church of Rome in his estimation.

As his long travels went on and on they failed to lighten either his mood or his prose. A first short publication describing his early travels appeared in 1614 under what was, for him, the happy title of *A Most Delectable and True Discourse of an Admired and Painfull Peregrination in Europe.* The initial printing quickly sold out and a second was issued in 1616. The original dedication to the king's then-favorite, Robert Carr, Earl of Somerset, and his wife, Lady Francis Howard, was changed in the reprint to "all Noble-minded Gentlemen, and Heroicke Spirits" — Carr and Howard were in the Tower of London, charged with the poisoning of Sir Thomas Overbury.

By 1632 Lithgow was presenting his expanded wanderings under the expanded title of *The Totall Discourse, of the Rare Adventures and Painfull Peregrinations of Long Nineteene Yeares Trauayles, from Scotland, to the Most Famous Kingdomes in Europe, Asia, and Affrica. Perfited by Three Dear Boughte Voyages, in Surueighing of Forty eight Kingdomes Ancient and Moderne; Twenty One Rei-Publickes, Ten Absolute Principalities, with Two Hundred Ilands. The Particular Names Whereof, Are Described in Each Argument of the Ten Diuisions of This History: And It Also Diuided in Three Bookes; Two Whereof, Neuer Heretofore Published. Wherein Is Contayned, and Exact Relation, of the Lawes, Religion, Policies, and Gouernment of All Their Princes, Potentates, and People. Together with the Grieuous Tortures He Suffered, by the Inquisition of Malaga in Spaine, His Miraculous Discouery and Delivery Thence: And of His Last and Late Returne from the Northerne Iles.* Clearly this was a man who didn't know when to stop.

In the later years of his life, when travel became difficult for him, he turned his attention to an account of an explosion at a Scottish castle called *A Briefe and Summary Discourse upon That Lamentable and*

Dreadfull Disaster at Dunglasses and a lengthy poetic work with the mournful title *The Gushing Teares of Godly Sorrow, Containing, the Causes, Conditions, and Remedies of Sinne, Depending Mainly on Contrition and Confession.* This moralistic poem invites the reader to dwell on "mans stinking flesh" as a "Mass of ill," a "Chaos of corruption," "rotten slime," and a "pudle of inruption" of "base filthynesse."

He had some cause for gloom. His journeys were stalked by bad luck and hard knocks. In contrast to Pietro della Valle, who seems to have been shielded by wealth and a kind of cosmic insouciance, Lithgow was robbed and beaten all over the world. Yet those beatings were only the prelude for his greatest torment, which would be saved for the end of his three main journeys.

Not much is known of Lithgow's origins. He was certainly not nobility, but his family doesn't seem to have been hard up either. He was educated at the Grammar School in the little market town of Lanark in Scotland. After leaving school he traditionally is said to have taken up with a certain Alice Lockhart, whose family considered themselves too high of station for the likes of Lithgow. One day her brothers followed the lovers and, surprising them in a compromising situation, the "four blood-shedding wolves," as he called them, cut off both of Lithgow's ears. This amused the good folk of Lanark no end: they pegged the poor boy with the moniker "Cut-Lugged Willie" and laughed him out of town. According to historian Boies Penrose, local residents were still enthusiastically pointing out the house where this incident took place more than two hundred years later.

Recently a Lithgow specialist named James Robert Burns has proposed that the object of Lithgow's youthful affections was not Alice Lockhart but a young woman from an even more upper-crust family named Helen Hamilton. However that may be, after this trouble Lithgow seems to have just kept on moving. Disdainful of stay-at-homes, whom he dismissed as "prattling Parrots, and sounding Cymbals," he resolved "to seclude my selfe from my soyle, and exclude my relenting sorrows." After warming up with walks through northern and central Europe, he began his three major journeys in 1608, when he left England for France; he would continue to Italy and on from there to Egypt and the Levant. His second journey, 1614–1616, took him to North Africa; his third, 1619–1621, to Spain.

On his first journey he was particularly disgusted by Rome, where he "sawe nothing but abomination, prophanation, and irreligious living." He had trouble keeping quiet about his religious beliefs, and "hardly escaped from the hunting of blood-sucking Inquisitors." In Penrose's estimation, "Lithgow's hatred of Catholicism…was so violent as to be in fact psychopathic, and his dour Calvinistic soul was so bitter that he would work himself into a raving frenzy at the mere thought of the Romish church." In Italy he also visited Naples, Venice, and other cities. He liked Venice best, in part because on the day he arrived "there was a gray Frier burning quick at S. Markes pillar, for begetting fifteene young Nopble Nunnes with child, and all within one yeare; he being also their Father confessor." Or so Lithgow claimed: his account is suspiciously similar to that of the English traveler Thomas Coryate, who visited Venice the year before and reported seeing hanging from a steeple the head of a friar who was supposed to have impregnated ninety-nine nuns.

He was less enthusiastic about nearby Padua, where he spent three months studying Italian. He considered the university a hotbed of depravity, rampant with the "monstruous filthinesse" of "beastly Sodomy" which was "to them a pleasant pastime, making songs, and singing Sonets of the beauty and pleasure of their Bardassi, or buggerd boyes."

Leaving this decadent scene, Lithgow set off through the Ionian islands, which were mainly under the control of Venice at the time. But his vessel was attacked by a Turkish galley, "which sudden affrighting newes overwhelmed us almost in despare." The other passengers urged surrender but Lithgow, who doubted that anyone would cough up a ransom for him, rallied a spirited defense. Seven men were killed in the fight, and Lithgow took a shot in the arm, but the ship was able to reach Cephalonia.

His wound treated by a Greek surgeon, Lithgow made his way to Crete. Ignoring advice not to venture into the interior of the island, he left most of his money behind in exchange and set off to see the sights. Sure enough, he was almost immediately attacked by "three Greeke murdering Renegadoes and an Italian Bandido: who laying hands on me, beate me most cruelly, robbed me of my clothes and stripped me naked, threatening me with many grievous speeches."

Stumbling into the town of Canea, he was befriended by some English soldiers. There he encountered a French galley slave who had been brought ashore bound in shackles. Lithgow got the captor drunk and freed the slave, disguising him as a woman in one of Lithgow's laundress's gowns. When this was discovered Lithgow was pursued by the furious slave owner and barely made it to the safety of a monastery.

When it was safe to come out he continued sailing from one Greek island to another. Again he was attacked by Turkish pirates, who took over his ship and imprisoned its captain, but Lithgow somehow escaped to shore.

His next vessel was not attacked by pirates. Instead it ran into a furious storm, in the face of which "every man looked (as it were) with the stampe of death upon his pale visage." Most of the passengers and crew were drowned, but again Lithgow and a few others made it to shore in a dinghy. Several days later they were rescued by Greek fishermen.

Arriving in Istanbul he had hardly touched down on the dock when he was set upon by four French "runnagats" who shouted "Adio Christiano!" and "beat me most cruelly." He was rescued by Turks from the crew of his ship.

In Istanbul he witnessed "men and women as usually sold here in Markets, as horses and other beasts are with us." Most of the slaves sold in Istanbul at this time were from the Balkans. Moved by her "pittifull lookes, and sprinkling teares," he purchased the release of a Dalmatian widow and found her a job as a barmaid. Lithgow overwintered in Istanbul, not unexpectedly forming the judgment that the city was

> A painted Whoore, the maske of deadly sin,
> Sweet faire without, and stinking foule within.

The following spring he scowled on to Cyprus, braving along the way "invasions of damnable Pirats, who gave us divers assaults to their own disadvantages." Arriving at this destination he repeated his pattern of rashly setting off to survey the interior and was promptly "encountered by the way with foure Turkes, who needs would have my mule to ride upon; which my Interpreter refused: But they in a revenge pulled me by the heeles from the Mules backe, beating me most pitifully, and left me almost for dead…. If it had not been for some compassionable Greekes, who by accident came by, and relieved me, I had doubtlesse immediately perished."

Lithgow was made of too stern a stuff to be held back by a bit of a beating. As usual he was soon back up to speed, but he reached Aleppo too late to catch the caravan to Baghdad as he had planned. He had to content himself with observing the city's strange customs, such as sending messages by carrier pigeon, smoking hookahs, and drinking coffee. Changing his plans, he now made his trip to Jerusalem, where he lodged with the Guardians of Mount Zion at the Francisco Monastery of Saint Salvatore, who arranged his eventful trip to the River Jordan.

In 1612, freshly tattooed with the mark of the holy city, and complaining about the eighteen pounds sixteeen shillings sterling his visit had cost him, he joined a caravan bound for Cairo in the company of six Germans. It proved to be an exceedingly difficult trip. Crossing the Sinai Desert, three of the Germans died of heatstroke, and when they

"The Author in the Libyan Desart" from *The Total Discourse, of the Rare Adventures, and Painefull Peregrinations* etc., London, 1632, by William Lithgow.

reached Cairo the remaining Germans visited the house of the Venetian consul, where they celebrated a little too vigorously for their strained systems and also passed away. Lithgow insisted that with his dying breath the last to go left the possessions of all six to him, but these were seized by the consul. Later an Ottoman court awarded Lithgow two-thirds of the total and one-third to the consul.

Having benefitted from its justice system, Lithgow formed a not completely negative impression of Cairo. "The Inhabitants here," he allowed, "were the first Inventors of the Mathematicall Sciences, of Letters, and of the use of Writing: Great Magicians and Astrologians, and are yet imbued with a special dexterity of Wit."

From Cairo he returned to Italy — "five sundry times assayled by the Cursayes and Pyrats" — and back to Scotland, where he published his first account of his journeys. His book was a hit, but Lithgow did not remain home for long. He was still restless, as he wrote in a poem that would be published in 1618:

> I loathe to live long in a private place,
> My soil I love, but I am born to wander,
> And I am glad when I extremes embrace.
> Sweet-sour delights must my contentment rander,
> So, so I walk to view hills, towns and plains,
> Each day new sights, new sights consume all pains.

In 1614 he set out again, this time hoofing it through the Netherlands and Germany. He paid a visit to King James's daughter, Elizabeth, and he looked up relatives of the German travelers who had died in Egypt during his last trip; they rewarded him handsomely for reporting on their final days. Along the way he picked up a young Scottish gentleman named David Bruce (presumably no beastly sodomy was involved). In Germany the two travelers were set upon and robbed, and would have been again in Italy, but the would-be thieves were so impressed by Lithgow having visited Jerusalem that they

> uncovered their heads, and did me homage, notwithstanding they were absolute murderers: Our lives and liberty is granted, and for a greater assurance, they took us both in to a great thicket of wood, where their timberd Cabine stood, and there made merry with us in good Wine and the best cheare their sequestrate cottage could afford.

Parting from his young companion, he continued on alone. Crossing a field in Sicily he made a strange discovery — he found two young noblemen lying dead, each killed by the other in a duel. "Upon which sight to speak the truth, I searched both their pockets, and found their two silken purses loaden with Spanish pistols." He not only helped himself to their money but also took their diamond rings off the young men's fingers. "In the mutability of time," he philosophized, "there is aye some fortune falleth by accident, whether lawful or not."

"The Modell of the Great City of Fez" from *The Total Discourse, of the Rare Adventures, and Painefull Peregrinations* etc., London, 1632, by William Lithgow.

He arrived in Tunis in the summer of 1615, where he made what seems a surprising friendship, for a person of his Calvinist sensibility, with the notorious renegade corsair captain Yusuf Reis (Jack Ward). Boies Penrose speculated that Lithgow's "shady exploit" in helping himself to the dead duelists' valuables "may have caused him to a feel a bond in common with others who were not particular about the rights of property." I think that following the success of his first book he was just thinking like an author, and he realized Ward would be a good story. He wrote:

> Here in Tunis I met with our English Captayne, generall Waird, once a great Pyrat, and Commaunder at Sea; who in despight of his denied acceptance in England, had turned Turke, and built there a faire Palace, beautified with rich Marble and Alabaster stones: With whome I found Domesticke, some fifteene circumcised English Runagates, whose lives and Countenances were both alike, even as desperate as disdainfull. Yet old Waird their maister was placable, and joined me

safely with a passing Land conduct to Algiers; yea, and diverse times in my ten dayes staying there I dyned and supped with him, but lay aboord in the French shippe.

Armed with Reis's safe pass, Lithgow continued to Algiers, where he stayed seventeen days. He also visited Fez and claimed to have made a bold journey deep into the Libyan desert. In February 1616, however, he "bad goodnight to Generous Waird and his forward Runagates" and sailed back to Sicily, suffering his usual misfortunes along the return journey to Scotland. There he managed to hold still for a year or two. Then he set off again, this time by way of Ireland, with the ultimate goal of visiting Ethiopia and the legendary domains in Africa of Prester John.

He never realized that ambition. Traveling through Spain, he found that outspoken Calvinists were not well received there. Sensing his danger, he made it out of Madrid and got as far as Malaga before he was surprised in an alleyway by nine officers, "who inclosing mee on both sides layd violent hands on mee, wrapping me up in a blacke frizado cloake, and gripping my throat to stop my crying, they carried me on their armes to the governours house, and inclosed me in a low Parlour." He was now in the hands of the Spanish Inquisition.

Someone had obtained a copy of his book, which condemned him to the torments appropriate to "an Arch-Hereticke to the Pope and the Virgin Mary." He was waterboarded. He was hung by his arms with weights on his feet. He was hung upside down by his big toes. He was flogged. He was beaten. Suspected of being a spy, he was put on the rack, and both of his legs were broken. Through it all he refused to confess or to abjure his beliefs. Finally he was informed that he had been condemned to be burned.

Then, suddenly, he was spared. The English consul had heard about his sufferings through a chance conversation and called in some favors at the Spanish court to get Lithgow released, barely alive. He was returned to England, where he was given scant chance of surviving, but he was nothing if not a tough old ornery cuss, and somehow he pulled through, "although my left Arme, and crushed bones be incurable."

In England Lithgow sued the Spanish government for damages and the return of money that had been confiscated from him. The Spanish ambassador promised him retribution, but he never delivered on the promise. The crippled Lithgow confronted the ambassador in London and "told him flatly in his face ... what he was." He so enraged the ambassador that he beat Lithgow severely. The English State Papers report that "Though the Scottish man took his blowes patientlie, yet he was committed to prison."

He remained in Marshalsea Prison for nine weeks for the crime of insulting an ambassador. His temper nothing soothed by this treatment, he was back in prison again the next year for unspecified offenses.

Failing to get the compensation he sought, his thoughts, incredibly, turned again to wandering. For the moment, however, he limited himself to hobbling around England and Scotland. He worked on a book called *Lithgowes Surveigh of Scotland* but never brought it to publication. He was no longer enthusiastic about his homeland. He was not impressed with his country's youth, who seemed to him devoted to

> Cards and Drunkenness, lashivious Lust:
> And all Prophananes, swearing and distrust.

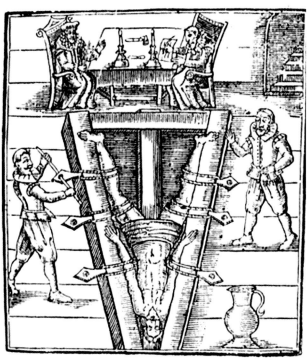

"The Author in the Racke at Malaga" from *The Total Discourse, of the Rare Adventures, and Painefull Peregrinations* etc., London, 1632, by William Lithgow.

In his later years he journeyed to the Netherlands, where he had a courtside seat for some of the battles of the Thirty Years War. He planned a trip to Russia but never undertook it.

In the end Lithgow became to the world just another old crank, and the exact year of his death went unremarked and unrecorded. He had survived, though, a quarter century after being broken on the rack. His travels might be seen, as James R. Burns suggests, as a kind of moral journey culminating in his final persona as a Protestant martyr. They also demonstrate that a dedicated traveler, touring not as a diplomat or sailor or pilgrim or merchant or anything other than a person curious about what lay farther down the road, could cover vast distances in the early modern world. And they show the extent to which such a traveler may carry preformed attitudes with him as a filter for experience and the extent to which, if his mind is not open, his attitudes to other ways of life may be hardened and constricted rather than loosened and expanded over the course of his travels.

Notwithstanding his tedious patches of moralistic ranting, Lithgow left behind one of the first major works of modern Western travel writing, his *Rare Adventures and Painful Peregrinations,* published in 1632, a decade after he had returned from Spain. Its final words could read as the sigh of resignation of a broken old man; or they could be heard as the good-bye of a bad-ass traveler determined to keep on moving: "And so farewell."

Experiences of slavery and piracy in the Mediterranean world also informed the work of a writer greater than Lithgow. Following a long convalescence after being injured in the Battle of Lepanto, where he had performed heroically and lost the use of one arm (though not the arm itself as is sometimes said), Miguel de Cervantes spent a few more years in military duty in the then-Spanish state of Naples and elsewhere. In 1575 he was finally on his way back to Spain. He was a passenger in *El Sol*, a Spanish galley that was part of a fleet of four ships. Approaching the coast of Spain, the fleet encountered bad weather, and the *Sol* became separated from the others. It was attacked and captured, after stout but futile resistance, by North African corsairs under the command of a renegade Albanian captain called Arnaut Mami.

Cervantes was taken to Algiers, where he would endure five years as a slave. He would make daring but unsuccessful escape attempts on four occasions before being ransomed in 1580. That he was not severely punished for his attempts at escape is intriguing, and many scholars have given their imaginations free rein in inventing explanations, especially since Cervantes later was forced to defend himself against a vague, anonymous accusation that he had engaged in some unspecified sexual impropriety during his years as a slave. In the end, all of the hypotheses may say more about the scholars than about Cervantes.

His experiences as a slave underlay some of his plays as well as the interpolated story "The Captive's Tale" and other parts of *Don Quixote;* the second part of the novel was published in 1615, not long before the author's death in 1616. According to the Spanish novelist Juan Goytisolo, it informed more than just those texts dealing explicitly with slavery: Cervantes's novel was conceived at a fundamental level, he says, from "the other shore" — it was his experience as a captive in Muslim North Africa that enabled him to elaborate the vision of Spanish society that informs his work.

Algiers, which had been part of the Ottoman empire for nearly a century, since the time of Suleiman I ("The Magnificent" or "The Lawgiver"), was one of the world's most cosmopolitan cities. Together with Tunis and Tripoli it formed a naval counterbalance to the Ottoman overland offensive in the Balkans, part of a pincer attack on Christian Europe. Unlike those cities, Algiers had been an insignificant coastal village until the sixteenth century, when its maritime advantages made it a boomtown. Its population had also been swollen by the arrival of Moors expelled from Spain.

By the early seventeenth century Algiers was the capital of a well-regulated state. Its economy was highly dependent on state-supported privateering: corsairs, legitimized by jihad, were taxed a percentage of their plunder. Silver was the basic currency.

The corsair system of Algiers was a meritocracy: if you were a good pirate it didn't matter much who you were or where you were from. Any corsair captain could rise to the supreme rank of admiral of the sea (*kapudan derya*) based on performance. Many corsair captains were devoted Muslims who considered themselves *mujahidin,* warriors for Islam. From the Muslim perspective corsair activity was a response to harassment by Spain, which had expelled its Moriscos — Muslims who were supposed to have converted to Christianity in order to stay in their Spanish homes — in 1609 and had made several attacks against the North African coast. Other corsair captains had baser motives. Renegades from many nations found shelter in Algiers, and some took advantage of the benefits (such as reduced taxes) of converting to Islam. The Spanish author of the *Topography and General History of Algiers* (1612), who is presumed to have been Antonio de Sosa, one of Cervantes's fellow captives, wrote that

There is no Christian nation in the world from which there are no renegades in Algiers. Beginning with the remote provinces of Europe, there are in Algiers renegade Muscovites, Reds ..., Bulgarians, Poles, Hungarians, Bohemians, Germans, Danes, Norwegians, Scots, Englishmen, Irishmen, Flemish, Burgundians, Frenchmen, Navarrese, Basques, Castilians, Galicians, Portuguese, Andalusians, Valencians, Aragonese, Catalans, Majorcans, Sardianians, Corsicans, Sicilians, Calabreses, Neapolitans, Romans, Tuscans, Genoise, Savoyans, Piedmontese, Lombards, Venetians, Slavs, Albanians ..., Greeks, Candiotas, Cretans, Cypriots, Surianos, Egyptians, and even Abejinos of Prester John and Indians from the Portuguese Indies, as well as from Brazil and New Spain.

By the 1580s, when Christopher Marlowe wrote *Tamburlaine,* Algiers and its renegade corsairs were infamous in Christian Europe; he alludes to

> the cruel pirates of Argier,
> That damned train, the scum of Africa,
> Inhabited with straggling runagates.

In Shakespeare's *The Tempest,* Algiers was the birthplace of Caliban's mother, a witch. Jean-Baptiste Gramaye, a French speaker from Flanders, who was held in the city in 1619, called it "the Whip of the Christian World, the terror of Europe, Bridle of Italy and Spain, Scourge of the Islands." Samuel Purchas, the early-seventeenth-century chronicler of voyages, became apoplectic on the topic of Algiers:

> the Whirlepoole of these Seas, the Throne of Pyracie, the Sinke of Trade and the Stinke of Slavery; the Cage of uncleane Birds of Prey, the Habitation of Sea-Devils, the Receptacle of Renegadoes of God, and Traytors to their Country....

The city, with its enclosed harbor, had acquired the reputation of invincibility. Its triangular configuration was bordered by the sea, mountains, and a ravine on the three sides — the design of the city was compared to a bent crossbow. Surrounded by twelve-foot-thick and forty-foot-high moated walls, it spread uphill from the bay to the Qassabah (Kasbah), manned by Turkish janissaries. Here was a strong fortress surrounded by its own octagonal walls and heavily armed with multiple tiers of guns. Larger than Rome, the city boasted many public baths and fountains; terraced gardens; a mint; mosques, chapels, and synagogues; and a theologi-

Opposite: Bird's-Eye View of Algiers, after Antonio Salamanca, from Braun and Hogenberg, *Civitates Orbis Terrarum* **(Cities of the World), vol. 2, 1575. Engraving.**

Georg Braun (1541–1622), a cleric of Cologne, edited the first comprehensive world atlas in six volumes between 1572 and 1617. The atlas contained several hundred prospects, bird's-eye views, and map views of cities around the world. Franz Hogenberg did the majority of the engravings, but the project enlisted more than a hundred artists and cartographers. The enterprise was an expression of the new globalization of the early modern world.

Algiers is correctly shown as a strongly fortified town advantageously placed on a harbor, although its triangular shape is not conveyed. The text in the cartouche reads, "View of Algiers, the most powerful town of the Saracens, built in the Numidian province of Africa. Situated on the edge of the Balearic Current in the Mediterranean Sea, across from Spain. Under Ottoman rule."

cal school. Houses were built close together; they often enclosed interior courtyards and were topped with roof gardens. It was possible to move from house to house by rooftop without descending to the narrow streets below. Officials lived in the heights by the Qassabah, while corsairs clustered in residences near the sea.

Governance of the city-state centered around the *ocak,* the garrison to which janissaries recruited elsewhere in the empire were assigned. As the janissaries gained seniority they moved into administrative positions in the Divan, the council of state. The Divan was for the most part a democratic institution in which policy was decided by vote of members. Native Algerines could not serve as janissaries and had little role in state governance — though on the city level they filled mayoral and city council positions — but they received exemption from many taxes and civic obligations.

According to the account of an early-seventeenth-century French writer, nearly eight hundred slaves were carried to Algiers in 1616. A modern estimate suggests that between 1520 and 1650 more than six hundred thousand captives were taken to the slave market. Many captives were chosen for work as pages or servants. Those with skills in specialized trades could work for merchants and keep up to a third of the income from their labor. The remainder did manual labor in quarries, public works, farms, or the shipyard; they were housed in special barracks, called bagnios, similar to those in which the janissaries lodged.

Slaves could obtain their freedom by converting to Islam, but this would complicate their return home, for "turning Turk" often meant an encounter with the Inquisition. Such *conversos* provided military and naval knowledge to Algiers and served as interpreters.

To prevent European states from joining forces against them, the city employed a subtle policy of shifting favoritism. Tributes, prisoner releases, corsair targets, and treaties favored one opponent or another. Beneficiaries of this system tended to be reluctant to team up with the less fortunate.

Algerian corsairs developed a type of vessel that was heavily armed and extremely fast by the standards of the time. Driven by sails, the corsair ships could easily overtake galleys powered by rowers. A Dutchman who had been living in Marseilles, named Siemen Danziker (called Simon Danser by the English), contributed to the development of this type of ship. According to John Smith, prior to the arrival in Algiers of Danziker and the Englishman Jack Ward, "the Moores knew scarce how to saile a ship," a claim that has the flavor of European condescension. William Lithgow claimed that Christian renegades taught the corsairs to cast cannon and use them in sea battles.

After turning renegade Danziker rose rapidly among the ranks of the corsairs and acquired the name Deli Reis — "Captain Devil." He is said to have captured forty ships that were then incorporated into the corsair fleet. Danziker also greatly expanded the range of corsair activity, traveling as far in search of prey as Iceland, which Algerian-based corsairs raided in 1616.

At some point recalling that he had left a wife and children in Marseilles, Danziker exchanged ten Jesuit priests he had captured off the coast of Valencia for the right to return to France, where he was granted full citizenship. His allegiances again reversed, he now attacked Algiers on behalf of the French. But he was captured and beheaded there, as the traveler William Lithgow looked on.

Though the most secure, Algiers was not the only corsair stronghold in North Africa. The other most formidable corsair captain of the early seventeenth century, Yusuf Reis (Jack Ward), operated out of Tunis. More advantageously located than Algiers for trade, Tunis was a more active commercial center, and less dependent on corsair revenue. But it possessed an excellent harbor and welcomed seamen who would convert to Islam and confine their raids to Christian ships. Reis and Danziger were sometimes a team and sometimes at odds. Perhaps a single town could not hold these two rough, powerful personalities. English taverns during the seventeenth century rocked with ballads about them:

> All the world about has heard
> Of Danseker and Captain Ward

Ward's date of birth is unknown, but in 1616 he seems to have been in his early sixties. He was a fisherman, "a fellow, poore, base and of no esteeme" — or so said a resentful ship master who had been taken prisoner by him and who wrote a chapbook about him that was published in 1609. He had apparently fought against Spain, and was one of many English buccaneers who were left adrift after the death of Elizabeth, when James reversed her policy of opposition and made peace with Spain. Many of these seamen, their raids no longer encouraged or supported, made their way to the Mediterranean and became corsairs. "After the death of Queen Elizabeth," wrote John Smith, the king "had no employment for those men of warre.... Those that were rich retired with that they had; those that were poore and had nothing but from hand to mouth, turned Pirats."

It is traditionally said that Ward entered piracy after serving aboard a ship called *The Lyon's Whelp*. When that ship put in at Portsmouth Ward learned of a barque harbored there that supposedly was richly stocked with the property of a recusant — a Catholic who refused to attend services of the Church of England — who was fleeing the country. The longer Ward talked with his shipmates over pint after pint of ale the richer this prize seemed and the easier to obtain. And indeed the seamen had no difficulty in seizing the barque from the two men on board, but unfortunately it did not contain the expected riches, which had been removed by their cautious owner. At this point there was no turning back. They continued down the English Channel until they came upon a French ship, which they commandeered. They went to Plymouth where they manned the ship with Ward's old alehouse acquaintances and set sail for the Mediterranean.

An Englishman's report to the state of Venice in 1608, following Ward's capture of a Venetian galley, contains this description of him:

> Captian Ward is about fifty years of age. Very short, with little hair, and that quite white; bald in front; swarthy face and beard, speaks little, and is almost always swearing. Drunk from morn till night. Most prodigal and plucky. Sleeps a great deal and often on board when in port. The habits of a thorough salt. A fool and an idiot out of his trade."

The following year Ward sailed to Ireland and from shelter there captured several vessels. Returning to the Mediterranean he took more ships and grew wealthy. Settling in Tunis, he made an alliance with the captain of the Janissaries by cutting him a 20 percent share of his loot; this provided him with a secure base. He married an Italian woman but continued to send money to the English wife he had left behind.

He seems to have more or less retired around 1612. He is said by this time to have become a devout Muslim and to have taken the name Yusuf Reis. He built himself a palatial house called "more fit for a prince than a pirate." According to one visitor, by this time he "always had a Turkish habit on" and "was to drink water and no wine."

Reis survived many sea battles over the course of his life but succumbed to plague in 1622 when he was about seventy. His life was turned into a play called *A Christian Turn'd Turk* by the English dramatist Robert Daborne in 1612. Reis had enjoyed a reputation in England as a likeable rogue who was thought to have mainly attacked the ships of Catholic nations (a questionable notion), but his conversion to Islam was troubling to his English admirers. Daborne finessed the issue by attributing his conversion not to a matter of faith but to his love for a beautiful Turkish woman.

Harsh as the conditions of slaves in the Muslim Mediterranean could be, unless they were galley slaves — which was virtually a death sentence — they could usually obtain their freedom through the payment of ransom or by converting to Islam. For some slaves, however, these were not options. One former slave who nonetheless rose to a position of prominence was Malik Ambar, who was born in the mid-sixteenth century in the remote highlands of Ethiopia, or Abyssinia as it was then known.

Ethiopia at that time was under the control of the Solomonic dynasty, so called because it claimed descent from Solomon; but Malik Ambar was probably from a non-Christian region, like the majority of Ethiopian slaves (called Habshis) at this time. His name then was Chapu. Only later did he acquire the name by which he is remembered today — "Malik" means "king" and "Ambar" means "ambergris," which is probably an allusion to his dark skin, since aged ambergris turns a dark gray to black color.

He was sold in a slave market on the Red Sea and taken to Baghdad, where he was purchased by a merchant who educated him and converted him to Islam. Most slaves were sold by the Solomonic Christians in exchange for Indian cottons, which were extremely popular at this time. Ambar was resold several times, eventually coming into the possession of a man named Chengiz Khan, who was chief minister of the sultanate of Ahmadnagar in the northwest of India's Deccan plateau. This region, together with Bijapur to its south, had the highest number of Habshi slaves in India. In fact, Chengiz Khan himself was a former slave.

Malik Ambar, like many Habshi slaves in Ahmadnagar, was purchased to augment the sultanate's military forces. Military slavery was an entirely different institution from the plantation slavery of the Americas. Because the loyalty of military slaves was critical, they were well cared for. The idea behind the institution of the military slave was that by removing warriors from their family ties, factionalism based on kinship could be held in check. The same idea was behind the janissary troops of the Ottomans, who were mainly preadolescent Christians from the Balkans, given up to the empire as a kind of tax called the *devshirme*; they were given military and Islamic training, and were supposed to remain celibate. It was also behind the extensive employment of eunuchs in the Chinese imperial court. In all of these contexts the childless men were also relied on as bodyguards and guards of the harem or the emperor's concubines.

Around 1575 Malik Ambar's master died, and his widow freed him. He

Malik Ambar, 1620s, by Hashim. From the Nasir al-Din Shah Album. Musée des Arts Asiatiques-Guimet, Paris, 7172 Ravaux (App. 6.4).

The album to which this image of Malik Ambar was attached, along with others from the royal Mughal court, came into the possession of the ruler of the Qajar region in present-day Azerbaijan during the nineteenth century. Most of the folios in the album are now in the Gulistan Palace Library in Tehran, where they have only occasionally been made accessible to scholars.

took a wife and rose to be a cavalry commander in charge of about 150 men. The Mughal emperor Akbhar, who pursued an aggressively expansionist policy, sought to conquer the sultanate of Ahmadnagar. In 1595 Mughal troops besieged the fortress in the city of Ahmadnagar, being turned back only by a spirited defense led by the sister of the recently deceased sultan. Five years later, however, the fortress fell to the Mughals. Malik Ambar took advantage of the ensuing chaos. The Mughals had imprisoned the Ahmadnagar sultan, but Malik Ambar found a young member of the royal family to install on the throne as figurehead ruler. He also arranged for the young sultan to marry his daughter.

For several years Malik Ambar and his main rival, a man named Raju Dakhni, led separate armies against the Mughals. Finally in 1606 Ambar confronted and defeated his rival in battle, and imprisoned him in the fortress in his new capital. Now the uncontested supreme military commander, he won victories against a rival state to the south; he held the coast against European powers; and, though he did not regain the city and fortress of Ahmadnagar, he defeated the Mughals in a series of clashes and won control of the countryside. With each victory more soldiers joined his side.

But by 1610 the puppet sultan had begun to resist some of Ambar's directives. One of his senior wives, a woman of Persian descent, goaded him to assert his independence. A Dutch observer reports that she called Ambar's daughter, a younger wife of the sultan, "a mere slave girl," and slandered Ambar besides. He was swift to respond: he had both the sultan and his Persian wife poisoned, and installed their five-year-old son as the new sultan.

Thanks to his military successes and his adroitness at palace intrigue, Malik Ambar enjoyed a long reign as the prime minister and was effectively the ruler of the Ahmadnagar sultanate. Observers agree that he was a skillful and evenhanded administrator. One of his main accomplishments was the rationalization of the tax system. He assessed the fertility of land holdings and imposed taxes based on a percentage of the actual produce, allowing the substitution of cash payments in place of a percentage of the yield. A Dutch visitor in 1617 reported that Ambar was "very much loved and respected by everyone and keeps good government."

The Mughal emperors Akbar and Jahangir both dispatched armies against him, winning only fleeting victories, as Ambar proved a master of guerilla tactics. He developed brigades of light cavalry that made quick harassing raids on enemy supply lines while avoiding directly engaging with the main Mughal military force. Jahangir grew obsessed with Malik Ambar. He called him "Ambar the black faced" and "Ambar of dark fate," and referred to his followers as "rebels of black fortune."

In the fall of 1616 Jahangir dispatched his son Khurram to lead a large force in an assault on the Ahmadnagar sultanate. Shortly before Khurram departed, Jahangir was sitting in his palace when he saw an owl fly onto a nearby roof. Because owls are associated with the night, like the blackness that so impressed Jahangir about his enemy, he associated Malik Ambar with owls. Calling for a gun, he shot at the bird and killed it, or so he wrote in his reign journal, the *Jahangirnama*. He subsequently commissioned a painting called "The Defeat of Malik Ambar," in which the association with owls is emphasized—a caption reads, "The head of the night-coloured usurper is become the house of the owl"—and his fantasy of defeating his nemesis was fulfilled, if only within the margins of the painting.

Khurram did defeat Malik Ambar, forcing him to pay tribute to the Mughals. Jahangir was so pleased with this result that on his son's return he rewarded him with the name by which he would later be known as emperor, Shah Jahan, "ruler of the world." But the victory proved temporary. Malik Ambar returned to battle and won back the lost territory. He continued to be a thorn in Jahangir's side until the two rival leaders died within a year of each other.

Malik Ambar died in 1626, when he was probably in his late seventies. Janhangir died in 1627; he was fifty-eight. Upon news of Ambar's death a Mughal chronicler graciously conceded that "this Ambar was a slave, but he was an able man." Seven years later his kingdom finally fell to the Mughals.

Because military slavery, unlike plantation slavery, did not make much use of women, the Habshis married Indian women and were gradually assimilated into society. By the eighteenth century the institution of Ethiopian slavery had ceased to exist in India, and the Habshis had virtually disappeared as a distinct group.

The plantation slavery of the Americans was a different institution entirely. Plantation farming—estates of hundreds of acres devoted to a single

The Submission of Rana Amar Singh to Prince Khurram, ca. 1620, by Nanha. Opaque watercolor on paper. 20 x 31 cm. Victoria and Albert Museum, IS 185-1984.

Prince Khurram, the future Shah Jahan, was delegated with subjugating various Indian kingdoms to Mughal rule. Among these was the important Rajput kingdom of Mewar, the last such kingdom to fall, in 1615. In the following year Prince Khurram went on to defeat Jahangir's nemesis, Malik Ambar, though his victory would turn out to be limited and temporary.

crop — was an Arab innovation copied by Europeans from sugar plantations
in the Levant. Long established in Brazil and other parts of Latin America,
plantation slavery was beginning to spread in the early seventeenth century
from the Caribbean to the British colonies of North America.

In May 1616 the governor of Bermuda welcomed the *Edwin,* a ship that
carried a variety of items useful to the young colony. The vessel "brought
with her also one Indian and a Negroe (the first thes Ilands ever had)."
The Indian, probably a Carib, a people originally from the north coast of
South America who had been used as slaves in the Americas since the conquest, was a novelty because Bermuda had no indigenous population. The
black man was a slave who was probably employed initially as a diver for
pearls. Since slavery was common throughout the early modern world, the
arrival of a single slave might seem an insignificant event. But it signaled
the beginning of the second phase in what would be the largest and most
inhumane relocation of peoples in world history.

Slave networks had long existed along the west coast of Africa. Because
land in that tropical climate was quickly exhausted as an agricultural resource, power depended not so much on the control of land as on the control of people. Slaves were acquired through warfare and traded up the coast.
They might have been treated harshly, but they were still perceived as people.
Typically their roles as slaves were not passed to their descendents. A slave in
the household of an important leader could be a person of influence.

So there were many varieties of slavery: Cervantes was kept as a slave
with a view to the payment of ransom. Malik Ambar was purchased as a
military slave to strengthen the Ahmadnagar sultanate's defenses against the
Mughals. Both emerged from their time as slaves into positions of influence.
The cruel American slave trade was different. It saw African slaves and their
descendants as chattel — not as people but simply as property. Under this
system slave status was inherited and continued in perpetuity.

The main initiators and the most active participants in the cross-Atlantic
slave trade were the Portuguese. As their maritime exploration and trade took
them more and more frequently up and down the coast of Africa, they began
to exchange textiles, guns, and other manufactured goods for slaves in African port cities and to carry the slaves across the Atlantic to the Americas.

The slaves were first taken to work in mines and farms in Central and
South America. Portuguese Brazil was an obvious destination. The mainland ports of Cartagena and Veracruz, which were rich with gold and silver from the mines of Mexico, Colombia, and Peru, became the official
slave-trading cities of Spanish America. The same ships that delivered the
slaves would then carry ore or agricultural products produced with slave

labor to Europe. There they loaded up again with manufactured goods and returned to Africa to repeat the cycle.

This trade was a factor in the development of a global economy. It was a potentially lucrative enterprise, because profits were made from each leg of the triangle. Eventually profits were increased by packing chained slaves tightly in order to deliver the largest possible cargo, even if many died along the way, though this was mainly a development of the eighteenth century.

The slave trade was responsible for a second wave of epidemic disease in the Americas. The first wave had occurred shortly after the first European contact — within twenty-five years of Columbus's first voyage Americans began dying of smallpox. Now unhealthy conditions aboard slave ships brought new diseases. Epidemics in 1616 and 1617 in Brazil were attributed to the arrival of slave ships.

Plantation economies grew so dependent on slavery that it became a habit that was tough to kick. Plantation slavery employed two varieties of slaves: house slaves worked as servants and performed menial household duties. Field slaves worked under harsh conditions in the fields. The average life expectancy of a sugar plantation slave was seven years. Women were enslaved as well as men to perform household duties and work as field hands, and also to protect the slave owner's investment from devaluation over time by replenishing the slave population. Children often began working around the age of seven.

Within a year after the arrival of the first slave, a Bermudan was exulting in "the "good store of neggars...brought from the West Indies." Within three years slaves were introduced to Jamestown, where John Rolfe had developed tobacco as a viable cash crop. Virginia would become one of the largest importers of African slaves. The first phase of slavery, from the conquest to about the early seventeenth century, was modest in its numbers compared to what was to follow. The introduction of slave economies through the Caribbean to North America by English, Portuguese, French, and Dutch traders marked the beginnings of the second and more devastating phase of New World slavery — the trade would accelerate during the second half of the seventeenth century, and more than three-quarters of the slaves brought to the Americas would be imported during the eighteenth and nineteenth centuries. The black slave brought to Bermuda in 1616 heralded the flood that would follow. The Americas had become slaves to slavery.

Movement of goods, including slaves, across vast distances required a multinational system of support for travel, and nowhere was travel more encouraged and supported than in the Muslim world, as Pietro della Valle was

discovering. The dapper Italian made a grand entrance into the holy city of Jerusalem — the head cameleer had dyed the camels with henna and bedecked them with trappings of yellow and crimson silk. He stayed three weeks seeing the sites of the city and observing the Easter celebrations of 1616, although his visit was marred somewhat by the high fever that struck his servant Tommaso.

From Jerusalem, unceremoniously tossing the invalid in a pannier slung over the back of a camel, he continued to Damascus. Here Tomasso decided he had had enough. Having visited Jerusalem, the party had completed its religious pilgrimage, yet della Valle, rather than returning home, seemed intent on journeying deeper into the lands of Islam. "Seeing himself in such a condition and such a place," della Valle tells us, "he became frightened and morose, and this only made him worse. His thoughts returned to his home and his family, to the comforts and delights of Italy; then despair seized him, and he gave himself up for lost." He was given last rites, but these were accompanied by herbs and infusions prepared by a Jewish healer. Reviving, Tommaso recanted his determination to return to Italy, assuring della Valle that he was prepared to go anywhere with him, even to India.

With that della Valle continued to Aleppo, where he spent three months. Aleppo was a cosmpolitan city, "for thither resort Jewes, Tartarians, Persians, Armenians, Egyptians, Indians, and many sorts of Christians, and injoy freedome of their consciences, and bring thither many kinds of rich merchandises," according to a late-sixteenth-century English merchant. Valuing its role as a trade crossroads, the city respected the varied faiths of the travelers. According to a chaplain attached to the Company of English Merchants there, "In Aleppo, as I have walked the streetes, both Turkes and Moores, and other Nations, would very reverently salute me.... They have not offered me or any of my companie wrong." The only insults he had suffered during ten years' travels in the region, he claimed, were from his own countrymen.

In Aleppo della Valle made a crucial decision. He ought, according to his original plan, to have gone to Istanbul to return to Italy. But he hadn't had enough. Always with an eye to the grand gesture, he conceived the notion of traveling to Persia to enlist in the service of Shah Abbas to fight against the enemy of Christian Europe, the Great Turk. Obtaining a forged passport from the Venetian consul in Aleppo, he and his his long-suffering servants Tomasso and Lorenzo and the painter shaved their heads and donned turbans. Thus disguised they joined a camel caravan and set off across the desert to Baghdad, a distance of nearly five hundred miles.

Della Valle did not realize then that he would not return to Italy for another ten years.

The extent to which the Islamic empires valued and encouraged travel and trade is demonstrated by their legacy of roadside caravanserai. These were fortified inns, usually built around a large central court, where travelers and caravans could take shelter and rest after a day's travel. Generally the structures presented a blank wall surmounted by towers to the outside world, since a minimum of openings made them easier to defend against thieves and invaders; some, however, were elaborately constructed, with domes, arcades, staircases, and friezes and ornamental motifs. A few also contained Turkish baths and small interior mosques. Besides an open courtyard there was usually a covered "winter hall" where pack animals could be protected during harsh winter nights.

In West Asia hundreds of caravanserai had been constructed by the end of the thirteenth century, and another wave of construction occurred throughout Anatolia, the eastern Mediterranean, and Egypt and North Africa during the early centuries of Ottoman rule. The result was an elabo-

Loading Bales onto a Camel, ca. 1630. Isfahan, Persia. Ink and colors on paper, 14 x 11 cm. British Museum, ME 1920.0917.0.279.3.

The tomb of Hatam, a sixth-century Arab renowned for his generosity, was a popular pilgrimage
site. In this image by the foremost
painter of Shah Abbas's court a
youth drinks wine and eats fruit in
a tent while other figures listen to
a lecture about the tomb or gaze
reverently at it.

rate network of resting places, spaced about twenty miles apart, that greatly
facilitated travel through the Islamic world. In Persia the greatest period of
caravanserai construction took place during the rule of Shah Abbas, while
in India Jahangir's father, Akbar, was notable for supporting caravanserai.
"The gracious sovereign cast an eye upon the comfort of travelers," wrote
Abul Fazl, the late sixteenth–early seventeenth century chronicler of Akbar's reign, "and ordered that in the serais on the high roads, refuges and
kitchens should be established." Two English merchants who traveled
these routes in 1615 and 1616 testified to the convenience of their resting
places: "Every five or six coss [about ten or fifteen miles], there are serais
built by the king or some great man, which add greatly to the beauty of the
road, are very convenient for the accommodation of travelers, and serve to
perpetuate the memory of their funders."

Most caravanserai were established and maintained through nonprofit
trusts called *waqfs*. Income from agriculture and shop rents was channeled
though waqfs to support institutions for the public good such as mosques,
baths, kitchens, cemeteries, and fountains. Maintenance of the Aya (Ha-
gia) Sofia in Istanbul was supported by a waqf, for example, as would be
the Taj Mahal in India, built by Jahangir's son and successor, Shah Jahan.
The institution was more popular and common in West Asia and North
Africa, however, than it was in India. Waqfs were also often used to keep
significant properties intact by preventing their being divided among a
donor's multiple heirs. In such a case one of the children would typically
be appointed custodian of the property that was transmitted to the waqf,
which tied up the property in perpetuity and prevented its subsequent
sale. At the same time that capitalism was increasingly a factor driving
economies in the new globalized world, especially in northern Europe,
nonprofit foundations remained important in supporting caravan routes
through the establishment and maintenance of caravanserai.

Merchant trade by means of the caravan routes was dominated by relatively small-scale peddlers, who sometimes traveled great distances. A late-
sixteenth-century Armenian merchant's account book, for example, shows
that he traveled as far as Lhasa in Tibet. That he stayed among an Armenian community there suggests the range of trade diasporas by means of
which residents abroad mediated and eased relations between traveling
merchants and local cultures.

But the caravan trade was erratic and unpredictable. Market and trade
conditions were obscure to individual peddlers, who were constantly attempting to obtain up-to-date information about the arrival of caravans
and the costs and sale prices of goods in geographically distant areas.

Without the buffer of middlemen prices fluctuated wildly, sometimes merely on the basis of rumors.

While the caravan merchants' transport costs were somewhat predictable, protection costs in the form of customs, bribes, and security expenses varied over routes and times depending on local situations. During the sixteenth century this situation remained unaffected by the Portuguese presence in the Indian Ocean and other parts of Asia, because the Portuguese mainly operated on top of existing market channels. Niels Steensgaard, who has looked closely at competing trade routes during this period, maintains that the Portuguese operations were primarily directed at gathering of tribute and taxes and only secondarily at trade — "the tax-gatherer turned merchant in order to maximize his revenue."

With the rise of the British and Dutch trade companies during the early seventeenth century, new political forces now operated in support of economic considerations rather than the other way around. The British and Dutch Companies internalized protection expenses so that their investors paid no more than cost for them. New maritime trade routes began to supplant the old overland caravan routes, which declined at this time rather than on the appearance of the Portuguese a century before.

After days of difficult travel through whirling sands, the caravan carrying Pietro della Valle was nearing Baghdad when tragedy struck — a thief sneaked into his tent and, uninterested in his books and manuscripts, made off with his fine Italian underwear.

Worse was to come. In Baghdad Tommaso — "because of some old rivalry he had with Lorenzo ever since Italy, springing from petty questions of precedence and some vain absurdities lodged in Tommaso's head for no cause whatsoever," della Valle said — knifed Lorenzo. Hearing the commotion della Valle rushed to the scene, and Lorenzo fell dead into his arms as Tomasso fled.

My horror at this I leave you to consider: first the ugliness of the crime in itself: life taken so evilly, and for no reason, from that poor man; then to see, under my protection, in my house, a person who for so long had served me so well so badly treated and betrayed; and then also what could be the consequence. We were in a country subject to the Turk, a country where we had no ambassador, nor consul, nor help whatsoever: very distant from the court, where justice is neither sought nor given, but only harsh treatment — especially to Christians.

Faced with this dilemma, della Valle called on the assistance of a renegade from Malta with whom he had become friendly. It was to this person's house that Tomasso had fled. They decided to wrap the body "in cotton bands because of all the blood still running, and to put it in a packing-case, well bound with cords." All night long della Valle scrubbed and cleaned away the blood that was everywhere, and in the morning he called an ordinary porter and had the package carried to the Turk's home, which was on the river. The next night he took the body from the container "and gave it burial in the middle of the Tigris." Della Valle had Tomasso sent away to Aleppo "with letters asking the Consul and other friends to send him at once to Christian shores, either with his assent or by force if he would not go otherwise."

Della Valle resumed touring the countryside. Baghdad was often confused at this time with Babylon, but della Valle realized that they were different places. Continuing the biblical theme of his journeys to this point, he set off down the Euphrates to locate the ruins, one of the first European travelers to do so. At night the party slept in tents, which Della Valle enjoyed: "I find the cleanliness of it makes it accommodation infinitely preferable to that afforded by our Italian inns, where a man is surrounded by unwashed individuals, and is served by greasy and sour-faced varlets, the mere sight of whom turns the stomach."

It was on the caravan to the ruins of Babylon that della Valle fell in love with Maani Gioerida. When an alarm went up that the caravan was about to be attacked, della Valle had been impressed with the eighteen-year-old's demeanor. Refusing to take cover, Maani had had stood her ground like a warrior. A month later, in December 1616, they were wed, as della Valle informed Dr. Schipano some fifty pages into the next letter he wrote. "It remains for me to tell you," he oddly wrote, "of my Babylonian love, which I name thus to differentiate it from my loves of Rome and elsewhere."

Now allied by marriage with a West Asian Christian family, della Valle continued his mission of making contact with Shah Abbas. Before setting out on the next caravan, he had a barber shave off the "Syrian" beard he had grown in his travels, to be replaced by the drooping mustachios that were all the rage in Persia, in emulation of the shah. The local barber "with great ceremony," he reported, "removed, all in one piece, my long and famous beard that I had preserved and combed with incredible labor throughout the length and breadth of Turkey during the sixteen months or so since I had left Constantinople." Confronted with the startling apparition of her husband's newly shaven face, Maani burst into tears.

Maani's mother was Armenian. The Armenian homeland was located at the southern end of the Caucasus Mountains, east of Turkey and north of Persia, near Mount Ararat. Like Baghdad, the chief Armenian city of Yerevan changed hands several times during the wars between Ottoman Turkey and Safavid Persia. Often the eastern part of Armenia would be controlled by the Persians and the western part by the Turks. But it was an area well situated for trade, and in developing their trade networks Armenians established small communities in far-flung parts of the world. The Armenian merchant diaspora extended from China to Tibet to India to Europe.

Shah Abbas was among the leaders most interested in developing his country's economy. He developed bazaars in his principal cities and put resources into making the caravan routes secure for travelers and improving caravanserai and the infrastructure of roads and bridges. Two English merchants who passed through Persia in 1615 remarked that under Abbas, "merchants are used with much favour, lest they should make complaints to the king, who will have the merchants kindly treated."

Persia's primary export was silk. To pump up the silk trade, Abbas nationalized the silk-producing northern regions, putting them under the control of Safavid treasury officials. Then he did something that profoundly affected the course of Armenian life: in 1605 Abbas forcibly resettled the entire Armenian community from its native region, called Julfa. The immediate cause of the relocation was a retreat that Abbas ordered in response to an Ottoman advance in the Armenian region. In the course of the retreat he instituted a scorched earth policy, destroying and depopulating villages as he went. The entire area was laid utterly to waste, leaving a barren landscape through which it would be difficult for a Turkish army to provision itself.

The refugee Armenian population was made to move to his new capital of Isfahan, where a new district was created for them, called, with Orwellian irony, New Julfa. There they employed their skills as merchants in trading Iranian silk. They also served as bankers and investors, and assisted in the collection of taxes.

Shah Abbas, ca. 1617, by Bishandas. Colors and ink on paper. 16 x 19 cm. Harvard University Art Museums, Gift of Stuart Cary Welch, Jr., 1999.304.

This sketch of Shah Abbas was made by an artist in the Mughal emperor Jahangir's court. The artist, Bishandas, was chosen to accompany a Mughal embassy to Persia because of his skill at portraiture.

The sketch, made when the shah was returning from a polo match, has a lively and spontaneous quality. The personaliy of the shah, captured by the artist in this casual moment, comes through more forcefully than in more carefully worked finished paintings.

Jahangir was pleased with his artist's work and rewarded him with an elephant upon his return.

The merchants of New Julfa were given autonomy and protection. They were allowed to retain their Christian religion. They became prosperous and thrived. They built churches, merchant centers, and schools. After Abbas died, however, the Safavid state weakened, both politically and economically; some Persians grew jealous of the Armenians' prosperity and privileges, and they later endured a more difficult existence. For a time, however, New Julfa represented a rare instance of forced relocation through which, painful though it must have been, both the state and the people were able to find new opportunities for growth.

While exploring around Baghdad Pietro della Valle heard reports of a European who was living the life of a nomadic Bedouin in the desert. He had been told "that when he goes to Aleppo...his dress and speech are such that the Arabs themselves would hold him a true Bedouin."

This mysterious figure was a Scot from "the Mearns" (Kincardineshire) named George Strachan, who was then about forty-three years old. Strachan was serving as physician to Amir Fayyad, a regional leader in the Euphrates area. Fayyad was nominally subject to the Ottomans but effectively independent. Strachan's apparent influence on him was intriguing, because it suggested to della Valle that a European could affect policy in West Asia.

Strachan had been educated in France, had taught in Italy, and had then traveled along much the same itinerary as della Valle. In fact, the two were comparable in several respects: both were Catholic, both were of noble lineage (though Strachan did not have della Valle's luxury of living off inherited wealth), both were trained in the classics (though Strachan was the better scholar), both had an interest in "Oriental" languages and culture.

It was common for Catholic Scots to be educated in France, but Strachan spent many years there, acquiring by all accounts a deep knowledge of many disciplines. He changed schools often — as many as four times in a single academic year — which probably attests to a certainly restlessness in his temperament. As the youngest of the sons in his family he did not have the ready-made opportunities of his older brothers, and he had to invent a life for himself. He toyed with the idea of becoming a Jesuit priest but in the end settled for the life of an itinerant scholar. Perhaps he was somehow unsuited to permanent employment in any one place for a length of time.

Anxious to add new languages to his arsenal that already included Latin, Greek, Hebrew, and modern European languages, he headed east. He was in Aleppo in 1615 when he learned that Amir Fayyad was in need of a physician. He had never studied medicine, but he acquired a couple of medical books and had a Flemish physician who was in Aleppo at the time teach him a few prescriptions. So armed, he presented himself to the amir as a doctor. By good judgment or good fortune, he helped his patient recover, and his reputation was made. He also won the support of the amir's wife by assuring him that frequenting other women was bad for his health. According to della Valle, "everybody is extremely kind to him, and now in the desert when you say 'Strachan' you need not say anything more."

Strachan later traveled to Isfahan and met della Valle there, and the two later met up again in India. Della Valle reported on Strachan's nomadic life and his move to Persia:

By those arts and manners, he lived in the desert under tents for two years, in the company of nomadic Arabs, and told me that he found that kind of life extremely pleasant, because of the continuous but slow wanderings, which are not tiresome, because of the noble sport of hunting diverse kinds of game, at which the most noble among them spent their time; but essentially because of the generous mode of freedom in which they live there: no enclosure in city walls, no subjection to the rule of anyone, except the prince [the amir], when he happens to be present. Finally, however, because the Emir was urging him to be circumcised, he resolved not to delay his departure. Therefore, at a time when the Emir's camp had settled in a certain place near Baghdad, he seized that opportunity to leave skillfully, with no little sorrow and affliction of her who believed herself his wife.

Strachan was probably not quite straight with della Valle about the women who "believed herself his wife." It was reported that they had in fact married. If so, it would mean that he had converted to Islam, although he denied this to della Valle.

In Isfahan Strachan taught Arabic classes and set about to compile a comprehensive Arabic dictionary. Among his students were Carmelite missionaries who reported that his instruction included two hours of reading and one hour of conversation each day. Unfortunately, he became involved in merchant activities with the British East India company and never completed his academic projects.

Eventually Strachan decided to move on to India. One of his main concerns before leaving Persia was to see to the many books of Islamic philosophy and literature he had acquired in his travels. He willed them to the Carmelite monastery in Rome. Della Valle endorsed the will. Many of the books are now in the Vatican library. After della Valle returned to Rome he lost track of his Scottish friend, and how Strachan spent his final years is unknown. But every once in a while a book shows up, like a Persian manuscript in the British Museum, that contains an interlineal translation that concludes "translated into Latin by George Strachan, Scot of the Mearns, 1634."

Scholars often traveled in search of teaching positions or patronage. The occultist scholar John Dee, for example, was advisor to Queen Elizabeth on astrological and scientific matters but later traveled in search of patronage to Poland, Bohemia, Austria, and elsewhere.

Scholars were also tossed and buffeted by the tumultuous politics of the time. Warfare created countless refugees. Korea, caught between China and

Japan, was often a battleground. Invasions from Japan led by Toyotomi Hideyoshi in 1592 and 1598 were among the most brutal ever, and are remembered by many Koreans today as the most devastating event in their difficult history. Japanese warriors sliced off enough ears and noses from enemy soldiers and civilians to create a huge mound with them near Kyoto, called the Mound of Ears (*Mimizuka*). The body parts were intended not only to inspire terror and serve as trophies of war but also to demonstrate samurai successes so that the warriors could be rewarded proportionally.

These conflicts were among the first large-scale modern wars involving huge armies, advanced military technology, and massive casualties. The invasions were intended as a prelude to the conquest of China. Many Korean artisans were forcibly transferred to Japan, where they had a major impact on the development of Japanese ceramic and textile technologies and aesthetics.

The Korean author Heo Gyun, who was over the course of his life a refugee, a diplomat, and a political dissident and reformer, was among those who fled from Hideyoshi's invaders. Heo, in his early twenties, was living in Seoul when the Japanese invaded. His young wife was pregnant. The Koreans were unprepared for the attack and offered little resistance.

As Heo and his wife fled the city they saw it burning behind them — slaves had set fire to government offices to destroy the records that bound them. They were heading for his hometown of Gangneung on the east coast of Korea, far from the centers of fighting, where Heo's father was governor. The refugees were traveling through a rugged mountainous region during the heat of summer. When Heo's wife went into labor there was no opportunity to find sanitary conditions. She died in childbirth, and their newborn son also died a few days later. Heo wrote a poem about his experience as a refugee fleeing the Japanese invasion:

Hideyoshi's Navy Attacking Busanjin Fortress, 1709, reworked 1760 by Byeon Bak. Colors on silk. Army Museum of San Gongneung-dong, Nowon-gu, Seoul 230-30. National Treasure no. 391.

This painting depicts the 1592 Japanese invasion of Korea. It is valued as a national treasure and an expression of the Korean spirit of resistance against overwhelming odds.

At the Refugee Camp

I
My home is in Changnung, east of a small market —
a thatched house with several small rooms, now empty.
So many of my scrolls were catalogued, but where are they now?
Perhaps thrown in a ditch, or buried under earth.

II
A few days ago, when court meetings adjourned, the wide street
filled with the *jingle* of waist pendants; ten thousand houses bubbled with
    courtesans
and fluttering flutes. Now the King has left his palace — the field for sing-
    ing and dancing
has become a battleground.

III
My father's grave is on the banks of the Han River.
At year's end, who will tend his tomb?
I look west to the pine trees, heartbroken — the sun sets
at the sky's edge — my handkerchief, wet with tears.

IV
The road's endless distance to West Castle's river border —
since leaving, it is difficult to send letters. I see only spears.
My refugee life, entrusted to others,
where will I enjoy clouds — spend a day in leisurely sleep?

V
Near the northern border, enemy swords still have not been broken.
When will the greedy pigs leave the central kingdom?
At day's end, beacon-post fires have all been quelled.
I sit, knowing the enemy will not confront this battle-ready mountain.

VI
A thousand foot castle wall surrounded by a hundred foot ditch —
the soldiers wield sharp arrows, strong bows, and long swords.
Clappers sound in front of the castle tents; soldiers speak with one another:
"Our governor will surely be defeated."

VII

At every station in my life, I've liked to act as a simple sick monk:
during hushed nights in my thatched house, I sit, facing a hooded candle.
It is difficult to melt away old habits of my luxurious life —
tomorrow on the plain, I plan a day of hawking.

VIII

At this river crossing, my friend, in the purple glow of evening, seemed
    a river spirit.
Once he left and letters ended, distance between us grew immense.
I cherish a memory of last year, during a moon like this night's,
when we rode side by side in the snow to fetch tea water.

The Japanese advance began to stall. Though Korea's army was out-matched, its navy — which had honed its skills defending the country against Japanese pirates — had success in disrupting the invaders' supply lines. As news of the invaders' brutality spread, impromptu militias rose up to supplement the inefficient and bureaucratic official military.

China's Ming court viewed the impending defeat of its tributary state with alarm. In 1593 the Wanli emperor dispatched a large army to fight the Japanese. Fierce battles devastated the countryside, as the two super-powers fought to stalemate. For several years an uneasy truce held while a negotiated settlement of the conflict was sought; then in 1597 the Japanese launched another attack. This time the Koreans were better prepared. Inconclusive fighting continued until September 1598, when Hideyoshi died. On his deathbed he ordered the withdrawal of Japanese forces.

Heo continued his scholarly studies throughout the long conflict. One of his teachers was a man named Lee Dal, a famous poet. In Heo Kyun's estimation Lee's "many splendid poems are acknowledged as being among the most brilliant collections of all the Tang-style poetry written in Korea since the Silla dynasty." Lee wrote in a simple, direct style (like that of Chinese poets from the Tang dynasty) that influenced both Heo Gyun and his sister, Heo Nanseolheon, one of Korea's foremost female poets. But Lee Dal's mother was a concubine, so he was unable to advance at court. This seemed to Heo Gyun a great injustice, and he became an advocate for reform.

As the century drew to a close Heo Gyun is believed to have written Korea's first novel in the vernacular language of ordinary people. Known as *The Tale of Hong Gildong* (Hong Gildong-jeon), it is traditionally attributed to him, though his authorship of the work has not been absolutely established. Hong Gildong has been called the Robin Hood of Korea. As an illegitimate son of a government minister, Hong was barred from normal paths of advancement. He studied martial arts and became the leader of a rebel band who fought for justice and the rights of the illegitimate, the disenfranchised, and the poor. Eventually he became governor of a utopian island where women, the common people, and the poor were given more opportunity than in traditional society. His story has remained popular in Korea, where it has inspired movies, television shows, cartoons, and video games.

After the withdrawal of the Japanese the Koreans were faced with what was essentially an occupying army of their Chinese allies. Heo Gyun was named an ambassador to the Ming court. Because of his deep familiarity with Tang dynasty Chinese poetry, he was popular with the Ming literati.

Gyun's sister, Nanseolheon, depressed following the deaths of her children after childbirth, committed suicide at the age of twenty-seven. Heo Gyun arranged the publication of her work in China, where it was received enthusiastically. It was said that demand for her work caused a paper shortage in Beijing.

Around 1616, back in Korea, Heo, now in his late forties, was appointed an official of the premier's office, but he would not remain in favor for long. Bitterly critical of many aspects of the Korean government, he posted an appeal on a public gate, which was seen as a rebellious act. He became involved in court disputes, and ended up holding the short stick. His dissident and reformist opinions had not gone unnoticed. In 1618 he was convicted of treason, his limbs were bound to oxen driven in separate directions, and he was drawn and quartered.

Pietro and Maani departed for Persia on Christmas day. To keep his departure a secret he let it be known that he was strolling out to admire the sunset and then joined the caravan after dark. Reaching Isfahan without incident, della Valle was struck, like all travelers to the Persian capital, by the excellence of its city planning and architecture. At the center of the city was the Maidan, an enormous square, seven times larger than the Piazza di San Marco in Venice, with which it was sometimes compared. It was "surrounded on all sides by symmetrical porticoes, uninterrupted by streets, with shops below selling various articles, and above with balconies and windows decorated with a thousand pretty ornaments." The result was a grand-scale "harmony of architecture" without parallel among the cities he had visited. Nor was there a match anywhere in Italy for the Chahar Bagh, the broad avenue designed by the shah.

Unfortunately, the shah was away on a campaign in Georgia at the time of della Valle's arrival, and he would be forced to wait a year for an audience. He passed the time by getting to know many of the city's literary figures and disputing religion with learned clerics. It was a cosmopolitan city. On one occasion della Valle met a Japanese man on his way to Europe who gave him a lesson in East Asian calligraphy. Maani made herself useful by becoming friendly with one of the wives of the shah's chief astrologer, an important figure in the capital. But the Flemish painter, who della Valle sadly reports had become intolerably insolent, abandoned the adventure in Isfahan, leaving behind an unfinished portrait of Maani that may have been the model for the engraving shown on p. 254.

Della Valle took matters into his own hands and went in search of Shah Abbas. Maani persuaded him to abandon his teetotaling ways. He would be forced to drink with the shah, she argued, so how could he refuse his own wife? She was upset about her failure to become pregnant, which she attributed to the "cold and wet humors" that entered into his blood as a result of his habit of drinking water. Della Valle had already fathered two illegitimate children in Italy, but he had been told by a Roman astrologer that he would not have many children. Rarely has a fortune proved so false.

When della Valle caught up with the shah he was welcomed with a fine banquet served by beardless young men, about eighteen to twenty years old, dressed in long stockings, thigh-length gowns worn tight at the chest, and little silk caps rimmed with fur. Musicians played softly while everyone chatted, waiting for the leader's arrival. At last he appeared,

> dressed in a cloth coat of a bright green color ... tied at the chest ... with orange laces. He wore violet hose, shoes of orange shagreen [untanned leather], a red turban, with silver stripes, swordbelt and top sash of many colors, and a sword of black shagreen and handle of white bone, which I think was from fishes' teeth.

The shah, della Valle added, was wearing his turban backwards on his head, a style that no one else in Persia was allowed to affect. Struck by this eye-catching outfit, della Valle must have realized he was in the presence of a kindred spirit, and indeed the two quickly became friendly.

After a time, della Valle's health began to decline, and he returned to the capital. He and Maani stayed there for three years. They were joined by Maani's parents, as well as an eight-year-old war orphan from Georgia whom Maani had adopted the year before, named Maria Tinatin de Ziba but always called Mariuccia. Her father had been killed in battle with the Persians, and she had been taken in by Carmelite missionaries. Adding to the entourage was a pride of Persian cats, a breed della Valle later introduced to Europe. But Maani's mother disliked life in Isfahan, and nine months later she returned to Baghdad with Maani's sisters.

During his time in the Persian capital della Valle observed the arrival of many diplomats from foreign nations. The emergent globalism of the early modern world resulted in a large number of embassies traveling vast distances, often achieving minimal results. Della Valle dismissed a pair of emissaries from Muscovy as "barbarous and rude...proud and uncouth, faithless, deceivers" whose dress was coarse and ugly, "pleated everywhere in the most haphazard manner. The waist is bound by an ugly belt, and a large hood...reaches halfway down the back." Another was the Mughal ambassador, whose habit of smoking a large hookah everywhere he went annoyed della Valle considerably. He brought with him a large quantity of gifts that included a menagerie consisting of water buffalo, elephants, rhinoceroses, and many other strange animals. An English emissary seemed to him a simple and unaffected fellow. Della Valle described Shah Abbas's handling of the diplomats. The shah sent subtle signals by keeping ambassadors waiting variable lengths of time or showing various kinds of preference to one or another. When a Turkish envoy ambassador arrived in Isfahan Abbas humiliated him in public, to the applause of a crowd of onlookers, but then negotiated with him in private.

One ambassador was an elderly Spaniard named Don Garcia de Silva y Figueroa, whom della Valle described as "white-haired but still very active," and whose increasing moodiness and disillusionment he documents. Don García de Silva y Figueroa was a longtime civil servant who had been passing his years placidly in the foreign office in Madrid before being appointed to head an embassy to Persia. His travails during this embassy, documented in a journal he kept of it, demonstrate some of the ordeals of international diplomacy during this time.

Silva y Figueroa's main qualifications for the assignment were that he was a person of high birth who had served in the military and the government, and he was respected as a geographer. He was charged with persuading Shah Abbas to wage war on the Ottomans, whose territories in North Africa were disrupting Spanish ships in the Mediterranean, and with ensuring the safety of Portuguese outposts in the Persian Gulf, particularly the strategically important city of Hormuz, which protected the gulf against access from the Indian Ocean. To this end he was supplied with diplomatic credentials dated August 1613. He was then sixty-three years old.

But it was not until the spring of 1614 that Silva y Figueroa actually embarked on his mission. It had been necessary to assemble suitable gifts

Page with a Golden Goblet, ca. 1610, by Riza-yi Abbasi. Colors and gold on brown paper. 8 x 16 cm. Musée du Louvre, Legs G. Marteau, inv. no. 7136 .

This drawing of a page by the leading painter of Shah Abbas's court may hint at the impression made by youthful attendants at banquets attended by Pietro della Valle and other visitors to the Safavid court. The shah increasingly took an interest in his young pages in his later years.

to impress the Persian ruler. Among the offerings were the sword Philip II had worn during his marriage ceremony; gold in the form of chains, cups, and gilded chests; silver in the form of a writing table and a table services; military armor and weapons; three hundred camel-loads of pepper; and much more, including even a mastiff "of notable generosity and strength." His ship, further delayed by high winds in Portugal, finally departed the second week of April.

During the journey down the coast of Africa Silva y Figueroa fumed about the "bestial obstinacy" of the ship's pilot. He considered him to have a cavalier attitude toward his navigational responsibilities, an opinion not diminished when, after it had already been announced that the ship had rounded the Cape of Good Hope, it appeared looming ahead a full two weeks later. The Cape was finally rounded in August.

Because of the lateness in rounding the Cape, the ship was unable to follow the preferred route through the Mozambique Channel, as this was considered too perilous any later than July 25. This meant that the ship would not touch land until arriving at Goa on the central Indian coast. By this time the water on board had gone bad, and the crew and passengers had become sick. Scurvy struck, with the result that most of those who survived did so with the loss of their teeth. When Pietro della Valle would encounter the ambassador in Persia he would observe that he had no teeth; whether he had embarked with a set is not known. Silva y Figueroa thought that the later phases of scurvy, which he called the "mal de Loanda," were a different ailment from the initial phase, and he detailed the symptoms:

> The second sickness is for the most part terrible and extremely dangerous. It is usually called the Mal de Loanda. It swells the feet and thighs with black or violent spots of the most evil and darkest quality, and then mounts upward to the belly and later the chest, at which point it kills immediately, without other pain or fever, all but those of the very strongest constitution. Only if the disease does not go higher than the thighs does the sufferer survive, for no effective remedy has been discovered during the hundred years that the malady has been known.

Adding to the torment were the hordes of rats that had multiplied over the months of the voyage and made themselves at home throughout the ship, including in the ambassador's cabin. "All their aggressiveness," Silva y Figueroa wrote in his journal, could have been endured, even with the constant screams that filled the night, had it not been for the attraction they felt for human flesh, especially at night, when whole troops of them, great and small (and the hotter it was the more there were) came out and roamed over the beds and faces of the passengers, not only causing annoyance and infection by their vile smell but also shamelessly biting many persons on their feet, hands, and faces, and any other parts that they found uncovered.

The ship finally touched land in Goa late in the fall, seven months after leaving Lisbon. Here, amid relentless heat, Silva y Figueroa met a chilly reception from the Portuguese authorities. Spain and Portugal had been united under one crown since 1580, but in this distant locale that union did not diminish the Portuguese viceroy's hostility to Spaniards. Despite the king's express instructions, the viceroy flatly refused to supply a ship to carry the ambassador on to Hormuz. Silva y Figueroa was forced to pass two full years in Goa before he managed to charter passage for himself on a small merchant vessel sailing out of Bassein (present-day Mumbai).

Contributing to the viceroy's indifference or hostility to Silva y Figueroa's mission was the increasing presence of the English in the region. It was becoming apparent that the days of Portuguese domination in the Indian Ocean were drawing to an end. This was an impression the viceroy, understandably, wished to undo. He figured a decisive sea victory over the English would reestablish Portuguese status. He fitted out an impressive armada of six galleons, two ships, two galleys, and sixty frigates bearing 2700 soldiers in addition to the sailors themselves. The armada shipped out under the personal leadership of the viceroy. Unfortunately, it was insufficiently provisioned for such a large body of men. The armada ran through its victuals before it could inflict serious harm on any English ships, and it had to hangdoggedly return to Goa.

Over the years Shah Abbas had grown weary of endless promises from Spain, the Vatican, and the Empire that they would assist in an assault on the Ottomans, and he was annoyed by the harassment of Persian merchants and high tariffs leveled against them by the Portuguese in Hormuz. Hormuz, an island commanding the entrance to the Persian Gulf, was of high strategic importance, but it depended on supplies of water from Bahrain and the mainland. The Persians overran the Portuguese outposts there and cut off these supplies. Arriving at Hormuz during this ominous atmosphere in April, the ambassador was forced to spend the summer there, impeded by the same Portuguese hostility he had encountered in Goa. Not until October did he manage to obtain passage on a camel caravan

Jahangir's Dream of the Visit of Shah Abbas, 1618–1620, by Abul Hasan. Freer Gallery of Art, Washington, DC, 45.9

Visual imagery played a role in international relations. The Mughal painter Abul Hasan makes a statement about the relative status of Jahangir and Shah Abbas in this painting. Diplomats had to be sensitive not just to practical concerns but also to issues of prestige.

headed to Isfahan. He was still traveling with the huge load of presents whose assembly had caused his initial delay, as well as an entourage of about a hundred people. Because of the heat his party traveled at night, stopping in caravanserai during the daytime. It was November by the time they reached the mountainous region near the city of Shiraz, and now they were held back by cold weather. They were forced to remain there until the following spring.

On setting out that spring Silva y Figueroa suddenly found himself deprived of his Armenian interpreter, whose decapitated body turned up lying by the road; neither his head nor his murderer were ever discovered. A complaint lodged with the Persian government went unanswered.

The ambassador did not reach Isfahan until May. Here, grouchy by nature or as a consequence of his long, difficult journey, he displayed a lack of flexibility about foreign customs that would render him a not entirely effective ambassador — but this scarcely mattered since he had been given an impossible assignment. He was informed by the Persians that all ambassadors must dismount from their horses and prostrate themselves before the royal palace as they went past it. This Silva y Figueroa flatly refused to do, insisting that he would honor the Persian ruler with the same gestures of respect that he would show to a European monarch and nothing more. While the Persians one by one kissed the threshold of the palace, the ambassador and his Spaniards remained seated on their horses. They did remove their hats, which must have seemed odd to the Persians, who left their turbans on even in the presence of the shah.

Shah Abbas, as it turned out, was not at the time present in his capital, having removed himself to the city of Kasvan. So the ambassador set out once again, arriving in Kasvan in mid-June, decked out in an elaborate formal costume that made it difficult for him to bend his knees and caused him to sweat profusely. The first order of business was making arrangements for the delivery of the diplomatic presents, which Silva y Figueroa proposed to send in advance of his audience. Shah Abbas would not hear of this, however, and insisted that they be broken up into multiple parcels to be carried in great show by no fewer than six hundred porters, a prospect that annoyed the impatient Spaniard.

Shah Abbas's proposal to make a show of the gift-giving was probably calculated to impress the Ottoman envoy who had arrived at his court just a few days before Silva y Figueroa. Under the leadership of Grand Vizier Kara Mehmed Pasha — called "The Ox" behind his back on account of his stocky build — the Turks had invaded Persia in 1616, penetrating as far as Yerevan in Armenia. The story is told that Mehmed Pasha and his aides were in a field tent planning strategy when an ox stuck its head through the flaps of the tent and stared intently at the Grand Vizier. His aides could barely suppress their laughter, but the formidable Mehmed was not amused. "Do you know what that animal has just said to me?" he asked. He answered his own question: "He said, 'I see who you are, but who are these jackasses around you?'"

Shah Abbas got the best of this strongman. He wisely avoided direct engagement: he left the city of Yerevan to its own defenses and instead attacked the Ottoman army's supply line. The strategy was successful, and Mehmed Pasha was forced to retreat. The retreat cost him his position as Grand Vizier, and within a few years he would be dead, strangled by a young janissary who had resisted his sexual advances. Under the circumstances, the Ottomans had temporarily been in no position to launch a new invasion. But now, under a new Grand Vizier, Turkish-Persian tensions were again heating up. The Turkish envoy represented a much more pressing concern to Shah Abbas than did anything concerning the Spanish or Portuguese. He hoped to avoid renewing conflict without having to relinquish any of the disputed territory.

The porters were garbed in the best outfits that could be found, and the party paraded through the town to the shah's garden. Here the Spaniards were told to sit on carpets spread out under a large tree and await the shah's appearance. After some time Silva y Figueroa, again uncomfortable in his constricting starched outfit, sent an indignant message demanding to be received immediately. He was then conducted to a pavilion, where the shah greeted him and instructed him to sit back down, this time on a carpet

In 1613 the Mughal emperor Jahangir sent an embassy under Khan Alam (Mirza Barkhurdar) to the Safavid court of Shah Abbas. He included a painter with the entourage, saying, "When I sent Khan Alam to Persia, I sent with him a painter named Bishandas, who was without equal in drawing likenesses, to take the likeness of the shah and his chief statesmen." On the Persian side the artist Rizza-yi Abassi also documented the meeting of the diplomats.

The embassy did not return to the Mughal court until 1620. During the early modern period both artists and diplomats often made journeys that were long in both distance and duration.

inside the pavilion. Encumbered with a long ceremonial sword in addition to his tight-fitting pants, the elderly ambassador found squatting on the carpet an excruciating experience. At last, two hours after sunset, dinner was served. The ambassador could scarcely conceal his contempt for the offering of chicken, mutton, rice, melons, and plums, though he did admire the table service, which was entirely made of gold. Already wobbly from hours of squatting, he was further destabilized by being obliged to partake, though he was a teetotaler, of wine that was poured out in copious quantities. By midnight, some eight hours after the beginning of the ceremonies, the weary ambassador's agony outweighed his sense of diplomatic etiquette, and he cried out that if he were not allowed to retire he would suffocate. He was allowed to outstretch his creaky limbs and depart.

He had not succeeded in discussing any affairs of state. That was not a discussion that Shah Abbas was in any hurry to have, for, having taken Bahrain and the coastal areas at the entrance to the Persian Gulf, he had little to fear from the Portuguese and their lonely outpost in Hormuz. Though charged with pressing for the return of those territories, Silva y Figueroa had not not been provided with inducements to make this happen, apart from empty promises of cooperation against the Turks. The shah had little expectation of military assistance from Spain. For years its assurances of action had proven hollow.

The presence of a deputation of Englishmen to the Persian court, Silva y Figueroa rightly judged, made his prospects even less promising. The first English Company ship visited Persia in 1616. The overture originated not in England but in India. English merchants had set up shop in Surat on India's northwest coast, having been encouraged by an initial exchange of goods there. But subsequent goods delivered to Surat turned out to be hard to move, and the English began looking around for other markets. They observed that the Portuguese control of the Persian Gulf was lax, and growing weaker. Silva y Figueroa had hoped to prevent the English from being received by Shah Abbas, but in his slow movement to the capital he had been passed by a swifter-moving English agent, who had got there first.

For three weeks the ambassador pressed for a meeting without results. Eventually he managed to surprise the shah while he was moving from one place to another, and he obtained an impromptu audience. The result was unsatisfactory, for Shah Abbas immediately went on the attack, demanding to know why the Europeans left Persia to fight the Turks all alone, why the pope could not unite the Christian powers, and why Spain limited itself to chasing a few corsairs around the western Mediterranean. He steered clear of the question of Hormuz and the gulf, and Silva y Figueroa was unable to bring it up. He considered his mission still unfulfilled.

Later the ambassador managed another conversation, in which he insisted on discussing the Hormuz situation and the Persian attack on its mainland supply bases. Because the Portuguese had exercised control over those regions through vassal kingdoms rather than directly, Shah Abbas was able to assert that he had made no move against Spain and Portugal, but only against those local kingdoms, who, he said, had taken land that rightfully belonged to Persia. The ambassador indignantly answered that Portugal had been in effective possession of the territories for a hundred years, and the shah could not claim they belonged to Persia. At which point the shah declared the discussion concluded.

There the matter stood for two more fruitless years. When at last he was given leave to return home, Silva y Figueroa suffered a debilitating attack of dysentery, delaying his journey to Hormuz. Arriving there, he again found the Portuguese in a state of panic over rumors of an impending attack from combined Persian and English forces (the fear was justified, and the assault would occur two years later). Pointing to the presence of English ships nearby, the Portuguese refused to take Silva y Figueroa to Goa. He was forced to spend another half year in Hormuz before he was able to find a local pilot who would convey him to India.

Back in Goa he encountered the same hostility that had met him on his outward trip, and he spent another half year before embarking in a small and rather rickety vessel that was bound for Lisbon. This ship got as far as Mozambique before it gave every indication of breaking apart, and it was forced to return all the way to Goa. There it deposited the poor ambassador, who had to cool his heals for another two years nine months. Goa was at the time suffering from a plaguelike epidemic. The Portuguese remained hostile. Silva y Figueroa was now more than seventy years old.

In 1622 the Persians and English defeated Hormuz, whereupon English and Dutch ships blockaded Goa. Silva y Figueroa's mission had achieved nothing. In 1624, eleven years after being appointed for his mission, he set sail for Lisbon. He never reached home. After the ship rounded the Cape of Good Hope, with a final entry estimating the vessel's position, his journal came to an abrupt end — he had died of the "mal de Loanda."

Sometimes it was hard to distinguish between ambassadors and adventurers. Such was the case with Anthony and Robert Sherley, who together with their brother Thomas figured prominently in relations between Europe and West Asia. In 1616 each of the three found himself in a different part of the world. Thomas, fifty-two years old, was in England, and likely in debtor's prison in London — at least, he is known to have been in King's Bench Prison in 1615 and Fleet Prison in 1617. Anthony, fifty-one, seems to have been in either Madrid or Granada. Robert, the youngest, was thirty-five; he was in Goa on the western India coast, waiting for passage to Lisbon. Each of the brothers was at his core an adventurer, with varying admixtures of soldier, diplomat, and con man mingled in, and each had followed a unique route to his present location.

They were the sons of Sir Thomas Sherley, senior, of the Sussex Sherleys, a somewhat down-on-its-heels family of good lineage. As a young man the first of the brothers fought in Ireland and the Netherlands. Already by this time he, like the father whose name he shared, was having difficulties with debt and, perhaps as much to escape his creditors as to raise funds, he determined on a career as a privateer. Obtaining some ships and a crew not overburdened by scruples, he attacked shipping in the North Atlantic and conducted raids on fishing villages along the coast of Portugal. The profit from these predations, however, does not seem to have gone far beyond covering his costs — on one occasion he had to borrow money using his ship as security in order to limp home in the damaged vessel. An observer reported on his return home from another one of his expeditions:

> Sr Thomas Sherley is returned with his navy royal, and yesterday … posted to the Court, as though they had brought tidings of the taking of Seville or some such town, whereas God knows they have sacked but two poor hamlets of two dozen houses in Portugal, the pillage wherof he gave to his army, reserving to himself only two or three peasants to ransome, of whom when he saw he could raise nothing, he would not bring them away for shame.

Undaunted, or desperate, Thomas decided to expand his range into the Mediterranean, where he hoped to obtain more valuable prizes. He attacked several vessels and lost fifty men in a fruitless attack on a Flemish ship.

As protests rained in from the various capitals of Europe, the English foreign office sought to defuse an international incident by promising to apprehend and punish him. Perhaps with a mind to putting distance between his fleet and possible pursuers, Thomas continued east at the command of three ships and attacked a Turkish vessel, but this proved a difficult battle, in which he lost a hundred men. To make matters worse, the spoils proved unequal to the high cost of the battle, and his rough crew grew mutinous. By the next day one of his ships had disappeared, and a second followed a few days later.

To restore a happy mood aboard his lone remaining vessel, Thomas quickly attacked the Greek island of Kea, but this venture turned out even worse than its predecessors — he was captured along with a few of his companions. The rest of the crew made it back to ship, where they remained in harbor for three days, weighing a possible rescue of their captain against the risk to their persons. In the end they simply sailed off.

The unfortunate Thomas was removed to a Turkish prison where he was held in chains awaiting ransom. Suspecting he might be worth more than they had initially demanded, his jailers put him to the rack to discover his identity. When they found out that he was the brother of the notorious Anthony Sherley, who they knew was inciting Shah Abbas of Persia to attack Turkey, he was treated more harshly, and his ransom was raised.

Queen Elizabeth had no use for the Sherleys and would not have minded seeing all three in Turkish prisons, but on assuming the throne James, who had corresponded with the Sherleys while still in Scotland, took a different tack (to the chagrin of Robert Cecil, his cold-blooded secretary of state). The king's personal intercession, along with a hefty ransom, won Thomas his release after about three years in Turkish captivity.

Back in England, Thomas discovered that he had new enemies. By stirring up trouble with Turkey he had complicated matters for the merchants of the Levant Company, whose fortunes depended on the smooth delivery of goods across Ottoman realms (both Anthony and Robert would later make great efforts to shift the Levant trade to maritime routes). The company spread the rumor that while in prison Thomas had "turned Turke" (converted to Islam), and he was carried off to the Tower of London.

He petitioned Cecil for pardon, writing "I have done nothinge out of malis, but have offended through weakness and ignorans." The charge of turning Turk didn't stick, and he was released. Twice married and with eighteen children, he was still obligated for the debt of seven thousand pounds that had been paid out as his ransom. While his brothers attained international notoriety, he remained forgotten, nagged by a plethora of petty troubles, and he grew morose and bitter.

In 1612, according to one observer's gossipy letter, "Sir Thomas Shirley, the younger, being in the King's Bench for debt, took the other day, a good quantity of poison, with intent to make himself away." The suicide attempt was unsuccessful, and 1615 found Thomas petitioning the king for relief from his debt. "Pardon my boldness, and then to vouchsafe to bow down your gracious eye upon this enclosed paper," his letter began obsequiously, "wherein your Majesty may behold (if you please) the true anatomy of a most ruined poor gentleman."

In 1617, while in Fleet Prison, Thomas, still brooding over the downturn in his fortunes that he blamed on his Turkish imprisonment, wrote a tiresome book called *Discours of the Turkes,* in which he belabored the argument that Turks "are all pagans and infidels, Sodomites, liars, and drunkards, proud, scornful, and cruel." In the end he sold off his ancestral home to raise funds, retired with his oversized family to a modest home on the Isle of Wight, and disappeared from the pages of history. There he died, the year unknown.

Anthony Sherley, only one year younger than Thomas, started out along a similar path. He too served in the military in the Low Countries. He was a protégée of the dashing Robert Devereux, second Earl of Essex, father of the Robert Devereaux who would be divorced by Lady Frances Howard on the grounds of impotence so she could marry the king's favorite, Robert Carr, an affair that lead ultimately to the Overbury murder and trial. The elder Devereaux had been Elizabeth's favorite until he was arrested following his command of an ill-fated campaign in Ireland. Imagining that he had the support and sympathy of the people, Devereaux led a farcical coup against the queen. Parading through the streets of London, he counted on swelling crowds to fall in with him and force Elizabeth from her throne. The crowds did not materialize, and he was beheaded for treason on the green of the Tower of London, as Walter Raleigh nonchalantly watched from a window, reportedly enjoying a smoke of tobacco.

Anthony Sherley was a good student of Devereaux's style, resembling his mentor in his flamboyance, smooth talk, grand aspirations, and lack of judgment. Devereaux's words, he once wrote, "were the star that guided me." In 1591 he had followed Devereaux during a campaign in Normandy in support of Henri IV. Henri rewarded him with a knighthood. This set Elizabeth off. "I will not have my sheep marked with a strange brand," she raged, "nor suffer them to follow the pipe of a strange shepherd!" It was a suitably inauspicious beginning to Anthony's checkered career. He was forced to formally renounce the title. Nonetheless, although he would never be offered an English title, he always thereafter styled himself "Sir Anthony."

In 1595 Sir Anthony married a cousin of the Earl of Essex. It was reported to be an unhappy union. Within three years he would leave the country, never to see her again. His destination was the Americas, where he led a raid against the Spanish on the island of Jamaica. The overall effect of this expedition was inconsequential. He then became involved in a plan to foment conflict among the Italian states. The pretext was a question of succession in the Duchy of Ferrara on the Adriatic coast south of Venice, but by the time Anthony's small party of men arrived the matter had already been settled. He sought some kind of service in Venice, but none was forthcoming. "All things appertaining to innovations or tumults in Italy lay dead," the dejected Anthony wrote home.

From his vantage point in Venice the only prospect he could see for stirring up the sort of trouble that might benefit a military adventurer (and for making plausible use of the unspent funding he had raised for the Ferrara expedition) lay in Persia. He booked passage from Venice with a band of about twenty-six men, including his seventeen-year-old brother, Robert. The Englishmen, pummeling and quarreling with some of the Italian passengers, made themselves so unpopular aboard ship that after stopping to eat at a port of call en route they discovered the seamen had quietly deposited their luggage and gone on without them. Anthony appealed to the English ambassador to Turkey for assistance, fabricating a story about being on a mission from the queen to the Red Sea. It was just one of many whoppers that would sustain him through his adventures.

Arriving at the Persian court by way of Aleppo and Baghdad, he followed up that fabrication with another, leading Shah Abbas to believe that he was an official representative of the queen — indeed, that he was her cousin, according to one Persian observer, who converted to Christianity and ended his life in Spain, where he wrote an account of Anthony and Robert Sherley in Persia. In fact, the plan Anthony Sherley advocated of a massive joint crusade against Turkey contradicted actual English policy, which sought to maintain détente with the Ottomans for the benefit of the

Levant trade. The English consul at Aleppo wrote regarding "the matters ... concerning Sir Anthony Sherley and his proceadinges" that little good would come of them, ironically wishing Sherley "better successe then wee by anie probabylyty can hitherto conjecture."

The timing of Sherley's arrival was fortuitous, as Shah Abbas was just then returning victorious from battle against the Uzbeks. Faced with wars on both the eastern and western sides of Persia, the shah had decided to concentrate all his initial energies on pacifying the east. This was possible because the Ottomans were engaged in war in the Balkans with Rudolf II, and skirmishing with Spain in the Mediterranean; even so, Persia did lose territory to the Ottomans in the early years of the shah's reign. Arriving triumphantly at the head of an army brandishing thousands of Uzbek heads on poles, Shah Abbas read in Sherley's appearance an affirmation of his growing international prestige.

After a few months the shah sent Anthony and a Persian named Husain Ali Beg as his agents to Europe. Robert Sherley was left behind, because, Anthony said, the shah had told him that "the company of my brother should give him great satisfaction in my absence." In fact Robert was being held as a hostage to ensure that Anthony performed his duties as expected.

From the beginning there was uncertainty about the status of the two emissaries. According to Anthony, he and Husain Ali Beg were designated by the shah as co-ambassadors. Translations of the embassy's diplomatic documents in the Vatican archives, however, appear to confirm Husain Ali Beg's contention that he was the sole ambassador and Anthony his traveling companion. But because Husain Ali Beg did not speak Latin or European languages he was dependent on Anthony's translation.

Together with Husain, Anthony returned to Europe by way of Moscow. The Muscovites, familiar with Persian diplomatic protocol, received Husain Ali Beg warmly but were cold to Anthony. The two travelers were provided with sixty-three presents for European heads of states. In a port on the White Sea north of Moscow, Anthony said he was putting these on an English ship headed for Rome on the grounds that this would safeguard them. The presents never reached Rome. Accused by Hussain of having sold them, Anthony replied that they had turned out to be unworthy as diplomatic gifts, and he had sent them back to Persia. They never arrived there either.

The embassy had hoped to visit eight European nations but in the end they were received only by the three that were already at war with Turkey: the Empire, the papal state, and Spain. From Muscovy the travelers took passage through the Norwegian Sea and North Sea into Germany and south to Prague, where they received a warm welcome but few firm commitments from Rudolf II. Some observers saw reason for caution in dealing with the Persian delegation: the Venetian ambassador at Rudolf's court, for example, immediately saw the contradiction in Anthony's performance, writing that "The English queen has friendly relations with Turkey and is not kindly disposed to the Habsburgs; what then does she intend with this embassy?"

Anthony and Husain continued to Rome, where they met with Pope Clement VIII, who also was encouraging but promised little beyond sincere prayers. In Italy tensions between the ambassadors reached the boiling point, and they came to blows. It was not an auspicious sign for Sherley's grand plan for a new crusade to defeat the Ottomans, who were still the greatest power in the regions of Europe and West Asia. One cardinal commented that "Since they, who are only two and are sent by the same prince on the same errand, cannot themselves agree, they will find it even more difficult to create unity among so many Christian princes and others with regard to overthrowing the Turkish Empire." Anthony sulked off, and Husain continued to Spain and Portugal on his own, eventually returning to Persia by way of Goa.

Anthony's subsequent career was something of an anticlimax to his first grand gesture in opening relations with Persia. He apparently spent a few years in Venice doing alchemical researches, or at least trying to find a way to profit from them. (One might wonder whether he had contact with Mordecai Modena at this time.) He was probably hard up for funds; while in Venice he was arrested for forcing his way into the house of a Persian merchant and attempting to seize his goods, claiming his status as a Persian ambassador gave him to right to do so.

From Italy he traveled to Spain, where he made the audacious proposal of creating a Mediterranean fleet at little expense to Spain by enlisting privateers — peace between England and Spain had put a damper on English privateers who, like his older brother, had formerly attacked Spanish vessels. He also intended, he said, to enlist the Barbary corsairs Ward and

Opposite: Letters from Robert
Sherley to Anthony Sherley,
1606, National Archives, London, ref. CO77/26 pp. 43–43v.

Robert Sherley was in his early
twenties went he sent these letters
from Persia to his older brother
Anthony. Robert had been left behind as a hostage when Anthony
was sent to the courts of Europe to
help represent Persian interests.
   Anthony failed to return to
Persia, and Robert upbraids his
brother for his failure to honor his
promises.

Danziker to help capture Turkish and Dutch prizes with which to finance the naval operations, and he initiated correspondence with them. Despite a complete lack of naval experience, the fast-talking Sherley managed to be appointed a Spanish admiral on the basis of this rather nutty proposal.

The project was not a success. Sherley returned to Spain "extreme poor in both purse and reputation," according to the English envoy there. He was pensioned off to Granada, where he would be far from the administrative centers of Madrid and Lisbon, and his ability to muck things up would be limited. There, like his older brother, he wrote a rather dull account of his adventures. In his later years he continued to put forth projects that failed to reach fruition, such as the proposal of a Spanish attack against James-town — which amounted to treason against England. He also advocated redirecting the Persian silk trade through maritime routes around Africa rather than overland through Ottoman lands, though again to no effect.

Although there was little to show from the first Persian embassy to Europe, it was well publicized, and it served to put Persia on the map for many Europeans. Together with the next Persian embassy, featuring the third of the Sherley brothers, it may have influenced the next wave of travelers to Persia, including Thomas Coryate, George Strachan, and Pietro della Valle.

Robert Sherley, left behind in Persia when his brother returned to Europe, remained there for eight years. According to a persistent legend — it is perpetuated to this day on several Wikipedia pages — he reformed and re-trained the Persian army and introduced firearms to the Persians. Certainly Shah Abbas extracted what military expertise he could from his European visitors. But the Persians were familiar with firearms before the Sherleys' arrival, and moreover the shah never made heavy use of them. It is doubtful that the Persian leader, fresh from his victory over the Uzbeks, required a great deal of schooling from a young pup like Robert.

But distance is a friend of legend, and Robert's reputation grew during his time abroad. In England it was reported that he had personally captured ninety Turkish generals. "The mighty Ottoman," Samuel Purchas said, "quaketh of a Sherly-Fever." He assured his readers that Sherley and his men once faced a hundred and sixty thousand Turks, of which only two thousand survived to flee the battle. Poems and plays were written about him and his brothers. No less a figure than Thomas Middleton would craft an account of him (though this was probably a work for hire commissioned by Thomas Sherley).

The tone of the letters, written in a childish hand, that Robert sent to Anthony tell a different story. In one he describes himself as "besids myself with the travailes and wants I am in, and the little hope I have of your retorne or of anie helpe from my delivry out of this Countrie." In another he upbraids his brother for failure to deliver on such promises as the sending of presents to the shah: this, Robert says, "hathe made me estimed a common lyar; brother for Gods sake, either performe, or not promis any thinge, because in this fasion you make me discreditt my-selfe, by reportinge things wch you care not to effecte."

Eventually Robert adjusted to his situation. He married a young Circassian Christian woman named Teresia Sampsonia (the Circassians, or Adyghe, are a people originally from the Caucasus region of the Black Sea in what is now southern Russia). Shah Abbas's reputation of tolerance toward Christians had reached Europe, and in 1608 a Carmelite mission arrived in Persia. Among the news the Carmelites delivered was the appointment of Anthony Sherley as head of a Spanish armada in the Mediterranean. This news rekindled the shah's fading hopes for a European alliance against Turkey. Robert was appointed ambassador for another embassy to Europe, and this time there would be no doubt about credentials.

Accompanied by his wife, Robert traveled to Moscow (where, unlike his brother, he was well received) and then struck out overland to Poland, making much better time than Anthony had by taking the arctic sea route around Scandinavia. He spent six months in Poland. Then, leaving Teresia behind, he continued on to Prague, where Rudolf II received him warmly and made him a Count Palatine. He continued to Italy and met with the pope — who made him a Count of the Sacred Palace of the Lateran — and other political leaders. The pope is supposed to have granted Robert the right to legitimize bastards. Sherley assured the pontiff that if the Ottomans fell Abbas would become a Christian.

Surviving documents indicate that two of Shah Abbas's prime objectives from this embassy were a cessation of European trade with Turkey and a sea attack to coordinate with a land offensive from Persia. Robert, perhaps influenced by his brother Anthony, recommended an attack on Cyprus in order to make the island a base for an incursion inland to Aleppo.

Throughout his travels Robert dressed in Persian garments, which capitivated his European audiences. His

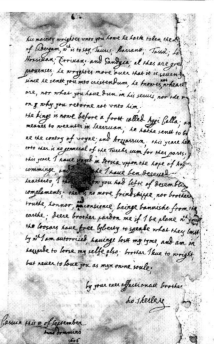

Robert Sherley, 1622, by Anthony Van Dyke. Oil on canvas, 133 x 200 cm. Petworth Castle, National Trust, UK acc. no. 38.

Like many Europeans, Van Dyke, who painted this portrait during the six years he spent in Italy (1621–1627), was fascinated by the Persian ambassador's costume.

portrait and Teresia's were painted several times, including by a young Anthony Van Dyke.

Like his brother's embassy, Robert's was received with expressions of friendship and vague promises of cooperation but few specifics or firm commitments. He continued to Spain. There he met a frosty reception. It might be that the Spaniards were simply wearying of Sherleys: the Council of Portugal declared Robert to be *tan inbencionero* — as much a teller of tales — as his brother; but they also had real limitations in their ability to engage in the eastern Mediterranean because of their ongoing involvement at that time in the Netherlands. At first they avoided meeting Robert at all, but eventually, concerned that he would carry his proposals to England with potentially negative consequences for Spain, they decided to pretend to negotiate in order to draw out the process as long as possible. Robert ended up spending a year in Spain, with nothing to show for his time in the end.

In Spain Robert found Anthony, disgraced following the failure of his naval ambitions, in a pathetic state. According to the English envoy, he was "so extreme poor, as if his brother did not relieve him he would doubtless suffer much misery":

> The poor man comes sometimes to my house, and is as full of vanity as ever he was, making himself believe that he shall one day be a great Prince, when for the present he wants shoes to wear.

Anthony continued to dream and scheme, but the grandiose proposals that he put foward daily now made him appear ridiculous. Robert gradually overcame the Sherley stigma and made a better impression, the English envoy judging that "those vices which in Sir Anthony do so abound, in this man may be found the contraries."

In September 1610 Sherley's position in Spain was undercut by the arrival of another Persian ambassador, a man named Janghiz Beg, who had left Persia a year after Sherley. Cooperation between the ambassadors proved nearly as difficult as had been the case with Anthony and Husain Ali Beg, and by June the following year, joined by Teresia after a separation of two years, he left the Spanish court for England.

Whatever Janghiz Beg's mission was, his performance of it evidently did not satisfy the shah: when he returned to Persia and bent to kiss the shah's foot he received a kick in the face. A few days later he was executed and his possessions seized. The reasons for this reception are disputed, but it is probably significant that an Ottoman peace envoy was present in the shah's court at the time. Peace with Turkey would enable Persia to address the problem of the Portuguese garrison in Hormuz, which was still harrassing Persian merchants.

Little as Spain wanted to negotiate with Sherley, they wanted him to negotiate with England even less. A warrant was put out for his arrest, but he slipped away to the Netherlands. Finding no enthusiasm for his propositions there, he continued to England, which he had left more than thirteen years before. He found his father in ill health and deep in dept and his brother Thomas in debtor's prison.

His proposals received a mixed reception. His plan to divert the silk trade to maritime routes was opposed by the Levant Company, but the royal family seemed well disposed to him. Teresia gave birth to the couple's first son, whom they named Henry after Prince Henry, who agreed to be godfather; Queen Anne was godmother. On the political front, however, nothing was achieved, and the Sherleys took passage to Persia, leaving Henry behind in the melancholy Thomas's squalid household crowded with children.

The voyage around the Cape set a speed record. The captain of the vessel was Christopher Newport, the most celebrated merchant captain of his day. He would travel as far as Java after delivering Sherley and his wife and still arrive back in England within a year and a half. Newport, a protégée of Francis Drake, spent two decades as a privateer attacking Spanish and Portuguese ships, mainly in Caribbean and Brazilian waters. Sometime around 1590 he lost one of his hands and is thought to have worn a hook in its place. The loss did not much hold him back. One of his subsequent prizes was a Portuguese carrack called the *Madre de Deus,* which he took off the Azores in 1592; its haul was the most valuable captured by any Englishman of his time. In 1609 Newport had captained the *Sea Venture,* the ship bound for Virginia carrying John Rolfe and his first wife, which wrecked on a Bermuda reef during a hurricane.

Newport had been in the employ of the English East India Company since 1612. On his next voyage he would carry Thomas Roe as the first official ambassador from James's court to the Mughals. That voyage, lasting from 1615 to 1617, is remarkable because no fewer than four journals survive from it: that of William Keeling, who was in overall command of the fleet of four ships; those of Walter Peyton and Thomas Bonner, captain and master of one of the vessels; and that of Roe himself (as far as Surat, where he disembarked). Besides the passengers, the fleet carried cargo consisting of iron bars, quicksilver, vermilion, ivory, glasses, mirrors, weapons, and fifty cases of "hote waters" (alcoholic spirits), among other goods. Newport would die in Java in 1617, at the age of fifty-seven.

Robert Sherley arrived in Persia in 1598, when he was eighteen years old. Left behind there by his brother Anthony, he married Teresia Sanpsonia, a Circasian Christian woman.

In 1608 Shah Abbas sent Robert on an embassy to Europe. Teresia traveled with him through parts of his journey to Poland, Germany, Italy, Spain, the Netherlands, and England. They returned to Persia in 1615 but were soon sent back to Europe. In 1628 they returned to Persia a final time.

The anonymous painter depicts Robert in an elaborate outfit topped by a stylish cloak that had been presented to him by the shah. He wears a turban and a silk sash in a Persian style. Sherley's Persian dress made a big impression on European observers.

Teresia, by contrast, is shown in an English-style silk dress, though her veil and crown are Persian. Her silk garments advertise products Persia was offering for trade.

She holds a pistol in her right hand and a pocket watch in her left, symbols of modern technology. The pistol may allude to Robert's supposed role in introducing firearms to Persia, as well as to Teresia's courage: she is said to have saved her husband's life against attackers on two occasions.

Sherley, set ashore at the mouth of the Indus, near the city of Karachi in present-day Pakistan, discovered that the Portuguese, determined not to allow him to carry any secret agreement forged in England back to the shah, had put a contract on his head. "If this [English trade] is put into practice," the Spanish Council of State had written, "it will be the destruction of Hormuz." The house where Robert and Teresia were staying was blown up, and several companions were killed in a harrowing series of incidents. Nonetheless, they managed to reach Jahangir's court in Agra, where the Mughal emperor graciously reimbursed Sherley for his losses so that he would have gifts to present to the shah on his return.

Between Lahore and Isfahan Robert and Teresia encountered the English travel writer Thomas Coryate, who was making the same journey in reverse. Coryate was pleased to discover that Robert was packing his books among his traveling luggage — it was the first time he had seen some in print. He was also grateful for the gift of forty shillings from Teresia.

They arrived at the Persian court in the summer of 1615, at a time when Shah Abbas was again putting out peace feelers to the Portuguese. The previous fall, when the Grand Vizier Nasuf Pasha was executed, the faction of the Ottoman government that favored peace with Persia, a position associated with Pasha, had lost out to the hawks. Faced with a resumption of hostilities with Turkey, the shah saw the need to calm down the situation in the south, so he was interested in reaffirming his friendship with Spain.

After such a long journey it is remarkable that the shah should immediately send Sherley away on another trip, but that is what happened. According to a Carmelite missionary present in Persia at the time, Sherley tried to talk the shah out of sending him away again, to no avail. Before his first ambassadorial journey to Europe Sherley had been forced to spend nearly a decade in Persia and was desperate to leave; now he was only to remain a few months, though he was desperate to stay.

Sherley had to retrace his steps to Hormuz in Portuguese territory, where he had recently only narrowly avoided being assassinated. But now the Portuguese received him sunnily. All was forgotten. Unfortunately, he missed the spring 1615 fleet to Lisbon and consequently had to spend nearly a year in Goa waiting for the next voyage. It was probably an uncomfortable year, as he was regarded with suspicion by all parties — the Spanish ambassador, Figueroa, was convinced he was conspiring with the

English, while the English ambassador Roe (who called Sherley a "charlatan") was certain that he was in league with the Portuguese.

Sherley arrived back in Lisbon in the fall of 1617. He would not leave the Spanish court until 1622. His mission there was not helped by the back-biting of his brother Anthony. Probably in the hopes of bettering his own prospects of obtaining employment from Spain, Anthony sent a letter to the court recommending that Robert not be received there (where he could contact the English ambassador) but instead be detained in Lisbon. Robert intercepted a reply to this, with predictable results. According to the English ambassador, "The two brothers are much fallen out and both by word and writing do all the harm they can in defaming each other, but I must needs confess that the Ambassador is the discreeter of the two."

It took a long time for Sherley to get an audience, and a longer time to hash out an understanding, but by spring 1619 Sherley had managed to achieve a draft agreement between Persia and Spain. How confident was he that Shah Abbas would ratify the agreement? It is suggestive that he put off returning to Persia for several years. Leaving the court in March 1622, he headed for Rome. There he disappears from the historical record until he shows up again in London in December 1623.

In London, ignoring the treaty he had drafted with Spain, he pitched an Anglo-Persian alliance. He met with King James in January. He assured the monarch that Shah Abbas would provide England with some 25,000 men to assist English efforts in Asia and would also redirect the silk trade to England in exchange for a delivery of English ships. Both the Levant Company and the East India Company doubted the validity of the offer, but James himself favored it. The argument went on for three years. In the end James determined to back the endeavor himself, with funding from various aristocrats. It was a scheme that would set him in direct competition with the East India Company.

The king's plan was scuttled by the arrival of letters indicating that favorable terms for Persian silk had already been obtained by Company representatives in Asia. Furthermore, just at this point Sherley's mission was again undercut by the arrival, in 1626, of another purported Persian ambassador, a peculiar character named Naqd Ali Beg.

Sherley called on Ali Beg together with a group of interested parties. An absurd altercation followed. One observer described it in these terms:

> Entring the Hall (where he [Ali Beg] was then sitting in a chair on his legs double under him, after the Persian Posture), and affording no motion of respect to any of us, *Sir Robert Sherley* gave him a salutation, and sate downe on a stoole neare him…. *Sir Robert Sherley,* unfolding his Letters [his ambassadorial credentials], and (as the Persian use is in reverence to their King) first touching his eyes with them, next holding them over his head, and after kissing them, he presented them to the Ambassador, that he receiving them, might performe the like observance, when he suddenly rising out of his chaire, stept to Sir *Robert Sherley*, snatcht his Letters from him, toare them, and gave him a blow on the face with his Fist, and while my Lord of *Cleaveland* stepping between kept off the offer of a further violence; the Persians Son next at hand flew upon Sire *Robert Shereley,* and with two or three blows more, overthrew him….

When things settled down Beg explained that he was outraged that Sherley had forged the Shah's signature. What he meant is unclear since the shah was illiterate, but he may have been referring to his official seal. Sherley, who "was in the meane time retyred behind the company" lost face from this encounter "for his default in his resolution, not to returne with blows (or words at least) the affront done him."

It was decided to send both ambassadors back to Persia, together with an English ambassador, to clear up the confusion about their status. Through Teresia, Sherley petitioned to keep the "barbarous heathen" Ali Beg separate from him during the journey. Meanwhile, the heathen himself had shacked up with a "lewd strumpet" whom he wanted to take aboard with him; this request was denied.

Landing at Surat in India, Robert and Teresia traveled by caravan to meet the shah. Among their party was a young man who later wrote an account of the journey. He reported that the caravanserai were excellent — the caravan was often welcomed with feasts and dances. At one stop along the way, in the town of Lar in the Punjab, he described a poet welcoming them with a lyrical oration, followed by a cacaphony of "barbarous jangling unmisical instruments." The fanfare was succeeded by an even more riotous display:

> A homely Venus, attired like a Bacchanal, attended by as many morris-dancers, began to caper and frisk their best lavoltas, so as every limb strove to exceed each other; the bells, cymbals, kettle-music and whistles storming such a Phrygic discord that, had it been night, it would have resembled an orgy to Bacchus, for glass-bottles emptied of wine

Foreign Ambassadors, 1616–1617, by Carlo Saraceni and workshop. Sala dei Corazzieri, Quirinale Palace, Rome.

Robert Sherley appears among several foreign ambasadors in these frescos in the Italian presidential palace in Rome.

clashing one against another, the loud braying of above two hundred asses, and mules ... and the continual shouting and whooping of above two thousand plebians all the way so amazed us that ... we thought never any strangers were bombasted with such a triumph.

Even more astonishing was a the performance of a yogi:

> He trod upon two sharp-edged scimitars with his bare feet; then laid his naked back upon them, suffering a heavy anvil to be set on his belly and two men to hammer out four horse shoes upon it as forcibly as they could beat; that trick ended, he thrust his arms and thighs through with many arrows and lances, then by mere strength of his head and agility of body lifted up (not less than a yard from the ground) a great stone weighing six hundred pounds; and then (as if he had done nothing) knitted his hair to an old goat's head, and with a scornful pull tore it asunder, crying *Allough Whoddow* (*i.e.* God be thanked), the standers by with a loud yell applauding him.

But the mood in the shah's court was more somber. Abbas was ill, and racked with remorse. Having grown suspicious of his sons, he had the crown prince, Mohammed Baqir Mirza, killed and his two other sons blinded and imprisoned. He is said to have particularly regretted the murder, and he was tortured by the unhappy turn his family life had taken. He did not, however, release his surviving sons from prison.

Sherley's draft agreement with Spain had reached Abbas in 1619 in advance of Sherley's return. The shah was in no hurry to have its proposals read to him, allowing it to age for several weeks before considering it. When the terms — including the return of conquered territories and the barring of English from Persia — were finally recited to him he laughed derisively and tore up the agreement.

Ali Beg had died the day the ship had landed in India. It was said that he took an overdose of opium rather than face the shah. Supporters of Sherley suggested, plausibly, that Ali Beg had been in cahoots with the English trade companies to discredit him. In Isfahan, according to an observer sympathetic to Sherley, Shah Abbas received him warmly, praising his many years of service. He said that if Ali Beg had not commited suicide he would have had him cut into pieces, mixed the pieces with dog shit, and burnt the lot in the market square. But an English Company agent reported that Sherley's credentials were not confirmed, that the Persians had no interest in English galleys since they had no sailors to man them, and that the shah commanded Sherley to leave his kingdom. In any case, after welcoming Sherley graciously the moping shah thereafter ignored him.

Spirits sagged. Everyone was sick. They declined rapidly, and within a few weeks both Sherley and the English ambassador died: the party had now lost all three of its ambassadors. Shah Abbas followed a few months later.

The shah's successors were unable to sustain his success and international prestige. His first successor was his grandson, who did not share Abbas's relative tolerance of other religions. Teresia was forced to flee Persia. She crossed Turkey, passed through Istanbul, and arrived in Rome. There she spent the years devoting herself to religion and charitable works. In 1658 she had Robert's remains delivered to Rome and buried in the Church of Santa Maria della Scala in the Trastevere district, where she lived until 1668, when she died at the age of seventy-nine.

The young travel writer who had accompanied Sherley composed an epitaph for him. "He had a heart as free as any man," he wrote. "His patience was more Philisophicall than his Intellect, having small acquaintance with the Muses: many Cities he saw, many hills climb'd over, and tasted severall waters.... Ranck mee with those that honour him."

> After land-sweats, and many a storme by Sea,
> This hillock aged Sherleys rest must be.
> He well had view'd Armes, men, and fashions strange
> In divers Lands. Desire so makes us range.

A quality of desperation underlies all of the Sherley brothers' machinations. With their family in decline and in debt in their native England, they sought their fortunes abroad, but brazen bluster could only sustain them for so long. Their agonizingly slow, endless journeying shows the difficulty of international diplomacy in the emerging global world of the early seventeenth century. Faced with changing situations and unable to communicate quickly from distant places with the governments they represented, they were forced to improvise. The closest either came to an international agreement was Robert's 1619 draft of a treaty between Spain and Persia, but by the time this agreement got back to Isfahan, changed relations with the representatives of England and Portugal in the Indian Ocean region had made it irrelevant. But it is not quite true to say the Sherleys accomplished nothing. As Niels Steensgaard has written of the embassies of Garcia de Silva y Figueroa and Anthony and Robert Shirley, ultimately they "chased away every illusion concerning common interests" between Spain and Persia.

The Sherleys had been frustrated by their inability to find sufficient conflict from which to profit. Warriors needed battles to be ensured of employment, because in peacetime standing armies were often modest in size or nonexistent. Johannes Kepler's father, Heinrich, traveled far from home seeking employment as a mercenary. Some English privateers became pirates or corsairs after King James made peace with Spain. And in Japan many samurai (particularly those who had served defeated masters) were forced to look for new occupations, since their fighting skills were less in demand after the establishment of the Tokugawa shogunate.

Yamada Nagamasa was one of the samurai who was searching for a new opportunity. He was born in Sunpu (present Shizuoka) in 1590. His father, it is said, was a kitchenware dealer. He was sent to a temple to study Zen Buddhism but instead chose to pursue the life of a warrior. He seems to have served as a palanquin bearer for his local daimyo. According to a Japanese biography written in the early twentieth century, he honed his fighting skills by vanquishing ghosts, witches, and monsters that were haunting temples.

Maybe they were the only opponents he could find. With the unification of the country and the end of its devastating civil wars, opportunities for the samurai class had become more limited. For this reason, many Japanese fighting men looked to maritime adventurism for new opportunities. In 1612 Yamada Nagamasa shipped out to Taiwan, and continued from there to Ayutthaya (Siam; present Thailand), where there was a community of Japanese expatriates.

By 1620 or 1621 he had become head of the Japanese enclave in Ayutthaya. At that time it was the second-largest Japanese community in Southeast Asia. Hard data is scarce and estimates vary, but the community of Japanese in Siam may have totaled about a thousand to fifteen hundred persons. (The Japanese population in Manila, around twice that size, was the largest expatriate community.)

Siam had sent its first official embassy to Japan in 1616. Similar recent histories helped to bring the two nations together. Just as Japan had stabilized and entered an era of relative peace with the establishment of the Tokugawa shogunate, so Siam had recently emerged from a period of disorder. The kingdom had been reconsolidated during the late sixteenth century, threats from Burma had been repulsed, and dominance over much of Cambodia and the Malaysian peninsula established. Ekathrosrot, who reigned in Ayutthaya during part of the first decade of the seventeenth century, sought to build on his predecessor's successes by improving the country's trade relations. In addition, both nations had existed in the shadow of China and had been forced to operate around the margins of that superpower. The two governments exchanged weapons, which hints at the possibility of a military alliance.

Besides encouraging trade with Japan, Ekathrosrot also provided a settlement district for Dutch merchants. The Dutch respected the Japanese presence in Siam and conceded them a monopoly on the Siamese-Japanese trade because they were concerned about continuing their own trade with Japan from outside the Siam corridor. The Japanese had already limited Portuguese and Spanish access because of their association with Jesuit missionaries. Jeremias Van Vliet, a Dutch merchant who was active in Siam, wrote that

> Some Japanese merchants for a long time frequented the Kingdom of Siam, and appeared there yearly with their junks, capital, and merchandise, principally in order to enjoy the profit which Siamese deer and ray-skins used to yield. Of these appetizing gains they became so greedy that (seeing the abundance of living in the country) some remained resident there, whereby the inclination of the Siamese Kings (who have always been fond of foreign merchants) toward the Japanese nation, especially on account of the quantity of silver that was yearly brought to Siam by traders in their junks, so increased that their Majesties sent various embassies with suitable presents and letters full of friendly compliments to the emperor of Japan.

Many of the Japanese in Ayutthaya, like Yamada Nagamasa, performed dual roles as as merchants and warriors. As merchants they exchanged silver from Japanese mines for gunpower, dyes, sugar, pepper, and skins; they also acquired textiles from India that had been transported to Siam. A Japanese daimyo wrote to a Siamese minister, "Friendship between neighbors … has nothing to do with distance. The waves are now quiet, and merchant vessels can go to and fro, to the mutual benefit of both countries." One merchant from Nagasaki is said to have married a daughter of the king, an indication of the merchants' prestige. As warriors, the Japanese samurai aided the Ayutthayan state against its traditional rival, Burma, and also served certain factions by intimidating rivals in internal power struggles. Japanese samurai were internationally renowned as warriors, and Japanese swords were the best in the world.

Besides warriors and merchants, some of the expatriate Japanese were refugee Christians who had taken advantage of the shipping connection to Siam to flee anti-Christian persecution in Japan carried out by Ieyasu and stepped up by his successor, Tokugawa Hidetada. Eventually more than three thousand Christians would be martyred in Japan. The Siamese, by contrast, appear to have been relatively tolerant of religious diversity. Yamada, though not himself a Christian, was supportive of the refugee faction. He is known to have provided a banquet for visiting Italian priests, as one reported in a letter back to Rome.

The Japanese maritime campaign was conducted by means of "Red Seal" ships. Functionally, these ships were rather like the mainstays of the VOC fleet — they were heavily armed merchant ships. In design they were influenced by Japanese exposure to Portuguese vessels: they resembled Western-style ships in having square sails and rudders. They were nearly the size of European galleons, holding more than two hundred passengers. They are called Red Seal ships after the vermilion-colored stamp from the shogunate that authorized them to ship out. Several such ships left each year for Siam during the early seventeenth century. Other destinations included the Philippines, Indonesia, India, and Vietnam.

It is difficult to separate legend from history in considering the role of the Japanese in Siam. In Japan Yamada Nagamasa has traditionally been viewed as a heroic figure, and his exploits applauded and exaggerated. In Thailand, where he is associated in popular culture with the Japanese occupation during World War II, his role has been downplayed. He must have served the king well, because he was rewarded with a royal title and entrusted with important responsibilities.

Following the death of King Songtham in 1628, a power struggle ensued between his brother and his son. Yamada successfully supported the cause of the son, but the struggle for power in the Ayutthayan court continued behind the scenes. Yamada, so the story goes, was sent to put down a revolt in the south, and he was victorious. But during the fighting he was wounded in the knee. A treacherous former ally is supposed to have dispatched a healer, purportedly to tend to him but actually with secret instructions to poison the wound. In 1629 or 1630 Yamada died. Shortly thereafter, relations between Japan and Siam came to an end. In 1636 the Japanese decreed that no citizen could go abroad, and no Japanese resident overseas could return to Japan.

At the helm of one of the Red Seal ships in 1616 was an Englishman named Will Adams. He was returning from a trip to Ayutthaya, his large ship loaded with 143 tons of sappanwood (*Caesalpinia sappan,* used as a red dye) and 3700 deer skins.

Like another famous seafaring man of the period, Yusuf Reis (Jack Ward), Adams was a native of Kent. He had entered the sea trade early, af-

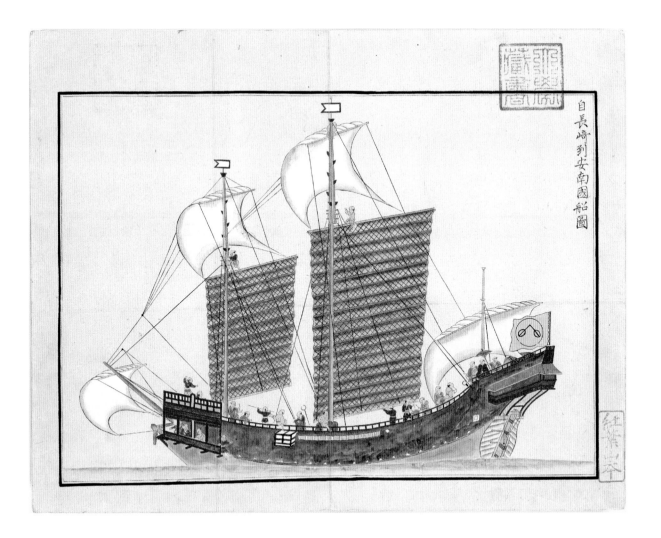

自長崎到安南國船圖

ter his father died when he was twelve. He had served under Francis Drake and saw naval service against the Spanish armada in 1588. In 1598 he hired on with an ill-fated fleet of five ships bound for the Pacific by way of the Straits of Magellan. After a brief raid in western Africa, the ships crossed the Atlantic. Two were lost to bad weather but three made it into the Pacific. Two of the remaining three ships, including the *Liefde* ("Charity"), with Adams and his brother Thomas on board, made it up the coast to present Ecuador. There Thomas and twenty other men were lost in a skirmish with natives. The third ship later turned up in Indonesia where its crew was killed by the Portuguese.

Now undermanned, the two remaining ships feared attack from the Spanish, so they set off across the north Pacific. Her companion vessel was lost to a typhoon but in April 1600 the *Liefe,* with only a couple dozen survivors, washed up in Japan. Among those to welcome them

Seventeenth-Century Red Seal Ship, before 1818. From the *Gaiban Shokan.* Colors on paper. National Archives of Japan.

This illustration of a trade ship heading from Nagasaki to Vietnam was part of a reference to a compilation of diplomatic documents of the Tokugawa shogunate prepared by Kondo Seisai (1771–1829).

were Portuguese priests who assured their Japanese hosts that the Dutch were pirates who should be crucified.

The Portuguese overplayed their hand. Their influence on the shogun was not as great as they imagined. Ieyasu had tolerated their presence because he thought they were necessary for the trade between Macau and Nagasaki to function smoothly; they were needed primarily as interpreters. But by this time the Portuguese had had a presence in Japanese for more than half a century. Some merchants had married Japanese women in Nagasaki. There was no longer any shortage of translators.

Adams was interrogated in several lengthy sessions by Ieyasu himself. Apparently the shogun was impressed by the thirty-six-year-old seaman. As Adams later reported, Ieyasu informed the Portuguese Jesuits that "we as yet had not doen to him nore to none of his lande any arme or damage; therefore against Reason and Justice to put us to death. If our countrey had warres the one with the other, that was no cause that he should put us to death."

Ieyasu recognized that Adams had a deep knowledge of large ocean-going vessels, and he employed him and another of the surviving sailors, a Dutchman named Jan Joosten, to assist his secretary of the navy, Mukai Shogen Tadakatsu (usually called Mukai Shogen), in the design and construction of Japan's Red Seal ships. From the voyage of one of these, which encountered a Dutch ship off Borneo, word got back to Europe of Adams's survival in Japan. But Adams had little contact with Europeans for several years, over which he became acculturated to Japan.

Adams and Joosten were given the rank of *hatamoto:* samurai in direct service of the shogun. Gradually Adams became the shogun's chief advisor and interpreter regarding relations with Europeans. He replaced the former advisor, the Jesuit linguist João Rodríguez Tçuzzu, who fell so far from the emperor's favor that he was sent away to Macau.

In a letter to Claudio Acquaviva, the Jesuit "general," Rodríguez characterized the Japanese as "wayward and inconstant," and unfit for admission to the order. Adams was more sympathetic to Japanese culture, so it is not surprising that Ieyasu would have preferred him. "The people of this Land of Japan are good of nature, curteous above measure, and valiant in war," he wrote. "Their justice is severely executed without any partiality upon transgressors of the law. They are governed in great civility. I mean, not a land better governed in the world by civil policy."

He married the daughter of a highway official, despite the fact that he had left a wife in England (he did manage to write to her and send her money). That problem was solved by Ieyasu pronouncing Will Adams the Englishman dead; in his place was born the white samurai Miura

Anjin—by this stroke his English wife was made a widow. With his Japanese wife he had a son named Joseph and a daughter named Susanna.

In 1613 an English captain arrived in Japan with the hope of establishing an English trade base there. (The Dutch complained that the English "dogged their footsteps all over the East," according to historian C. R. Boxer, "only venturing to trade in places where the Hollanders had already broken the back of Iberian resistance.") He was appalled at the extent to which Adams had adopted Japanese customs. He complained that Adams insisted on giving "admirable and affectionated commendations of Japan" and concluded "It is generally thought amongst us that he is a naturalized Japaner." What might have set the captain off is the low valuation Adams placed on his cargo.

The captain claimed that Adams and Mukai Shogen had discussed an invasion of the Philippines, planned for sometime in 1616. But Mukai apparently doubted the ability of the Japanese navy to confront larger Western-style warships. The death of Ieyasu put such plans on hold as Mukai was making efforts to upgrade the Japanese fleet.

Beginning in 1614 Adams became involved in the Red Ships trade. The trip from which he was returning in 1616 was his second to Ayutthaya. Unfortunately for him, Ieyasu died shortly before he reached Japan. Thereafter Adams' influence diminished. But he did make two more trade expeditions to Cochinchina (Vietnam). He died in 1620. His son, Joseph, inherited his title of Miura Anjin and prospered through the sea trade until the closure of the country, after which information about the family is lost.

In the Quirinale, the residence of the Italian president in Rome, are frescoes painted by Agustino Tassi, Carlo Saraceni, and Giovanni Lanfranco in 1616 and 1617. These painters were masters of architectural detail and perspective foreshortening, and both of those skills are on display in the frescoes, as figures lean over balconies and crane, peer, and bend in myriad directions. Some sections of the paintings depict the Persian embassy of Robert Sherley — he looks young and rather overwhelmed. Another panel shows an ambassador from the Congo, Emanuele Ne Vunda.

Another ambassador, who had come to Rome from a much more distant location, is also depicted. His name was Hasekura Tsunenaga, and he was a diplomat in the service of the influential daimyo Date Masamune. In 1616, at the time the frescoes were painted, Haskura was on his way to Mexico from Europe and was planning his return trip across the Pacific.

Date Masamune was a strongman who was originally based on Japan's west coast, on what Korea calls the East Sea and Japan calls the Sea of

Japan. He bridged the gap between Japan's warring years and the new Edo era of peace. Having lost an eye to smallpox during childhood, and affecting battle gear that featured an enormous crescent moon on the helmet, the "one-eyed dragon" (*dokuganryū*) cut a flamboyant figure.

His family relations were turbulent. His mother favored his younger brother and reportedly tried to poison Masamuno on his behalf. The attempt failed and she ended up fleeing the region. Masamuno put an end to his brother's pretensions to rule by killing him. Soldiers under his command also killed his father, although this happened while he was being held hostage. He defeated this enemy and had the kidnappers and their families tortured and killed.

Fierce though he was, Date was no match for the power of the unifier of Japan, Toyotomi Hideyoshi, and he was forced to become his vassal. He assisted Hideyoshi in his ill-fated, bloody invasion of Korea. After Hideyoshi's death Date championed the cause of Tokugawa Ieyasu. This turned out to be the right horse to back, and Date was rewarded by being transferred to the Sendai domain on the east coast of Japan. The largest and most prosperous domain in northern Japan, Sendai was roughly equivalent to modern Miyagi Prefecture, near the epicenter of the devastating 2011 earthquake.

Date sought to increase trade in Sendai, so he encouraged foreign visitors, even missionaries. One missionary who found shelter in Date's region was a Spanish Franciscan named Luis Sotelo, who had traveled between Japan and Mexico on more than one occasion. In 1613 Sotelo jouneyed to Tokyo from Sendai to inaugurate a new church. This was during one of Ieyasu's crackdowns on missionaries. Seven who had been arrested with Sotelo were executed, but he was released at the request of Date, who had plans for him.

Date's ambitious plan was to send an embassy to Philip III of Spain and Pope Paul V in Rome. The embassy would travel through Mexico, and Date hoped to initiate a trade channel between Japan and Acapulco. The project was at least approved by, and perhaps conceived in collaboration with, the Bakufu, the shogunal government in Edo. Sotelo may have put a bug in Date's ear. He was keen on the embassy, because such a journey could increase the influence of his Franciscan order, which had so far been in the shadow of the Jesuits in East Asia. At the head of the embassy was one of Date's retainers who had served with him during the Korean campaign, a man named Hasekura Tsunenaga. Sotelo would accompany him.

Mukai Shogen sent his chief carpenter to assist in the construction of a vessel in the style of a Western galleon, which may have been recon-

structed from a ship that had wrecked on Japanese shores. The construction involved thousands of workers and was completed in a month and a half. Besides Sotelo, another Spaniard, Sebastian Vizcaino, lent technical assistance. Vizcaino, who was in his mid-sixties, was a veteran soldier and sea captain. Widely traveled, he had at one time been stationed in New Spain, where he was assigned to survey the California coast to locate harbours that could be used by galleons making the return trip from Manila to Acapulco. He visited San Diego Bay, Point Lobos, Santa Catalina Island, Carmel, Monterey Bay, Sierra Point, and Coyote Point, all of which owe their names to him.

In 1611–1612 Vizcaino received permission from the Bakufu to perform a similar survey of harbors on the east coast of Japan, with the idea that they could be a stopping-over point for Manila-Acapulco galleons. Ieyasu is said to have had misgivings about this project and to have consulted

Will Adams. Adams, who was no friend of the Spanish, replied that in Europe such activity would be seen as reconnaissance for a possible military invasion. It appears that Vizcaino was allowed to finish his survey, but was always viewed with suspicion thereafter.

With the arrogance of a Spaniard who had lived in the Americas, where the Spanish conquest had seemed surprisingly easy, Vizcaino made matters worse by adopting a condescending attitude toward the Japanese. Ieyasu had made it clear that he was only interested in trade and did not want any missionaries sent to Japan. Vizcaino scornfully rejected this, telling one daimyo that the king of Spain cared nothing about trade with Japan "nor any temporal interest, for God had given him many kingdoms and dominions.... All nations should be taught the Holy Catholic Faith and thus be saved."

Ieyasu was having nothing of it. He provided the embassy with a message to the viceroy of New Spain that read:

> The doctrine followed in your country differs entirely from ours. Therefore, I am persuaded that it would not suit us. In the Buddhist sutras it is said that it is difficult to convert those who are not disposed to being converted. It is best, therefore, to put an end to the preaching of your doctrine on our soil. On the other hand, you can multiply the voyages of merchant ships, and thus promote mutual interests and relations. Your ships can enter Japanese ports without exception. I have given strict orders to this effect.

The ship was christened the *San Juan Bautista.* It set sail with Vizcaino as captain in October of 1613, carrying 180 persons, including 60 who were attached to the embassy. In an odd echo of the Persian embassies of the Sherleys, there was subsequently some dispute about whether Hasekura or Sotelo should be viewed as the primary ambassador, but the Western nations the embassy visited all treated Hasekura as the ambassador, and it is difficult to believe that Date or Ieyasu would have placed their mission in the hands of a Franciscan friar.

The ship reached the Philippines the next month and made excellent time across the Pacific, arriving in Acapulco the following January. While in Mexico the embassy was witnessed by a native writer named Don Domingo de San Antón Muñón Chimalpahin Quanhtlehuanitzin, who has come to be known by the mercifully shortened name Chimalpahin. He was associated with a church in Mexico City. His book, written in Nahuatl and translated as *Annals of His Time,* is one of the most significant documents of the period by a native American from Mexico. Nothing like the work of the Peruvian writer Guaman Poma, the book is in the tradition of Nahuatl annals. Such books were community documents recording events of their time, and they were, for the most part, devoid of personal items and editorializing. Traditionally Nahuatl annals would have combined texts and images, but by Chimalpahin's time the use of images had severely declined. What Chimalpahin has given us instead is a lengthy text detailing events concerning his parish.

Chimalpahin had described the arrival of a previous group of Japanese:

> They wear something like an ornamented jacket, doublet, or long blouse, which they tie at their middle, their waist; there they place a *catana* of metal, which counts as their sword, and they wear something like a *mantilla*. And their footwear is soft, softened leather called chamois, counting just like foot-gloves that they put on their feet. They seem bold, not gentle and meek people, going about like eagles.

According to Chimalpahin there had been a falling out in Acapulco between Vizcaino and the Japanese, apparently over the disposition of gifts the embassy had brought with them. On March 4, 1614, he reports that an advance party of Japanese reached the city on that day, but Hasekura, Sotelo, and Vizcaino were trailing behind. "Señor Vizcaino is also still coming slowly, coming hurt; the Japanese injured him when they beat and stabbed him at Acapulco, as became known here in Mexico City, because of all the things coming along that had been made his responsibility in Japan, that the great ruler there, the emperor, gave him to be gifts on arrival."

Vizcaino finally arrived in the city during Lent, on March 17. The remainder of the party followed one week later. Chimalpahin describes Hasekura as "a great personage." He understands the purpose of the mission to be primarily religious: "The reason their ruler the emperor in Japan sent this lordly emissary and ambassador here is to go to Rome to see the holy father, Paul V, and to give him their obedience concerning the holy church."

While from the Japanese side the religious aspect of the embassy seems unclear — a Japanese historian characterized it as a mix of some who wanted to use the kingdom of heaven for trade and others who wanted to use trade for the kingdom of heaven — once on Western soil the party left no doubt about its embrace of Christianity. Sixty-three Japanese were baptized in Mexico. Hasekura was the exception: he would be baptized in Europe as a publicity stunt.

After several months, leaving some members behind to continue developing trade relations with Mexico, the reduced embassy sailed from Veracruz to Spain, where Hasekura had an audience with Philip III and, astonishingly, assured him that all of Japan was ready to convert to Christianity. He proposed an alliance with Spain, and Sotelo added that this would forestall the efforts of the Dutch. Philip said he would think about it.

Hasekura was baptized by the king's chaplain and given the Christian name Felipe. The Duke of Lerma was appointed his godfather. Then the embassy continued to Italy. They arrived in Genoa, where one observer described their appearance:

> One of them was of Japanese nationality and was called Don Filippo Fasecura; the other a Spaniard of Sevilla, Luigi Sotelo by name, a Franciscan priest of the order of the "Osservanza." They have with them a train of twenty-eight persons, for the most part Japanese, and these all are with the exception of one, of low stature, olive coloured; they have small eyes, little beard, and greatly resemble each other. Fasecura was dressed in a long black-velvet tunic, over which he wore another, shorter one, of black silk; his stockings were of yellow silk, made almost like gloves, that is, with the big toe separated from the rest; and with leathern soles, and he also wore a black felt hat. The ambassador and his companions had their hair close shaved on the top of their head and on the rest of the head it was long and tied up on the back like a tail. He carried a most beautiful scimitar and also a sword. The other gentlemen wore similar tunics but less rich. They all ate with little chop-sticks. Father Sotelo wore the habit of the order and also acted as interpreter.

The swords of the Japanese were especially admired. It was said that "their swords cut so well that they can cut a soft paper just by putting it on the edge and by blowing on it."

Continuing to Rome, the embassy repeated its performance for Pope Paul V. A letter from Date Masamune was produced that said that while he was not himself a Christian he would welcome and protect Franciscan monks. In exchange, he asked the pope to put in a good word for him with the king of Spain for the purpose of trade. But the embassy, with its Franciscan bias, was received in Rome with little ceremony because of opposition from the Jesuits. The pope told Hasekura he would think about it, and consult with Philip.

Retracing its steps, the embassy returned to Spain, where Philip told Hasekura that he could not sign a treaty since he represented only a regional lord and not the official Japanese government. By this time word of Ieyasu's expulsion of foreign missionaries had reached Spain.

His futile mission now as complete as it would ever be, Hasekura sailed from Spain to Mexico in 1617, but six of his party remained behind in Coria del Rio, near Seville, where there are today about seven hundred residents with the surname Japón. After spending a couple of years in the Philippines, he returned to Sendai in 1620, seven years after departing Japan. (At this point he had only twelve remaining companions.) He found the situation there entirely changed. A few months after the embassy's departure Ieyasu had issued his edict expelling all missionaries from Japan. Tokugawa Hidetada had succeeded Ieyasu in 1616 and closed Japan's doors even more tightly, barring nearly all foreigners from the country.

Opinion differs about whether Hosekura's conversion was genuine. Was his baptism merely a diplomatic ploy? He is said to have abjured the faith once back in Japan, but this seems contradicted by reports that some of his descendants remained Christians.

The embassy had accomplished nothing of political value, and in fact was an embarrassment to Date Masamune, who felt the need to write an apologetic letter to Hidetada, tactfully reminding him of the Bakufu's involvement in the enterprise. Hasekura was tarred with the failure of the embassy, and his status greatly reduced. Life isn't fair.

He still made out better than Sotelo. The Franciscans wanted to send him to Mexico, but he had not abandoned hope for a Japanese mission. Disguised as a merchant, he sailed from Manila to Nagasaki aboard a Chinese junk. There he was promptly seized and burnt alive, tied to a pole fixed to a pile of wood. To prolong his agony the fire was kept low for as long as possible before being allowed to rage.

The next Japanese embassy to Europe would not occur for another two and a half centuries. A theme park devoted to Hasekura's embassy,

Japanese Embassy to Rome, 1616, perhaps by Agostino Tassi and workshop. Fresco, Sala Regia, Quirinale Palace, Rome.

In the foreground of this image from the Quirinale the Japanese ambassador, Hasekura Tsunenaga, confers with the Franciscan missionary Luis Sotelo.

featuring a replica of the *San Juan Bautista,* was created in 1993 in the harbor of Ishinomaki from which the embassy departed. The city was one of the worst hit by the 2011 tsunami, but the replica ship miraculously survived. According to Japanese newspaper reports, there is talk of using it as a symbol of the town's hoped-for reconstruction.

In the years when Japan was active in Southeast Asia there was a small Japanese community in Vietnam, where many factions vied for control. The Le dynasty, based around Hanoi in the north, was the longest-ruling Vietnamese dynasty. But several other powerful family groups, including the Trinh, the Nguyen, and the Mac, were also powerful. When the Mac succeeded in driving the Le from Hanoi around 1520 Trinh and Nguyen factions established a new state in the south, which they claimed was the legitimate successor of the Le. Combining forces, they defeated the Mac and regained Hanoi.

Cooperation between the Trinh and the Nguyen ended there, however. A northern leader, Trinh Tung, claimed to be the legitimate heir of the Le dynasty, while a southern leader, Nguyen Phuc Nguyen, championed his own cause. Trinh Tung ruled in the north from around 1570 until 1623. Nguyen Phuc Nguyen, who succeeded his dynamic father in 1613, ruled in the south until 1635. Both claimed to be working in the cause of a figurehead Le emperor, whom both mostly ignored. Tensions would build up until the outbreak of the Trinh–Nguyen War, which would drag on from 1627 until 1672, exhausting both sides.

Into this heated environment came Chinese, Japanese, and Europeans. The Chinese had long had an interest in Vietnam. The prestige of the Le dynasty derived from having driven them out following the early, expansionist days of the Ming. But many aspects of Chinese culture remained, including Confucianism as a philosophy of governance. Now, as the Ming dynasty teetered toward its final days, more Chinese arrived, not this time as conquerors but in search of new opportunities. Japanese came as adventurers, merchants, and Christian refugees. Europeans — the first to arrive were the Portuguese — included merchants and missionaries.

Among the latter was a Jesuit named Christoforo Borri. In Italy his name had been rendered as Borro or Burro, but during his overseas mission he used such names as Brono or Bravo so as "not to offend the Portuguese ears with the word *boro*, which in their language does not sound good."

Perhaps he would have been better to stick with *burro,* since he was as obstinate and difficult as a donkey. He entered the Jesuit order with a view to teaching, but throughout his life he never entirely came to terms with the order, or it with him. His first known trouble occurred not long after Galileo published his *Starry Messenger* in 1610. Borri aspired to be a scientist, and in particular an astronomer, like Galileo. Like Galileo, he obtained a position as a professor of mathematics, teaching at the Collegio de Brera in his home town of Milan. But he lacked the charisma or the political acumen and negotiating skills of a Galileo, and his life would take a different course.

Borri's life, like that of his fellow astronomer Kepler, was determined by a youthful inspiration. Influenced by Tycho Brahe, Borri decided that the heavens were neither solid nor empty: they were liquid. Moreover, he said, there were three of them: one containing the moving planets, one containing the fixed stars, and the heavenly realm beyond. It was an idea just radical enough to offend traditionalists but not quite radical enough to please bold thinkers enthralled with Copernicanism. Nonetheless, for the next couple of decades, until his death in 1632, he never abandoned his pet idea. Nor, in all that time, did he convince many people to take it seriously.

Certainly his own Jesuit order did not favor it. Faculty at Borri's school had been instructed to toe the party line in teaching astronomical subjects. Borri probably failed to comply, or he might have come to odds with his superiors for some other reason. Throughout his life he rubbed a lot of people the wrong way. Whatever the reason, sometime between 1610 and 1614 he got canned.

It was a devastating blow for the young scholar. His deepest desire was to win acclaim as a brilliant mathematician and astronomer, but he was now cut off from academia. He had not developed a network of contacts that would enable him to stay current with developments in his field. So he shipped out to do missionary work overseas. He had formulated a theory about a new way to determine longitude, and he needed to get readings from distant places to develop it. His system involved measuring and mapping the deviation between magnetic and true north in different parts of the world, so Asia was an ideally distant location for him to acquire the readings he needed.

The year 1616 found him sailing from Goa to Macau: having departed Lisbon in April 1515, he would have arrived in Goa in the fall and then had to wait until the following spring for the next voyage to Macau. But he was not to remain there long: what with the persecution of missionaries in Nanking in 1616 and the need for new missionaries in Vietnam, Borri retraced his steps to Cochinchina, as the Europeans called southern Vietnam (they called northern Vietnam "Tonkin"). It is not known whether he antagonized members of the order during his brief stay in Macau, but he seems quickly to have proved unpopular in Vietnam.

The Jesuit mission in Vietnam during Borri's time consisted of four or five priests. A surviving letter from one of them, a Portuguese named Antonio de Pina, is full of criticism of his colleagues. According to de Pina, "Whenever something happens, if I don't go, no one else goes." De Pina also says that the other priests made no effort to learn the Vietnamese language. Of his superior he says, "Whether he says a word or not, it comes to about the same."

Olga Dror and K. W. Taylor, who have done a masterful job of reconstructing Borri's story from the fragments of documentation that remain, speculate that de Pina's letter suggests that the Vietnam mission was divided by the Jesuit order's "Rites Controversy." Some missionaries, of whom the best known is Matteo Ricci — another was Roberto de Nobili, who, working in southern India, learned Sanskrit and comported himself as a Brahman — believed that the best opportunities for conversion resulted from being informed about the local culture and working from within its belief system as much as possible. Ricci considered Confucianism a philosophy rather than a religion, and so he situated Christian ideas in a Confucian context. His successor, Nicolas Longobardi, took a harder line. According to him, before a Chinese could embrace Christianity he would have to renounce the teachings of Confucius. Just as in Europe there was no room for Galileo's deviation from official teachings about the heavens, so in overseas missions there must be no compromise in religious purity and rigor.

It's not certain what Borri thought about this issue, but he demonstrated little interest in Vietnamese culture. Although he claimed the language was easy to learn he never became adept in it and was unable to use it effectively in missionary work — the meager evidence available suggests that he made few conversions. He did not even master the transliteration system that his own colleagues had developed. He stayed for five years in Vietnam and left as clueless as he had arrived about the differences between Taoism and Buddhism.

Borri was recalled to Macau. He said that he was forced to leave Vietnam on account of illness. But an Italian Jesuit who wrote about the Vietnamese mission said its modest successes owed

> no part to Father Christoforo Borri...who was recalled by his superiors to Macau; not, as he wrote, to be put in the hand of physicians there, who would heal his body, because it was not ailing; but to cure his soul, that is, to return it from anxiety to fervor of the spirit.

On the other hand, another Jesuit (though writing a century later) called Borri "once the most praised among the evangelical laborers."

Borri returned to Macau and stayed there about a year, teaching at a Jesuit college. Even though he won an award for gallantry when the town was shelled by the Dutch, he was soon on his way back to Goa. There he crossed paths with Pietro della Valle, who would be his biggest supporter in his remaining years. Della Valle was fascinated with his scientific theories and activities. According to Dror and Taylor, "After Borri's death, della Valle seemed to be the only person interested in his legacy."

Borri sailed for Europe on the same ship that was to carry the unfortunate ambassador Garcia de Silva y Figueroa, who would die of scurvy off the Azores before reaching his homeland. He taught for a while in Lisbon and continued to advocate for his celestial and navigational theories. He tried to win a cash prize the Spanish and Portuguese had offered to anyone who could solve the problem of determining longitude. While it is difficult to assess how accurate Borri's system, the details of which have been lost, actually was, his presentation to the court was described as a fiasco. One observer called it "presumptuous and bizarre." Another said his work had "little reliability and solidity."

Borri made one last try. In October 1616 the Dutch captain Dirk Hartog had made landfall at Shark Bay on the west coast of Australia (150 years before Captain James Cook's better publicized journey to Australia's east coast). Borri called for an expedition there as a test of the navigational apparatus he had invented. But the Spanish empire had grown weary. The council responded with some truth that the king "already had more land than he could maintain; it is not worthwhile to search for more."

Failing to make headway in Portugal and Spain, Borri returned to Rome and pressed his case to the pope. He pressed it a little too hard. Della Valle reported that "In Rome, Father Borri had a lot of troubles with his superiors, who did not like his direct contacts with the pope." He also had "great troubles with the Spaniards." Della Valle does not specify the exact nature of these troubles, which may have involved complaints about his missionary activities or his behavior at court.

In the end Borri was removed from the Jesuit order. Della Valle said that he had received a papal dispensation to transfer to the Cistercian order (famous as brewers of the Trappist ales of Belgium). Others said that, in an echo of the dismissal from his teaching post that had long ago launched his career as a traveler, he had been drummed out of the order. It was also said that he wore out his welcome with the Cistercians within a few weeks, but won a court order protesting his dismissal.

"On his way to announce his victory in court to the prelate," a priest wrote in a letter, "an accident happened, which put him into bed, where

he died the following day." The fatal "accident" was reported to have been a stroke. He was forty-nine. The year before his death he had published a book about Vietnam, called *An Account of Cochin-China,* and it is mainly for that artifact of an episode that he regarded as a sidetrack in his scientific career, rather than for the astronomical and navigational activities that he considered his life's work, that he has been remembered, to the extent that he has been remembered at all. His correspondence with Pietro della Valle went unnoticed until it was discovered in the Vatican archives in 1947.

The Death of Maani Gioerida, 1664–1665, from *Der Voortrefelkyke Reisen van Pietro della Valle,* a Dutch translation of Della Valle's travels. Engraving.

Della Valle tried ineffectually to be of assistance to the Christian communities in Persia. His letters document local Christian activities such as Armenian weddings for which the bride's face is covered with gold leaf "like we use on macaroons." But his enthusiasm for the shah as a benefactor of Christianity faded, in parallel with the shah's own disillusionment with the empty promises of the European powers. Unable to affect a great deal of change in the condition of Persian Christians, and still weak from illness, della Valle decided it was time to return to Italy. Once again he set out in a caravan, with Maani, their adopted daughter Mariuccia, and two servants in tow. This time his destination was Hormuz. Fearful of traveling through Ottoman lands after his long residence in Persia, he hoped to return to Europe from there by sea.

En route to Hormuz della Valle stopped in the ancient Persian capital of Persepolis to copy inscriptions off the walls of its ruins — his drawings would be the first versions of its cuneiform writing to appear in the West. Then he received the happy news that the wine regimen seemed to have done its job — Maani was at last pregnant. "We swam in a sea of joy," he wrote, "spending all our time in laughter and amusement."

Their joy was short-lived. Hormuz was a war zone. English forces had allied with the Persians against the Portuguese outpost. Della Valle's party was forced to retreat to wait for the situation to settle down. During this time Mariuccia became ill with acute diarrhea. She would recover. Maani tended to her. Then she too became ill, as did Pietro.

Maani delivered a stillborn son prematurely. She was devastated that the child had died before receiving baptism. They had agreed to name the child Persindo, "since it had been conceived in Persia and, if all had gone well, would have been born in India." Maani's fever increased day by day. She had an unquenchable thirst. Every physical and spiritual remedy was attempted. She only grew worse. Then:

One day, one of the Muslim women who served her came, out of kindness and in very high spirits, with the news that she had consulted a famous fortune-teller who had assured her that it was certain that Signora Maani would be completely cured on the following Friday. This information terrified me, for I considered that divination — and Muslim divination in particular — could only be a black art; that the Devil, being at once the father of lies and a source of knowledge, could foretell the future that lay hidden from us. I was persuaded that by this answer he meant that Signora Maani would *die* on the following Friday — as in fact she did.

She was twenty-three. Her bereaved husband composed a now-lost sequence of twenty-three sonnets he entitled *My Tears.*

Della Valle felt it important to bury his wife on Christian soil. So he did something extraordinary. Lacking customary embalming fluids, he had local women remove his wife's organs and preserve her corpse with camphor. But the heart, he stipulated, must remain inside — Maani would need it at the Last Judgment. The women complied, and to demonstrate that they had carried out his instructions they brought Maani's heart to show him. "Imagine my feelings," he wrote, "when I saw the heart of her whom I loved best in the world brought in to me on a saucer!"

A coffin was made of mango wood, nailed shut, and wrapped in waxed cloth inside an outer layer of leather. Carrying this macabre item, della Valle, still severely ill, made his way to the town of Lar. Expected to die, he surprised everyone by recovering in a couple of months. Soon he seemed more or less his old sociable self, conversing with the learned men of Lar, who impressed him more than the literati of the capital had. He delighted in the roof-mounted fans that delivered fresh air into stuffy houses, an innovation he hoped to introduce to Europe.

At length he learned he might obtain passage to India on English ships docked at Hormuz. He ordered two new containers similar to the one containing his wife but twice as deep. It would be necessary to hide his wife's body, because no captain would set sail with a corpse on board. He disguised the contents of Maani's container by surrounding her body with layers of clothing.

His next concern was to get Mariuccia on board, because women were not generally allowed sea passage. Disguising her as a boy, he managed to smuggle her aboard. In February 1623, a year after Maani's death, he arrived in Surat in South Asia.

Over the summer and fall of 1615 an enormous caravan was making its way from Persia to India. Among its number was an odd Englishman from a little village in Somerset, who was traveling by foot. Having conceived a fancy to take a ride on an elephant, he was bound for India. His name was Thomas Coryate.

Coryate has been described as a fool. Which he might have been, but he was no dummy. He was the canny sort Shakespeare had in mind when he wrote "This fellow is wise enough to play the fool."

Apparently he looked the part, though this is not evident from depictions of him that appear on the title page and elsewhere in his great travel book, *Coryat's Crudities*. Yet a contemporary claimed that "he carried folly (which the charitable call merriment) in his very face. The shape of his head had no promising form, being like a sugar-loaf inverted, with the little end before, as composed of fancy and memory, without any common sense."

He was a joker, and the butt of jokes. The son of a parson, he was born in the rectory of the village of Odcombe. He attended Oxford but didn't complete his degree and seems to have spent a few years just hanging out in the village. Around the time James acceded to the throne he decided to try his luck in London.

He soon mixed in the literary scene. It wasn't hard to find, since many of the city's writers had made a tavern called the Mermaid Inn their unofficial clubhouse. Ben Jonson presided there, and luminaries such as Edmund Spencer and Will Shakespeare must have flung witticisms back and forth from time to time. Into this high-powered company Coryate presented himself as a sort of presumptuous rube. He spoke in an outlandish, overblown style that matched his appearance, and the Mermaid wags adopted him as a sort of jester-mascot. John Donne called him "that great lunatic." No entertainment was complete, some said, without a helping of sweetmeats and Coryate.

The role of amiable buffoon was not the end of Tom's aspirations. He was determined to make his name as a man of letters, and he hit upon an inspired means of doing so: he would walk to Venice and back and record his journey in what could serve as a guidebook to travelers on the continent. Many young Englishmen were undertaking tours of Europe, but there was no book available to guide them.

In 1608 he crossed the channel and arrived in Calais, having "varnished the exterior parts of the ship with the excrementall ebullitions of my tumultuous stomach." He traveled through France and Italy to Venice — "this thrise worthie citie, the fairest Lady, yea the richest Paragon and Queene of Christendome" — which was the high point of his tour. He was impressed by its gondolas, which he said numbered ten thousand, and its courtesans, who were barely fewer in number. The Piazza di San Marcos, he commented, marked "the greatest magnificence of architecture to be seene, that any place under the sunne doth yeelde."

He visited the Jewish ghetto, where he was startled to discover that Jews resembled other human beings. He had been led to expect a Jew to be "a weather beaten warp-face fellow, sometimes a phrenticke and lunaticke person" but was forced to concede that "some fewe of those Jewes, especially some of the Levantines, to bee such goodly and proper men" with "most elegant and sweet featured persons."

Venice, he concluded, was well worth the trip:

> Had there bin an offer made unto me before I took my journey to Venice, eyther that foure of the richest mannors of Somerset-shire (wherein I was borne) should be gratis bestowed upon me if I never saw Venice, or neither of them if I should see it, although certainly those mannors would do me much more good in respect to a state of livelihood to live in the world, then the sight of Venice: yet notwithstanding I will ever say while I live, that the sight of Venice and her resplendent beauty, antiquities, and monuments, hath by many degrees more contented my minde, and satisfied my desires, than those four Lordshippes could possibly have done.

Reluctantly bidding Venice good-bye, Coryate returned to England through Switzerland, Germany, and the Netherlands, and set himself to writing. He spent some two years writing up his six-month journey, only to find himself in the position of many an aspiring author, with a manuscript but no publisher. He called the book *Coryat's Crudities, Hastily Gobbled Up in Five Months Travels in France, Savoy, Italy, Rhetia Commonly Called the Grisons Country, Helvetia alias Switzerland, Some Parts of High Germany and the Netherlands; Newly Digested in the Hungry Aire of Odcombe in the County of*

Somerset, and Now Dispersed to the Nourishment of the Travelling Members of the Kingdome. It was an excellent though very long guide to European travel, for Coryate was a sharp observer who had diligently visited the major sites and assembled pertinent statistics and information about each place he visited. But it seems no one was willing to take a chance on publishing it — at least, Coryate ended up self-publishing, whether by choice or necessity.

Faced with this dilemma Coryate devised a shrewd marketing maneuver — calling on his friends at the Mermaid Inn, he engineered the most elaborate book blurb in the history of publishing. With the backing of his sometime patron Prince Henry, he solicited rhymed testimonials from many of England's literary luminaries as a preface to the book. The Mermaid wits vied with one another to create the slyest and most ridiculous couplets. Among those who contributed were John Donne, Ben Jonson, Inigo Jones, and Thomas Campion. A sample gives a taste of the verses:

> First, th'Author here glutteth Sea, Haddocke and Whiting
> With spuing, and after the world with his writing.

> A Punke here pelts him with egs. How so?
> For he did but kisse her, and so let her go.

> Old Hat here, torne Hose, with Shoes full of gravell,
> And louse-dropping Case, are the Armes of his travel.

> Here France, and Italy both to him shed
> Their hornes, and Germany pukes on his head.

> But here, nether trusting his hands, nor his legs,
> Beeing in feare to be rob'd, he most learnedly begs.

As usual, Coryate was the butt of their humor, but he seems not to have minded. His promotional stratagem worked, and once the book was published in 1611 his faith in it was confirmed. Despite clocking in at some eight hundred pages it became an enormous hit and an indispensable guidebook for travelers.

He followed the *Crudities* with some supplemental writings, but its success fueled his appetite for larger undertakings. He resolved to travel for ten years, ride upon an elephant, and deliver an oration to an Asian potentate. He would travel almost entirely on foot.

While traveling through Turkey on his way to Persia, he was robbed of his bankroll near Baghdad, so he was forced to travel on a shoestring, relying on the kindness of strangers. He reached Isfahan without further incident and spent two months there, but he was frustrated in his desire to meet Shah Abbas. He joined an enormous caravan to India, consisting of six thousand people and five thousand animals. Traveling with this large party he encountered Robert Sherley and his wife, Teresia, among a caravan headed the opposite direction. He was flattered that Sherley was carrying his books and, considering the loss of his funds, was especially grateful to the kind and thoughtful Teresia "who bestowed fortie shillings upon mee in Persian money."

In India Coryate visited Lahore, Delhi, and Agra. He reached Ajmere, Gujarat, at that time the site of Jahangir's court (which he moved often), where he was greeted by the English ambassador, Thomas Roe, whom he had previously met at the Frankfurt Book Fair on his way back to England from Venice. Roe wrote that the

> fates have sent Coryate hither, and now he lives in my house. He came hither afoote, hath passed by Constantinople, Jerusalem, Bethlem, Damascus, and (breefly) thorowgh all the Turks territory: seene every post and pillar: observed every tombe, visited the monuments of Troy, Persia, and this King's dominions, all afoote with most unwearied legges: and is now for Samarcand in Tartarya, to kisse Tamberlans tombe; from thence to Susa, and to Prester Jhac in Ethiopia, where he will see the hill Amara, all afoote; and so foote it to Odcombe. His notes are already too great for portage....

Sadly, those voluminous notes have been lost. Coryate fell ill with dysentary, and he died in Surat, in the company of some of his countrymen. They reported that his last words were "Sack, sack, is there such a thing as sack? I pray give me some sack." What might have been an invaluable book of early travel through the lands of Islam was lost to history. We have only some letters that he sent home, which were collected and published as *Greeting from the Court of the Great Mogul* in London in 1616.

Before he died Coryate realized some of his ambitions. He had walked from the Levant all the way to India. He had ridden upon an elephant, as illustrated in the 1616 volume (p. 30). And, in August 1616, he delivered an oration to Jahangir. He did so standing in the street and screaming up at the startled emperor, who looked down from an upstairs window. Apparently Coryate addressed the emperor in excellent Persian, which he had studied with the same diligence with which he approached all his undertakings. He began by exalting Jahangir with flowery praise. He explained that he had walked to Jahangir's lands in order to ride an elephant and see the Ganges. He concluded with his intention to visit Samarkand and he requested the emperor's permission to visit Timor's tomb.

The emperor replied that he was unable to grant the permission because Samarkand was outside his dominion. But he tossed Coryate a purse containing £10. Sometimes it paid to play the fool.

Thomas Coryate was indifferent to mountains and their vistas. He was most attracted to fertile flat or rolling farmlands. He regarded the Alps not as a destination but an impediment to his travels. He was uninspired by Lake Como.

At the same time that Coryate was hoofing it through Persia and India, a traveler in China was also walking great distances and making notes on his travels for future publication. He was an unusually tall man, who covered ground quickly with long strides. He was described as "nimble as an ape, sturdy as an ox." His complexion was dark, and he was said to have "a Taoist look." A friend wrote that "after traveling for several hundred *li,* he would clamber up a broken rock to a withered tree and burnt pines in order to gather together some tassels. He would then dash off a record of his journey, which was as good as a writing manual."

Born Xu Honzu, he was best known by his pen name of Xu Xiake ("traveler among sunset clouds"), which was given to him by his friend the landscape painter Chen Jiru. Like Coryate he preferred to travel on foot and to be completely independent. "When I travel," he wrote, "I require neither a horse nor a companion; rather than traveling together, it would be better if you could simply point out the way to me."

Xu Xiake did not merely reject horses and companions. In scaling mountains he was searching for what he called the "ultimate void." Although he wrote that "in my boundless roaming there is nothing I wish to omit," he admitted that he was particularly "obsessed with mountains." On one occasion, reaching the peak of Mount Jinhua, he wrote:

> As the evening sun went down, a clear moon sustained the light, and all of nature was still; the sky was awash with blue.... I thought back to the mediocrity of the lower world: who else had experienced this clear light?
>
> Even if others climbed towers and let out screams of delight, or sipped wine by the riverside, if they saw our solitary ascent of the peaks of ten thousand mountains to a place where paths end and roads cease

and we are completely beyond the mortal world, they would see it was a true paradise. I was not frightened by the crowds of mountain spirits and strange beasts hemming me in, let alone the unmoving silence, for I was wandering with the Ultimate Void."

His contemporaries agreed that Xu's travels were a form of obsession: Chen Jiru wrote that "in his long travels Xu was neither an official nor a trader, nor was he on a social outing — he was just obsessed with the landscape." Another scholar echoed that he was "born with a strange obsession."

He was born to a well-to-do scholar household. His father, Xu Yuan, was described as a "recluse." His mother, Wang Ruren, was characterized as a remarkably knowledgeable woman who was devoted to gardening and weaving. According to the painter and art theorist Dong Qichang, under whom a friend of Xu's studied, Xu Xiake's father "did not like to consort with officials. It was his wife who shaped their second son into such an exceptional person."

Xu had a younger brother who was the child of a concubine. Before his death his father told his mother that the family estate could be divided only among her two sons; the son of the concubine did not require any inheritance. But she included the youngest boy and divided it into three parts anyway.

Xu Xiake spent long days talking with his mother, who outlived his father by twenty-one years. She too seemed fond of travel, and the two often journeyed together. Once he was on a mountain top when his heart started pounding. He hurried down to discover that his mother was ill. After that he tried not to range too far away from her. Only after her death did he feel free to undertake his longest excursions.

Xu inherited his father's reclusive tendencies. He had no interest in taking exams and becoming an official. He considered mountain climbing and travel a sufficient calling. Rejecting life at court in order to literally rise above the troubles of the late Ming, he clambered up many of China's major mountains, always striving to reach the highest point. In 1616 he scaled Mount Huang, which became a popular destination around this time. (There was an explosion of paintings of the mountain during the late Ming and early Qing dynasties. Among the many who painted Mount Huang around this time were Ding Yunpeng, 1547–ca. 1621; Xiao Yuncong, 1596–1673; Zheng Min, 1607–after 1682; Hong Ren, 1610–1663; Kun Can, 1612–after 1674; Dai Benxiao, 1621–ca. 1694; Mei Qing, ca. 1623–1697; and Shi Tao, 1642–1718.)

Opposite: Morning Sun over the Heavenly Citadel, 1614, by Ding Yunpeng. Ink and colors on paper. 212.7 x 55.4 cm. Andrew R. and Martha Holden Jennings Fund, 1965.28.

Mount Huang, a focus of artistic attention and a travel destination during the late Ming, was actually a series of peaks, including one called Heavenly Citadel. Ding Yunpeng, a devout Buddhist, would have regarded his subject as a highly spiritual place.

For Xu the mountain was a living being that was always changing. Something of an early environmentalist, he regarded damage to the natural world as wounds to a living body, of which every part was unique. As he climbed Mount Huang, he wrote, "Looking around in every direction, every step brought new strangeness." The attitude may owe something to Dong Qichang's theory of painting. "If on a mountaintop you should chance to see an unusual tree," the artist advised, "you should approach it from four different angles."

But Dong Qichang was more interested in the essence of landscape than particular vistas. There was also a strain of thought in the late Ming that was more concerned with what Timothy Brook has called "the particularity of place." Some artists were attempting to capture the specificity of subjects such as aspects of Mount Huang. Enabled in part by an explosion in printing, writers all over China were publishing route books (produced mainly by and for merchants) and gazetteers — sourcebooks of knowledge about local geography, customs, and events. Travel diaries were also becoming popular, though Xu carried the form to new literary heights. But his travel account would exist only in handwritten manuscripts until it finally saw print for the first time in 1776.

By Xu's time some mountains had become popular tourist destinations. One traveler described staying at the base of Mount Tai, which received eight hundred thousand visitors a year. He stayed in a large inn that contained twenty kitchens. At the end of a day on the mountains visitors were entertained with operas or lute performances.

Regarded as a link between heaven and earth, mountains had been associated with spiritual qualities since ancient times. The Yellow Emperor, the legendary founder of Chinese civilization, was said to have acquired the secret of immortality on Mount Huang, which became home to many immortals. Many monks and hermits who withdrew from the Ming court retreated to mountain huts. Buddhist and Taoist temples were established on Mount Huang early on. By Xu's time the mountain was not necessarily viewed in a strictly Buddhist or Taoist sense, but it could still fill visitors with what James Cahill has called a "quasi-religious sense of the sublime." Xu's friend who was a a student of Dong Qichang's wrote a poem about Xu that concludes:

Neither a Buddhist
Nor a Taoist immortal
But half stubborn, half deranged
He stirs up Heaven and Earth, year after year
Until the mulberry groves wither
And the blue sea runs dry

Mountains were thought to contain "cave paradises" that provided a channel to the realm of the immortals. Many people were afraid to enter caves because of the spirits that inhabited them, but Xu, in whom some writers have seen the beginning of a new, more scientific experience of discovery, explored them thoroughly.

His rejection of travel companions was far from absolute. A friend wrote of him:

> He would travel with a servant, or sometimes with a monk and just a staff and a cloth bundle, not worrying about carrying a traveling bag or supplies of food. He could endure hunger for several days, eating his fill when he found some food. He could keep walking for several hundred *li,* ascending sheer cliffs, braving bamboo thickets, scrambling up and down, hanging over precipices on a rope.... He used towering crags for his bed, streams and gullies for refreshment and found companionship amongst fairies, trolls, apes, and baboons, with the result that he became unable to think logically and could not speak. However, as soon as we discussed mountain paths, investigated water sources or sought out superior geographical terrain, his mind suddenly became clear again.

Julian Ward, author of a study of Xu Xiake, cites this passage as an example of "his bravery, his independence of thought and action and above all, his complete devotion to travel."

Though not wholly either a Buddhist or a Taoist, Xu was respectful of both beliefs. In 1636 he undertook his greatest adventure, a three-year journey to southwest China — an area that had only recently come under Chinese control — in the company of two servants and a Buddhist monk named Jingwen, who was undertaking a pilgrimage to a sacred mountain called Mount Chickenfoot. Jingwen carried with him a manuscript of the Buddhist Lotus Sutra, which he had copied out in his own blood. Xu reports that other travelers kept their distance from him because when he was ill he refused to bathe in the river for fear of polluting it.

Banditry was a problem for Xu Xiake just as it was for travelers in Europe and West Asia, such as William Lithgow. Traveling by boat, Xu's party moored in a remote spot on the Xiang River. Xu was sitting in the boat gazing at the moon. He heard the sound of sobbing on the riverbank, which continued for more than two hours. He began to compose a mournful poem, while the monk Jingwen went to see what was the matter — he learned that a teenaged boy was fleeing from his cruel eunuch master. Just then bandits attacked, hoping by hollering and waving swords to frighten away the travelers and seize their boat and possessions. To prevent this Xu threw the sail and his money-box overboard, but his foot got caught in the towrope, dragging him down. As he struggled up for air a servant beat the bandits back.

Later Jingwen fell ill with dysentery and died. "We had a life-and-death pledge to go to the mountains," Xu wrote in a poem. "Now gazing eastward alone, to continue brings pain."

Xu became ill with malaria. "My head and limbs were covered in spots, which gathered up in piles in the folds of my skin," he wrote, "while my left ear and left foot twitched." Then his servant suddenly disappeared. "For a master and his servant to be three years away from home, their forms and shadows inseparable, only for me to be abandoned one morning ten thousand *li* from home," Xu said, "is too much to bear." A few days later Xu's diaries come to an abrupt end. He was carried halfway home in a sedan chair, covering 2,550 kilometers in 150 days. He completed his journey by boat on the Yangtse River, covering 1700 kilometers in under a week.

At home he is said to have shown little interest in visitors. Instead he lay in bed, absently stroking oddly shaped rocks. He died at the age of fifty-four in 1641, fifteen months after his final diary entry. On his deathbed he said, "Life is a lodging, death a return. I now long in my journeying to be transformed." Amid the chaos of the fall of the Ming dynasty Xu's manuscript of his travels was lost. Fortunately, nearly complete copies preserved by friends survive.

In Surat, India, Pietro della Valle was, like Xu Xiake, considering the sanctity of nature. He toured the countryside, visiting a community of Jains, who "looked upon all nature, even lifeless objects, as animate, and took the most elaborate precautions to prevent the accidental death of even the smallest animalculae." He was particularly impressed by an animal hospital where sick birds were nursed back to health.

From Surat he continued to Goa in a Portuguese vessel. He recorded his impressions of the city:

> The city ... is very big and is built partly on the level and partly on some charming hills, from whose summits can be seen in the distance the entire island and the sea, with the mainland all about, offering a delightful view. The buildings of the city are good, large and commodious, mostly arranged to capture the breeze, which is very strong (this is necessary because of the occurrences of great heat), and also to withstand the heavy rains of the three months of *pausecal,* June, July, and August.... The buildings, however, do not display much ornamentation, nor any fine craftsmanship, being rather plain and nearly all without decoration.... The population of Goa is numerous, but the greater part are slaves, black and wretched, mostly naked, or else so very ill-dressed, that they seem to me to spoil rather than enhance the city. The Portuguese are fairly few, and though they used to be rich, today, on account of many losses suffered following the incursions of the Dutch and the English into those seas, they do not possess great wealth.

Again he adapted to the local style, changing his drooping Persian mustaches into the upswept Portuguese style and adding a goatee and a single earring to complete a rather Bohemian look. He attended a masquerade party dressed in an outfit embroidered with tears to represent his grief at the death of his wife.

Altogether he stayed in India for more than two years. In December 1625 he sailed for Basra on the Persian Gulf. The city was a semi-independent part of the Ottoman empire; the Portuguese used it as their base on the Gulf following the loss of Hormuz. When della Valle arrived it was under attack from the Persians. Tense days followed, but the Persians suddenly withdrew, and at last he was able to make his way by caravan across Syria to Italy.

He arrived in Naples in February 1626, where he was welcomed by Dr. Schipano, and reached Rome that April. There he was hailed as "Il Fantastico." But he still preferred "Il Pellegrino," the pilgrim. While in Rome, awaiting the arrival of his wife's casket, which he had shipped separately, he met the Basque "lieutenant nun," Catarina de Erauso. "She is tall and broadly built for a woman; you could never tell by her stature that she was not a man," he reported. "Her face is not deformed, though not pretty and rather worn with age. With her short black hair, cut in men's fashion with a little lock, she looks more like a eunuch than a woman. Her clothes and sword are Spanish, and her waist is tightly laced. In brief, you would take her rather for a weather-beaten soldier than for an amorous courtier. Only her hands — which are rather plump and fleshy, though strong and robust — and the way she moves them, betray that she is a woman."

At length Maani's body arrived. Before burying her, he opened her casket for one last look:

> I found the flesh of the head, which I could see through a tear in the shroud, to be wholly eaten away, nothing remaining but the bone; at this I was not surprised, for the brain had not been removed and this had caused the decomposition. The rest of the body appeared to be better preserved; but because the face was no longer to be seen, I would not unfold the linen to look further. Having renailed the amba wood coffin I enclosed it in a leaden one which I had well soldered. On this, near to the feet, I had placed a large plate engraved with a great cross and the following epitaph:

Maani Gioeridae heroinae

Praestantissimae

Petri de Valle peregrine uxoris

Mortales exuvae

Maani Gioeridae heroine

Most excellent

Wife of the pilgrim Pietro della Valle

Her mortal remains

Della Valle delivered a funeral oration for his wife in which he praised her as the epitome of feminine virtue. Her oratory, he said, surpassed that of Demosthenes and Cicero. Her beauty … at that point della Valle broke down in tears. There are two accounts of the reception to della Valle's theatrical oration. One says that when he dissolved into tears the mourners began to sob along with him. The other reports that they broke into laughter.

Before long della Valle remarried. His wife was Mariuccia, the orphan girl Maani had adopted. Together they had fourteen sons, some of whom would publish the letters that their father had sent to Dr. Schipano during his years of travel. According to one writer, in later years a whiff of camphor could at times be detected in della Valle's study. Its source was never located.

Epilogue: Christmas, His Masque

On Christmas Day in 1616 the English royal court gathered in Whitehall to watch a masque by Inigo Jones and Ben Jonson called *Christmas, His Masque*. It is remembered today mainly for marking the first appearance of a character called Father Christmas.

> He is attir'd in round Hose, long Stockings, a close Doublet, a high crownd Hat with a Broach, a long thin beard, a Truncheon, little Ruffes, white Shoes, his Scarffes, and Garters tyed crosse, and his Drum beaten before him.

In January, the masque *The Golden Age Restored* had portrayed James's court as ushering in a new era of peace, justice, and wisdom, marking a return to an imagined idyllic past. In June, James gave a speech that he considered of special importance: it is the final item in his *Collected Workes,* published the same year. In it he concluded that "As every fish liues in his owne place, some in the fresh, some in the salt, some in the mud: so let euery one liue in his owne place, some at Court, some in the Citue, some in the Countrey, especially at Festiual times, as Christmas and Easter."

Both the masque and the speech expressed the wish to staunch changes taking place in a world in motion. Every day more people came to London, a development James deplored and blamed on the influence of women:

> To dwell in London, is apparently the pride of the women: For if they bee wiues, then their husbands; and if they be maydes, then their fathers must bring them vp to London; because the new fashion is to bee had no where but in London: and here, if they be vnmarried they marre their marriages, and if they be married, they loose their reputations, and rob their husbands purses....

Christmas, His Masque completed James's 1616 agenda calling for return to the simple, unchanging virtues of the supposedly glorious past. Father Christmas embodied revival of innocent rural festivals of mummers and morris dancers in the face of London's wicked temptations. But the clock could not be turned back. The world was changing too fast. Civil war would break out during the rule of his son Charles, whose beheading foretold a coming age of revolutions. The golden age was not restored.

Opposite: The Chongzhen Emperor Slays One of His Daughters (detail), 1655. From *De Bello Tartarico* by Martino Martini.

By midcentury the world had been transformed. Northern Europeans began to outpace southern Europeans for influence in the new world of maritime globalism. Developing their North American colonies through reliance on African slave labor, they would expand aggressively into both continents. Spain and Portugal would have increasing difficulty governing Latin America, whose share of the global economy would diminish.

The Ottoman empire would reach its greatest extent. The Mughals remained powerful, but the seeds of English colonialism were sown. European expansion in Southeast Asia would also lay the groundwork for later colonial history.

The last emperor of Ming China was the Wanli emperor's grandson, whose reign name, Chongzhen, means "honorable and auspicious." Facing the fall of his capital, he drew his sword and killed most of the members of his household. "Why must you be born in this family?" he shouted at his second daughter, who was sixteen and about to be married. She survived but lost her left arm.

The Chongzhen emperor hanged himself from a tree. China would not again be governed by its native people until its Manchu rulers were overthrown in 1911.

Some Significant Dates

POLITICS AND RELIGION

Events

1351–1767 Kingdom of Ayutthaya (Siam/Thailand)
1368–1644 Ming dynasty, China
1392–1910 Joseon dynasty, Korea
1405–1421 Zhang He leads voyages of Chinese treasure fleets
1450s Movable metal type printing reengineered in Europe
1453 Ottomans capture Constantinople, rename it Istanbul
1491 Treaty of Tordesillas divides the world
1497 Vasco da Gama reaches India by sea
1501–1722 Safavid dynasty, Iran
1545–1563 Council of Trent
1550 Portuguese allowed to trade in Japan
1555 Peace of Augsburg
1555 First Jewish ghetto established in Venice
1567–1609 Netherlands provinces unite, revolt against Spain
1571 Ottomans defeated at Battle of Lepanto
1572 St. Bartholomew's Day Massacre, France
1573–1620 Reign of the Wanli emperor, China
1575–1580 Cervantes is held as a slave in Algiers
1580–1640, Spain and Portugal are merged in Iberian union
1587 Mary Queen of Scots is executed
1588–1648 Reign of Christian IV of Denmark
1589 Battle of Mombasa
1590s Irish rebel against English
1598 Henri IV of France issues Edict of Nantes
1603–1617 Ahmed I is Ottoman sultan
1605–1621 Paul V is Roman Catholic pope
1605–1627 Reign of Mughal emperor Jahangir
1607–1618 War between Burma and Siam
1608 French settle at Quebec
1608–1623 Reign of Gwanghaegun (Yi Hon) of Korea
1609 Moriscos (converted Muslims) expelled from Spain
1610–1643 Reign of Louis XIII of France
1613 Marriage of Frederick, Elector Palantine, and Elizabeth of England
1615–1618 Giovanni Bembo is Doge of Venice
1615–1868 Tokugawa (Edo) shogunate, Japan
1616–1619 Tepehuanes Revolt, Mexico
1616–1620 Smallpox epidemic strikes New England tribes
1616 Cardinal Richelieu named French Secretary of State
1616 Thomas Roe establishes first British embassy in India
1616 Jesuits expelled from Ming court in China
1616 Tokugawa Ieyasu dies, Japan
1616 Vincenz Fettmilch is beheaded, Jews return to Frankfurt
1616 Nurhaci, founder of Qing dynasty, declares himself emperor
1616 Thomas Overbury murder scandal, London, ends with the conviction of the Earl and Countess of Somerset
1616 Fort San Diego, overlooking Acapulco Bay, completed

1618–1648 Thirty Years War
1643–1644 Fall of Ming dynasty, beginning of Qing dynasty, China

People

Shah Abbas of Iran, 27 January, 1571–19 January, 1629
Akbar, Mughal emperor, 1556–1605
Anne of Denmark, 12 December, 1574–2 March, 1619
Bembo, Giovanni, 21 August, 1543–16 March, 1618
Catherine de Medici of France, 13 April, 1519–5 January, 1589
Christian IV of Denmark, 12 April, 1577–28 February, 1648
De Silva, Juan, d. April 19, 1616
Elizabeth I of England, 7 September, 1533–24 March, 1603
Galigai, Leonora, 19 May, 1568–8 July, 1617
Godunov, Boris Feodorovich, c. 1551–April, 1605
Henri IV of France, 13 December, 1553–Paris, 14 May, 1610
Hosokawa Gracia, 1563–August 25, 1600
Ignatius of Loyola, 1491–31 July, 1556
Jahangir, 20 September, 1569–8 November, 1627
James VI of Scotland, I of England, 19 June, 1566–27 March, 1625
Kanō Anisen, 1570–1616
Kanō Tanyu, 1602–1674
Louis XIII of France, 27 September, 1601–14 May, 1643
Marie de Médicis, 26 April, 1575–3 July, 1642
Mary I of Scotland, 8 December, 1542–8 February, 1587
Nurhaci, 21 February, 1559–30 September, 1626
Nur Jahan, 1577–1645
Pope Paul V, 17 September, 1552–28 January, 1621
Philip (Felipe) III of Spain, 14 April, 1578–31 March, 1621
Powhatan (Wahunsenacawh), d. 1618
Raleigh, Walter, c. 1552–29 October, 1618
Romanov, Mikhail Fyodorovich, 12 July, 1596–13 July, 1645
Rudolf II of Austria, 18 July, 1552–20 January, 1612
Tokugawa Hidetada, 2 May, 1579–14 March, 1632
Tokugawa Ieyasu: 31 January, 1543–1 June, 1616
Toyotomi Hideyoshi, 2 February, 1536–18 September, 1598
Wallenstein, Albrecht von, 24 September, 1583–25 February, 1634
Wang Yangming, 1472–1529
Wanli emperor, 4 September, 1563–18 August, 1620

TRADE AND TRAVEL

Events

1557 China allows Portuguese to establish a port at Macau
1565 First Spanish settlement in the Philippines
1596 Dutch ships arrive in Indonesia
1602 Dutch East India Company (VOC) founded
1607 Jamestown first successful British settlement in No. America
1616 First African slave brought to Bahamas
1616 Dirk Hartog makes the second recorded landfall in Australia by a European
1616 Willem Schouten rounds Cape Horn
1616 Matoaka (Pocahontas) travels to London
1616 The Tokugawa shogunate, Japan, restricts most foreigners to the ports of Nagasaki and Hirado

1616 Pope Paul V welcomes the embassy of the Japanese samurai Hasekura Tsunenaga in Rome
1616 Peter Paul Rubens begins a series of classical tapestries
1616 Rene Descartes graduates from the University of Poitiers
1616 Pietro Della Valle marries Maani Gioerida in Baghdad
1616 Will Adams travels to Siam

People
Adams, Will, 24 September, 1564–16 May, 1620
Coryate, Thomas, 1577–1617
Della Valle, Pietro, 1586–1652
Erauso, Catalina de, perhaps 1592–1650
Lithgow, William, 1582–1645
Magellan, Ferdinand, c. 1480–27 April, 1521
Malik Ambar, 1546–1626
Matoaka (Rebecca Rolfe/Pocahontas), c. 1595–21 March, 1617
Reis, Yusuf (Jack Ward), c. 1553–1622
Rolfe, John, c. 1585–1622
Schouten, Willem Cornelisz, c. 1567–1625
Sherley, Robert, c. 1581–13 July 1628
Spielbergen, Joris van, 1568–1620
Xu Xiake, 5 January, 1587–8 March, 1641
Yamada Nagamasa, c. 1550–1630

SCIENCE, TECHNOLOGY, MEDICINE
Events
1543 Copernicus, *On the Revolutions of the Heavenly Bodies*
1596 Kepler, *The Cosmic Mystery*
1610 Galileo, *The Starry Messenger*
1613 Heo Jun, *Mirror of Eastern Medicine*
1616 Galileo meets Pope Paul V in Rome
1616 Edward Wright, *Admirable Table of Logarithmes*
1619 Kepler, *The Harmony of the World*

People
Bacon, Francis, 22 January, 1561–9 April, 1626
Boot, Adrian, c. 1590–1648
Bourgeois, Louise, c. 1563–1636
Galilei, Galileo, 15 February, 1564–8 January, 1642
Gilbert, William, 1544–1603
Heo Jun, 1537–1615
Kepler, Johannes, 27 December, 1571–15 November, 1630
Martínez, Enrico, d. 1632
Stevin, Simon, 1548 or 1549–1620
Taqi al-Din, 1526–1585
Tycho Brahe, 14 December, 1546–24 October, 1601

CULTURE
Events
1604–1611 King James Bible
1611 Thomas Coryate, *Coryat's Crudities*
1616 Blue Mosque completed, Istanbul
1616 Artemisia Gentileschi admitted to the Academie del Disegno of Florence

1616 John Donne appointed Reader in Divinity, Lincoln's Inn
1616 First appearance of Father Christmas, in a Christmas masque by Ben Jonson
1616 Ben Jonson, *Workes* and *The Devil Is an Ass*
1616 Shakespeare, first folio
1616 Thomas Middleton, *The Witch*
1616 Dorothy Leigh, *The Mother's Blessing*
1616 Banabe Rich, *My Lady's Looking Glass*
1616 Domenico Belli, *L'Orfeo Dolente*
1617 Jacques Olivier, *Alphabet of Women's Imperfections and Malice*

People
Abul Hasan, born 1588 or 1589
Andreae, Johan Valentin, 17 August, 1586–27 June, 1654
Avercamp, Hendrick, baptized 27 January, 1585–15 May, 1634
Boehme, Jacob, c. 1575–17 November, 1624
Brueghel, Jan, the Elder, 1568–13 January, 1625
Cervantes, Miguel de, 29 September, 1547–23 April, 1616
De Vega, Lope, 25 November, 1562–27 August, 1635
Dong Qichang, 1555–1636
Donne, John, 1572–31 March, 1631
Fletcher, John, 1579–1625
Fludd, Robert, 17 January, 1574–8 September, 1637
Francken II, Frans, 1581–6 May, 1642
Frith, Mary (Moll Cutpurse), c. 1584–July 26, 1659
Gentileschi, Artemisia, 8 July, 1593–ca. 1656
Goltzius, Hendrik, January or February, 1558–1 January, 1617
Góngora y Argote, Luis de, 11 July, 1561–24 May, 1627
El Greco, 1541–7 April, 1614
Guaman Poma de Ayala, Felipe, c. 1535–after 1616
Heo Gyun, 1569–1618
Jonson, Ben, June, 1572–6 August, 1637
Jones, Inigo, 15 July, 1573–21 June, 1652
Maier, Michael, 1568–1622
Middleton, Thomas, 18 April, 1580–1627
Modena, Leon, 23 April, 1571–24 March, 1648
Montaigne, Michel de, 28 February, 1533–13 September, 1592
Monteverdi, Claudio Giovanni Antonio, baptized 15 May, 1567–29 November, 1643
Mulla Sadra, c. 1571–1636
Rubens, Peter Paul, 28 June, 1577–30 May, 1640
Shakespeare, William, baptised 26 April, 1564–23 April, 1616
Stampa, Gaspara, 1523–1554
Tang Xianzu, 24 September, 1550–29 July, 1616
Wroth, Mary, 1587–perhaps 1653

LONDON

SEVILLE

JAMESTOWN

MEXICO CITY   VERACRUZ

ACAPULCO

CAPE VERDE ISLANDS

CARTAGENA

CALLAO / LIMA

POTOSÍ

CAPE HORN

AMSTERDAM •
LISBON
• PRAGUE
• MOSCOW
ALGIERS•
• ROME
TUNIS•
ISTANBUL•
BEIJING•
• NAGASAKI
• ALEPPO
NANJING•
BAGHDAD•
• ISFAHAN
• MACAU
• HORMUZ
HANOI•
• MANILA
GOA•
AYUTTHAYA•
(SIAM)
• MELAKA
BATAVIA•
(JAKARTA)
• MOZAMBIQUE

Source Notes

This section and the reading list that follows attempt to acknowledge the most significant of the many debts I owe to other writers. Comprehensive bibliographies of all of the many topics in this book are impossible; instead, I try to list works, mainly in English, that I have particularly relied on or that serve as useful points of entrance to some of the main subjects (the notes are arranged roughly in order of the appearance of topics in the text). Omissions are failures of record keeping not signs of ingratitude, and I apologize for them. Isaac Newton wrote, "If I have seen further, it is only by standing on the shoulders of giants," and I would be shortsighted indeed were it not for the inspired work of the countless scholars I have depended on.

General

There are, it turns out, a number of books devoted to single years. Some, like Ray Huang's fascinating *1587: A Year of No Significance,* which is a study of a year in the reign of the Wanli emperor, and Christopher Lee's *1603: The Death of Queen Elizabeth I, the Return of the Black Plague, the Rise of Shakespeare, Piracy, Witchcraft, and the Birth of the Stuart Era,* whose concerns are amply announced by its copious subtitle, focus on specific regions. Others, like Felipe Fernández-Armesto's *1492: The Year the World Began* and David Andress's *1789: The Threshold of the Modern Age,* attempt a more global viewpoint (both of these authors see in their years, despite a difference of nearly three centuries, the beginnings of many aspects of the modern world. Probably any year, looked at closely enough, will reveal seeds of modernity).

As this book is about to go to print, Charles C. Mann's *1493* is receiving a lot of attention. Mann had previously published a book entitled *1491.* I have not read these books (I'm just now beginning *1493*), but my impression is that the attention is well deserved. I believe that Mann treats his years primarily as symbols of the world before and after the Columbian encounter, so his enterprise is different in nature from those that try to focus more literally on a single calendar year.

Sometime after starting this project I recalled reading reviews of John E. Wills's *1688: A Global History,* which seemed likely to be the most similar of the global histories to my own. So, for fear of being unduly influenced by Wills's approach, I made sure not to read his book until after I had completed a draft of this one. I did read other of Wills's fine work, such as his *The World from 1450 to 1700* and his contributions to the *Cambridge History of China.* When I finally reviewed that excellent book, I saw that there is minimal overlap and it takes a somewhat different approach.

Victor Lieberman, professor of history at the University of Michigan, has attempted macrohistories of the early modern period, looking for points of similarity across diverse cultures, in groundbreaking books such as *Strange Parallels: Southeast Asia in Global Context, c. 800–1830* and *Beyond Binary Histories: Re-imagining Eurasia to c. 1830* (a collection of essays in which several scholars challenge or expand on the analysis he presents in a foundation essay).

Timothy Brook's *Vermeer's Hat: The Seventeenth Century and the Dawn of the Global World* is a stimulating book that is especially strong on connections between China and the Netherlands. Its main focus is somewhat later in the seventeenth century than this book's. Brook is a scholar of the Ming dynasty whose enlightening and readable surveys of the period include *The Confusions of Pleasure,* a cultural history of Ming China that focuses not on large-scale political events but on changing attitudes and patterns of everyday life; *The Troubled Empire,* a history of the Yuan and Ming dynasties; and *The Chinese State in Ming Society.*

Taking as one of its goals the correcting of European biases of traditional histories, Charles H. Parker's *Global Interactions in the Early Modern Age, 1400–1800* offers a whirlwind tour of four hundred years of early modern globalism. *Globalization in World History,* edited by A. G. Hopkins, sounds like it should be even broader in scope but is actually a collection of essays from various contributors that are mostly related to aspects of early modern and modern history. Hopkins outlines several stages of globalism, according to which the early seventeenth century would represent aspects of "archaic" and "proto" globalism, in which state, economic, and industrial components are not yet fully integrated.

Stephen Dale's recent *The Muslim Empires of the Ottomans, Safavids, and Mughals* provides an especially helpful overview of the three great Islamic empires of this period. Catherine B. Asher and Cynthia Talbot's *India before Europe* provides a good overview of India around this time. *Destiny Disrupted* by Tamim Ansary corrects long-standing Western biases. Jerry Brotton's breezy *The Renaissance Bazaar: From the Silk Road to Michelangelo* surveys Asian influences on Europe, mostly via the Ottomans, and mainly from an earlier period than that of this book.

Opposite: The Old Philosopher Chilo Lacedæmonius, 1616, by Jacob de Gheyn III (1596–1641), from the series *Septem Sapientum Græciæ Icones* (Seven Wise Men of Greece). Etching on paper, 253 mm. x 185 mm. British Museum, AN468768001.

Andrew J. Newman's admirably detailed *Safavid Iran* may be tough sledding for the nonspecialist.

Ashin Das Gupta is excellent on trade in the Indian Ocean region (see too a collection of essays in his honor edited by Rudrangshu Mukherjee). Other books on the Indian Ocean region include works by Sugata Bose, Richard Hall, and M. Pearson. For Southeast Asia, in addition to Lieberman, see works by Anthony Reid.

There are many books devoted to the early modern period in Europe. Good bibliographies are available online from scholars associated with Cambridge, CUNY, and UCLA; a web search for "early modern" + "reading list" should turn up these and similar results. Merry Wiesner-Hanks's *Early Modern Europe, 1450–1789* is a solid introduction that combines thematic and chronological perspectives. Henry Kamen's *Early Modern European Society* focuses on social developments rather than large-scale political events. Theodore Rabb's *The Last Days of the Renaissance* examines the shift from the early Renaissance to the later early modern period leading to the age of revolutions. H. G. Koenigsberger's *Early Modern Europe 1500–1789,* though getting a little long in the tooth, remains a convenient primer.

William J. Bernstein's *Splendid Exchange* is a wide-reaching study of global trade through history.

Preface and Prologue

For NICOLAAS GEELKERCKEN see J. Keuning's article in *Imago Mundi.* Geelkercken's map also appears (as does the map by Franc-Antoine de la Porte on the front flap of the hardcover jacket) in Rodney Shirley's *The Mapping of the World,* where it is dated later in the seventeenth century.

In *Writing Women in Jacobean England,* Barbara Kiefer Lewalski has written cogently on THE COUNTESS OF BEDFORD and her role as Penthesilea in *The Masque of Queens.* Texts of the masques discussed in the prologue and epilogue of this book can be found online, as can many other works from the early seventeenth century. In many such cases I have assumed interested readers can locate the texts easily enough and have not given up space in "Selected Reading" for this.

On JAMES I, QUEEN ANNE, AND MARY, QUEEN OF SCOTS, Alan Stewart's *The Cradle King* is solid and thorough (though the narrative does not always sustain momentum). Antonia Fraser's illustrated *King James VI of Scotland, I of England* is sympathetic to the royal family.

Victor Lieberman has discussed what he calls the "charter states," or GOLDEN AGES, embraced by several early modern states. The discussion of the different KINDS OF POLITICAL AUTHORITY of the Islamic empires owes a large debt to Stephen Dale.

BEN JONSON "returns again and again to the myth of the Golden Age, evoking classical and mythological glories with affecting nostalgia and fervid optimism," according to Claude Summers and Ted-Larry Pebworth in *Ben Jonson Revised,* a critical study that rises above the level of many in the Twain series. James Hirsh's *New Perspectives on Ben Jonson* collects fairly recent essays on the author. David Riggs's *Ben Jonson: A Life* is a reliable biography. On the masques in particular, see works by A. D. Cousins and Alison V. Scott, David Lindley, and Stephen Orgel. Jonson's 1616 folio *Workes* was reissued in facsimile in 1976.

On the connection between East Asian and Renaissance European printing technology, see my "Gutenberg and the Koreans," available online through search.

Among many resources related to the VOC and the other NORTHERN EUROPEAN TRADE COMPANIES is Nick Robins's *The Corporation that Changed the World: How the East India Company Shaped the Modern Multinational.* Niels Steensgaard's *Carracks, Caravans and Companies* considers the impact of the companies on preexisting trade networks in West Asia and the Indian Ocean region. In *A Splendid Exchange* William J. Bernstein does a good job of highlighting differences between the Dutch and English companies.

The story of THE SIEGE OF RUN is told in Giles Milton's rousing *Nathaniel's Nutmeg.* For a shorter version, see William J. Bernstcin's *Splendid Exchange;* it also includes a section on JAN PIETERSZOON COEN.

Silk and Silver

Information on ADRIAN BOOT and, to a lesser degree, ENRIQUE MARTINEZ is sparse. In "The Fortification of Acapulco, 1615–1616" Engel Sluiter provides a progress report from the supervisor of the fortification project and discusses Boot's role in that context. Louisa Schell Hoberman's "Technological Change in a Traditional Society: The Case of the Desague in Colonial Mexico" discusses the Mexico City drainage disputes. Valerie L. Mathes also touches on these issues in "Enrico Martínez of New Spain." *Mapping and Empire* by Reinhartz and Saxon also briefly discusses the two figures.

Late in my research I discovered the work of Priscilla Connolly and Roberto Mayer, who have investigated the transmission of the works of Adrian Boot and Juan Gómez de Trasmonte. These include a plan and view of Mexico City and views of Acapulco and Veracruz: three are shown here (pp. 32, 39, and 81). According to Connolly and Mayer, "Scholars have generally considered these coloured prints to be the only accurate representations of seventeenth-century Mexico City, Acapulco and Veracruz." They believe that the originals of these works were drawings, which were probably among the booty of a ship captured by the Dutch pirate Piet Hein in 1628. That would explain how they made their way to the Netherlands, where they were converted into oil paintings, now lost, by David Vinckboons, and then watercolors by his son Johannes Vingboons (ca. 1617–1670). Johannes, they say, inscribed the watercolors with the names of the artists of the original drawings.

Connolly and Mayer report on as yet unpublished work on Adrian Boot by Victor Manuel Ruiz Naufal and Jean-Pierre Berthe, so perhaps the engineer's life will soon come into better focus.

William Lytle Schurz's *The Manila Galleon* remains the best overview of the MANILA–ACAPULCO GALLEONS. Additional information can be found in Henry Kamen's *Empire: How Spain Became a World Power, 1492–1763* and *European Entry into the Pacific* by Dennis O'Flynn, Arturo Giraldez, and James Sobredo. See also Carla Rahn Phillips, *Six Galleons for the King of Spain.*

Thomas K. Peterson, author of *Secrets of the Manila Galleon* (www.proaxis.com/~tpeterson/), which deals with the galleons in their heyday from 1650 to 1780, kindly referred me to Bruce Cruikshank's website, "Manila Galleon Listing"(https://sites.google.com/site/manilagalleonlisting/), which details the voyages of the galleons year by year. In an e-mail Cruikshack told me "I am not an expert on the galleons but was frustrated that there was not a list and that there were so many gaps and contradictions in the data. There are still gaps but I've tried to identify or eliminate the contradictions." This is helpful work indeed.

For JORIS VAN SPILBERGEN see J.A. Villiers, *The East and West Indian Mirror, Being an Account of Joris Van Speilbergen's Voyage Round the World.* Peter Gerhard's account of pirates on the west coast of New Spain is a highly readable summation. Tonio Andrade has described how the Dutch East India Company tried to lead a coalition of pirates to war against China.

Among general books on SILK are Philippa Scott's *The Book of Silk,* Anne E. Wardwell and James C. Y. Watt's *When Silk Was Gold: Central Asian and Chinese Textiles,* and Shelagh Vainker's *Chinese Silk: A Cultural History.* Chinese silk technology is exhaustively covered in Joseph Needham's *Science and Civilization in China.*

The best known translations of the SHI JING, or Classic of Songs, are by James Legge, Arthur Waley, and Ezra Pound. The translations here are my own reworkings based mainly on the collective work of previous translators.

There has been much written about THE WANLI EMPEROR. The *Cambridge History of China,* Ray Huang's *1587, a Year of No Significance,* and the works of Timothy Brook are good places to start. The *Cambridge History* is also a good source on the treasure fleets of ZHENG HE.

Sanjay Subrahmanyam has written on THE PORTUGUESE IN ASIA. Jay A. Levenson's *Encompassing the Globe* was a companion book to an exhibition at the Freer and Sackler Galleries. Jorge Flores's *Goa and the Great Mughal* accompanied an exhibition at the Museu Calouste Gulbenkian in Lisbon.

On the subject of GUAM I consulted Robert F. Rogers's *Destiny's Landfall: A History of Guam.*

Henry Kamen's *Empire: How Spain Became a World Power, 1492–1763* has a good chapter on MANILA AND THE PHILIPPINES. The *Cambridge History of China* is another useful source.

Jonathan Spence has written persuasively on MATTEO RICCI. D.E. Mungello's *Curious Land: Jesuit Accommodation and the Origins of Sinology* is a comprehensive account of JESUIT MISSIONARIES IN CHINA. Joanna Waley-Cohen's *The Sextants of Beijing* contains a chapter on China and Catholicism. C.R. Boxer's *The Christian Century in Japan 1549–1650* remains a prime source on CHRISTIAN MISSIONARIES IN JAPAN.

Rodrigo Rivero Lake's *Namban: Art in Viceregal Mexico* is richly illustrated.

Jane E. Mangan's *Trading Roles* explores aspects of life in POTOSÍ that I have not been able to get into here, focusing more on its trade interactions than on the experience of native miners. For more on Potosí, see Bartolome Arzáns de Orsúa y Vela's *Tales of Potosí,* which is available in English translation with a helpful introduction, and Peter J. Bakewell's *Miners of the Red Mountain: Indian Labor in Potosi, 1545–1650.* Eduardo Galeano's *Memory of Fire* trilogy is a beautiful, wrenching retelling of Latin American history.

Rolena Adorno dominates the study of GUAMAN POMA. See "Selected Reading" (p. 369) for a list of titles.

Peter J. Bakewell's *Silver Mining and Society in Colonial Mexico* is an account of events in ZACATECAS, and Charlotte M. Gradie discusses THE TEPEHUAN REVOLT OF 1616 in her book of that title.

Shakespeare's Sisters
I am indebted to Naomi J. Miller for making the connection between Mary Wroth and Virginia Woolf's comments about Shakespeare's hypothetical sister, which inspired the title of this chapter.

Margaret L. King's *Women of the Renaissance* surveys the roles of women at all levels of European society, while Dorothy Ko sheds new light on aspects of women in China in *Teachers of the Inner Chambers: Women and Culture in Seventeenth-Century China.*

Camilla Townsend's *Pocahontas and the Powhatan Dilemma* is a good survey of the subject; Townsend was the first, I think, to suggest MATOAKA (POCAHONTAS) may have suffered from Stockholm Syndrome. Helen Rountree's excellent *Pocahontas, Powhatan, Opechancanough: Three Indian Lives Changed by Jamestown,* which is informed by anthropological research, is more detailed; it views events from the Powhatan perspective. Paula Gunn Allen's speculative *Pocahontas: Medicine Woman, Spy, Entrepreneur, Diplomat* purports to illuminate its subject by means of the affinity of a shared native American point of view. Books such as Philip Barbour's *Pocahontas and Her World* now sound dated.

In "Pocahontas at the Masque" Karen Robertson claims that "It would be a mistake to see her as only a trophy of colonization or tragic victim." Somehow she is able to discern in the surviving fragments of Matoaka's life "traces of a subjectivity not simply produced within European discourses of the savage, but a self constructed within a different set of cultural assumptions."

Terrence Malick's picturesque and evocative romantic fantasy of John Smith and Pocahontas, *The New World,* takes considerable liberties with the historical story, shifting around dates and characters for purposes that are not always clear to me. It all works within the film's own self-defined bounds so long as you don't expect historical fidelity. Like the Disney *Pocahontas,* Malick's film imagines a romance between Matoaka and John Smith. A couple of actors from the Disney film reappear in it: Irene Bedard, who did the speaking voice of Disney's Pocahontas, plays her mother in Malick's film, while Christian Bale also had roles in both productions.

Tom Cain has discussed the ideology of colonization in the works of JOHN DONNE.

Joseph Quincy Adams's *Shakespearean Playhouses* discusses playhouse-inns such as the Bell Savage and the White Hart. For more on THE BELL SAVAGE INN AND PLAYHOUSE, see Herbert Berry's article in *Medieval and Renaissance Drama in England.*

Much of the writing on LADY MARY WROTH has been oriented to feminist interpretation of her work, so that until recently it has been difficult to obtain some basic facts about her life. Gary F. Waller's tortured *The Sidney Family Romance* adds an additional layer of Freudian theory (to convey the fluidity of gender Waller often puts the word "man" within quotes). Happily, this omission has recently been rectified by Margaret P. Hannay's admirable biography, *Mary Sidney, Lady Wroth*. For readers not ready to tackle such a substantial work, the best brief biography I know appears in Josephine A. Roberts's *The Poems of Lady Mary Wroth*. Naomi Miller focuses on Wroth's "female vision of community." Bernadette Andrea sees her subtly working the margin between self-effacement and self-assertion. Nona Fienberg views her work as an interior journey of self-discovery. Ann Rosalind Jones compares her work to that of Gaspara Stampa. See also Katharina M. Wilson's *Women Writers of the Renaissance and Reformation*.

The case of the Chinese wet nurse who committed suicide appears in Timothy Brook's *The Confusions of Pleasure*.

Silvia Brown and Christine W. Sizemore are among those who have written on DOROTHY LEIGH.

Wendy Perkins's *Midwifery and Medicine in Early Modern France* is the most substantial study of LOUISE BOURGEOIS. I found Bridgette Sheridan's "At Birth: The Modern State, Modern Medicine, and the Royal Midwife Louise Bourgeois in Seventeenth-Century France" to be helpful. See also Natalie Zemon Davis, *Society and Culture in Early Modern France: Eight Essays*. For an overview of early modern midwifery, see Hilary Marlin's *The Art of Midwifery: Early Modern Midwives in Europe*.

Ellison Findly's biography *Nur Jahan, Empress of Mughal India* was my main source for NUR JAHAN.

There has been a lot written about the YOSHIWARA PLEASURE DISTRICT, *ukiyo-e* paintings, and Japanese courtesans and geisha, though most focuses on a later historical period. For my present purposes, Cecilia Segawa Seigle's *Yoshiwara: The Glittering World of the Japanese Courtesan* was most helpful.

GASPARA STAMPA has been annointed a member of the core Western canon by the self-appointed arbiter Harold Bloom, and there is a generous body of material on her. Ann Rosalind Jones's *The Currency of Eros: Women's Love Lyric in Europe, 1540–1620* and Katharina M. Wilson's *Women Writers of the Renaissance and Reformation* contain essays on Stampa that can provide an entry for further research.

The Norton Critical edition of Thomas Middleton and Thomas Dekker's THE ROARING GIRL, edited by Jennifer Panek, includes fourteen critical essays.

There has been a fair amount written on CATALINA DE ERAUSO, most of it, unsurprisingly, strongly oriented to gender studies, and for the most part rather repetitive. One might hope for future scholars to address the basic factual problems of her biography, which are substantial (it is difficult to reconcile various dates associated with her). A section in Stephanie Merrim's *Early Modern Women's Writing and Sor Juana Inés de la Cruz* is one of the better treatments of de Erauso. Sherry Velasco, in *The Lieutenant Nun: Transgenderism, Lesbian Desire, and Catalina de Erauso*, does a particularly good job of considering the cultural reception of de Erauso's story. Among others who have written on her are Jerome R. Adams and Eva Mendieta. *Lieutenant Nun: Memoir of a Basque Transvestite in the New World* is a competent recent translation by Michele Stepto and Gabriel Stepto of the memoir attributed to de Erauso.

R. Ward Bissell's *Artemisia Gentileschi and the Authority of Art: Critical Reading and Catalogue Raisonné* provides an exellent overview of the career of ARTEMISIA GENTILESCHI. David Topper and Cynthia Gillis have explored the possibility of influence from Galileo's work with parabolas on her painting. See also works by Keith Christiansen, Elizabeth Cropper, and Mary D. Garrard.

Creative Imitation

For DONG QICHANG (Tung Ch'i-ch'ang in the old Wade-Giles transliteration system), see the two-volume *The Century of Tung Ch'i-ch'ang*, but be aware you will need a wheelbarrow to get it home. Additional resources include the *Proceedings of the Tung Ch'i-Ch'ang International Symposium* and *The Compelling Image* and *The Distant Mountains* and other works by James Cahill.

Pieter Roelofs's *Hendrick Avercamp: Master of the Ice Scene* and Ariane Van Suchtelen's *Holland Frozen in Time: The Dutch Winter Landscape in the Golden Age* are richly illustrated resources on the ice scene paintings of HENDRICK AVERCAMP. Bravo to LACMA for making high-resolution images of *Winter Scene on a Frozen Canal* (pp. 144–145) and other works freely available online on the grounds that they are in the public domain. More museums should follow LACMA's example.

Brian Fagan's wide-ranging *The Little Ice Age: How Climate Made History, 1300–1850* is the most accessible and appealing book on the LITTLE ICE AGE that I know of. Another source to consult is H. H. Lamb's more technical *Climate, History and the Modern World*.

For HENDRICK GOLTZIUS I found Huigen Leeflang and Ger Luijten's handsomely illustrated *Hendrick Goltzius (1558–1617): Drawings, Prints and Paintings* most helpful.

I am indebted to Theodore K. Rabb (*The Last Days of the Renaissance*) for the argument, which I have closely followed here, that the painting career of PETER PAUL RUBENS reflects a progression from glorification of militarism to revulsion for it. Mark Lamster's *Master of Shadows* is a readable book on the painter's diplomatic career, although it strains at times in an effort to cast Rubens's diplomatic work as something akin to a spy adventure. Kristin Lohse Belkin's *Rubens*, from Phaidon Press, is a convenient concise introduction to the artist.

Tsueno Takeda's *Kano Eitoku* is a clear if somewhat dated introduction to the KANO SCHOOL OF JAPANESE PAINTING. Sandy Kita studies IWASA MATABEI in *The Last Tosa: Iwasa Katsumochi Matabei, Bridge to Ukiyo-e*.

There are many good books on MUGHAL PAINTING. One of my favorites is *Painting the Mughal Experience* by Som Prakash Verma, whose other books on this topic include one devoted to the Mughal painter Mansur. I also relied heavily on Orataoaditya Pal's *Master Artists of the Imperial Mughal Court*. Susan Stronge's *Made for Mughal Emperors* is an excellent recent title focusing on life in and around the workshops of Akbar, Jahangir, and Shah Jahan. Other helpful titles include Ashok Kumar Srivastava's *Mughal Painting: An Interplay of Indigenous and Foreign Traditions*, Wheeler M. Thackston's illustrated and annotated translation of the *Jahangirnama*, and Elaine Wright's *Muraqqa'*.

Sheila Canby dominates RIZA-YI ABBASI studies. Her *The Rebellious Reformer* is a beautifully produced book (though lacking an index and difficult to navigate since the images are not in numerical order) providing the best guide to the artist's life and work. Unfortunately, it can b-e hard to find — there seems not to be a single copy in the entire University of California system. Another excellent book by Canby is *Shah Abbas and the Remaking of Iran* (where reproductions tend to be larger). For more titles by Canby, see the list of Selected Reading.

Information about CHEN JIRU and WU BIN relies on *The Distant Mountains* and other works by James Cahill, and on Chinese painting in general I have at times consulted curators in the Chinese art department at the Asian Art Museum, San Francisco.

Witch Hunters and Truth Seekers
John Henry's slim *The Scientific Revolution and the Origins of Modern Science* is a great little sourcebook on themes in EARLY MODERN EUROPEAN SCIENCE.

Recent books on JOHANNES KEPLER are not necessarily improvements over earlier works. Max Caspar's 1959 *Kepler* remains the standard biography, but Arthur Koestler's *The Watershed,* which was originally part of his *The Sleepwalkers,* is well written (and shorter); Koestler strongly admires Kepler and favors him over Galileo. James A. Conner's *Kepler's Witch* is a biography framed around his mother's witchcraft trial. Despite repetitions, it is a sincere and useful book, but HarperOne should be ashamed of their failure to adequately copy edit it, a failure that leaves the reader confronting many embarrassing sentences such as "She was, like her father, a practical woman." Books by Kitty Ferguson and Joshua and Anne-Lee Gilder focus on Kepler's relationship with Tycho Brahe.

There is a wealth of material on GALILEO. Stillman Drake's many publications remain the core texts in English. Drake helped to recast the scientist as a defender of the faith rather than a challenger of it. James Reston's *Galileo: A Life* is a good more recent work aimed at a more general audience. William R. Shea focuses on Galileo's fertile middle period. Dava Sobel's *Galileo's Daughter* fleshes out a relationship I've only touched on here. There is a helpful list of further reading as well as a useful chronology at the online Galileo Project: http://galileo.rice.edu/lib/bibliography.html.

In books like *Islamic Mathematical Astronomy* and *Islamic Science and the Making of the European Renaissance,* respectively, David A. King and George Saliba have led recent investigation into SCIENCE IN THE ISLAMIC WORLD. John Freely also discusses connections between Islamic and European science. *Islamic Science* by Seyyed Hossein Nasr is an illustrated overview, while *Science, Tools and Magic* by Francis Maddison and Emilie Savage-Smith is a beautifully illustrated look at Islamic scientific instuments. *Astrolabes of the World,* originally published in 1932 by a curator at the Ashmolean Museum in Oxford, is scholarly and valuable but marred by passages expressing the prejudices of the time, such as "It has been pointed out that the Koran does not contain a single precept that is favourable to the study of Natural Science. It is therefore scarcely a matter for surprise that for the first century after the Hegira in A.D. 622, the thoughts of the fanatical followers of Mohammed were directed to spread their creed by sword rather than by reason."

Majid Fakhry has written on ISLAMIC PHILOSOPHY,

and Ibrahim Kalin has produced substantial work on MULLA SADRA. The *Encyclopaedia of Islam* and the online *Encyclopædia Iranica* are generally helpful on science, philosophy, and other topics related to the Islamic world.

Nicholas Goodrick-Clarke's *The Western Esoteric Traditions* is a fine, readable introduction to the history of ESOTERIC THOUGHT in the West.

Francis Yates's politically oriented *The Rosicrucian Enlightenment* is the work on ROSECRUCIANISM to which most others refer. It includes the text of the *Chemical Wedding of Christian Rosenkreutz. The Rosicrucian Enlightenment Revisited,* a collection of papers from two conferences held in 1995 and 1997, updates and expands on Yates's work with mixed success. Susanna Åkerman has discussed the spread of Rosicrucianism in Northern Europe.

Though a tad stuffy, George Perrigo Cooper's *Theories of Macrocosms and Microcosms in the History of Philosophy* remains a useful guide to the topic of MACROCOSMS AND MICROCOSMS.

On the INNER ALCHEMY of Taoism I like Stephen Little's *Taoism and the Arts of China,* and of course Joseph Needham also has much to say on inner alchemy and on Chinese science in general. A more recent work updating and complementing Needham's is *On Their Own Terms* by Benjamin A. Elman.

I have followed David Tod Roy in my understanding of THE PLUM IN THE GOLDEN VASE (*Jin Ping Mei*).

Carl J. Ernst's "Being Careful with the Goddess: Yoginis in Persian and Arabic Texts" is the groundbreaking work on Pietro della Valle and the Kamarupa Seed Syllables. It is available from Manohar Publishers. An online version can be found through a web search. Mircea Eliade wrote on Tantrism in his book *Yoga.*

Andrew Weeks's *Boehme: An Intellectual Biography of the Seventeenth-Century Philosopher and Mystic* is inescapable on JACOB BOEHME. At a more general level, Nicholas Goodrick-Clarke's *The Western Esoteric Traditions* is, again, good on this, as on other topics. Antoine Faivre and Jacob Needleman's *Modern Esoteric Spirituality* includes a chapter on Boehme by Pierre Deghaye.

There seems to be no thorough comparative global study of WITCHCRAFT AND WITCH HUNTS. Despite its subtitle, Wolfgang Behringer's *Witches and Witch-Hunts: A Global History,* though interesting, is more a sociological investigation of witchcraft than a true global history. Behringer's primary research has been in early modern European witchcraft, as his *Witchcraft Persecutions in Bavaria: Popular Magic, Religious Zealotry and Reason of State in Early Modern Europe* suggests. Michael D. Bailey's *Magic and Superstition in Europe* is a good single-volume overview. Other titles include Carlo Ginzburg's *Night Battles,* Brian Levack's *New Perspectives on Witchcraft, Magic, and Demonology,* Lyndal Roper's *Witch Craze,* and Charles Zika's *Exorcising Our Demons.*

In the discussion of THOMAS MIDDLETON and his relation to some of the plays of Shakespeare I have followed Gary Taylor and John Lavagnino from their comprehensive *Thomas Middleton and Early Modern Textual Culture: A Companion to the Collected Works,* which is a model of modern scholarship. Following are the lyrics to "Come Away, Hecate, Come Away," from Middleton, *The Witch,* and Shakespeare and Middleton, *The Tragedy of Macbeth:*

Come Away, Hecate, Come Away

Come away, come away, Hecate,
Hecate, O come away.
I come, I come, I come, I come, I come
With all the speed I may
With all the speed I may
Where's Stadlin? Here!
Where's Puckle? Here!
And Hoppo too, and Helway too.
We lack but you, we lack but you.
Come away, make up the count,
I will but 'noint, and then I mount.
I will but 'noint, and then I mount.
Here comes one down to fetch his dues,
A kiss, a coll, a sip of blood.
And why thou stay'st so long I muse, I muse,
Since the art's so fresh and good.
O, art thou come? What news, what news?
All goes well to our delight.
Either come, or else refuse, refuse.
Now I am furnished for the flight,
Now I go, O now I fly
Malkin, my sweet sprite, and I
O what a dainty pleasure is this
To ride in the air
When the moon shines fair
And laugh, and sing, and toy, and kiss.
Over woods, high rocks, and mountains,
Over seas and crystal fountains,
Over steeples, towers, and turrets,
We flight tonight 'mongst troops of spirits.
No ring of bells to our ears sounds,
No howl of wolves, nor yelps of hounds,
No nor the noise of water breach,
Nor cannon's throat our height can reach.

For FRANS FRANCKEN II, see works by Arthur K. Wheelock, Jr. and Ursula Alice Härting.

Readers interested in the witch RANGDA should consult Natasha Reichle's fine *Bali: Art, Ritual, Performance.*

On THE HARMONY OF THE SPHERES AND THE PYTHAGOREAN TRADITION, see Siglind Bruhn's offbeat but scholarly *The Musical Order of the World: Kepler, Hesse, Hindemith* and Kitty Ferguson's *The Music of Pythagoras* (which is aimed at a more popular audience), as well of course as Kepler's own *The Harmony of the World* and liner notes to Hindemith's opera. Ferguson has recently taken up the subject of Pythagoras again in a book entitled *Pythagoras: His Lives and the Legacy of a Rational Universe,* published by Icon Books, which I have not had the opportunity to review.

Hereward Tilton has written on MICHAEL MAIER. *Atalanta Fugiens* is available in an attractive edition from Phanes Press.

Mark R. Cohen has edited and translated LEON MODENA's *Life of Judah* under the title *The Autobiography of a Seventeenth-Century Venetian Rabbi.*

Christopher R. Friedrichs's "Politics or Pogrom?" makes a good starting point for investigating the FETTMILCH UPRISINGS.

Works on MILLENNARIANISM include those by John M. Court, Matt Goldish and Richard Henry Popkin, David S. Katz and Popkin, and Karl A. Kottman. The story of Shah Abbas and the Nuqtavis is told by Sanjay Subrahmanyam in *Beyond Binary Histories.*

For a comprehensive history of the THIRTY YEARS WAR, see Peter H. Wilson's *The Thirty Years War: Europe's Tragedy.*

Siglind Bruhn relates PAUL HINDEMITH to the Pythagorean tradition in *The Musical Order of the World: Kepler, Hesse, Hindemith.*

World in Motion
Although I learned early on that Giovanni Lanfranco, Agostino Tassi, and Carlo Saraceni worked on the QUIRINALE FRESCOES, shown on pp. 252, 321, and 335, I had difficulty determining which artists worked on which panels. Rudolf Wittkomer writes of these frescoes in *Art and Architecture in Italy 1600–1750,* "The division of hands between the artists participating is not easily established." I tried many different approaches to resolving the question (among them posting an appeal on my blog, *blog.rightreading.com*) and finally wrote to nine academic specialists in early modern Italian painting. Seven failed to respond, and another responded that she could be of no assistance. Happily, Eunice Howe of USC was the exception. She suggested that the image on p. 252 was by Lanfranco based on its similarity to a study in the British Museum and suggested some avenues for further research. Later I discovered that the Lanfranco attribution is confirmed in an article by Walter Vitzthum. One of the images on p. 321 is identified as by Saraceni in Ann Ottani Cavina's book on the artist, and the image on p. 335 is identified as by Tassi in Steffi Roettgen's mammoth *Italian Frescoes of the Baroque Era, 1600–1800.* There are discussions of the frescoes in Kate Lowe's *'Representing Africa'* and in *The Image of the Black in Western Art* by David Bindman, Henry Louis Gates, Jr., and Karen C.C. Dalton.

PIETRO DELLA VALLE's *Viaggi* are available online in the original Italian. A condensed version has been convincingly translated into English by George Bull as *The Pilgrim: The Travels of Pietro Della Valle.* Another readable translation and retelling of della Valle's journeys, supplemented by observations from contemporaneous travelers, is Wilfred Blunt's *Pietro's Pilgrimage: A Journey to India and Back at the Beginning of the Seventeenth Century.* Translations from the *Viaggi* in this book are usually drawn from Bull or Blunt, sometimes reworked by me.

On British travelers in general, Boies Penrose's still readable *Travel and Discovery in the Renaissance* and *Urbane Travelers 1591–1635,* though not in a style currently in favor, are lively, artful, and amusing. Samuel C. Chew's *The Crescent and the Rose: Islam and England During the Renaissance,* also long in the tooth, remains a first-rate account of the influence of contacts with the the Islamic world on English Renaissance and early modern literature.

My primary source for the particulars of THE HAJJ during this period was Suraiya Faroqhi's *Pilgrims and Sultans: The Hajj Under the Ottomans, 1517–1683.*

The journeys of WILLIAM LITHGOW are detailed in Boies Penrose's *Urbane Travelers* and, more recently, in

Clifford Edmund Bosworth's *An Intrepid Scot.* Lithgow's book is in print in a paperback version, but it does not include the later travels.

B.G. Tamaskar's *The Life and Work of Malik Ambar* is unfortunately rather dry, but Richard Eaton's *A Social History of the Deccan, 1300–1761* has a good chapter on MALIK AMBAR. *The Encyclopaedia of Islam* is, as often, helpful.

Philip Curtin has done foundational work on the Atlantic slave trade and plantation SLAVERY. Charles H. Parker's *Global Interactions in the Early Modern Age, 1400–1800* contains a substantial section on the slave trade, and John E. Wills's *The World from 1450 to 1700* has a brief but cogent one. Consult Virginia Bernhard's *Slaves and Slaveholders in Bermuda 1616–1782* for a good history of Bermuda slavery. See also works by F.P. Bowser, Robert C. Davis, G.A. Beltrán, Susie Minchin and Linda A. Newson, and John Leddy Phelan.

María Antonia Garcés discusses CERVANTES's years as a slave in *Cervantes in Algiers: A Captive's Tale.* Her book has been much praised and has won awards; for a dissenting view, see a review in the *Bulletin of the Cervantes Society of America* by Michael McGaha. See also A.M. Rodríguez-Rodríguez on Antonio de Sosa and slavery in Algiers. Donald McCrory's biography of Cervantes is sound and readable.

William Spencer's *Algiers in the Age of the Corsairs* is a little jewel on the subject of ALGIERS and the OTTOMAN CORSAIRS of NORTH AFRICA. Another book on this subject is John B. Wolf's *The Barbary Coast.* On the subject of SIEMEN DANZIKER and YUSUF REIS (JACK WARD), particularly from the standpoint of their impact on English literature, see Samuel C. Chew's *The Crescent and the Rose: Islam and England During the Renaissance.*

The Encyclopedia of Islam and Stephen Dale's *The Muslim Empires of the Ottomans, Safavids, and Mughals* proved the best sources on the Islamic WAQFS.

For GEORGE STRACHAN see G.L. Dellavida, *George Strachan: Memorials of a Wandering Scottish Scholar of the Seventeenth Century.*

My main sources for HEO GYUN are *Borderland Roads: Selected Poems of Hŏ Kyun,* translated and with an introduction by Ian Haight and Tae-young Ho, and the chapter devoted to him in Kichung Kim's *Introduction to Classical Korean Literature.* The poem "At the Refugee Camp" is reprinted from *Borderland Roads* by permission of White Pine Press.

Probably the best single resource on THE JAPANESE INVASIONS OF KOREA is Kenneth M. Swope's *A Dragon's Head and a Serpent's Tail: Ming China and the First Great East Asian War, 1592–1598.* On a related topic, Swope has an article on the Wanli emperor as a military leader in *Culture, Courtiers, and Competition: The Ming Court (1368–1644),* edited by David M. Robinson.

Though it does show its age, I like A.C. Wratislaw's "The Diary of an Embassy" on GARCIA DE SILVA Y FIGUEROA.

It's not hard to find information on THOMAS, ANTHONY, AND ROBERT SHERLEY. Some good places to start would be Boies Penrose's *The Sherleian Odyssey,* Samuel C. Chew's *The Crescent and the Rose,* and Sheila R. Canby's *Shah 'Abbas: The Remaking of Iran.*

The story of Robert Devereaux's farcical coup attempt is well told in James Shapiro's excellent *A Year in the Life of William Shakespeare.*

Kennon Breazeale's "Whirligig of Diplomacy" and Yoshiteru Iwamoto's "Yamada Nagamasa and His Relations with Siam," both from the *Journal of the Siam Society,* are helpful on YAMADA NAGAMASA. See also Chaiwat Khamchoo and E. Bruce Reynolds, *Thai-Japanese Relations in Historical Perspective.* Khien Theeravit's dissertation on this topic can be found online.

On AYUTTHAYA, with an emphasis on its art, see Forrest McGill's *The Kingdom of Siam.*

On WILL ADAMS, see books by William Corr and Giles Milton. His story was made into a novel by the twentieth-century Japanese novelist Shusaku Endo, translated into English by Van C. Gessel as *The Samurai.*

Surprisingly little work appears to have been done on Date Masamune and the embassy of HASEKURA TSUNENAGA to Europe. One of the best sources in English remains G. Meriweather's 1893 account in the *Transactions of the Asiatic Society of Japan.* CHIMALPAHIN'S *Annals* have been translated with helpful annotations and supplementary information by James Lockhart, Susan Schroeder, and Doris Namala.

Views of Seventeenth-Century Vietnam by Olga Dror and K.W. Taylor masterfully tells the story of CHRISTOFORO BORRI in Vietnam (and elsewhere).

The story of THOMAS CORYATE has often been told, so I have not devoted a lot of space to it here. Michael Strachan's *The Life and Adventures of Thomas Coryate* is probably the best place to start, after Coryate's own works. Strachan has, among other things, compiled a comprehensive list of the members of Coryate's circle, including those who contributed verses to the *Crudities,* those who were invited to a "Convivium Philosophicum" at a tavern in which Coryate participated, and those who are mentioned in Coryate's letters. See also Boies Penrose's *Urbane Travelers 1591–1635,* Katharine Craik's *Reading Sensations in Early Modern England,* and Samuel C. Chew's *The Crescent and the Rose.*

The section on XU XIAKE relies heavily on Julian Ward's *Xu Xiake (1586–1641): The Art of Travel Writing.* Xu also appears in Timothy Brooks's *The Confusions of Pleasure.* Susan Naquin's *Pilgrims and Sacred Sites in China* contains an essay by James Cahill on Huang Shan paintings as pilgrimage pictures. For a contemporary poetic take informed by the Chinese attitude to mountains, see Gary Snyder's *Mountains and Rivers Without End.*

Stephen Bertman, in a brief online summary of Pietro della Valle's life and travels for *Biblical Archaeology Review,* mentions the "aroma, faint but pungent, not unlike camphor" that lingered in della Valle's home.

Epilogue: Christmas, His Masque

Christmas, His Masque was probably performed on Christmas day, but the exact date cannot be verified. This section owes a debt to Leah Sinanoglou Marcus's "'Present Occasions' and the Shaping of Ben Jonson's Masques."

Youth Reading, 1620s, by
Riza-yi Abbasi. Opaque
watercolor on paper. 8 x 14
cm. British Museum, inv. no.
1920.9.17.0298.3.

Selected Reading
See also Source Notes, p. 361.

Abril Curto, Gonzalo. "Conflictos culturales y estrategias discursivas en dos textos de la América colonial hispana." Article, 2003. http://eprints.ucm.es/4915/.

Adams, Jerome R. *Notable Latin American Women: Twenty-Nine Leaders, Rebels, Poets, Battlers and Spies, 1500–1900.* Jefferson, NC: Mcfarland and Company, 1995.

Adams, Joseph Quincy. *Shakespearean Playhouses.* 1917. Reprint Gloucester, Mass.: P. Smith, 1960.

Adams, Percy G. "The Discovery of America and European Renaissance Literature." *Comparative Literature Studies* 13, no. 2 (1976): 100–115.

Adams, Percy G. *Travel Literature and the Evolution of the Novel.* Lexington: University Press of Kentucky, 1983.

Adorno, Rolena. *Guaman Poma and His Illustrated Chronicle from Colonial Peru: From a Century of Scholarship to a New Era of Reading.* Copenhagen: Museum Tusculanum Press, 2001.

Adorno, Rolena, and Ivan Boserup. *New Studies of the Autograph Manuscript of Felipe Guaman Poma De Ayala's Nueva Coronica y Buen Gobierno.* Copenhagen: Museum Tusculanum Press, 2003.

Adorno, Rolena. *The Polemics of Possession in Spanish American Narrative.* New Haven: Yale University Press, 2008.

Adorno, Rolena. *Guaman Poma: Writing and Resistance in Colonial Peru.* Austin: University of Texas Press, 1986.

Ahmed I. *Letters from the Great Turke Lately Sent Vnto the Holy Father the Pope and to Rodulphus Naming Himselfe King of Hungarie, and to All the Kinges and Princes of Christendome.* London: John Windet; reprinted Da Capo Press, 1971.

A. K. C. "Mughal Painting (Akbar and Jahangir)" in *Museum of Fine Arts Bulletin* 16, no. 93 (Feb. 1918): 2–8.

Åkerman, Susanna. *Rose Cross over the Baltic: The Spread of Rosicrucianism in Northern Europe.* Boston: Brill, 1998.

Alam, Muzaffar, and Sanjay Subrahmanyam. *Indo-Persian Travels in the Age of Discoveries, 1400–1800 .* Cambridge: Cambridge University Press, 2007.

Alderson, A. D. "Sir Thomas Sherley's Piratical Expedition to the Aegean and His Imprisonment in Constantinople." *Oriens* 9, no. 1 (1956): 1–40.

Allen, Paula Gunn. *Pocahontas: Medicine Woman, Spy, Entrepreneur, Diplomat.* San Francisco: HarperSanFrancisco, 2003.

Alvarez, J. L. "Don Rodrigo de Vivero et la Destruction de la Nao 'Madre de Deos' (1609 à 1610)." Pierre Humbertclaude, S. M., trans. *Monumenta Nipponica* 2, no. 2 (Jul. 1939): 479–511.

Ames, Glenn J., and Ronald S. Love. *Distant Lands and Diverse Cultures: The French Experience in Asia, 1600–1700.* Westport, CT: Praeger, 2003.

Andrade, Tonio. "The Company's Chinese Pirates: How the Dutch East India Company Tried to Lead a Coalition of Pirates to War against China, 1621–1662." *Journal of World History* 15, no. 4 (December 2004): 415–444.

Andrade, Tonio. *How Taiwan Became Chinese: Dutch, Spanish, and Han Colonization in the Seventeenth Century.* Columbia: Columbia University Press, 2008.

Andrea, Bernadette. "Pamphilia's Cabinet: Gendered Authorship and Empire in Lady Mary Wroth's *Urania.* *English Literary History* 68, no. 2 (Summer, 2001): 335–358.

Ansary, Tamim. *Destiny Disrupted: A History of the World through Islamic Eyes.* New York: PublicAffairs, 2009.

Arzáns de Orsúa y Vela, Bartolome. *Tales of Potosí.* Providence, RI: Brown University Press, 1975.

Asher, Catherine B., and Cynthia Talbot. *India before Europe.* New York: Cambridge University Press, 2006.

Aughterson, Kate. *Renaissance Woman: A Sourcebook: The Construction of Femininities in England 1520–1680.* New York: Routledge, 1995.

Axworthy, Michael. *A History of Iran: Empire of the Mind.* New York: Basic Books, 2008.

Bailey, Michael D. *Magic and Superstition in Europe: A Concise History from Antiquity to the Present (Critical Issues in History).* Lanham: Rowman and Littlefield, 2006.

Bakewell, Peter J. *Silver Mining and Society in Colonial Mexico, Zacatecas 1546–1700.* New York: Cambridge University Press, 1972.

Bakewell, Peter J. *Miners of the Red Mountain: Indian Labor in Potosi, 1545–1650.* Albuquerque: University of New Mexico Press, 1984.

Bandelier, Adolph F., and Madeleine Turrell Rodack. "History of the Colonization and Missions of Sonora, Chihuahua, New Mexico and Arizona to the Year 1700." *Journal of the Southwest* 30, no. 1 (Spring 1988): 47–120.

Barbour, Philip. *Pocahontas and Her World a Chronicle of America's First Settlement in Which Is Related the Story of the Indians and the Englishmen, Particularly Captain John Smith, Captain Samuel Argall, and Master John Rolfe.* Boston: Houghton Mifflin, 1970.

Barker, Andrew. "A Report of Captaine Ward and Danseker, Pirates." http://zeerovery.nl/history/barker01.htm.

Barnhart, Richard M. "Dong Qichang and Western Learning: A Hypothesis in Honor of James Cahill." *Archives of Asian Art* 50 (1997/1998): 7–16.

Barton, Anne. *Ben Jonson: Dramatist.* New York: Cambridge University Press, 1984.

Bassett, D. K. "European Influence in South-East Asia, c.1500–1630." *Journal of Southeast Asian History* 4, no. 2 (Sep. 1963): 134–165.

Beach, Milo Cleveland. "The Mughal Painter Abu'l Hasan and Some English Sources for His Style" in *The Journal of the Walters Art Gallery,* Vol. 38 (1980): 6–33.

Bearman, P. J., Th. Bianquis, C. E. Bosworth, E. van Donzel, and W.P. Heinrichs et al., eds. *Encyclopædia of Islam,* 2nd Edition (12 vols.). Leiden: E. J. Brill, 1960–2005.

Behringer, Wolfgang. *Witchcraft Persecutions in Bavaria: Popular Magic, Religious Zealotry and Reason of State in Early Modern Europe.* Cambridge: Cambridge University Press, 2002.

Behringer, Wolfgang. *Witches and Witch-Hunts: A Global History.* Cambridge, UK: Polity Press, 2004.

Belkin, Kristin Lohse. *Rubens.* London: Phaidon, 1998.

Beltrán, G. A. "The Slave Trade in Mexico." *Hispanic American Historical Review* 24, no. 3 (1944): 412–431.

Bernhard, Virginia. *Slaves and Slaveholders in Bermuda 1616–1782.* Columbia: University of Missouri Press, 1999.

Bernini, Giovanni-Pietro. *Giovanni Lanfranco (1582–1647).* Parma: Centro Studi della Val Bagenza, 1985.

Bernstein, William J. *A Splendid Exchange: How Trade Shaped the World.* New York: Atlantic Monthly, 2008.

Berry, Herbert. "The Bell Savage Inn and Playhouse in London." *Medieval and Renaissance Drama in England* 19 (2006): 121–143.

Bertman, Stephen. "Il Fantastico: The Strange Pilgrimage of Pietro Della Valle," *Biblical Archaeology Review,* http://www.bib-arch.org/online-exclusives/il-fantastico.asp.

Bindman, David, Henry Louis Gates, Jr., and Karen C. C. Dalton. *The Image of the Black in Western Art.* Cambridge: Belknap Press, 2010.

Bissell, R. Ward. *Artemisia Gentileschi and the Authority of Art: Critical Reading and Catalogue Raisonné.* University Park, PA : Pennsylvania State University Press, 1999.

Bissell, R. Ward. "Artemisia Gentileschi—A New Documented Chronology." *The Art Bulletin* 50, no. 2 (Jun. 1968): 153–168.

Blunt, Wilfrid. *Pietro's Pilgrimage: A Journey to India and Back at the Beginning of the Seventeenth Century.* Philadelphia: J. Barrie, 1953.

Boehme, Jacob. *Confessions.* New York: Harper, 1954.

Boehme, Jacob. *The Signature of All Things.* Cambridge: James Clarke and Co., 1969.

Boehme, Jacob. *Six Theosophic Points and Other Writings.* Michigan: University of Michigan, 1971.

Borah, W. "Un gobierno provincial de frontera en San Luis Potosí (1612–1620)." *Historia Mexicana* 13, no. 4 (1964): 532–550.

Borg, Barbara E., and Glenn W. Most. "The Face of the Elite." *Arion* 8, no. 1. Third Series (April 1, 2000): 63–96.

Bose, Sugata. *A Hundred Horizons: The Indian Ocean in the Age of Global Empire.* Cambridge: Harvard University Press, 2009.

Bosworth, Clifford. *An Intrepid Scot: William Lithgow of Lanark's Travels in the Ottoman Lands, North Africa and Central Europe, 1609–21.* Aldershot, England: Ashgate, 2006.

Bowser, F. P. *The African Slave in Colonial Peru, 1524–1650.* Stanford, California: Stanford University Press, 1974.

Boxer, C. R. *The Christian Century in Japan 1549–1650.* Berkeley: University of California Press, 1967.

Boxer, C. *The Portuguese Seaborne Empire, 1415–1825.* London: Hutchinson, 1977.

Breazeale, Kennon. "Whirligig of Diplomacy: A Tale of Thai-Portuguese Relations, 1613–9." *Journal of the Siam Society* 94 (2006).

Briganti, Giuliano. *Il Palazzo del Quirinale.* Rome: Istituto Poligrafico dello Stato, 1962.

Brokaw, Galen. "The Poetics of Khipu Historiography: Felipe Guaman Poma de Ayala's 'Nueva corónica' and the 'Relación de los quipucamayos.'" *Latin American Research Review* 38, no. 3 (2003): 111–147.

Brook, Timothy. *The Chinese State in Ming Society.* New York: Routledge, 2004.

Brook, Timothy. *The Confusions of Pleasure: Commerce and Culture in Ming China.* Berkeley: University of California Press, 1998.

Brook, Timothy. *The Troubled Empire: China in the Yuan and Ming Dynasties.* Cambridge: Belknap Press of Harvard University Press, 2010.

Brook, Timothy. *Vermeer's Hat: The Seventeenth Century and the Dawn of the Global World.* New York: Bloomsbury Press, 2007.

Brotton, Jerry. *Trading Territories: Mapping the Early Modern World.* Ithaca: Cornell University Press, 1998.

Brotton, Jerry. *The Renaissance Bazaar: From the Silk Road to Michelangelo.* New York: Oxford University Press, 2002.

Brown, Claudia. *Weaving China's Past: The Amy S. Clague Collection of Chinese Textiles.* Phoenix: Phoenix Art Museum, 2001.

Brown, Silvia, ed. *Women's Writing in Stuart England: The Mothers' Legacies of Dorothy Leigh, Elizabeth Joscelin, and Elizabeth Richardson.* Gloucestershire: Sutton Publishing, 1999.

Bruhn, Siglind. *The Musical Order of the World: Kepler, Hesse, Hindemith.* Hillsdale, NY: Pendragon, 2005.

Bryson, Bill. *Shakespeare: The World as Stage.* New York: Harper Perennial, 2008.

Buisseret, David. "Spanish Military Engineers in the New World Before 1750." In Dennis Reinhartz and Gerald D. Saxon, eds., *Mapping and Empire: Soldier-Engineers on the Southwestern Frontier.* Austin: University of Texas Press, 2005. 44–56.

Cahill, James. *Compelling Image: Nature and Style in Seventeenth-Century Chinese Painting* (The Charles Eliot Norton Lectures, 1978–1979). Cambridge: Harvard University Press, 1982.

Cahill, James. *The Distant Mountains: Chinese Painting of the Late Ming Dynasty, 1570–1644.* New York: Weatherhill, 1982.

Cahill, James. "Late Ming Landscape Albums and European Printed Books." In Sandra Hindman, ed., *The Early Illustrated Book: Essays in Honor of Lessing J. Rosenwald.* Washington: Library of Congress, 1982.

Cahill, James. *Fantastics and Eccentrics in Chinese Painting.* New York: Asia Society, 1967.

Cahill, James. *The Painter's Practice: How Artists Lived and Worked in Traditional China.* New York: Columbia University Press, 1994.

Cahill, James. *The Restless Landscape: Chinese Painting of the Late Ming Period.* Berkeley: University Art Museum, 1971.

Cain, Tom. "John Donne and the Ideology of Colonization." *English Literary Renaissance* 31, no. 3 (September 2001): 440–476.

Canby, Sheila R. *The Golden Age of Persian Art, 1501–1722.* New York: Harry N. Abrams, 2000.

Canby, Sheila R. *Persian Painting.* Northhampton, Mass.: Interlink, 2005.

Canby, Sheila R. *Shah 'Abbas: The Remaking of Iran.* London: British Museum Press, 2009.

Caraman, Philip. *The Lost Paradise: The Jesuit Republic in South America.* New York: Seabury Press, 1976.

Carvalho, Pedro. *Luxury for Export: Artistic Exchange Between India and Portugal Around 1600.* Boston: Isabella Stewart Gardner Museum / Gutenberg Periscope Pub., 2008.

Casale, Giancarlo. *The Ottoman Age of Exploration.* Oxford: Oxford University Press, 2010.

Caspar, Max. *Kepler.* Translated and edited by C. Doris Hellman. New York: Abelard-Schuman, 1959.

Cavazzini, Patrizia. *Painting as Business in Early Seventeenth-Century Rome.* Pennsylvania: Pennsylvania State University Press, 2008.

Chang, Tien-Tse. "The Spanish-Dutch Naval Battle of 1617 outside Manila Bay." *Journal of Southeast Asian History* 7, no. 1 (Mar. 1966): 111–121.

Chew, Samuel C. *The Crescent and the Rose: Islam and England During the Renaissance.* New York: Octagon, 1974.

Chimalpahin Cuauhtlehuanitzin, Domingo. *Annals of His Time: Don Domingo De San Anton Munon Chimalpahin Quauhtlehuanitzin.* James Lockhart, Susan Schroeder, and Doris Namala, eds. and trans. Stanford: Stanford University Press, 2006.

Christensen, Thomas. "Gutenberg and the Koreans: Did Asian Printing Traditions Influence the European Renaissance?" http://www.rightreading.com/printing/gutenberg.asia/gutenberg-asia-1-introduction.htm.

Christian, John L, and Nobutake Ike. "Thailand in Japan's Foreign Relations." *Pacific Affairs* 15, no. 2 (Jun. 1942): 195–221.

Christiansen, Keith. "Becoming Artemisia: Afterthoughts on the Gentileschi Exhibition." *Metropolitan Museum Journal* 39 (2004): 10, 101–126.

Clark, G. N. "The Barbary Corsairs in the Seventeenth Century." *Cambridge Historical Journal* 8, no. 1 (1944): 22–35.

Clark, G. N. *The Seventeenth Century,* Oxford : The Clarendon Press, 1929.

Clayton, L. A. "Trade and Navigation in the Seventeenth-Century Viceroyalty of Peru." *Journal of Latin American Studies* 7, no. 01 (1975): 1–21.

Cleary, J. C. *Worldly Wisdom: Confucian Teachings of the Ming Dynasty.* Boston: Shambhala, 1991.

Cobb, Gwendoline B. "Supply and Transportation for the Potosi Mines, 1545–1640." *Hispanic American Historical Review* 29, no. 1 (1949), 24–45.

Cohn, Norman Rufus Colin. *Cosmos, Chaos, and the World to Come: The Ancient Roots of Apocalyptic Faith.* New Haven: Yale University Press, 1993.

Conner, James A. *Kepler's Witch: An Astronomer's Discovery of Cosmic Order Amid Religious War, Political Intrigue, and the Heresy Trial of His Mother.* San Francisco: HarperOne, 2004.

Connolly, Priscilla, and Roberto Mayer. "Vingboons, Trasmonte and Boot: European Cartography of Mexican Cities in the Early Seventeenth Century." *Imago Mundi* 61, no. 1 (January 2009): 47–66.

Cooper, George Perrigo. *Theories of Macrocosms and Microcosms in the History of Philosophy.* New York: Columbia University Press, 1922.

Corr, William. *Adams the Pilot: The Life and Times of Captain William Adams, 1564–1620.* Folkestone, Kent: Japan Library, 1995.

Coryate, Thomas. *Coryat's Crudities.* Glasgow: MacLehose and Sons, 1905.

Coryate, Thomas. *Greeting from the Court of the Great Mogul.* New York and Washington D.C.: Da Capo Press, 1968.

Court, John M. *Approaching the Apocalypse: A Short History of Christian Millennarianism.* London: I. B. Tauris, 2008.

"The Court and Times of James the First." http://www.archive.org/stream/courttimesofjame01bircuoft#page/n7/mode/2up.

Cousins, A.D., and Alison V. Scott, *Ben Jonson and the Politics of Genre.* Cambridge: Cambridge University Press, 2009.

Craik, Katharine. *Reading Sensations in Early Modern England.* New York: Palgrave Macmillan, 2007.

Croissant, Doris. *Japan und Europa 1543–1929.* Berlin: Argon, 1993.

Cropper, Elizabeth. "New Documents for Artemisia Gentileschi's Life in Florence." *The Burlington Magazine* 135, no. 1088 (Nov. 1993): 760–761.

Cruikshank, Bruce. "Manila Galleon Listing." https://sites.google.com/site/manilagalleonlisting/.

Cruysse, Dirk Van Der. *Siam and the West, 1500–1700.* Seattle: University of Washington Press, 2002.

Cunningham, Michael R. *Masterworks of Asian Art.* London: Thames and Hudson, 1998.

Curtin, Philip D. *The Rise and Fall of the Plantation Complex: Essays in Atlantic History.* Cambridge: Cambridge University Press, 1994.

Dale, Stephen F. *The Muslim Empires of the Ottomans, Safavids, and Mughals.* Cambridge: Cambridge University Press, 2010.

Dalrymple, David. "Memorials and Letters Relating to the History of Britain in the Reign of James the First." http://books.google.com/books?id=DlRjAAAAMAAJ&dq=dalrymple+memorials&source=gbs_navlinks_s.

Danielson, Dennis. *The Book of the Cosmos: Imagining the Universe from Heraclitus to Hawking.* Cambridge: Perseus Publishing, 2000.

Das Gupta, Ashin. *The World of the Indian Ocean Merchant, 1500–1800: Collected Essays of Ashin Das Gupta.* Oxford: Oxford University Press, 2001.

Davis, Natalie Zemon. *Society and Culture in Early Modern France: Eight Essays.* Stanford: Stanford University Press, 1975.

Davis, Robert C. "Counting European Slaves on the Barbary Coast." Past and Present, no. 172 (August 2001): 87–124.

Dennis, Richard. *The Book of the Cosmos: Imagining the Universe from Heraclitus to Hawking.* Cambridge: Perseus, 2000.

De la Cerda Silva, R. "Los Tepehuanes." *Revista Mexicana de Sociologia* 5, no. 4 (1943): 541–567.

Della Valle, Pietro. *The Pilgrim: The Travels of Pietro Della Valle.* George Bull. ed. London: Hutchinson, 1990.

Della Valle, Pietro. "Viaggi Di Pietro della Valle, Il Pellegrino: La Turchia, La Persia, E L'india by Pietro Della Valle." http://www.onread.com/book/Viaggi-Di-Pietro-Della-Valle-Il-Pellegrino-La-Turchia-La-Persia-E-L-india-659436.

Della Valle, Pietro. "Viaggi di Pietro della Valle." http://books.google.com/books?id=C-QNHn2XkCQC&ots=S41qtajNOP&dq=Viaggi%20Di%20Pietro%20Della%20Valle.

Dellavida, G. L. *George Strachan: Memorials of a Wandering Scottish Scholar of the Seventeenth Century.* Aberdeen: Third Spalding Club, 1956.

Den Dooven, Pierre. "La Sorcellerie au Ban de Spa." http://users.skynet.be/maevrard/sorcelleriespa.html.

Drake, Stillman. *Essays on Galileo and the History and Philosophy of Science.* N. M. Swerdlow and T. H. Levere, eds. Toronto: University of Toronto Press, 1999.

Drake, Stillman. *Galileo.* New York: Hill and Wang, 1980.

Drake, Stillman. *Galileo at Work: His Scientific Biography.* Chicago: University of Chicago Press, 1978.

Dressing, David. *Social Tensions in Early Seventeenth-Century Potosí* (Ph.D. diss.) Tulane University, 2008. http://proquest.umi.com/pqdweb?did=1432776441&sid=1&Fmt=2&clientId=79356&RQT=309&VName=PQD.

Dror, Olga, and K. W. Taylor. *Views of Seventeenth-Century Vietnam.* Ithaca: Southeast Asia Program Publications, Southeast Asia Program, Cornell University, 2006.

Dunn, Richard. *The Age of Religious Wars, 1559–1715.* New York: Norton, 1979.

Dutton, Richard. *Ben Jonson: To the First Folio.* Cambridge: Cambridge University Press, 1983.

Eaton, Richard M. *A Social History of the Deccan, 1300–1761: Eight Indian Lives.* New York: Cambridge University Press, 2005.

Eldem, Edhem, Daniel Goffman, and Bruce Masters. *The Ottoman City Between East and West: Aleppo, Izmir, and Istanbul.* New York: Cambridge University Press, 1999.

Eliade, Mircea. *Yoga: Immortality and Freedom.* William R. Trask, trans. Princeton: Princeton University Press, 1970.

Elliott, J. H. *Imperial Spain: 1469–1716.* Boston: Penguin, 2002.

Elman, Benjamin. *On Their Own Terms: Science in China, 1550–1900.* Cambridge: Harvard University Press, 2005.

"Encyclopædia Iranica," http://www.iranica.com/.

Endō Shūsaku. *The Samurai: A Novel.* New York: Harper and Row, 1982.

Eraly, Abraham. *The Mughal Throne: The Saga of India's Great Emperors.* London: Phoenix, 2004.

Erauso, Catalina de (attrib.). *Historia de la Monja Alferez.* Joaquin Maria de Ferrer, ed. Echévarri: Editorial Amigos del Libro Vasco, 1986 (facsimile of Paris: Julio Dido, 1829, edition).

Erauso, Catalina de (attrib.). *Lieutenant Nun: Memoir of a Basque Transvestite in the New World.* Boston: Beacon Press, 1996.

Erauso, Catalina de (attrib.), and Juan Pérez de Montalbán. *The Nun Ensign and La Monja Alférez.* Translated by James Fitzmaurice-Kelly. London: T. Fisher Unwin, 1908.

Erdoğan, Sema. *Sexual Life in Ottoman Society.* Istanbul: Dönence, 1996.

Ernst, Carl J. "Being Careful with the Goddess: Yoginis in Persian and Arabic Texts." In Pallabi Chakravorty and Scott Kugle, *Performing Ecstasy: The Poetics and Politics of Religion in India.* Delhi: Manohar Publishers, 2009.

Evenden, Doreen. *The Midwives of Seventeenth-Century London.* New York: Cambridge University Press, 2000.

Fagan, Brian. *The Little Ice Age : How Climate Made History, 1300–1850.* New York: Basic Books, 2000.

Faivre, Antoine, and Jacob Needleman. *Modern Esoteric Spirituality.* New York: Crossroad, 1992.

Fakhry, Majid. *A History of Islamic Philosophy.* New York: Columbia University Press, 1970, 1983.

Faroqhi, Suraiya. *Approaching Ottoman History: An Introduction to the Sources.* Cambridge: Cambridge University Press, 1999.

Faroqhi, Suraiya. *Pilgrims and Sultans: The Hajj Under the Ottomans, 1517–1683.* London: I. B. Tauris, 1994.

Ferrier, R. W. "The Armenians and the East India Company in Persia in the Seventeenth and Early Eighteenth Centuries." *The Economic History Review* 26, no. 1. New Series (January 1, 1973): 38–62.

Fei, Si-yen. *Negotiating Urban Space: Urbanization and Late Ming Nanjing.* Cambridge: Harvard University Asia Center, 2009.

Ferguson, Kitty. The *Music of Pythagoras : How an Ancient Brotherhood Cracked the Code of the Universe and Lit the Path from Antiquity to Outer Space.* New York: Walker and Co., 2002.

Ferguson, Kitty. *Tycho and Kepler: The Unlikely Partnership That Forever Changed Our Understanding of the Heavens.* New York: Walker and Co., 2002.

F. H. "The Pocahontas Portrait." *The Virginia Magazine of History and Biography* 35, no. 4 (Oct. 1927): 431–436.

Fienberg, Nona. "Mary Wroth's Poetics of the Self." *Studies in English Literature, 1500–1900,* vol. 42, no. 1, *The English Renaissance* (Winter, 2002): 121–136.

Findly, Ellison. *Nur Jahan, Empress of Mughal India.* New York: Oxford University Press, 1993.

Finkel, Caroline. *Osman's Dream: The History of the Ottoman Empire.* New York: Basic Books, 2006.

Flores, Jorge. *Goa and the Great Mughal.* London: Scala, 2004.

Flynn, Dennis O., and Arturo Giráldez. "Arbitrage, China, and World Trade in the Early Modern Period." *Journal of the Economic and Social History of the Orient* 38, no. 4 (1995): 429–448.

Flynn, Dennis O., Arturo Giráldez, and James Sobredo, eds. *European Entry into the Pacific: Spain and the Acapulco-Manila Galleons.* Aldershot: Ashgate, 2001.

Folsach, Kjeld, Nationalmuseet (Denmark). *Sultan, Shah, and Great Mughal: The History and Culture of the Islamic World.* Copenhagen: National Museum, 1996.

Fontenay, Michel. "L'Empire Ottoman et le risque corsaire au XVIIe siècle." *Revue d'histoire moderne et contemporaine (1954–)* 32, no. 2 (Apr./Jun. 1985): 185–208.

Foster, William. *Early Travels in India 1583–1619.* Oxford: Oxford University Press, 1921.

Fraser, Antonia. *King James VI of Scotland, I of England.* New York: Knopf, 1975.

Freely, John. *Aladdin's Lamp: How Greek Science Came to Europe through the Islamic World.* New York: Alfred A. Knopf, 2009.

Friedrichs, Christopher R. "Politics or Pogrom? The Fettmilch Uprising in German and Jewish History." *Central European History* 19, no. 2 (June 1986): 186–228.

"Galileo Timeline," *The Galileo Project.* http://galileo.rice.edu/chron/galileo.html.

Garcés, María Antonia. *Cervantes in Algiers: A Captive's Tale.* Nashville: Vanderbilt University Press, 2005.

Garrard, Mary D. *Artemisia Gentileschi around 1622: The Shaping and Reshaping of an Artistic Identity.* Berkeley: University of California Press, 2001.

Gelber, Harry. *The Dragon and the Foreign Devils: China and the World, 1100 B.C. to the Present.* New York: Walker and Company, 2007.

Gemelli Carreri, Juan Francisco. *Las Cosas Mas Considerables Vistas en la Nueva España.* Mexico: Ediciones Xochitl, 1946.

Gerhard, Peter. *Pirates on the West Coast of New Spain, 1575–1742.* Edinburgh: A. H. Clark, 1960.

Gernet, Jacques. *A History of Chinese Civilization.* Cambridge Cambridge: Cambridge University Press, 1982.

Gibbs, Sharon. *Planispheric Astrolabes from the National Museum of American History.* Washington: Smithsonian Institution Press, 1984.

Gilder, Joshua, and Anne-Lee Gilder. *Heavenly Intrigue: Johannes Kepler, Tycho Brahe, and the Murder Behind One of History's Greatest Scientific Discoveries.* New York: Doubleday, 2004.

Ginzburg, Carlo. *The Night Battles: Witchcraft and Agrarian Cults in the Sixteenth and Seventeenth Centuries.* John and Anne Tedeschi, trans. Boston: Penguin, 1985.

Goldish, Matt, and Richard Henry Popkin. *Jewish Messianism in the Early Modern World.* Millenarianism and Messianism in Early Modern European Culture, vol. 1. Dordrecht: Kluwer Academic, 2001.

Goodrick-Clarke, Nicholas. *The Western Esoteric Traditions: A Historical Introduction.* Oxford: Oxford University Press, 2008.

Goodwin, Jason. *Lords of the Horizons: A History of the Ottoman Empire.* New York: H. Holt, 1999.

Gradie, Charlotte M. *The Tepehuan Revolt of 1616: Militarism, Evangelism, and Colonialism in Seventeenth-Century Nueva Vizcaya.* Salt Lake City: University of Utah Press, 2000.

Greenblatt, Stephen J. *Renaissance Self-Fashioning: More to Shakespeare.* Chicago: University of Chicago Press, 1981.

Greer, Germaine, Susan Hastings, and Jeslyn Medoff. *Kissing the Rod: An Anthology of Seventeenth Century Women's Verse.* New York: Farrar Straus Giroux, 1989.

Gunther, Robert. *The Astrolabes of the World: Based Upon the Series of Instruments in the Lewis Evans Collection in the Old Ashmolean Museum at Oxford, with Notes on Astrolabes in the Collections of the British Museum, Science Museum, Sir J. Findlay, Mr S. V. Hoffman, the Mensing Collection, and in other Public and Private Collections.* London: The Holland Press, 1932, reprinted 1976.

Gurney, J. D. "Pietro della Valle: The Limits of Perception." *Bulletin of the School of Oriental and African Studies, University of London 49,* no. 1 (January 1, 1986): 103–116.

Hajek, Lubor. *Indian Miniatures of the Moghul School.* London: Spring Books, 1960.

Hakluyt, Richard. *Hakluyt's Voyages to the New World: A Selection.* Edited by David Freeman Hawke. Indianapolis: Bobbs-Merrill, 1972.

Hall, Richard. *Empires of the Monsoon: A History of the Indian Ocean and Its Invaders.* London: HarperCollins, 1996.

Hanna, Willard. *Bali Chronicles: A Lively Account of the Island's History from Early Times to the 1970s.* Singapore: Periplus, 2004.

Hannay, Margaret P. *Mary Sidney, Lady Wroth.* Farnham, Surrey: Ashgate, 2010.

Hansson, Anders, ed. *The Chinese at Play: Festivals, Games and Leisure.* London: Kegan Paul, 2002.

Hantman, J. L. "Between Powhatan and Quirank: Reconstructing Monacan Culture and History in the Context of Jamestown." *American Anthropologist* 92, no. 3 (1990): 676–690.

Härting, Ursula Alice. *Frans Francken der Jüngere (1581–1642): Die Gemälde mit Kritischem Oeuvrekatalog.* Freren: Luca, 1989.

Hearn, Maxwell K. *Splendors of Imperial China: Treasures from the National Palace Museum, Taipei.* New York: Metropolitan Museum of Art, 1996.

Heinemann, Margot. *Puritanism and Theatre.* New York: Cambridge University Press, 1980.

Henry, John. *The Scientific Revolution and the Origins of Modern Science.* Houndsmills, Basingstoke, Hampshire: Palgrave Macmillan, 2008.

Hirsh, James, ed. *New Perspectives on Ben Jonson.* Madison, NJ: Fairleigh Dickinson University Press, 1997.

Ho, Wai-kam, and William Rockhill. *Eight Dynasties of Chinese Painting: The Collections of the Nelson Gallery-Atkins Museum, Kansas City, and the Cleveland Museum of Art.* Cleveland: Cleveland Museum of Art 1980.

Hŏ Kyun. *Borderland Roads: Selected Poems of Hŏ Kyun.* Translated by Ian Haight and Tae-young Ho. Buffalo: White Pine, 2009.

Hŏ Nansŏrhŏn. *Vision of a Phoenix: The Poems of Hŏ Nansŏrhŏn.* Translated by Yang-hi Choe-Wall. Ithaca: East Asia Program, Cornell University, 2003.

Ho, Wai-Ching. *Proceedings of the Tung Ch'i-Ch'ang International Symposium.* Kansas City Mo.: Nelson-Atkins Museum of Art, 1991.

Hoberman, Louisa Schell. "Technological Change in a Traditional Society: The Case of the Desagüe in Colonial Mexico." *Technology and Culture* 21, no. 3 (1980): 386–407.

Hofstadter, Dan. *The Earth Moves: Galileo and the Roman Inquisition.* New York: W. W. Norton, 2009.

Hopkins, A. G., ed. *Globalization in World History.* New York: W. W. Norton, 2002.

Horne, Alistair. *La Belle France.* New York: Knopf, 2005.

Hough, W. "Oriental Influences in Mexico." *American Anthropologist* 2, no. 1 (1900): 66–74.

Huang, Ray. *1587, a Year of No Significance: The Ming Dynasty in Decline.* New Haven: Yale University Press, 1981.

Huang, Ray. *China: A Macro History.* London: East Gate, 1997.

Hyland, Paul. *Raleigh's Last Journey: A Tale of Madness, Vanity, and Treachery.* New York: HarperCollins, 2003.

Israel, Jonathan. *Dutch Primacy in World Trade, 1585–1740.* Oxford: Oxford University Press, 1990.

Iwamoto, Yoshiteru. "Yamada Nagamasa and His Relations with Siam." *Journal of the Siam Society* 95 (2007), 73–84.

Jahangir. *The Jahangirnama: Memoirs of Jahangir, Emperor of India.* Edited by Wheeler M. Thackston. New York: Oxford University Press, 1999.

Jardine, Lisa, and Alan Stewart. *Hostage to Fortune: The Troubled Life of Francis Bacon.* New York: Hill and Wang, 1999.

Johnson, Merle and Francis. J. Dowd. *Howard Pyle's Book of the American Spirit.* New York: Harper Brothers, 1923.

Jones, Ann Rosalind. *The Currency of Eros: Women's Love Lyric in Europe, 1540–1620.* Bloomington: Indiana University Press, 1996.

Jonson, Ben. *The Workes of Benjamin Jonson.* London: William Stansby, 1616; reprinted in facsimile, London: Scolar, 1976.

Kalin, Ibrahim. *Knowledge in Later Islamic Philosophy: Mulla Sadra on Existence, Intellect, and Intuition.* Oxford: Oxford University Press, 2010.

Kamen, Henry. *Early Modern European Society.* New York: Routledge, 2000.

Kamen, Henry. *Empire: How Spain Became a World Power, 1492–1763.* New York: HarperCollins, 2003.

Kamen, Henry. *The Spanish Inquisition: A Historical Revision.* New Haven: Yale University Press, 1998.

Kamen, Henry. *Who's Who in Europe 1450–1750.* London: Routledge, 2000.

Kaplan, Benjamin. *Divided by Faith: Religious Conflict and the Practice of Toleration in Early Modern Europe.* Cambridge: Belknap Press of Harvard University Press, 2007.

Katz, David, and Richard H. Popkin. *Messianic Revolution: Radical Religious Politics to the End of the Second Millennium.* New York: Hill and Wang, 1999.

Kepler, Johannes. *The Harmony of the World.* Trans. E. J. Aiton, A. M. Duncan, and Judith Veronica Field. Philadelphia: American Philosophical Society, 1997.

Kerr, Robert. "A General History and Collection of Voyages and Travels, Volume 9." http://www.gutenberg.org/files/13055/13055-h/13055-h.htm.

Kerridge, Eric. *The Agricultural Revolution.* New York: Augustus M. Kelley, 1968.

Keuning, J. "Nicolaas Geelkerken." *Imago Mundi* 11 (1954): 174–177.

Khamchoo, Chaiwat, and E. Bruce Reynolds. *Thai-Japanese Relations in Historical Perspective.* Bangkok: Institute of Asian Studies, Chulalongkorn University, 1988.

Kim, Kichung. *An Introduction to Classical Korean Literature: From Hyangga to P'ansori.* Armonk NY: M. E. Sharpe, 1996.

King, David A. *Astronomy in the Service of Islam.* Aldershot, Hampshire: Variorum, 1993.

King, David A. *Islamic Astronomical Instruments.* London: Variorum Reprints, 1987.

King, David A. *Islamic Mathematical Astronomy.* Aldershot, Hampshire, Great Britain: Variorum, 1993.

King, Margaret L. *Women of the Renaissance.* Chicago: University Of Chicago Press, 1991.

Kita, Sandy. *The Last Tosa: Iwasa Katsumochi Matabei, Bridge to Ukiyo-e.* Honolulu: University of Hawaii Press, 1999.

Kitagawa Tomoko. "The Conversion of Hideyoshi's Daughter Go." *Japanese Journal of Religious* Studies 34, no. 1, 9–25.

Klein, Herbert S. *A Concise History of Bolivia.* Cambridge: Cambridge University Press, 2003.

Knight, Michael, and He Li. *Power and Glory: Court Arts of China's Ming Dynasty.* San Francisco: Asian Art Museum, 2008.

Ko, Dorothy. *Teachers of the Inner Chambers: Women and Culture in Seventeenth-Century China.* Stanford : Stanford University Press, 1995.

Koenigsberger, H. G. *Early Modern Europe 1500–1789.* London: Longman, 1987.

Koestler, Arthur. *The Sleepwalkers: A History of Man's Changing Vision of the Universe.* New York: Penguin, 1990.

Koestler, Arthur. *The Watershed: A Biography of Johannes Kepler.* New York: Doubleday, 1960.

Kottman, Karl A. *Catholic Millennarianism: From Savonarola to the Abbé Grégoire.* Millennarianism and Messianism in Early Modern European Culture, vol. 2. Dordrecht: Kluwer Academic, 2001.

Lach, Donald F. *Asia in the Making of Europe.* Chicago: University of Chicago Press, 1965.

Lamb, H. H. *Climate, History and the Modern World.* London: Methuen Young Books, 1982.

Lancre, Pierre. *On the Inconstancy of Witches: Pierre De Lancre's Tableau De L'inconstance Des Mauvais Anges Et Demons (1612).* Edited by Gerhild Scholz Williams. Tempe Ariz: Arizona Center for Medieval and Renaissance Studies, 2006.

Lane-Poole, Stanley. *The Story of the Barbary Corsairs.* New York: G. P. Putnam's Sons, 1890.

Leeflang, Huigen, and Ger Luijten. *Hendrick Goltzius (1558–1617): Drawings, Prints and Paintings.* Amsterdam: Waanders Publishers, 2003.

Leonard, Irving A. *Baroque Times in Old Mexico: Seventeenth-Century Persons, Places, and Practices.* Ann Arbor: University of Michigan Press, 1959.

Levack, Brian. *New Perspectives on Witchcraft, Magic, and Demonology.* New York: Routledge, 2002.

Levenson, Jay A. *Encompassing the Globe: Portugal and the World in the Sixteenth and Seventeenth Centuries.* Washington: Smithsonian Books, 2007.

Levi, Anthony. *Cardinal Richelieu: And the Making of France.* New York: Carroll and Graf, 2000.

Levi Della Vida, Giorgio. *George Strachan: Memorials of a Wandering Scottish Scholar of the Seventeenth Century.* Aberdeen: Third Spalding Club, 1956.

Lewalski, Barbara Kiefer. "Writing Women and Reading the Renaissance." *Renaissance Quarterly,* vol. 44, no. 4 (Winter, 1991): 792–821.

Lewalski, Barbara Kiefer. *Writing Women in Jacobean England.* Boston: Harvard University Press, 1993.

Lieberman, Victor. *Beyond Binary Histories: Re-Imagining Eurasia to c.1830.* Ann Arbor: University of Michigan Press, 1999.

Lieberman, Victor. *Strange Parallels: Southeast Asia in Global Context, c. 800–1830.* Cambridge: Cambridge University Press, 2003.

Lillehoj, Elizabeth. *Critical Perspectives on Classicism in Japanese Painting, 1600–1700.* Honolulu: University of Hawaii Press, 2004.

Lindley, David. *Court Masques: Jacobean and Caroline Entertainments, 1605–1640.* Oxford: Oxford University Press, 1995.

Lithgow, William. *The Rare Adventures and Painful Peregrinations of William Lithgow.* Edited by Gilbert Phelps. London: Folio Society, 1974.

Little, Stephen. *Taoism and the Arts of China.* Berkeley: University of California Press, 2000.

Los Angeles County Museum of Art. *Masterpieces from the Shin'enkan Collection: Japanese Painting of the Edo Period.* New York: Harper and Row, 1986.

Lowe, Kate. "'Representing' Africa: Ambassadors and Princes from Christian Africa to Renaissance Italy and Portugal, 1402–1608." *Transactions of the Royal Historic Society* 17 (2007), 101–128.

Luengo, Jose Maria S. *A History of the Manila-Acapulco Slave Trade (1565–1815).* Tubigon, Bohol, Philippines: Mater Dei, 1996.

Luijten, Ger. *Dawn of the Golden Age: Northern Netherlandish Art, 1580–1620.* Amsterdam: Rijksmuseum, 1993.

McCrory, Donald. *No Ordinary Man: The Life and Times of Miguel de Cervantes.* London: P. Owen, 2002.

McGaha, Michael. "Cervantes in Algiers : A Captive's Tale (review)" *Cervantes: Bulletin of the Cervantes Society of America,* 23.2 (2003): 437–442.

McGill, Forrest, ed. *The Kingdom of Siam: The Art of Central Thailand, 1350–1800.* San Francisco: Asian Art Museum, 2005.

Maddison, Francis, and Emilie Savage-Smith. *Science, Tools and Magic: The Nasser D. Khalili Collection of Islamic Art.* London: Nour Foundation, 1997.

Maier, Michael. *Atalanta Fugiens: An Edition of the Fugues, Emblems, and Epigrams.* Grand Rapids, Mich.: Phanes, 1989.

Mangan, Jane. *Trading Roles: Gender, Ethnicity, and the Urban Economy in Colonial Potosí.* Durham, NC: Duke University Press, 2005.

Mannarelli, Mari a Emma. *Private Passions and Public Sins: Men and Women in Seventeenth-Century Lima.* Albuquerque: University of New Mexico Press, 2007.

Marcus, Leah Sinanoglou. "'Present Occasions' and the Shaping of Ben Jonson's Masques." *ELH* 45, no. 2 (July 1, 1978): 201–225.

Margolis, Howard. *It Started with Copernicus: How Turning the World Inside Out Led to the Scientific Revolution.* New York: McGraw-Hill, 2002.

Mark, Peter, and José da Silva Horta. "Two Early Seventeenth-Century Sephardic Communities on Senegal's Petite Côte." *History in Africa* 31 (January 1, 2004): 231–256.

Marlin, Hilary, ed. *The Art of Midwifery: Early Modern Midwives in Europe.* New York : Routledge, 1993.

Martin, John Rupert. *Rubens Before 1620.* Princeton: Princeton University Press, 1972.

Mather, James. *Pashas: Traders and Travellers in the Islamic World.* New Haven: Yale University Press, 2009.

Mathes, Valerie L. "Enrico Martínez of New Spain." *The Americas* 33, no. 1 (Jul. 1976): 62–77.

Matsumoto Tadashige. *Stories of Fifty Japanese Heroes*. Tokyo: Koseikaku, 1929.

Matthee, Rudi. "Anti-Ottoman Politics and Transit Rights: The Seventeenth-Century Trade in Silk between Safavid Iran and Muscovy." *Cahiers du Monde Russe* 35, no. 4 (October 1, 1994): 739–761.

Melikian-Chirvani, Assadullah Souren. *Le Chant du Monde: L'Art de l'Iran Safavide 1501–1736*. Paris: Musée du Louvre, 2007.

Mendieta, Eva. *In Search of Catalina de Erauso: The National and Sexual Identity of the Lieutenant Nun*. San Francisco: Center for Basque Studies, 2009.

Meriwether, G. "A Sketch of the Life of Date Masamune and an Account of His Embassy to Rome." *Transactions of the Asiatic Society of Japan* 21 (November 1893).

Merrim, Stephanie. *Early Modern Women's Writing and Sor Juana Inés de la Cruz*. Nashville: Vanderbilt University Press, 1999.

Michael, Franz H. *The Origin of Manchu Rule in China: Frontier and Bureaucracy as Interacting Forces in the Chinese Empire*. 1942. Reprint, Paris: Octagon Books, 1965.

Middleton, Thomas. *Thomas Middleton: The Collected Works*. Gary Taylor and John Lavagnino, eds. Oxford: Oxford University Press, 2007.

Miller, Naomi J. *Changing the Subject: Mary Wroth and Figurations of Gender in Early Modern England*. Lexington: University Press of Kentucky, 1996.

Miller, Naomi J. "'Not Much to Be Marked': Narrative of the Woman's Part in Lady Mary Wroth's *Urania*." *Studies in English Literature, 1500–1900*, vol. 29, no. 1, *The English Renaissance* (Winter, 1989): 121–137.

Milton, Giles. *Nathaniel's Nutmeg, or, the True and Incredible Adventures of the Spice Trader Who Changed the Course of History*. New York: Farrar, Straus and Giroux, 1999.

Milton, Giles. *Samurai William: The Englishman Who Opened Japan*. New York: Farrar, Straus and Giroux, 2003.

Minchin, Susie, and Linda A. Newson. *From Capture to Sale: The Portuguese Slave Trade to Spanish South America in the Early Seventeenth Century*. Leiden: Brill, 2007.

Modena, Leon. *The Autobiography of a Seventeenth-Century Venetian Rabbi: Leon Modena's Life of Judah*. Mark R. Cohen, ed. and trans. Princeton: Princeton University Press, 1988.

Morse, Anne. *Drama and Desire: Japanese Paintings from the Floating World, 1690–1850*. Boston: Museum of Fine Arts Boston, 2007.

Mote, Frederick. *Imperial China, 900–1800*. Cambridge: Harvard University Press, 1999.

Mukherjee, Rudrangshu. *Politics and Trade in the Indian Ocean World: Essays in Honour of Ashin Das Gupta*. Oxford: Oxford University Press, 2003.

Mungello, D. E. *Curious Land: Jesuit Accommodation and the Origins of Sinology.* Honolulu: University of Hawaii Press, 1985, 1989.

Murad, Abdal-Hakim. "Ward the Pirate." http://www.masud.co.uk/ISLAM/ahm/ward.htm.

Nagaoka. "Full text of 'Histoire des relations du Japon avec l'Europe aux XVIe et XVIIe siècles.'" http://www.archive.org/stream/histoiredesrela00nagagoog/histoiredesrela00nagagoog_djvu.txt.

Naquin, Susan, and Joint Committee on Chinese Studies (U.S.). *Pilgrims and Sacred Sites in China*. Berkeley: University of California Press, 1992.

Naylor, Thomas H, and Charles W. Polzer, S. J. *The Presidio and Militia on the Northern Frontier of New Spain: A Documentary History, Volume I, 1570–1700*. Tucson: University of Arizona Press, 1986.

Needham, Joseph, and Lu Gwei-Djen. *Chemical and Chemical Technology: Spagyrical Discovery and Invention; Physiological Alchemy. Science and Civilization in China 5*. Cambridge: Cambridge University Press, 1983.

Needham, Joseph. *Chemistry and Chemical Technology. Spinning and Reeling. Science and Civilization in China 9*. Cambridge: Cambridge University Press, 1988.

Nasr, Seyyed Hossein. *Islamic Science: An Illustrated Study*. London: World of Islam Festival, 1976.

Newman, Andrew J. *Safavid Iran: Rebirth of a Persian Empire*. New York: I. B. Tauris, 2006.

Nicoll, Allardyce. *Stuart Masques and the Renaissance Stage*. New York: Benjamin Blom, 1938, reprinted 1963.

O'Flynn, Dennis, Arturo Giraldez, and James Sobredo, eds. *European Entry into the Pacific: Spain and the Acapulco–Manila Galleons*. Aldershot: Ashgate Pub Ltd, 2001.

Ogborn, Miles. "Writing Travels: Power, Knowledge and Ritual on the English East India Company's Early Voyages." *Transactions of the Institute of British Geographers* 27, no. 2. New Series (January 1, 2002): 155–171.

Orgel, Stephen. *The Jonsonian Masque*. Cambridge: Harvard University Press, 1965.

Oteiza Iriarte, Tomás. *Acapulco: La Ciudad de las Naos de Oriente y de las Sirenes Modernas: Historia*. Mexico: Editorial Diana, 1973.

Ottani Cavina, Ann. *Carlo Saraceni*. Milan: Mario Spagnol, 1968.

Overton, Mark. *Agricultural Revolution in England: The Transformation of the Agrarian Economy 1500–1850*. New York: Cambridge University Press, 1996.

Paludan, Ann. *The Imperial Ming Tombs: Text and Photographs*. Hong Kong: Hong Kong University Press, 1981.

Panek, Jennifer, ed. *The Roaring Girl: Authoritative Text, Contexts, Criticism*. New York: W. W. Norton, 2011.

Pang, Mae Anna. *Asian Art in the Collections of the National Gallery of Victoria*. Melbourne: National Gallery of Victoria, 2003.

Parker, Charles H. *Global Interactions in the Early Modern Age, 1400–1800*. Cambridge: Cambridge University Press, 2010.

Parker, Geoffrey. *Europe in Crisis: 1598–1648*. Malden, Mass.: Blackwell, 2001.

Parker, Geoffrey, and Leslie M. Smith. *The General Crisis of the Seventeenth Century*. Boston: Routledge and Kegan Paul, 1978.

Parry, J. H. *The Age of Reconnaissance: Discovery, Exploration and Settlement 1450 to 1650*. New York: Praeger, 1969.

Peabody Essex Museum. *Geisha: Beyond the Painted Smile*. New York: George Braziller, 2004.

Pearson, M. *The Indian Ocean*. London: Routledge, 2007.

Pearson, M. N. "'Objects Ridiculous and August': Early Modern European Perceptions of Asia." *The Journal of Modern History* 68, no. 2 (1996): 382–397.

Pendergast, James T. "The Massawomeck: Raiders and Traders into the Chesapeake Bay in the Seventeenth Century." *Transactions of the American Philosophical Society, New Series* 81, no. 2 (1991): i–101.

Penrose, Boies. *Sea Fights in the East Indies in the Years 1602–1639*. Cambridge: Harvard University Press, 1931.

Penrose, Boies. *The Sherleian Odyssey, Being of the Travels and Adventures of Three Famous Brothers During the Reigns of Elizabeth, James I, and Charles I*. Taunton: Wessex, 1938.

Penrose, Boies. *Travel and Discovery in the Renaissance, 1420–1620.* Cambridge: Harvard University Press, 1963.

Penrose, Boies. *Urbane Travelers 1591–1635.* Philadelphia: University of Pennsylvania Press, 1942.

Peterson, Thomas K. *Secrets of the Manila Galleons.* Corvallis, Or., 2007.

Phelan, John Leddy. "Free Versus Compulsory Labor: Mexico and the Philippines 1540–1648." *Comparative Studies in Society and History* 1, no. 2 (Jan. 1959): 189–201.

Phillips, Carla Rahn. *Six Galleons for the King of Spain: Imperial Defense in the Early Seventeenth Century.* Baltimore: Johns Hopkins University Press, 1986.

Platonov, S. F. *The Time of Troubles: A Historical Study of the Internal Crisis and Social Struggle in Sixteenth- and Seventeenth-Century Muscovy.* John T. Alexander, trans. Lawrence: The University Press of Kansas, 1970.

Polenghi, Cesare. "The Japanese in Ayudhya in the First Half of the 17th Century." http://www.samurai-archives.com/jia.html.

Poma, Huaman. *Letter to a King: A Peruvian Chief's Account of Life under the Incas and under Spanish Rule.* New York: E. P. Dutton, 1978.

Price, J. L. *The Dutch Republic in the Seventeenth Century.* New York: St. Martin's, 1998.

Qaisar, Ahsan Jan. *The Indian Response to European Technology and Culture (A.D. 1498–1707).* Delhi: Oxford University Press, 1982.

Rabb, Theodore K. *Jacobean Gentleman:Sir Edwin Sandys, 1561–1629.* Princeton: Princeton University Press, 1998.

Rabb, Theodore K. *The Last Days of the Renaissance: And the March to Modernity.* New York: Basic Books, 2006.

Rabb, Theodore K. *Renaissance Lives: Portraits of an Age.* New York: Basic Books, 2001.

Reff, D. T. "The 'Predicament of Culture' and Spanish Missionary Accounts of the Tepehuan and Pueblo Revolts." *Ethnohistory* 42, no. 1 (1995): 63–90.

Reichle, Natasha. *Bali: Art, Ritual, Performance.* San Francisco: Asian Art Museum, 2011.

Reid, Anthony. *Charting the Shape of Early Modern Southeast Asia.* Chiang Mai, Thailand: Silkworm Books, 1999.

Reid, Anthony. *Southeast Asia in the Age of Commerce, 1450–1680.* New Haven: Yale University Press, 1988.

Reinhartz, Dennis, and Gerald D. Saxon. *Mapping and Empire: Soldier-Engineers on the Southwestern Frontier.* Austin: University of Texas Press, 2005.

"Relações de Portugal com a Pérsia - Resumo." http://www.cham.fcsh.unl.pt/garciasilvafigueiroa/resumo_eng.html.

Repetti, W. C. "A Guide to Old Manila." *Monumenta Nipponica* 2, no. 1 (Jan. 1939): 287–290.

Reston, James. *Galileo: A Life.* New York: HarperCollins Publishers, 1994.

Riggs, David. *Ben Jonson: A Life.* Cambridge: Harvard University Press, 1989.

Rivero Lake, Rodrigo. *Namban: Art in Viceregal Mexico.* Madrid: Estilomexico Editores, 2005.

Roberts, Josephine A., ed.. *The Poems of Lady Mary Wroth.* Baton Rouge: Louisiana State University Press, 1992.

Robertson, Karen. "Pocahontas at the Masque." *Signs* 21, no. 3 (Spring 1996): 551–583.

Robins, Nick. *The Corporation that Changed the World: How the East India Company Shaped the Modern Multinational.* London: Pluto Press, 2006.

Robinson, B. W. "Shāh 'Abbās and the Mughal Ambassador Khān 'Ālam: The Pictorial Record." *The Burlington Magazine* 114, no. 827 (February 1, 1972): 58–63.

Robinson, David M. *Culture, Courtiers, and Competition: The Ming Court (1368–1644).* Cambridge: Harvard University Asia Center, 2008.

Robinson, Francis. *The Mughal Emperors and the Islamic Dynasties of India, Iran, and Central Asia, 1206–1925.* New York: Thames and Hudson, 2007.

Rodriguez, M. "The Genesis of Economic Attitudes in the Rio De La Plata." *Hispanic American Historical Review* 36, no. 2 (1956): 171–189.

Rodríguez-Rodríguez, A. M. "The Spectacle of Torture and Death in *A Topography and General History of Algiers.*" *HIOL: Hispanic Issues On Line,* no. 7 (2010): 175–186.

Roelofs, Pieter. *Hendrick Avercamp: Master of the Ice Scene.* Amsterdam: Rijksmuseum / Nieuw Amsterdam, 2009.

Roettgen, Steffi. *Italian Frescoes of the Baroque Era, 1600–1800.* New York: Abbeville, 2007.

Rogers, Robert F. *Destiny's Landfall: A History of Guam.* Honolulu : University of Hawaii Press, 1995.

Rogers, Howard. *Masterworks of Ming and Qing: Painting from the Forbidden City.* Lansdale PA: International Arts Council, 1988.

Roper, Lyndal. *Witch Craze: Terror and Fantasy in Baroque Germany.* New Haven: Yale University Press, 2004.

Ross, D., and others. "A Letter from James I to the Sultan Ahmad." *Bulletin of the School of Oriental and African Studies* 7, no. 2 (1934): 299–306.

Ross, E. Denison. *Sir Anthony Sherley and His Persian Adventure, Including Some Contemporary Narratives Relating Thereto.* London: G. Routledge and Sons, 1933.

Rountree, Helen. *Pocahontas Powhatan Opechancanough: Three Indian Lives Changed by Jamestown.* Charlottesville: University of Virginia Press, 2005.

Rountree, Helen. "Powhatan Indian Women: The People Captain John Smith Barely Saw." *Ethnohistory* 45, no. 1 (1998): 1–29.

Rountree, Helen. "Powhatan Priests and English Rectors: World Views and Congregations in Conflict." *American Indian Quarterly* 16, no. 4 (1992): 485–500.

Rowe, William T. *China's Last Empire: The Great Qing.* Cambridge, Mass.: Belknap Press, 2009.

Saliba, George. *Islamic Science and the Making of the European Renaissance.* Cambridge: MIT Press, 2007.

Saliba, George. "Whose Science is Arabic Science in Renaissance Europe?" http://www.columbia.edu/~gas1/project/visions/case1/sci.3.html.

Savage-Smith, Emilie. *Magic and Divination in Early Islam.* Aldershot, Hants: Ashgate/Variorum, 2004.

Scammell, G. V. "European Exiles, Renegades and Outlaws and the Maritime Economy of Asia c. 1500–1750." *Modern Asian Studies* 26, no. 04 (1992): 641–661.

Schurz, William Lytle. *The Manila Galleon.* New York: Dutton, 1939.

Schurz, William Lytle. "Mexico, Peru, and the Manila Galleon." *Hispanic American Historical Review* 1, no. 4 (1918): 389–402.

Scoffing Scholar of Lanling (Tang Xianzu?), *The Plum in the Golden Vasse, or Ching Ping Mei* (5 vols.). Translated by David Tod Roy. Princeton: Princeton University Press, 1993-2011.

Scott, Philippa. *The Book of Silk.* New York: Thames and Hudson, 2001.

Seigle, Cecilia Segawa. *Yoshiwara: The Glittering World of* the Japanese Courtesan. Honolulu: University of Hawaii Press, 1993.

Shah, Idries. *The Sufis.* New York: Anchor Books, 1990.

Shapiro, James. *A Year in the Life of William Shakespeare: 1599.* New York: HarperPerennial, 2006.

Shaver, Anne. "A New Woman of Romance." *Modern Language Studies,* vol. 21, no. 4 (Autumn, 1991): 63–77.

Shea, William R. *Galileo's Intellectual Revolution; Middle Period, 1610–1632.* New York: Science History Publications, 1972.

Sheridan, Bridgette. "At Birth: The Modern State, Modern Medicine, and the Royal Midwife Louise Bourgeois in Seventeenth-Century France." *Dynamis : Acta Hispanica ad Medicinae Scientiarumque. Historiam Illustrandam,* 19 (1999), 145–166.

Shirahara, Yukiko. *Japan Envisions the West: 16th–19th Century Japanese Art from Kobe City Museum.* Seattle: Seattle Art Museum, 2007.

Shirley, Rodney. W. *The Mapping of the World: Early Printed World Maps 1472–1700.* London: Holland Press, 1983.

Sizemore, Christine W. "Early Seventeenth-Century Advice Books: The Female Viewpoint." *South Atlantic Bulletin* 41, no. 1 (January 1, 1976): 41–48.

Sluiter, Engel. "Dutch Maritime Power and the Colonial Status Quo, 1585–1641." *The Pacific Historical Review,* 11, no. 1 (1942): 29–41.

Sluiter, Engel. "The Fortification of Acapulco, 1615–1616." *The Hispanic American Historical Review* 29, no. 1 (Feb. 1949): 69–80.

Smart, Ellen. "The Death of Ināyat Khān by the Mughal Artist Bālchand," in *Artibus Asiae,* Vol. 58, No. 3/4 (1999), 273–279.

Smith, John. "The Generall Historie of Virginia, New-England, and the Summer Isles: With the Names of the Adventurers, Planters, and Governours From Their First Beginning Ano: 1584. To This Present 1624...." Documenting the American South. http://docsouth.unc.edu/southlit/smith/menu.html (accessed April 27, 2010).

Smoley, Richard, and Jay Kinney. *Hidden Wisdom: A Guide to the Western Inner Traditions.* New York: Arkana, 1999.

Sobel, Dava. *Galileo's Daughter: A Historical Memoir of Science, Faith, and Love.* New York: Walker and Company, 1999.

Solano, L. R. "La Nueva España y las Filipinas." *Historia Mexicana* 3, no. 3 (1954): 420–431.

Souza, T. R. de. "Bocarro's Account of Goa-based Trade in the Early 17th Century." *Indian Economic and Social History Review* 12, no. 4 (December 1975).

Spence, Jonathan. *The Memory Palace of Matteo Ricci.* New York: Viking, 1984.

Spencer, William. *Algiers in the Age of the Corsairs.* Norman: University of Oklahoma Press, 1976.

Srivastava, Ashok Kumar. *Mughal Painting: An Interplay of Indigenous and Foreign Traditions.* New Delhi: Munshiram Manoharlal Publishers, 2000.

Srivastava, S. P. *Jahangir: A Connoisseur of Mughal Art.* New Delhi: Abhinav Publications, 2001.

Steensgaard, Niels. *Carracks, Caravans and Companies: The Structural Crises in the European-Asian Trade in the Early Seventeenth Century.* Scandinavian Institute of Asian Studies monograph series, no. 17. Copenhagen: Lund, Studentlitteratur, 1973.

Steinmann, Linda K. "Shah 'Abbas and the Royal Silk Trade 1599–1629." *Bulletin (British Society for Middle Eastern Studies)* 14, no. 1 (January 1, 1987): 68–74.

"Stemmata Shirleiana." http://openlibrary.org/books/OL24182907M/Stemmata_Shirleiana.

Stewart, Alan. *The Cradle King: The Life of James VI and I, the First Monarch of a United Great Britain.* New York: St. Martin's Press, 2003.

Strachan, Michael. *The Life and Adventures of Thomas Coryate.* Oxford : Oxford University Press, 1962.

Stierlin, Henri. *Turkey: From the Selçuks to the Ottomans.* Köln: Taschen, 2002.

Stronge, Susan. *Made for Mughal Emperors: Royal Treasures from Hindustan.* London: I. B. Tauris, 2010.

Subrahmanyam, Sanjay. *Penumbral Visions: Making Polities in Early Modern South India.* Ann Arbor: University of Michigan Press, 2001.

Subrahmanyam, Sanjay. *The Portuguese Empire in Asia, 1500–1700: A Political and Economic History.* London: Longman, 1993.

Suchtelen, Ariane van. *Holland Frozen in Time. The Dutch Winter Landscape in the Golden Age.* Waanders Uitgevers, 2001.

Sullivan, Michael. *The Arts of China.* Berkeley: University of California Press, 2008.

Summers, Claude J., and Ted-Larry Pebworth. *Ben Jonson Revised.* New York: Twayne, 1999.

Summerson, John. *Inigo Jones.* Baltimore: Penguin, 1966.

Swope, Kenneth M. *A Dragon's Head and a Serpent's Tail: Ming China and the First Great East Asian War, 1592–1598.* Norman: University of Oklahoma Press, 2009.

Takisawa, O. "La Delegación Diplomática Enviada a Roma por el Señor Feundal Japonés Date Masamune" (2009).

Tamaskar, B. G. *The Life and Work of Malik Ambar.* London: Idarah-I Adabiyat-I Delli, 1978.

Tambs, Lewis A. "Brazil's Expanding Frontiers." *The Americas* 23, no. 2 (October 1966): 165–179.

Taylor, Gary, and John Lavagnino. *Thomas Middleton and Early Modern Textual Culture: A Companion to the Collected Works.* New York: Oxford University Press, 2008.

Taylor, P. S. "Spanish Seamen in the New World during the Colonial Period." *Hispanic American Historical Review* 5, no. 4 (1922): 631–661.

Thirsk, Joan. *Alternative Agriculture: A History: From the Black Death to the Present Day.* New York: Oxford University Press, 1997.

Thirsk, Joan. *Economic Policy and Projects: The Development of a Consumer Society in Early Modern England.* New York: Oxford University Press, 1978.

Thirsk, Joan. *The English Rural Landscape.* New York: Oxford University Press, 2000.

Thompson, D. E. "Joris van Speilbergen's Journal and a Site in the Huarmey Valley, Peru." *American Antiquity* 32, no. 1 (1967): 113–116.

Thurston, H. "The First Beatified Martyr of Spanish America: Blessed Roque Gonzalez (1576-1628)." *Catholic Historical Review* 20, no. 4 (1935): 371–383.

Tilton, Hereward. *The Quest for the Phoenix: Spiritual Alchemy and Rosicrucianism in the Work of Count Michael Maier (1569–1622).* New York: Walter de Gruyter, 2003.

Topper, David, and Cynthia Gillis. "Trajectories of Blood: Artemisia Gentileschi and Galileo's Parabolic Path." *Woman's Art Journal* 17, no. 1 (Spring-Summer 1996): 10–13.

Townsend, Camilla. *Pocahontas and the Powhatan Dilemma.* New York: Hill and Wang, 2004.

Tremblay, G. "Reflecting on Pocahontas." *Frontiers, A Journal of Women's Studies* 23, no. 2 (2002): 121–125.

Tromans, Nicholas. *The Lure of the East: British Orientalist Painting*. New York: Yale University Press, 2008.

Tsueno Takeda. *Kano Eitoku*. Translated by H. Mack Horton and Catherine Kaputa. New York: Kodansha International, 1977.

Tuan, Hoang Anh. *Silk for Silver: Dutch-Vietnamese Relations, 1637–1700*. Koninklijke Brill NV, Leiden: Brill Academic Publishers, 2007.

Tuveson, Ernest. *Millennium and Utopia: A Study in the Background of the Idea of Progress*. Berkeley: University of California Press, 1949.

Twitchett, Denis. *The Cambridge History of China*. Cambridge: Cambridge University Press, 1998.

Vainker, Shelagh. *Chinese Silk: A Cultural History*. New Brunswick, NJ: Rutgers University Press, 2004.

Van Suchtelen, Ariane. *Holland Frozen in Time: The Dutch Winter Landscape in the Golden Age*. Zwolle: Waanders, 2001.

Vaporis, Constantine. *Breaking Barriers: Travel and the State in Early Modern Japan*. Cambridge: Council on East Asian Studies, Harvard University, 1994.

Vaughan, Alden T. *Transatlantic Encounters: American Indians in Britain, 1500–1776*. New York: Cambridge University Press, 2008.

Velasco, Sherry. *The Lieutenant Nun: Transgenderism, Lesbian Desire, and Catalina de Erauso*. Austin: University of Texas Press, 2001.

Verma, Som. *Mughal Painter of Flora and Fauna Ustad Mansur*. New Delhi: Abhinav, 1999.

Verma, Som. *Painting the Mughal Experience*. Oxford: Oxford University Press, 2005.

Villiers, J. A. *The East and West Indian Mirror, Being an Account of Joris Van Speilbergen's Voyage Round the World*. London: Hakluyt Society, 1906.

Vitzthum, Walter. "Lanfranco at the Quirinal–Two New Documents." *The Burlington Magazine* 107, no. 750 (1965): 468–471.

Vlieghe, Hans. *Flemish Art and Architecture, 1585–1700*. New Haven: Yale University Press, 1998.

Von Glahn, Richard. *Fountain of Fortune: Money and Monetary Policy in China, 1000-1700*. Berkeley: University of California Press, 1996.

Von Glahn, Richard. "Myth and Reality of China's Seventeenth-Century Monetary Crisis." *The Journal of Economic History* 56, no. 2 (June 1996): 429–454.

Waley-Cohen, Joanna. *The Sextants of Beijing: Global Currents in Chinese History*. New York: W. W. Norton, 1999.

Waller, Gary F. *The Sidney Family Romance: Mary Wroth, William Herbert, and the Early Modern Construction of Gender*. Detroit: Wayne State University Press, 1993.

Wandel, Lee Palmer, and Robin W. Winks. *Europe in a Wider World, 1350–1650*. New York: Oxford University Press, 2003.

Ward, Julian. *Xu Xiake (1586–1641): The Art of Travel Writing*. London: Curzon, 2000.

Wardwell, Anne E., and James C. Y. Watt. *When Silk Was Gold: Central Asian and Chinese Textiles*. New York: Metropolitan Museum of Art, 1997.

Watson, William. *The Arts of China 900–1620*. New Haven: Yale University Press, 2000.

Weber, Eugen. *Apocalypses: Prophecies, Cults, and Millennial Beliefs through the Ages*. Cambridge: Harvard University Press, 1999.

Weeks, Andrew. *Boehme: An Intellectual Biography of the Seventeenth-Century Philosopher and Mystic*. Albany: State University of New York Press, 1991.

Welch, Anthony. "Painting and Patronage under Shah 'Abbas I." *Iranian Studies* 7, no. 3/4 (July 1, 1974): 458–507.

Wiesner-Hanks, Merry. *Early Modern Europe, 1450–1789*. Cambridge: Cambridge University Press, 2006.

Wheelock, Arthur K. *Flemish Paintings of the Seventeenth Century*. Washington: National Gallery of Art, 2005.

White, David. *Sinister Yogis*. Chicago: University of Chicago Press, 2009.

White, John, ed. *The Rosicrucian Enlightenment Revisited*. Hudson NY: Lindisfarne Books, 1999.

Wills, Jr., John E. *1688: A Global History*. New York: W.W. Norton, 2001.

Wills, Jr., John E. *The World from 1450 to 1700*. New York: Oxford University Press, 2009.

Wilson, Katharina M., ed. *Women Writers of the Renaissance and Reformation*. Athens: University of Georgia Press, 1987.

Wilson, Peter H.. *The Thirty Years War: Europe's Tragedy*. Cambridge: Belknap Press, 2009.

Wittkomer, Rudolf. *Art and Architecture in Italy 1600–1750. Vol. 1: The Early Baroque 1600–1625*. Revised by Joseph Connors and Jennifer Montagu. New Haven: Yale University Press, 1958, 1999.

Wolf, John B. *The Barbary Coast: Algeria under the Turks*. New York and London: W. W. Norton and Co., 1979.

Wratislaw, A. C. "The Diary of an Embassy." *Blackwood's Magazine,* October 1924.

Wright, Elaine Julia. *Muraqqa': Imperial Mughal Albums from the Chester Beatty Library, Dublin*. Alexandria, VA: Art Services International, 2009.

Yates, Frances. *The Rosicrucian Enlightenment*. New York: Routledge, 2002.

Yavuz, Ayşil Tükel. "The Concepts That Shape Anatolian Seljuq Caravanserais." *Muqarnas* 14 (January 1, 1997): 80–95.

Zika, Charles. *Exorcising Our Demons: Magic, Witchcraft, and Visual Culture in Early Modern Europe*. Boston: Brill, 2003.

Acknowledgments

Many people have been generous with assistance, and if anything's wrong it's their fault. Haven't you always wanted to read that in an author's acknowledgments? Tolerating my nights and weekends devoted to this project, Carol Christensen made helpful suggestions and embodied beauty, wisdom, and compassion. Ellen Christensen offered sensible, thoughtful, and creative insights. Claire Christensen shared her knowledge of Turkey. Peter Laufer was encouraging early on, and a supporter throughout. Jane Vandenburgh read early drafts of opening sections, and her enthusiasm was motivating.

Thanks are due to colleagues at the Asian Art Museum in San Francisco. Former director Emily Sano read the book in manuscript, and I was heartened by her positive response. Chief curator Forrest McGill made helpful comments on the Persian painter Riza-yi Abbasi in particular. Susie Cantor shared resources on Low Country painting. Qamar Adamjee was of special assistance, and the entire curatorial staff — Michael Knight for China, Melissa Rinne for Japan, Kumja Kim for Korea, Natasha Reichle for Southeast Asia, along with too many others to list here — informed my understanding of Asian art and culture. (Similarly, my understanding of Latin American culture derives in part from my work with Julio Cortázar, Carlos Fuentes, and many others.)

Jack Shoemaker at Counterpoint Press, who believed in this book early on, was a pleasure to work with — I am fortunate to have so congenial an editor. Laura Mazer provided steady guidance. Barrett Briske, who is able to distinguish an italic from a roman period in 7.65-point type, caught a number of errors in copy editing. James Donnelly's attentive and perceptive responses to the text exceeded what anyone could reasonably expect of a proofreader.

Eunice Howe of USC was generous and helpful on the Quirinale frescoes (for more on this see p. 366). Gary Snyder kindly read the manuscript during a busy period of travel and shared his response, for which I am deeply grateful. It was wonderful to receive a hand-written note from Evan Connell expressing positive sentiments: years ago I worked as an editor on his *Son of the Morning Star* and other books. Ren Weschler's artfully crafted blurb arrived around the time I was reading his brilliant *Everything That Rises: A Book of Convergences,* compounding my pleasure. I am also profoundly grateful to John E. Wills, Jr., for consenting to read and comment on the book even though we had no previous acquaintance.

Thanks to Rod Clark, a friend since high school, for publishing an excerpt in the fiftieth issue of *Rosebud* magazine. Thanks also to the Asian Art Museum, San Francisco, and the J. Paul Getty Museum, Los Angeles, for providing high-resolution images of works in their collections; to Art Resource, NY, for permission to reproduce works from the Metropolitan Museum, New York (pp. 55 and 71), and the Skulpturensammlung, Staatliche Kunstsammlungen, Dresden, Germany (p. 257); to Dennis Maloney of White Pine Press for permission to reproduce "At the Refugee Camp" by Heo Gyun (pp. 296–297); to New Directions for permission to quote from "The Signature of All Things" by Kenneth Rexroth, from *The Collected Shorter Poems,* copyright ©1949 by Kenneth Rexroth. Reprinted by permission of New Directions Publishing Corp. (p. 227); to the Eisei-Bunko Museum for permission to reproduce the Western-style bell of the Hosokawas (p. 66); to Juliette Crane of Sue Bond Public Relations and the Khalili Trust for permission to reproduce the planispheric astrolabe, SC153 (p. 207), from The Nasser D. Khalili Collection of Islamic Art; to the Museo Galileo for permission to reproduce Galileo's calculating device (p. 199); and to the Phoenix Art Museum and the kind assistance of Claudia Brown, Leesha M. Alston, and Momoko Welch for permission to reproduce the throne cover in the museum's collection (p. 53).

Index

Page references in *italics* denote captions to illustrations.

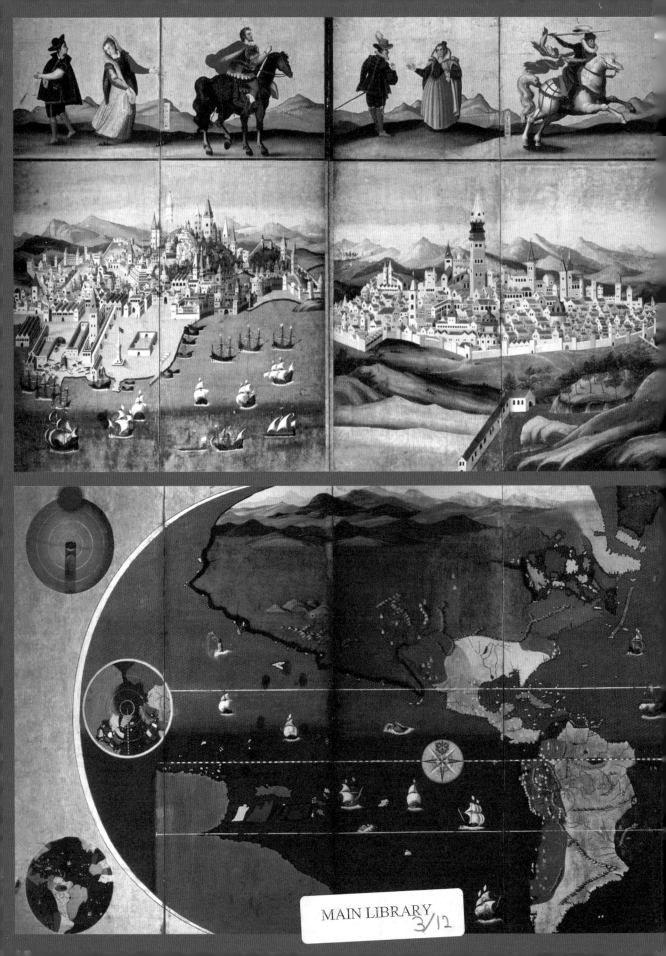